The Best American Political Writing 2005

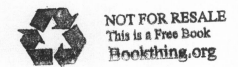

The Best American Political Writing 2005

Edited by Royce Flippin

Thunder's Mouth Press
New York

THE BEST AMERICAN POLITICAL WRITING 2005

Published by
Thunder's Mouth Press
An Imprint of Avalon Publishing Group Inc.
245 West 17th St., 11th Floor
New York, NY 10011

AVALON
publishing group incorporated

Library of Congress Cataloging-in-Publication Data is available.

ISBN: 1-56025-771-7
ISBN 13: 978-1-56025-771-4

9 8 7 6 5 4 3 2 1

Book design by Sue Canavan
Printed in the United States of America
Distributed by Publishers Group West

This book is dedicated to the next generation
of the Lipsitz-Flippin family:
Michael Shields, Stephen Shields, Brian Nole,
Bobby Flippin, Alex Burchins, Andrew Burchins,
Michael Flippin, Molly Burchins,
Ryan Flippin, and Christopher Flippin

CONTENTS

Part Two: Politics in the Bush Era—Four More Years

National Conversation: Social Security Reform

Part Three: The Democrats Look to 2006 . . . and Beyond

Part Four: The State of the Union

National Conversation: Politics, Morality, and Religion

Part Five: Iraq and the War on Terrorism

Part Six: America in an Uncertain World

Acknowledgments

I want to express my thanks and appreciation to all those who gave their permission or helped in securing permission to reprint the work of the many fine writers and publications represented in this anthology—as well as to all of the thousands of authors, columnists, bloggers, and letter writers who enrich our political discourse on a daily (sometimes hourly) basis.

Special thanks go to Michael O'Connor, my partner in crime at Avalon Publishing Group, who waded through hundreds of pieces with me during the selection process. Thanks also to Thunder's Mouth publisher John Oakes for continuing to back this anthology series, and to Avalon publicist Karen Auerbach and the Avalon design and production team for their work on the book. I'm also grateful to Taylor Smith for his sage advice on permissions.

Finally, a huge thank-you to my wife, Alexis Lipsitz Flippin, for her ever-present love, support, and friendship—and to my springer spaniel, Bailey, for making sure I start each day bright and early.

Preface

Welcome to the fourth edition of our anthology series. *The Best American Political Writing 2005* contains thirty-one articles and essays that saw print in the twelve-month period from June 2004 through May 2005—a year that opened with the fiercely fought presidential campaign and George W. Bush's subsequent reelection (described in detail in Nancy Gibbs's *Time* magazine account, "In Victory's Glow," on p. 3), and hit its midpoint with the inspiring election in Iraq and Bush's second-term call for Social Security reform (you can see ex-Bush adviser N. Gregory Mankiw plead his former boss's case in his *New Republic* essay "Personal Dispute," on p. 117). Since then, however, both the rebuilding of Iraq and the president's domestic initiatives have been foundering. By late spring, the president's approval ratings had sunk to just above 40 percent, Republicans in Congress were beginning to talk openly about developing an exit strategy for Iraq, and Bush's signature proposal for private Social Security accounts was all but dead.

The year's roller-coaster trajectory serves as a reminder that, at its heart, politics is an ongoing war of ideas. Elections just set the boundaries for this war; the rest of the time, the fighting occurs in the halls of legislatures, in TV and radio broadcasts, and, most of all, in America's newspapers, magazines, blogs, and books. For despite the widely-lamented decline in newspaper sales and the perpetual struggle of both print and online publications to stay profitable—and with all due respect to the power of television—the written media in the U.S. remains our main conduit for new and important information and opinions. It's also the arena in which the major battles over ideas invariably take place.

That being said, what *were* the big themes being tossed around during this notably contentious year? Using the selections in this year's anthology as a guide, here are a few that spring to mind:

Presidents who govern by thin margins should be prepared to reach out. George Bush has consistently had the support of no more than half of the electorate—a fact borne out in both elections—but he's governed as if he had a conservative mandate. This helped get him get reelected (by avoiding his father's mistake of neglecting his conservative base), but it has also made it increasingly difficult to govern. Republicans and Democrats in Washington are at loggerheads—as Jeffrey Toobin's *New Yorker* story about the scrap over judicial filibusters, "Blowing Up the Senate," (p. 73) vividly illustrates—leaving the minority Democrats united like never before, as evidenced by their unyielding opposition to Bush's plan for Social Security private accounts (for reasons spelled out by the *New Republic*'s Jonathan Chait in "Blocking Move," on p. 123).

The president has run into similar problems abroad, where his unilateralist tendencies have made international cooperation harder to come by. As *Newsweek*'s Fareed Zakaria notes ruefully in his otherwise laudatory column "What Bush Got Right" (p. 287), America's image has taken a huge hit overseas. Meanwhile traditional U.S. alliances have been strained— needlessly, some would say—by a lack of diplomatic "lubrication" (as John Lewis Gaddis notes in his *Foreign Affairs* essay "Grand Strategy in the Second Term," on p. 350), and by the Administration's dubious record on human rights, encapsulated in Jane Mayer's chilling *New Yorker* article "Outsourcing Torture" (p. 315).

The cultural divide is real—but not as big as you might think. For sure, the past year had its share of culturally-rooted conflicts—headlined by the showdown over whether or not to remove the feeding tube of Terry Schiavo, the brain-damaged Florida woman. In his *Weekly Standard* essay "How Liberalism Failed Terri Schiavo" (p. 268), Eric Cohen makes a vigorous case for keeping Schiavo alive. On the other hand, *Nation* columnist Katha Pollitt's "Backward Christian Soldiers" (p. 265) is an equally eloquent denunciation of the growing intrusions by the religious Right and their Republican allies into people's personal lives.

At the same time, though, the culture clash between what Hanna Rosin calls "traditionalists" and "modernists" in her *Atlantic Monthly* piece "Beyond Belief" (p. 276) may be not be as all-consuming as it's cracked up to be. For one thing, as the *New Yorker*'s Louis Menand makes clear in his fascinating dissection of the presidential vote, "Permanent Fatal Errors" (p. 46), post-election analysis shows that Bush's victory turned much more on national security issues than on any sense of shared "values." Similarly, in "Bipolar Disorder" (p. 201), which ran as a companion piece to Rosin's in the *Atlantic*, Jonathan Rauch digs up some academic research suggesting that most Americans are in remarkably close agreement on most issues. And *Esquire* writer James McManus's cry from the heart to allow federal funding for stem-cell research, in his wrenching "Please Stand By While the Age of Miracles Is Briefly Suspended," (p. 245) expresses an ethical sentiment that cuts across religious and cultural boundaries.

The Democrats have a credibility problem when it comes to national defense. I realize this is a fairly obvious one, but the theme comes up again and again (and again) in pieces like "Kerry's Undeclared War" (p. 21), Matt Bai's profile of contender John Kerry from the *New York Times Magazine*, "The Unbranding" (p. 155), Jeffrey Goldberg's *New Yorker* article on the Democratic Party's struggle to reshape its image on national defense, and "A Fighting Faith" (p. 167), an essay by the *New Republic*'s Peter Beinart on the need for liberals to toughen up. You can also glimpse a real-life Democratic hawk in the making in Jennifer Senior's entertaining *New York* magazine profile of Hillary Clinton, "The Once and Future President Clinton" (p. 182).

George Bush's foreign policy is working—sort of. This is another theme that was expressed repeatedly during the past year by writers of all stripes. Democracy may be struggling to be born in Iraq and Afghanistan, but it seems to be in the air everywhere. Tom Junod, who admits he loathes the president, asks in his *Esquire* article "The Case for George W. Bush" (p. 12) whether Bush might be on the right track after all with his pro-democracy doctrine; and the *New Republic*'s Martin Peretz echoes the thought in "The Politics of Churlishness: Giving George W. Bush His Due on Democracy" (p. 291). On the down side, however, as James Fallows observes in his *Atlantic Monthly* article "Bush's Lost Year" (p. 364), there is a concern that our push for democratic progress abroad may be occurring at the cost of our own national security. No one said that running the world would be easy. Fortunately, military strategist Thomas P. M. Barnett is on hand to tell our commander in chief exactly what to do next, in his highly readable *Esquire* essay, "Mr. President, Here's How to Make Sense of Your Second Term, Secure Your Legacy, and, Oh Yeah, Create a Future Worth Living" (p. 341).

The press doesn't have it easy. Just read Eric Alterman's article from the *Nation*, "Bush's War on the Press" (p. 84), about the Administration's stifling control over information, and Michael Massing's essay "Iraq, the Press and the Election" (p. 299), about journalists caught between bombs and mortar fire on the one hand, and editors who just don't want to hear about it on the other. Then you'll know what I mean.

Like the previous editions of *Best American Political Writing*, this year's selections are grouped into different sections by topic: Part One is devoted to the presidential election of 2004. Part Two, the latest incarnation of our ongoing "Politics in the Bush Era" section, covers the political wheelings and dealings of the Bush administration and the rest of America's political leadership. Part Three, "The Democrats Look to 2006 . . . and Beyond," reports on the Democratic Party's struggle to regain power. Part Four, "The State of the Union," contains selections that address issues of national significance. Part Five, "Iraq and the War on Terrorism," and Part Six, "America in an Uncertain World," both showcase articles and essays about U.S. foreign policy. Part Five concentrates on the Mideast and American anti-terror policy, while Part Six focuses more broadly on America's global concerns.

Finally, we've also included two installments of the "The National Conversation," each presenting a variety of views on a controversial subject. The first section features different perspectives on President Bush's second-term push for Social Security reform, and the second section contains several writers' views on the role of morality and religion in politics—a subject that's becoming an increasingly prominent part of the national dialogue.

As this is being written, Iraq is still groping its way toward a coherent national government. Meanwhile, violence continues to erupt there at a numbing rate. American troop deaths now top 1,700, and political support for the war here at home is oozing away, with a majority of those polled now indicating that, in their view, the war wasn't worth it. The Senate Democrats, clinging to what leverage they still possess, are stubbornly maintaining their filibuster of the nomination of John Bolton, Bush's crusty pick to be UN ambassador, while Congressional Republicans—keenly aware that Congress's approval rating is the lowest it's been in years—are reluctantly trying to cobble together some type of Social Security bill, all the while keeping one worried eye on the 2006 elections that loom on the horizon.

Sounds like it's going to be another banner year for political writing!

—Royce Flippin
June 2005

The Best American Political Writing 2005

Part One:
The 2004 Presidential Election

In Victory's Glow: The Extraordinary Triumph of President George W. Bush

Nancy Gibbs

Reported by John Dickerson, Perry Bacon Jr., Matthew Cooper, Michael Duffy, Karen Tumulty, Eric Roston, Wendy Cole, Mitch Frank, Nathan Thornburgh, Nancy Harbert, Marc Hequet, Sandeep Kaushik, Brad Liston, Wendy Malloy, Tim Padgett, Michael Peltier, Betsy Rubiner, Sean Scully, and Stacy Willis

Time | November 3, 2004

Like the 2000 contest before it, the 2004 presidential election had its share of twists and turns. On the afternoon of Election Day, normally-reliable exit polls showed John Kerry well ahead in a number of key states. Democrats across the country allowed themselves a brief moment of hope—only to have their optimism dashed by the evening's first official results, which showed George Bush running much more strongly than the polls had suggested.

In the end, Bush's reelection was sealed just before noon on Wednesday when Kerry called to concede. Piling up a record 62 million votes, Bush beat Kerry with 50.7 percent of the popular vote (to Kerry's 48.3 percent), and a 286 to 251 edge in the Electoral College, as he swept a wide swath of states across the country's interior. In the process, Bush finally silenced those who still claimed his 2000 election—in which he trailed Al Gore by some 500,000 votes in the popular tally—was illegitimate.

Bush's victory could also be seen as vindication of his policies—but only up to a point. Yes, his triumph was unquestioned. (The Democrats' post-election rumblings centered mainly on Ohio's disgracefully long voter lines and malfunctioning touch-screen voting machines, but even in that tightly-contested state, Bush's 100,000-vote margin was decisive enough to preclude any real challenges. Meanwhile, Ralph Nader was not a factor this time around, polling a meager .38 percent of the national vote.) Still, Bush's win was anything but a landslide. For one thing, Kerry's 59 million votes were also more than any U.S. presidential candidate had ever gotten before—suggesting widespread dissatisfaction with the incumbent. Further-more, Bush's margin of victory, taken as a percentage of the popular vote, was the smallest of any sitting U.S. president in history.

In other words, Bush got reelected in a squeaker—and for that, he can thank his indefatigable political operation and its leader, chief cook, and bottlewasher, Karl Rove. In this post-election report, Nancy Gibbs, together with a team of Time *reporters based across the country, examines how Rove and Co. made it happen. . . .*

Tuesday was the night the ghosts died in the Bush White House. There was the ghost of his last campaign, which Bush lost among voters but won in the court. There was the ghost of his father's last campaign, when even winning a war was not enough to earn a second term. And then there was the ghost of Tuesday afternoon, when the entire Bush campaign team was haunted by the possibility that they had got it all wrong, as the first exit polls came in and nothing, but nothing, was going their way.

When it was finally over, the President who had become a radical champion of democracy's power to change the world became the living symbol of how it works. He made his decisions and moved on; the voters made theirs, in one of the most extraordinary displays of political passion seen in a generation. About 120 million voted, 15 million more than in 2000, with Bush beating Senator John Kerry by about 51 percent to 48.5 percent. He became the first President since 1988 to win a majority of the popular vote, he gained seats in both houses of Congress, and for good measure, he knocked off not just the Democratic nominee but the party's Senate leader as well. The love-hate presidency of George W. Bush was neither an accident of ideology nor a product of these times. Asked as he left the Crawford, Texas, polling station about the polarized feelings he inspires in voters, Bush replied, "I take that as a compliment. It means I'm willing to take a stand." He saw his task as leading and never looking back, and only that night did he learn whether enough people had decided to fall into line behind him to allow him to carry on. In a triumphant speech at the Ronald Reagan Building in D.C., after a long and winding election night, Bush declared victory. "America has spoken, and I am humbled by the trust and the confidence of my fellow citizens. With that trust comes a duty to serve all Americans, and I will do my best to fulfill that duty every day as your President."

Moments earlier, Kerry had stood before his supporters at Boston's Faneuil Hall, where his campaign began. To stamp out any delusions, he was very clear about the finality of his decision: "We cannot win this election," he said. Then, his voice breaking, he reminded his supporters that after an election, "we all wake up as Americans" and called for the healing to commence.

The kid who was born serious, who was greeted on campus with kazoos buzzing *Hail to the Chief*, who was tagged on national TV at age 27 as a future President, who marinated in the Senate among 99 other aspiring Presidents for 19 years before launching a bid for the White House that this time a year ago saw him barely twitching at about 10 percent in the polls, had shown exactly the kind of toughness his opponents claimed he lacked. He mortgaged his house, recast his team, renovated virtually every position he had ever taken and shook the grave dust off his suit several times before arriving at history's door. And then it closed in his face on a day when for a moment it had seemed to blow wide open.

In the end, an election that was supposed to be about all the ways we are divided at least brought us together at 193,000 polling places in democracy's messy leap of faith. Turnout was huge even in states where the result was assured. In Ohio the polls closed at 7:30, but the lines were so long that people were still voting at midnight. Some people admitted they just did not want to face their neighbors or their children at the end of the day and say they had not bothered to show up. Others said if you don't vote, you can't complain and did not want to be mute at a time like this. In the end, polls suggested that the single issue that mattered most was not the Iraq war or terrorism, not the economy, but the questions of values that simmered beneath the headlines throughout the campaign.

If the outcome still showed a public divided, it produced a government somewhat less so. Thanks to their sweeping victories Tuesday, the Republicans ensured that the very real challenges facing Bush in a second term—from Iraq as it heads toward elections, to entitlements as they drift toward insolvency, to Supreme Court appointments and the social issues that most deeply divide the public—would be addressed by a party with a rare monopoly of power in all three branches of government and a mandate, however slim, that did not exist four years ago. All of which points to the great mystery ahead: With reelection no longer the organizing principle of George Bush's presidency, what will guide his next four years, when the only judge left is history?

• • •

For a President who loves the game and knew this was his last campaign, Bush sounded on Tuesday morning like a man at peace. "This election is in the hands of the people," he said after he voted, "and I feel very comfortable with that." He was host of a gin-rummy tournament on Air Force One as he headed from Crawford back to the White House to wait out the results. It was on the plane that strategist Karl Rove started calling around to get the results of early exit polls. But the line kept breaking down. The only information that came through as the plane descended was a Black-Berry message from an aide that simply read: "Not good." Not long afterward, Rove got a more detailed picture and told the President and senior aides the bad news. Florida Governor Jeb Bush had been saying the state was looking good, and the Bush team had expected to be ahead in Ohio. But Kerry was leading everywhere. "I wanted to throw up," said an aide onboard. Bush was more philosophical: "Well, it is what it is," he told adviser Karen Hughes. On the ground in Arlington, Virginia, that afternoon, chief strategist Matthew Dowd was walking around Bush campaign headquarters looking like a "scientist whose formulas were all wrong," said a top Bush staff member. Dowd had designed the strategy for targeting voters, and the exit polls were undermining his every theory. It would take him six long hours to crack the code. When the actual vote counts started coming in at 8 P.M., Dowd noticed that in South Carolina, Virginia and Florida the numbers were what the Republicans expected them to be; the President was outperforming the exit polls. "We've got to go talk to the press. The exit polls are wrong," Dowd said.

The emotional route of Kerry's day passed Bush's somewhere halfway, traveling from wild hope to stunned despair. After one last dawn campaign visit, a triple-witching photo op on the Iowa-Wisconsin-Minnesota border, Kerry flew back to Boston for his ritual Election Day lunch at the Union Oyster House. Superstitious, he wore his lucky Red Sox cap, carried an Ohio buckeye in one pocket and a clover in the other and refused to let his speechwriters work on election-night speeches of any flavor. But he wasn't relying entirely on voodoo. He spent the afternoon doing satellite interviews in key markets, 38 interviews over four hours.

All along, the Republicans predicted they would beat the Democrats in the final 72 hours because the Dems were relying on hired help whereas the GOP was running its ground game with volunteers. At Bush campaign rallies throughout the year, anyone who came through security was asked to register. If they were already registered, they were asked to volunteer. Those who had already volunteered were scheduled to go on buses after the President left so that they could walk precincts and knock on doors. The chance to get close enough to shake the President's hand was not reserved for big donors, as in the past. The ones who got the lucky bracelet that allowed them into that proximity were the ones who promised to work in the phone bank after the event.

The GOP knew that every last disciple would be needed because the Democrats had so much money to spend this time. The liberal 527 America Coming Together (ACT), which overall spent $125 million registering voters and turning them out, had 30,000 paid foot soldiers in Ohio alone, making ACT, for a day, the state's biggest employer. And alongside ACT was an army of free-lancers and first-timers and recruits from every Democratic activist group, matching the Republican faithful step for step.

For all the warnings of turmoil on Election Day, most people were on their best behavior. Even at war, there was civility. In New Mexico a law student policing the polls for the Democrats lent her cell phone to her Republican counterpart. In Merrimack, New Hampshire, volunteers from MoveOn.org passed out hot cocoa to activists holding signs outside the polling place— Republicans and Democrats alike. "We might be a battleground state," said voter-protection volunteer Chris L'Estrange in Des Moines, Iowa, "but there's not much of a battle." Florida state troopers suspended safety checkpoints for the day to avoid any accusations of trying to suppress turnout.

For weeks, both campaigns had suspected it could all come down to Ohio, a state no Republican has ever lost and still won the White House. More than two-thirds of precincts were using punch-card ballots, with their potentially hanging chads. So Democrats acquired 611 punch-card machines, some of them discarded from Florida and Michigan and others found on eBay, so volunteers could hold little seminars outside key precincts on how to vote correctly. Republicans dispatched vote counters to every county election board so they would give the campaign an early read about where Bush might be lagging. Back at campaign headquarters in Washington, the information streamed toward operatives sitting at laptops watching their maps change color. A county colored blue meant that Bush was doing better than he had in 2000. The Ohio map just kept getting more blue. In some places it bled dark blue, almost purple, indicating areas where Republicans had improved 10 percent from four years ago.

Three times over the course of the day, poll watchers from both parties could enter precincts and scan the lists of voters to see who had turned out and who had not. Then they called their war rooms so volunteers—the Republicans called them flushers—could call the voters who hadn't yet cast a ballot, give a pep talk, offer a ride. In Franklin County the board of elections handed out more than 800 cell phones to the nonpartisan precinct judges there so they could call the board to report any problems or ask questions. In the end "the good people of central Ohio have kept their cool heads," said Doug Preisse, chairman of the Franklin County Republican Party.

Remaining cool through the night was a little harder for the candidates. Bush was with his father in the White House residence, having highly technical conversations about turnout models by phone with campaign manager Ken Mehlman. Bush wanted to know who was on talk radio making his case and whether everything was being done to win every possible vote. "He's like a political director who is President," said a Bush official. Once it was clear that the early rumors of a Kerry sweep were all wrong, the networks were playing it very safe about calling states. The job of declaring who would be the next President—and when the country might know— would fall to the campaigns.

In the old family dining room of the residence, Rove set up his computers. Bush called him regularly to ask about what was happening in certain precincts and districts. Finally, after midnight, the President was on the phone with his communications director, Dan Bartlett, discussing Ohio. Bartlett explained why the networks would be reluctant to call the key swing state. Bush then said, "Well, they just called it," although only NBC and Fox had. The room erupted into cheers. Bartlett held out the phone so Bush could hear. "Congratulations, Mr. President," Bartlett said, "You won the presidency." But it would be nearly 15 more hours before the President could come out and say so himself.

Bush was ahead in Ohio by 130,000 votes. But about the same number of provisional ballots—given to voters whose eligibility had been challenged— remained unopened. In elections gone by, that gap would still have been enough to put the state in Bush's column, but most networks exercised uncharacteristic caution.

As the night wore on, Bush officials spoke informally to the Kerry camp, urging Kerry to concede. Kerry advisers replied that their candidate would come to his own conclusion in good time. Undeterred, Mehlman reached out to John McCain's advisers, trying to get the Arizona Senator to call on Kerry to give in. McCain's advisers said Kerry would come to the decision on his own, as he ultimately did. Shortly after dawn, Kerry advisers gathered one last time to go over the Ohio math. By 9:30, the conclusion was clear: Kerry simply did not have the numbers. Campaign manager Mary Beth Cahill called Kerry at his town house. Within 10 minutes, he had called her back to say he agreed. At 11 A.M., Kerry called Bush to concede. He congratulated the President and urged him to unify the country. Bush called Kerry "an admirable and worthy opponent."

What finally swayed those near mythical voters who managed to make it until Tuesday without making up their minds? The weight that voters attached to values suggests that Rove's single-minded attention to the goal of turning out 4 million more evangelical voters than in 2000 may have paid off. On the other hand, there were voters like Jeffrey Wilson, 21, a student at the University of South Florida in Tampa, a gay Catholic raised in a conservative family but registered as a Democrat, who finally went with Bush. It wasn't the war that mattered. "I think they're both for stepping things up and cleaning up the mess we've created," he said. Instead it was a matter of character. "I just don't feel that I really trust John Kerry to do what he says he's going to do." For Andrea Levin, 39, of Seattle, who voted for Al Gore in 2000, it was the return of Osama bin Laden, who released a videotape taunting Bush four days before Election Day, that made the difference. "When he made his presentation, looking all spiffed up, and condemned the President's foreign policy, I saw that as a clear sign that I should vote for Bush."

Historians will have an easy time arguing that the race was always Bush's to lose; he scarcely ever ran behind, from Labor Day on. A country will seldom discharge a Commander in Chief during wartime, particularly one who had sustained a higher level of approval for longer than any modern U.S. President. Economist Ray Fair devised a model that weighs inflation and growth rates, and by his formula, Bush looked on track to win 58 percent of the popular vote. And he was running against a New England Senator so stiff, he creaked, when no non-Southern Democrat has won in 44 years.

So consider the obstacles Bush overcame and the rules that were broken by his victory. Since the country previously met at the polls, voters have encountered a record deficit, job losses, airport shoe searches, rising bank-ruptcies and bruising battles over stem-cell research and the definition of marriage. On the eve of Election Day, fully 55 percent of voters said the country was moving in the wrong direction. Only 49 percent approved of the job the President was doing, and anything below 50 percent is sup-posed to be fatal to an incumbent. A war that Bush promised would cost no more than $50 billion a year is running at nearly three times that. He was attacked by well-organized and well-funded detractors who described him as a liar, a fraud, a drug abuser, a warmonger, an incurious zealot, an agent of the Saudis, a puppet of his goblin Vice President. And he faced an opponent with a long record of public service, a shiny record from a war Bush had avoided and a Democratic base suffused with a cold and implacable hatred, a group that had never been so united—not over the war, not over tax policy or job losses or health care but simply in the pur-pose of bringing this presidency it so despised to an end.

Bush says the war on terrorism is not a clash of civilizations, but this campaign was, by his careful design. He never really pretended to have much to say to Democrats beyond I will keep you safe. He relied largely instead on inspiring those who agreed with him already, who don't want to see gay couples kissing on the evening news, think stem-cell research has been oversold and believe abortion on demand is a sin. Even Republicans who dis-agreed with him on one or more issues—the fiscal conservatives who prefer less extravagant government spending, the civil libertarians who would like a less intrusive Patriot Act—were still prepared to side with him. His 97 per-cent approval rate within his party surpassed even Ronald Reagan's. Bush plainly understood that his best weapon against Kerry was less what Bush did than who he was. You may disagree with me, he said at every stop, but you know where I stand.

That message alone was meant to be a source of comfort, particularly since he was also telling voters that everything had changed since the last time they elected a President and no amount of wishful thinking could turn the calendar back. After a happy and lucky decade, the U.S. is locked in a war that will last the rest of our lives. "The outcome of this election will set the direction of the war against terror," Bush said Saturday in Grand Rapids, Michigan. Of Kerry, he argued that if you don't even admit it's a war, you can't be trusted to fight it. Critics who saw his faith in contagious democracy as naive may have missed the point that the American people have always been attracted to the idea. At the very least, voters may not punish a President for placing such hope in the principles they value most.

Having said that, surveys had consistently found that a majority of voters were ready to fire Bush—provided they had an acceptable alternative. That suggests how much Bush's success owes to Kerry's failure. The Senator never needed to be as likable as Bush to win, as Kerry proved when he defeated the popular Governor William Weld in their 1996 Senate race. Kerry just needed to be plausible. His supporters saw his serial explanations of his Iraq-war position as a mark of thoroughness and subtlety; opponents were alarmed by a sense that he was guided by no core beliefs but was only searching for a politically safe place to land. Bush was proud of setting a vision and then delegating even big decisions to a small group of advisers; Kerry was famously surrounded by enough advisers to fill a small liberal-arts college but still spent four weeks agonizing over the right font for his campaign logo. Kerry's résumé of élite schools, a prosecutor's office and the U.S. Senate honored his deliberative process; the presidential campaign proved too fast for it, and Bush never missed a chance to portray Kerry as the hollow man, ever expedient, always cautious, incapable of taking a stand and sticking to it.

Bush needed to demonize Kerry to make him an unacceptable alternative. The strategy carried some risk: negative ads over the summer portrayed Kerry as such a ridiculous, windsurfing, flip-flopping fop that when the cartoon version of Kerry didn't show up for the debates, Bush suffered in contrast. It was a rare miscalculation by a politician who understands well the value of low expectations. But overall, Bush succeeded in making Kerry appear an élitist emphatically defending moderation at a time when nothing less than passion would do. In Boston at their convention, the Democrats held a tasteful remembrance of 9/11. A month later in New York City, the Republicans unleashed a battle cry, and the contrast was plain: the party of victims vs. the party of warriors.

The past four years have rewired our politics in ways that guaranteed this election would be a historic one, whatever the outcome. The presidency simply matters more. To the delight of his supporters and the outrage of his opponents, George W. Bush governed as though he had won a mandate four years ago and, through his radical assertion of presidential power, showed what a difference it makes who is in the White House. With Congress all but dysfunctionally deadlocked, the spotlight for four years has focused entirely on the Executive Branch.

But in a second Bush term, Congress may be even more bitterly divided, making any legislative agenda hard to achieve. The initial goodwill that produced the No Child Left Behind Act is gone. The post-9/11 sense of national unity that produced the Patriot Act is gone. Bush has recently relied on disciplined party-line votes and seldom even pretended to try to reach a compromise with Democrats. He has admitted that this state of affairs is a disappointment, given his promise to unite and not divide. In an interview with *Time* in August, he blamed the rancor on entrenched special interests, as though he were more victim than leader. Washington, he said, turned out to be a nastier place than Texas. But it is natural when the lines are so tightly drawn that neither side wants to hand the other a victory that it can take to the voters next time around.

For Kerry's supporters, there is some consolation that Bush will have to take responsibility for finishing what he started in Iraq. For Bush's supporters, there is an obligation to recognize that the intense effort of the other side was as much an expression of love of country as any pledge, hymn or flag. For people on both sides, there is relief that the day affirmed the sustaining virtue of American democracy. However fierce the battle and however high the stakes, on Election Day citizens go to the polls, close a curtain and cast their vote—and then go home to honor the outcome because we have only one President at a time.

The Case for George W. Bush (I.e., What If He's Right?)
Tom Junod

Esquire | August 2004

One of the biggest things going for George W. Bush in the 2004 presidential campaign was the sense among many voters that, whether or not you agreed with all of the president's politics, his basic instinct to push back hard against a dangerous world was a correct one. Yes, we could be pursuing the war on terror more diplo-matically; and yes, the administration had manipulated the intelligence on Saddam Hussein's WMDs and was stumbling through the rebuilding of Iraq—but still, the president had taken the bull by the horns at a time when dithering was not an option. Plus, maybe he was onto something with his democracy-building project.

In this essay, published the summer before the election, Tom Junod considers the possibility that Bush's stubborn moral certainity about "the evil of global ter-rorism," as distasteful as it may be to some, could be what's standing between us and disaster—and that liberals just don't get it . . .

It happened again this morning. I saw a picture of our president—my president—and my feelings about him were instantly rekindled. The pic-ture was taken after his speech to the graduating seniors at the Air Force Academy. He was wearing a dark suit, a light-blue tie, and a white shirt. His unsmiling visage was grim and purposeful, in pointed contrast to the face of the elaborately uniformed cadet standing next to him, which was lit up with a cocky grin. Indeed, as something more than a frozen moment—as a political statement—the picture might have served, and been intended to serve, as a tableau of the resolve necessary to lift this nation out of this steep and terrible time. The cadet represented the best of what America has to offer, all devil-may-care enthusiasm and willingness to serve. The presi-dent, his hair starting to whiten, might have represented something even more essential: the kind of brave and, in his case, literally unblinking lead-ership that generates enough moral capital to summon the young to war. Although one man was essentially being asked to stake his life on the wisdom of the other, both were melded in an attitude of common purpose, and so both struck a common pose. With the cadet bent slightly forward and the commander in chief leaning slightly back, each man cocked his right arm and made a muscle. They flexed! I didn't know anything about the cadet. About President George W. Bush, though, I felt the satisfaction of absolute certainty, and so uttered the words as essential to my morning as my cup of Kenyan and my dose of high-minded outrage on the editorial page of the *Times*: "What an asshole."

Ah. That feels better. George W. Bush is an asshole, isn't he? Moreover, he's the first president who seems *merely* that, at least in my lifetime. From Kennedy to Clinton, there is not a single president who would have been capable of striking such a pose after concluding a speech about a war in which hundreds of Americans and thousands of Iraqis are being killed. There is not a single president for whom such a pose would seem entirely characteristic—not a single president who might be tempted to confuse a beefcakey photo opportunity with an expression of national purpose. He has always struck me as a small man, or at least as a man too small for the task at hand, and therefore a man doomed to address the discrepancy between his soul and his situation with displays of political muscle that succeed only in drawing attention to his diminution. He not only has led us into war, he seems to get off on war, and it's the greedy pleasure he so clearly gets from flexing his biceps or from squaring his shoulders and setting his jaw or from landing a plane on an aircraft carrier—the greedy pleasure the war president finds in playacting his own attitudes of belligerence—that permitted me the greedy pleasure of hating him.

Then I read the text of the speech he gave and was thrown from one kind of certainty—the comfortable kind—into another. He was speaking, as he always does, of the moral underpinnings of our mission in Iraq. He was comparing, as he always does, the challenge that we face, in the evil of global terrorism, to the challenge our fathers and grandfathers faced, in the evil of fascism. He was insisting, as he always does, that the evil of global terrorism is exactly that, an evil—one of almost transcendent dimension that quite simply must be met, lest we be remembered for not meeting it . . . lest we allow it to be our judge. I agreed with most of what he said, as I often do when he's defining matters of principle. No, more than that, I thought that he was defining principles that desperately needed defining, with a clarity that those of my own political stripe demonstrate only when they're decrying either his policies or his character. He was making a moral proposition upon which he was basing his entire presidency—or said he was basing his entire presidency—and I found myself in the strange position of buying into the proposition without buying into the presidency, of buying into the words while rejecting, utterly, the man who spoke them. There is, of course, an easy answer for this seeming moral schizophrenia: the distance between the principles and the policy, between the mission and "Mission Accomplished," between the war on terror and the war in Iraq. Still, I have to admit to feeling a little uncertain of my disdain for this president when forced to contemplate the principle that might animate his determination to stay the course in a war that very well may be the end of him politically. I have to admit that when I listen to him speak, with his unbending certainty, I sometimes hear an echo of the same nagging question I ask myself after I hear a preacher declaim the agonies of hellfire or an insurance agent enumerate the cold odds of the actuarial tables. Namely: What if he's right?

As easy as it is to say that we can't abide the president because of the gulf between what he espouses and what he actually *does*, what haunts me is the possibility that we can't abide him because of us—because of the gulf between his will and our willingness. What haunts me is the possibility that we have become so accustomed to ambiguity and inaction in the face of evil that we find his call for decisive action an insult to our sense of nuance and proportion.

The people who dislike George W. Bush have convinced themselves that opposition to his presidency is the most compelling moral issue of the day. Well, it's not. The most compelling moral issue of the day is exactly what he says it is, when he's not saying it's gay marriage. The reason he will be difficult to unseat in November—no matter what his approval ratings are in the summer—is that his opponents operate out of the moral certainty that he is the bad guy and needs to be replaced, while he operates out of the moral certainty that terrorists are the bad guys and need to be defeated. The first will always sound merely convenient when compared with the second. Worse, the gulf between the two kinds of certainty lends credence to the conservative notion that liberals have settled for the conviction that Bush is distasteful as a substitute for conviction—because it's easier than conviction.

In 1861, after Confederate forces shelled Fort Sumter, President Abraham Lincoln suspended the writ of habeas corpus from Philadelphia to Washington and thereby made the arrest of American citizens a matter of military or executive say-so. When the Chief Justice of the Supreme Court objected to the arrest of a Maryland man who trained troops for Confederate muster, Lincoln essentially ignored his ruling. He argued that there was no point fixating on one clause in the Constitution when Southern secession had shredded the whole document, and asked, "Are all the laws *but one* to go unexecuted, and the government itself go to pieces, lest that one be violated?" During the four-year course of the Civil War, he also selectively abridged the rights of free speech, jury trial, and private property. Not that the war went well: His army was in the habit of losing long before it learned to win, and Lincoln did not find a general to his liking until he found Ulysses S. Grant, whose idea of war was total. He financed the bloodbath by exposing the nation to ruinous debt and taxation, and by 1864 he had to contend with an antiwar challenge from Democrats and a political challenge from a member of his own Cabinet. On August 23, 1864, he was motivated to write in a memorandum that "it seems exceedingly probable that this administration will not be reelected," and yet his position on peace never wavered: He rejected any terms but the restoration of the union and the abolition of slavery. The war was, from first to last, portrayed as *his* war, and after he won landslide reelection, he made a vow not only to stay the course but to prosecute it to the brink of catastrophe and beyond: "Fondly do we hope—fervently do we pray—that this mighty scourge of war may speedily pass away. Yet, if God wills that it continue, until all the wealth piled by the bond-man's two hundred and fifty years of unrequited toil shall be sunk, and until every drop of blood drawn with the lash, shall be paid by another drawn with the sword, as was said three thousand years ago, so still it must be said 'the judgments of the Lord, are true and righteous altogether.' "

Today, of course, those words, along with Lincoln's appeal to the better angels of our nature, are chiseled into the wall of his memorial, on the Mall in Washington. And yet if George Bush were to speak anything like them today, we would accuse him of pandering to his evangelical base. We would accuse him of invoking divine authority for a war of *his* choosing, and Maureen Dowd would find a way to read his text in light of the cancellation of some *Buffy* spin-off. Believe me: I am not comparing George W. Bush to Abraham Lincoln. The latter was his own lawyer as well as his own writer, and he was alive to the possibilities of tragedy and comedy—he was *human*—in a way that our president doesn't seem to be. Neither am I looking to justify Bush's forays into shady constitutional ground by invoking Lincoln's precedents with the same; I'm not a lawyer. I am, however, asking if the crisis currently facing the country—the crisis, that is, that announced itself on the morning of September 11, 2001, in New York and Pennsylvania and the District of Columbia—is as compelling a justification for the havoc and sacrifice of war as the crisis that became irrevocable on April 12, 1861, in South Carolina, or, for that matter, the crisis that emerged from the blue Hawaiian sky on December 7, 1941. I, for one, believe it is and feel somewhat ashamed having to say so: having to *aver* that 9/11/01 was a horror sufficient to supply Bush with a genuine moral cause rather than, as some would have it, a mere excuse for his adventurism.

We were attacked three years ago, without warning or predicate event. The attack was not a gesture of heroic resistance nor the offshoot of some bright utopian resolve, but the very flower of a movement that delights in the potential for martyrdom expressed in the squalls of the newly born. It is a movement that is about death—that honors death, that loves death, that fetishizes death, that worships death, that seeks to accomplish death wherever it can, on a scale both intimate and global—and if it does not warrant the expenditure of what the self-important have taken to calling "blood and treasure," then what does? Slavery? Fascism? Genocide? Let's not flatter ourselves: If we do not find it within ourselves to identify the terrorism inspired by radical Islam as an unequivocal evil—and to pronounce ourselves morally superior to it—then we have lost the ability to identify any evil at all, and our democracy is not only diminished, it dissolves into the meaninglessness of privilege.

Yeah, yeah, I know: Nobody who opposes Bush thinks that terrorism is a *good* thing. The issue is not whether the United States should be involved in a war on terrorism but rather whether the war on terrorism is best served by war in Iraq. And now that the war has defied the optimism of its advocates, the issue is no longer Bush's moral intention but rather his simple competence. He got us in when he had no idea how to get us out. He allowed himself to be blinded by ideology and blindsided by ideologues. His arrogance led him to offend the very allies whose participation would have enabled us to win not just the war but the peace. His obsession with Saddam Hussein led him to rush into a war that was unnecessary. Sure, Saddam was a bad guy. Sure, the world is a better place without him. But . . .

And there it is: the inevitable *but*. Trailed by its uncomfortable ellipsis, it sits squirming at the end of the argument against George Bush for very good reason: It can't possibly sit at the beginning. Bush haters have to back into it because there's nothing beyond it. The world is a better place without Saddam Hussein, but . . . but *what?* But he wasn't so bad that we had to do anything about him? But he wasn't so bad that he was worth the shedding of American blood? But there are other dictators just as bad whom we leave in place? But he provided Bush the opportunity to establish the doctrine of preemptive war, in which case the cure is worse than the disease? But we should have secured Afghanistan before invading Iraq? But we should have secured the cooperation of allies who were no more inclined to depose Saddam than they—or we, as head of an international coalition of the unwilling—were to stop the genocide in Rwanda ten years before? *Sure, genocide is bad, but . . .*

We might as well credit the president for his one great accomplishment: replacing *but* with *and* as a basis for foreign policy. The world is a better place without Saddam Hussein, *and* we got rid of him. And unless we have become so wedded to the politics of regret that we are obligated to indulge in a perverse kind of nostalgia for the days of Uday and Qusay, we have to admit that it's hard to imagine a world with Saddam still in it. And even before the first stem-winder of the Democratic convention, the possibility of even limited success in Iraq has reduced the loyal opposition to two strategies: either signing up for the oversight role they had envisioned for the UN, or else declaring the whole thing a lost cause, in their own war of preemption.

Of course, Iraq might be a lost cause. It might be a disaster unmitigated and unprecedented. But if we permit ourselves to look at it the way the Republicans look at it—as a historical cause rather than just a cause *assumed* to be lost—we might be persuaded to see that it's history's judgment that matters, not ours. The United States, at this writing, has been in Iraq fifteen months. At the same point in the Civil War, Lincoln faced, well, a disaster unmitigated and unprecedented. He was *losing*. He didn't lose, at least in part because he was able to both inspire and draw on the kind of moral absolutism necessary to win wars. Bush has been unable to do the same, at least in part because he is undercut by evidence of his own dishonesty, but also because moral absolutism is nearly impossible to sustain in the glare of a twenty-four-hour news cycle. In a nation incapable of feeling any but the freshest wounds, Bush cannot seek to inspire moral absolutism without his moral absolutism becoming itself an issue—indeed, *the* issue. He cannot seek to engender certainty without being accused of sowing disarray. And he cannot speak the barest terms necessary for victory in *any* war—that we will stay the course, through good or through ill, because our cause is right and just, and God is on our side—without inspiring a goodly number of his constituents to aspire to the moral prestige of surrender.

• • •

There is supposed to be a straight line between Bush's moral absolutism—between his penchant for calling our enemies "evil-doers" or even, well, "enemies"—and Guantánamo, and then between Guantánamo and the case of Jose Padilla, and then between Padilla and the depravities of Abu Ghraib. More than a mere demonstration of cause and effect, the line is supposed by those opposed to a second Bush presidency to function as a geometric proof of the proposition that the American position in Iraq is not only untenable but ignoble. It's supposed to prove that victory in any such enterprise is not worth the taint and that withdrawal is tantamount to victory, because it will save the national soul. In fact, it proves something quite different: It proves that just as the existence of the animal-rights movement is said to depend on the increasing American distance from the realities of the farm, the liberal consensus on the war in Iraq depends on the increasing American distance from the realities of soldiering. All Abu Ghraib proves is what Lincoln made clear in his writings, and what any soldier has to know from the moment he sizes up another soldier in the sight of his rifle: that war is undertaken at the *risk* of the national soul. The moral certainty that makes war possible is certain only to unleash moral havoc, and moral havoc becomes something the nation has to rise above. We can neither win a war nor save the national soul if all we seek is to remain unsullied—pristine. Anyway, we are well beyond that now. The question is not, and has never been, whether we can fight a war without perpetrating outrages of our own. The question is whether the rightness of the American cause is sufficient not only to justify war but to withstand war's inevitable outrages. The question is whether—if the cause is right—we are strong enough to make it remain right in the foggy moral battleground of war.

In 1861, Abraham Lincoln suspended the writ of habeas corpus, and historians today applaud the restraint he displayed in throwing thousands of American citizens in jail. By the middle of 2002, George W. Bush had declared two American citizens enemy combatants, and both men are still in jail at this writing, uncharged. Both presidents used war as a rationale for their actions, citing as their primary constitutional responsibility the protection of the American people. It was not until two years later that Congress took up Lincoln's action and pronounced it constitutionally justified. Our willingness to extend Bush the same latitude will depend on our perception of what exactly we're up against, post-9/11. Lincoln was fighting for the very soul of this country; he was fighting to preserve this country, as a country, and so he had to challenge the Constitution in order to save it. Bush seems to think that he's fighting for the very soul of this country, but that's exactly what many people regard as a dangerous presumption. He seems to think that he is fighting for our very survival, when all we're asking him to fight for is our security, which is a very different thing. A fight for our security? We can handle that; it means we have to get to the airport early. A fight for our survival? That means we have to live in a different country altogether. That means the United States is changing and will continue to change, the way it did during and after the Civil War, with a fundamental redefinition of executive authority. That means we have to endure the constitutional indignity of the president's declaring Jose Padilla an enemy combatant for contemplating the still-uncommitted crime of blowing up a radioactive device in an American city, which seems a constitutional indignity too great to endure, unless we think of the constitutional indignities we'd have to endure if Padilla had actually committed the crime he's accused of planning. Unless we think of how this country might change if we get hit again, and hit big. In defending his suspension of habeas corpus, Lincoln sought to draw the distinction between liberties that are absolute and those that are *sustainable* in time of war. Bush seems to be relying on the same question, and the same distinction, as an answer to all the lawyers and editorial writers who suggest that if Jose Padilla stays in jail, we are losing the war on terror by abrogating our own ideals.

Losing the war on terror? The terrible truth is that we haven't begun to find out what that really means.

I will never forget the sickly smile that crossed the president's face when he asked us all to go shopping in the wake of 9/11. It was desperate and a little craven, and I never forgave him for it. As it turned out, though, his appeal succeeded all too well. We've found the courage to go shopping. We've welcomed the restoration of the rule of celebrity. For all our avowals that nothing would ever be the same, the only thing that really changed is our taste in entertainment, which has forsaken the frivolity of the sitcom for the grit on display in *The Apprentice*. The immediacy of the threat was replaced by the inexplicability of the threat level. A universal war—the war on terror—was succeeded by a narrow one, an elective one, a personal one, in Iraq. Eventually, the president made it easy to believe that the threat from within was as great as the threat from without. That those at home who declared American moral primacy were as dangerous as those abroad who declared our moral degeneracy. That our national security was not worth the risk to our soul. That Abu Ghraib disproved the rightness of our cause and so represented the symbolic end of the war that began on 9/11. And that the very worst thing that could happen to this country would be four more years of George W. Bush. In a nation that loves fairy tales, the president seemed so damned *eager* to cry wolf that we decided he was just trying to keep us scared and that maybe he was just as big a villain as the wolf he insisted on telling us about. That's the whole point of the story, isn't it? The boy cries wolf for his own ends, and after a while people stop believing in the reality of the threat.

I know how this story ends, because I've told it many times myself. I've told it so many times, in fact, that I'm always surprised when the wolf turns out to be real, and shows up hungry at the door, long after the boy is gone.

Kerry's Undeclared War
Matt Bai

The New York Times Magazine | October 10, 2004

Throughout the 2004 campaign, George Bush and John Kerry both strove mightily to present themselves as effective wartime leaders. The importance of the leadership issue is what led Kerry to place such emphasis on his Vietnam service, and it's also why the Republicans attacked his wartime record with such ferocity. Still, for all his attempts to position himself as a hawk on Al Qaeda, Iraq, and other foreign-policy fronts, Kerry was never able to convey a clear, concise vision of where he wanted to take the country and, in particular, how he intended to wage the fight against terrorism—a fact reflected in the pre-election polls, which consistently indicated that a majority of people did not feel Kerry would make the country safer.

In this profile, which appeared a few weeks before the election, Matt Bai gives us a snapshot of the Democratic challenger in full campaign mode (Kerry's wary reaction to an innocent question about bottled water is priceless), and explores why

Kerry's anti-terror policy remained so "ethereal." One reason, Bai suggests, is that while Kerry had a detailed grasp of the terrorism threat—as it turns out, the danger posed by "nonstate" actors is an issue he's worked on for years—his wonkish understanding of the problem made it hard for him to frame his position in lofty, post-9/11 terms. . . .

As New York and Washington were under attack on Sept. 11, 2001, a film crew happened to come upon John Kerry leaving the Capitol. The brief moment of footage, included in a BBC documentary called *Clear the Skies,* tells us something, perhaps, about Kerry in a crisis. The camera captures Congressional aides and visitors, clearly distraught and holding onto one another, streaming down the back steps of the Capitol building in near panic, following the bellowed instructions of anxious police. Off to one side of the screen, there is Kerry, alone, his long legs carrying him calmly down the steps, his neck craning toward the sky, as if he were watching a gathering rainstorm. His face and demeanor appear unworried. Kerry could be a man lost in his thoughts who just happens to have wandered onto the set of a disaster film.

"I remember looking up at the sky as I walked down the steps," Kerry told me recently, when I asked him about the film clip. He said that he and other members of the Senate's Democratic leadership had just watched on television as the second plane hit the World Trade Center, and shortly after that they heard the sonic boom of an explosion and saw, through a large window, the black smoke rise from the Pentagon. "We'd had some warning that there was some airplane in the sky. And I remember seeing a great big plane—I think it was a 747 or something—up there, but it wasn't moving in a way that, you know, I was particularly concerned. I remember feeling a rage, a huge anger, and I remember turning to somebody and saying, 'This is war.' I said, 'This is an act of war.' "

After leaving the Capitol on that terrible day, Kerry walked across the street to his office in the Russell Senate building, where he made sure that his staff had been evacuated and was safe. Reluctant to leave Capitol Hill, he watched TV coverage in his office and saw the second tower fall. He called his older daughter, Alexandra, who was living in New York, and his wife, Teresa, who was in Washington. Those who saw Kerry that morning recall mainly that he was furious, an emotion, those close to him say, that comes easily to him in times of trial. He thought it was a mistake to shut down the Capitol, to show terrorists that they had the power to send the United States government into hiding.

"You know, my instinct was, Where's my gun?" Kerry told me. "How do you fight back? I wanted to do something." That evening, sitting at home, he called an aide and said he wanted to go to New York that very night to help the rescuers; he was ultimately convinced that such a trip was logistically impossible. In the days ahead, Kerry would make two trips to ground zero to see what remained of the carnage.

With the terrorist attacks of 9/11, the geopolitical currents that Washington had spent half a century mastering shifted all at once. It isn't clear how long it took Kerry—a senator for nearly 20 years and, in September 2001, an undeclared candidate for the presidency—to understand the political magnitude of that change. George W. Bush and his advisers got it almost instantly. Few men get to be president, and far fewer get to be president at a critical, transformative moment; Bush, seizing the opportunity, recast himself as the accidental protagonist of a new and dramatic national narrative. Less than a year removed from a disputed election, he set about elbowing his way into the small pantheon of modern presidents—F.D.R. after Pearl Harbor, Kennedy during the Cuban Missile Crisis—who led the nation in profound moments of peril.

Before the smoke had even dissipated over Manhattan, Bush presented the country with an ambitious, overarching construct for a new era in foreign relations. "The war on terror," as he put it, was this generation's test of military and ideological resolve, different from the ones that came before with regard to tactics, perhaps, but not in the magnitude of the challenges or the ambition of the enemy. Bush explained that Al Qaeda and its allies and imitators would constitute a new kind of menace in the years ahead, stealthier and less predictable than past enemies. And yet, in their opposition to American principles and the threat they posed to the nation, he suggested, the Islamic terrorists were the equivalent of Hitler and Stalin, and defeating them would require the same steel and the same conviction that guided America in the last century's campaigns.

While Bush and much of the country seemed remade by the historic events of 9/11, Democrats in Washington were slow to understand that the attacks had to change them in some way too. What adjustments they made were, at first, defensive. Spooked by Bush's surging popularity and the nation's suddenly ascendant mood of patriotism, Democrats stifled their instinctive concerns over civil liberties; and whatever their previous misgivings about intervention, many Congressional Democrats, a year after the terrorist attacks, voted to give Bush the authority to invade Iraq.

What few Democrats did at the time was think creatively about the new world of foreign policy. The candidates who began their runs for the presidency last year, from Dennis Kucinich and his peace platform on the left to Joe Lieberman and Dick Gephardt on the other side of the spectrum, attacked the president's foreign policy from different directions, but if any new ideas emerged during those months, they were soon drowned out by the booming anti-war voice of Howard Dean. When Kerry emerged as the most palatable alternative, he at first ran mostly on the viability of his personal story, focusing more on his combat experience in Vietnam than on any plan to fight Al Qaeda or remake Iraq. Only since Labor Day has Kerry begun to sharpen his distinctions with Bush on national security and foreign policy. In a series of combative speeches and statements, and in a crisp performance at the first head-to-head debate, Kerry has argued that Bush's war in Iraq is a disaster, that troops should be brought home before the end of the next presidential term and that the Iraq war is a "profound diversion" from the war on terror and the real showdown with Al Qaeda.

What Kerry still has not done is to articulate clearly a larger foreign-policy vision, his own overarching alternative to Bush's global war on terror. The difference between the two men was clear during the foreign-policy debate in Florida ten days ago. Kerry seemed dominant for much of the exchange, making clear arguments on a range of specific challenges— the war in Iraq, negotiations with North Korea, relations with Russia. But while Kerry bore in on ground-level details, Bush, in defending his policies, seemed, characteristically, to be looking at the world from a much higher altitude, repeating in his brief and sometimes agitated statements a single unifying worldview: America is the world's great force for freedom, unsparing in its use of preemptive might and unstinting in its determination to stamp out tyranny and terrorism. Kerry seemed to offer no grand thematic equivalent.

Inside liberal think-tanks, there are Democratic foreign-policy experts who are challenging some of Bush's most basic assumptions about the post-9/11 world—including, most provocatively, the very idea that we are, in fact, in a war. But Kerry has tended to steer clear of this conversation, preferring to attack Bush for the way he is fighting terrorism rather than for the way in which he perceives and frames the threat itself.

The argument going on in Washington has its roots in the dark years of the cold war. Just about everyone agrees that many factors contributed to America's triumph over world communism—but people differ on which of those factors were most important. The neo-conservatives who shaped Reagan's anti-Soviet policy and now shape Bush's war on terror have long held that the "twilight struggle" with the Soviet empire was won primarily as a result of U.S. military intervention in several hemispheres and of Reagan's massive arms buildup, without which democracy and free markets could not have taken hold. Many liberals, on the other hand, have never been comfortable with that premise; while they acknowledge that American military power played a role, they contend that the long ideological struggle with communism ended chiefly because the stifling economic and social tenets of Marxism were unsustainable, and because a new leader emerged— Mikhail Gorbachev—who understood that. They see Islamic fanaticism, similarly, as a repressive ideology, born of complex societal conditions, that won't be defeated by any predominately military solution.

In the liberal view, the enemy this time—an entirely new kind of "non-state actor" known as Al Qaeda—more closely resembles an especially murderous drug cartel than it does the vaunted Red Army. Instead of military might, liberal thinkers believe, the moment calls for a combination of expansive diplomacy abroad and interdiction at home, an effort more akin to the war on drugs than to any conventional war of the last century.

Even Democrats who stress that combating terrorism should include a strong military option argue that the "war on terror" is a flawed construct. "We're not in a war on terror, in the literal sense," says Richard Holbrooke, the Clinton-era diplomat who could well become Kerry's secretary of state. "The war on terror is like saying 'the war on poverty.' It's just a metaphor. What we're really talking about is winning the ideological struggle so that people stop turning themselves into suicide bombers."

These competing philosophies, neo-conservative and liberal, aren't mutually exclusive, of course. Neo-cons will agree that military operations are just one facet, albeit the main one, of their response to terrorism. And liberals are almost unanimous in their support for military force when the nation or its allies face an imminent and preventable threat; not only did the vast majority of liberal policy makers support the invasion of Afghanistan, but many also thought it should have been pursued more aggressively. Still, the philosophical difference between the two camps, applied to a conflict that may well last a generation, is both deep and distinct. Fundamentally, Bush sees the war on terror as a military campaign, not simply to protect American lives but also to preserve and spread American values around the world; his liberal critics see it more as an ideological campaign, one that will turn back a tide of resentment toward Americans and thus limit the peril they face at home.

Perhaps the most pressing question of the presidential campaign is where John Kerry stands in this debate. The man who would be the first Vietnam veteran to occupy the Oval Office has doggedly tried to merge both world-views, repeatedly vowing to fight both a more fierce and a more restrained, multifaceted war on terror. Aides say this is evidence of his capacity to envision complex solutions for a complex world; voters, through the summer and early fall, seemed less impressed. In a typical poll conducted by *The Washington Post* and ABC News just before the first presidential debate, only 37 percent of the respondents agreed with the statement that Kerry would make the country safer. A *New York Times*/CBS News poll conducted in mid-September found that half the respondents thought Bush would make the right decisions to protect the nation from terrorism, compared with only 26 percent who said the same thing about Kerry.

More surprising than the poll numbers, though, is the sense of frustration, expressed not just by voters but by some in Kerry's own party, that even at this late hour, Kerry's long-term strategy for defeating the terrorists remains so ethereal. "You will lose, and we will win," Kerry told America's enemies in the most memorable line of his convention speech in late July. "The future doesn't belong to fear. It belongs to freedom." But *how* will we win? How do you root out and destroy Islamic radicals while at the same time capturing the "hearts and minds" of Islamic students? When John Kerry said, on Sept. 11, 2001, "This is war," what precisely did he mean?

On an evening in August, just after a campaign swing through the Southwest, Kerry and I met, for the second of three conversations about terrorism and national security, in a hotel room overlooking the Ferris wheel on the Santa Monica pier. A row of Evian water bottles had been thought-fully placed on a nearby table. Kerry frowned.

"Can we get any of *my* water?" he asked Stephanie Cutter, his commu-nications director, who dutifully scurried from the room. I asked Kerry, out of sheer curiosity, what he didn't like about Evian.

"I hate that stuff," Kerry explained to me. "They pack it full of minerals."

"What kind of water do you drink?" I asked, trying to make conversation.

"Plain old American water," he said.

"You mean tap water?"

"No," Kerry replied deliberately. He seemed now to sense some kind of trap. I was left to imagine what was going through his head. *If I admit that I drink bottled water, then he might say I'm out of touch with ordinary voters. But doesn't demanding my own brand of water seem even more aristocratic? Then again, Evian is French—important to stay away from anything even remotely French.*

"There are all kinds of waters," he said finally. Pause. "Saratoga Spring." This seemed to have exhausted his list. "Sometimes I drink tap water," he added.

After months of having his every word scrutinized by reporters and mocked by Republicans, Kerry appeared to sense danger in the most mun-dane of places. Interviewing him reminded me at times of what I'd read in *Tour of Duty*, the historian Douglas Brinkley's flattering account of Kerry's service in Vietnam. The Swift boat crews on the Mekong Delta and the Ca Mau Peninsula did not aspire to be heroic, although they were. Kerry and the young sailors were given patrol missions that seemed unnecessarily dangerous; their job was essentially to prove the point that Americans could traverse the windy rivers of the delta, rife with Vietcong, and lure the enemy out into the open. They traveled slowly and kept watch in all direc-tions, and if their leader got them from point A to point B and back again without serious casualties, he had done his job.

Kerry seems to find presidential politics in the era of Karl Rove as treacherous as riverine warfare, and he has run for the presidency in much the same way. From the beginning, Kerry's advisers said that the election would be principally a referendum on Bush, whose approval ratings, reflecting public anxiety over Iraq and a sluggish economy, were consis-tently low for a president seeking reelection. All Kerry had to do to win, the thinking went, was to meet a basic threshold of acceptability with voters and avoid doing or saying anything that might be fatally stupid. The river-banks were lined with hostile Republicans and reporters, lying in wait for him, and Kerry's goal as he sailed upriver was simple: Stay down. Exercise caution. Get to November in one piece.

Which is exactly what it's like to interview Kerry as he runs for the presidency; he acts as if you've been sent to destroy him, and he can't quite figure out why in the world he should be sitting across from you. When I met him for our first conversation, in his cabin aboard the 757 that shuttles his campaign around the country, Kerry didn't extend his hand or even look up to greet me when I entered, and he grew so quickly and obviously exasperated with my questions about his thoughts and votes on Iraq that he cut the interview short. (Embarrassed aides later told me he had been abruptly roused from a nap.) He was far more gracious in our subsequent conversations about terrorism and foreign policy, but he still spent a lot of the time repeating phrases from his stump speech. ("You will lose, we will win," and so on.) What some politicians—Bill Clinton comes to mind—might have considered an opportunity to persuade and impress voters, Kerry seemed to regard only as an invitation to do himself harm.

Kerry's guardedness has contributed to the impression that he does not think clearly or boldly about foreign policy. In his short but fascinating book titled *Surprise, Security, and the American Experience*, the Yale historian John Lewis Gaddis suggests that Bush's framework for fighting terrorism has its roots in the lofty, idealistic tradition of John Quincy Adams and Woodrow Wilson. (The book was so popular in the White House that Gaddis was invited over for a discussion.) "What Bush is proposing is quite long-term, quite radical and quite Wilsonian," Gaddis told me when we spoke; when I asked him about Kerry, he said: "I don't know where Kerry is on this. I don't have the slightest clue."

Kerry's adversaries have found it easy to ridicule his views on foreign policy, suggesting that his idea of counterterrorism is simply to go around arresting all the terrorists. This is what Dick Cheney was getting at when he said last month that there was a danger, should Kerry be elected, that "we'll fall back into the pre-9/11 mind-set, if you will, that in fact these terrorist attacks are just criminal acts, and that we're not really at war." These barbs have some resonance, largely because Kerry is so obviously defensive about them; talking to him, you sometimes get the sense that he would gladly throw on a pair of night-vision goggles and abduct a member of his own staff if he thought it would prove he could be as tough on terror as his opponent. (When I asked one Kerry adviser what it was that voters needed to know about Kerry and terrorism, he replied without hesitation. "That he's strong and tough," he said. "In the case of John Kerry, unlike Dick Cheney and George W. Bush, he's looked people in the face and shot them dead.")

It's perhaps not surprising, then, that Kerry hasn't been eager to challenge Bush's grand notion of a war on terror; such a distinction might sound weak, equivocal or, worse yet, nuanced. It's equally unsurprising that, in the recent *Times* poll, 57 percent of the respondents said Kerry hadn't made his plans for the country clear, and 63 percent believed he said what he thought people wanted to hear, rather than what he actually thought. This reflected savage Republican attacks on Kerry's character, to be sure, but it probably also had something to do with the fact that he hadn't made his plans clear and seemed to be saying what he thought people wanted to hear.

When I asked Kerry's campaign advisers about these poll numbers, what I heard from some of them in response was that Kerry's theories on global affairs were just too complex for the electorate and would have been ignored—or, worse yet, mangled—by the press. "Yes, he should have laid out this issue and many others in greater detail and with more intellectual creativity, there's no question," one adviser told me. "But it would have had no effect."

This is, of course, a common Democratic refrain: Republicans sound more coherent because they see the world in such a rudimentary way, while Democrats, ten steps ahead of the rest of the country, wrestle with profound policy issues that don't lend themselves to slogans. By this reasoning, any proposal that can be explained concisely to voters is, by definition, ineffective and lacking in gravitas. Other Kerry aides blame the candidate and his coterie of message makers, most of whom are legendary for their attack ads but less adept at thinking about broad policy arguments. "If you talk about this the right way, then the American people, or most of them, will get it," one of Kerry's informal advisers told me. "But you've got to have guts."

This is the Republican line on Kerry—that he lacks guts. Kerry's often wobbly attempt to be both like and unlike Bush in his approach to terrorism and the war in Iraq enabled the Bush team, by the time Kerry and I spoke in August, to portray him, devastatingly, as a "flip-flopper" who careens from one position to another. In our conversation, Kerry seemed unusually sensitive to these allegations, to the point where he seemed unwilling to admit to having evolved or grown in the way that politicians—or human beings, for that matter—generally do. When I asked Kerry how Sept. 11 had changed him, either personally or politically, he seemed to freeze for a moment.

"It accelerated—" He paused. "I mean, it didn't change me much at all. It just sort of accelerated, confirmed in me, the urgency of doing the things I thought we needed to be doing. I mean, to me, it wasn't as transformational as it was a kind of anger, a frustration and an urgency that we weren't doing the kinds of things necessary to prevent it and to deal with it."

Kerry did allow that he, like other Americans, felt less safe after 9/11. "Look, until a few months ago," he said, referring to the time before he was enveloped in a Secret Service escort and whisked around on charter planes, "I was flying like everybody else, you know, going through things. Absolutely, I've looked at people very carefully on an airplane. I'd look at shoes. I'd check people who I thought might be a little squirrelly. Going into crowded events, I feel very much on the alert."

Bush attacked Kerry earlier in the campaign over this question of whether the war on terror was really a war. ("My opponent indicated that he's not comfortable using the word 'war' to describe the struggle we're in," Bush said, although whether Kerry had actually said that is debatable.) Now that I'd heard Holbrooke and others say flat out that we *weren't* in an actual war, I wanted to hear what Kerry thought. Is this a real war, or a metaphorical one? I asked him. Is "war" the right word to use?

"There's a danger in it," Kerry said, nodding. "But it's real," he went on, meaning the war itself. "You know, when your buildings are bombed and 3,000 people get killed, and airplanes are hijacked, and a nation is terrorized the way we were, and people continue to plot to do you injury, that's an act of war, and it's serious business. But it's a different kind of war. You have to understand that this is not the sands of Iwo Jima. This is a completely new, different kind of war from any we've fought previously."

Kerry told me he would stop terrorists by going after them ruthlessly with the military, and he faulted Bush, as he often does, for choosing to use Afghan militias, instead of American troops, to pursue Osama bin Laden into the mountains of Tora Bora, where he disappeared. "I'm certainly, you know, not going to take second seat to anybody, to nobody, in my willingness to seek justice and set America on a course—to make America safe," Kerry told me.

"And that requires destroying terrorists. And I'm committed to doing that. But I think I have a better way of doing it. I can do it more effectively."

This was a word that Kerry came back to repeatedly in our discussions; he told me he would wage a more "effective" war on terror no less than 18 times in two hours of conversations. The question, of course, was how.

"I think we can do a better job," Kerry said, "of cutting off financing, of exposing groups, of working cooperatively across the globe, of improving our intelligence capabilities nationally and internationally, of training our military and deploying them differently, of specializing in special forces and special ops, of working with allies, and most importantly—and I mean most importantly—of restoring America's reputation as a country that listens, is sensitive, brings people to our side, is the seeker of peace, not war, and that uses our high moral ground and high-level values to augment us in the war on terror, not to diminish us."

This last point was what Kerry seemed to be getting at with his mantra of "effectiveness," and it was in fact the main thrust of his campaign pitch about terrorism. By infuriating allies and diminishing the country's international esteem, Kerry argued, Bush had made it impossible for America to achieve its goals abroad. By the simple act of changing presidents, the country would greatly increase its chances of success in the global war on terror. Both candidates, in fact, were suggesting that the main difference between them was one of leadership style and not policy; just as Bush had taken to arguing that Kerry was too inconstant to lead a nation at war, Kerry's critique centered on the idea that Bush had proved himself too stubborn and arrogant to represent America to the rest of the world.

But when you listen carefully to what Bush and Kerry say, it becomes clear that the differences between them are more profound than the matter of who can be more effective in achieving the same ends. Bush casts the war on terror as a vast struggle that is likely to go on indefinitely, or at least as long as radical Islam commands fealty in regions of the world. In a rare moment of either candor or carelessness, or perhaps both, Bush told Matt Lauer on the *Today* show in August that he didn't think the United States could actually triumph in the war on terror in the foreseeable future. "I don't think you can win it," he said—a statement that he and his aides tried to disown but that had the ring of sincerity to it. He and other members of his administration have said that Americans should expect to be attacked again, and that the constant shadow of danger that hangs over major cities like New York and Washington is the cost of freedom. In his rhetoric, Bush suggests that terrorism for this generation of Americans is and should be an overwhelming and frightening reality.

When I asked Kerry what it would take for Americans to feel safe again, he displayed a much less apocalyptic worldview. "We have to get back to the place we were, where terrorists are not the focus of our lives, but they're a nuisance," Kerry said. "As a former law-enforcement person, I know we're never going to end prostitution. We're never going to end illegal gambling. But we're going to reduce it, organized crime, to a level where it isn't on the rise. It isn't threatening people's lives every day, and fundamentally, it's something that you continue to fight, but it's not threatening the fabric of your life."

This analogy struck me as remarkable, if only because it seemed to throw down a big orange marker between Kerry's philosophy and the president's. Kerry, a former prosecutor, was suggesting that the war, if one could call it that, was, if not winnable, then at least controllable. If mobsters could be chased into the back rooms of seedy clubs, then so, too, could terrorists be sent scurrying for their lives into remote caves where they wouldn't harm us. Bush had continually cast himself as the optimist in the race, asserting that he alone saw the liberating potential of American might, and yet his dark vision of unending war suddenly seemed far less hopeful than Kerry's notion that all of this horror—planes flying into buildings, anxiety about suicide bombers and chemicals in the subway—could somehow be made to recede until it was barely in our thoughts.

Kerry came to his worldview over the course of a Senate career that has been, by any legislative standard, a quiet affair. Beginning in the late '80s, Kerry's Subcommittee on Terrorism, Narcotics and International Operations investigated and exposed connections between Latin American drug dealers and BCCI, the international bank that was helping to launder drug money. That led to more investigations of arms dealers, money laundering and terrorist financing.

Kerry turned his work on the committee into a book on global crime, titled *The New War*, published in 1997. He readily admitted to me that the book "wasn't exclusively on Al Qaeda"; in fact, it barely mentioned the rise of Islamic extremism. But when I spoke to Kerry in August, he said that many of the interdiction tactics that cripple drug lords, including governments working jointly to share intelligence, patrol borders and force banks to identify suspicious customers, can also be some of the most useful tools in the war on terror.

"Of all the records in the Senate, if you don't mind my saying, I think I was ahead of the curve on this entire dark side of globalization," he said. "I think that the Senate committee report on contras, narcotics and drugs, et cetera, is a seminal report. People have based research papers on it. People have based documents on it, movies on it. I think it was a significant piece of work."

More senior members of the foreign-relations committee, like Joe Biden and Richard Lugar, were far more visible and vocal on the emerging threat of Islamic terrorism. But through his BCCI investigation, Kerry did discover that a wide array of international criminals—Latin American drug lords, Palestinian terrorists, arms dealers—had one thing in common: they were able to move money around through the same illicit channels. And he worked hard, and with little credit, to shut those channels down.

In 1988, Kerry successfully proposed an amendment that forced the Treasury Department to negotiate so-called Kerry Agreements with foreign countries. Under these agreements, foreign governments had to promise to keep a close watch on their banks for potential money laundering or they risked losing their access to U.S. markets. Other measures Kerry tried to pass throughout the '90s, virtually all of them blocked by Republican senators on the banking committee, would end up, in the wake of 9/11, in the USA Patriot Act; among other things, these measures subject banks to fines or loss of license if they don't take steps to verify the identities of their customers and to avoid being used for money laundering.

Through his immersion in the global underground, Kerry made connections among disparate criminal and terrorist groups that few other senators interested in foreign policy were making in the '90s. Richard A. Clarke, who coordinated security and counterterrorism policy for George W. Bush and Bill Clinton, credits Kerry with having seen beyond the national-security tableau on which most of his colleagues were focused. "He was getting it at the same time that people like Tony Lake were getting it, in the '93–'94 time frame," Clarke says, referring to Anthony Lake, Clinton's national security adviser. "And the 'it' here was that there was a new nonstate-actor threat, and that nonstate-actor threat was a blended threat that didn't fit neatly into the box of organized criminal, or neatly into the box of terrorism. What you found were groups that were all of the above."

In other words, Kerry was among the first policy makers in Washington to begin mapping out a strategy to combat an entirely new kind of enemy. Americans were conditioned, by two world wars and a long standoff with a rival superpower, to see foreign policy as a mix of cooperation and tension between civilized states. Kerry came to believe, however, that Americans were in greater danger from the more shadowy groups he had been investigating—nonstate actors, armed with cellphones and laptops—who might detonate suitcase bombs or release lethal chemicals into the subway just to make a point. They lived in remote regions and exploited weak governments. Their goal wasn't to govern states but to destabilize them.

The challenge of beating back these nonstate actors—not just Islamic terrorists but all kinds of rogue forces—is what Kerry meant by "the dark side of globalization." He came closest to articulating this as an actual foreign-policy vision in a speech he gave at U.C.L.A. last February. "The war on terror is not a clash of civilizations," he said then. "It is a clash of civilization against chaos, of the best hopes of humanity against dogmatic fears of progress and the future."

This stands in significant contrast to the Bush doctrine, which holds that the war on terror, if not exactly a clash of civilizations, is nonetheless a struggle between those states that would promote terrorism and those that would exterminate it. Bush, like Kerry, accepts the premise that America is endangered mainly by a new kind of adversary that claims no state or political entity as its own. But he does not accept the idea that those adversaries can ultimately survive and operate independently of states; in fact, he asserts that terrorist groups are inevitably the subsidiaries of irresponsible regimes. "We must be prepared to stop rogue states and their terrorist clients," the National Security Strategy said, in a typical passage, "before they are able to threaten or use weapons of mass destruction against the United States and our allies and friends."

By singling out three states in particular—Iraq, North Korea and Iran—as an "axis of evil," and by invading Iraq on the premise that it did (or at least might) sponsor terrorism, Bush cemented the idea that his war on terror is a war against those states that, in the president's words, are not with us but against us. Many of Bush's advisers spent their careers steeped in cold-war strategy, and their foreign policy is deeply rooted in the idea that states are the only consequential actors on the world stage, and that they can—and should—be forced to exercise control over the violent groups that take root within their borders.

Kerry's view, on the other hand, suggests that it is the very premise of civ-ilized states, rather than any one ideology, that is under attack. And no one state, acting alone, can possibly have much impact on the threat, because terrorists will always be able to move around, shelter their money and con-nect in cyberspace; there are no capitals for a superpower like the United States to bomb, no ambassadors to recall, no economies to sanction. The U.S. military searches for bin Laden, the Russians hunt for the Chechen ter-rorist Shamil Basayev and the Israelis fire missiles at Hamas bomb makers; in Kerry's world, these disparate terrorist elements make up a loosely affil-iated network of diabolical villains, more connected to one another by tac-tics and ideology than they are to any one state sponsor. The conflict, in Kerry's formulation, pits the forces of order versus the forces of chaos, and only a unified community of nations can ensure that order prevails.

One can infer from this that if Kerry were able to speak less guardedly, in a less treacherous atmosphere than a political campaign, he might say, as some of his advisers do, that we are not in an actual war on terror. Wars are fought between states or between factions vying for control of a state; Al Qaeda and its many offspring are neither. If Kerry's foreign-policy frame is correct, then law enforcement probably is the most important, though not the only, strategy you can employ against such forces, who need pass-ports and bank accounts and weapons in order to survive and flourish. Such a theory suggests that, in our grief and fury, we have overrated the military threat posed by Al Qaeda, paradoxically elevating what was essen-tially a criminal enterprise, albeit a devastatingly sophisticated and global one, into the ideological successor to Hitler and Stalin—and thus confer-ring on the jihadists a kind of stature that might actually work in their favor, enabling them to attract more donations and more recruits.

This critical difference between the two men running for the presidency, over what kind of enemy we are fighting and how best to defeat it, is at the core of a larger debate over how the United States should involve itself in the Muslim world. Bush and Kerry are in agreement, as is just about every expert on Islamic culture you can find, that in order for Americans to live and travel securely, the United States must change the widespread percep-tion among many Muslims worldwide that America is morally corrupt and economically exploitative. It is this resentment, felt especially strongly among Arab Muslims, that makes heroes of suicide bombers. The question vexing the foreign-policy establishment in Washington is how you market freedom. Is the establishment of a single, functioning democracy in the Middle East enough to win the "hearts and minds" of ordinary Muslims, by convincing them that America is in fact the model for a free, more open society? Or do you need to somehow strike at the underlying conditions—despotism, hopelessness, economic and social repression—that breed fundamentalism and violence in the first place?

"You've got to do something to acknowledge the gulf that exists between the dispossessed Arab world and us, because it's huge," says Bob Kerrey, the former Democratic senator who is now president of New School University and who served on the independent 9/11 commission. "We don't have enough money, we don't have enough parents who are willing to give up their sons and daughters, to win this with our Army, Air Force, Navy, Marine Corps and Coast Guard. We don't have the bodies to do it. So if you don't have a real agenda of hope that's as hard-headed and tough as your military and law-enforcement agenda, we're not going to win this thing."

The neo-conservatives have advanced a viral theory of democracy. In their view, establishing a model democracy in the Arab world, by force if necessary, no matter how many years and lives it takes, would ultimately benefit not only the people of that country but also America too. A free and democratic Iraq, to take the favorite example, will cause the people of other repressive countries in the region to rise up and demand American-style freedom, and these democratic nations will no longer be breeding pools for nihilistic terrorists. Like so much of Bush's policy, this kind of thinking harks directly back to the cold war. The domino theory that took hold during the 1950's maintained that an ideological change in one nation—"going" communist or democratic—could infect its neighbor; it was based in part on the idea that ideologies could be contagious.

Bush crystallized the new incarnation of this idea in his convention speech last month, notable for the unapologetic sweep and clarity of its vision. "The terrorists know that a vibrant, successful democracy at the heart of the Middle East will discredit their radical ideology of hate," the president said. "I believe in the transformational power of liberty. As the citizens of Afghanistan and Iraq seize the moment, their example will send a message of hope throughout a vital region. Palestinians will hear the message that democracy and reform are within their reach, and so is peace with our good friend Israel. Young women across the Middle East will hear the message that their day of equality and justice is coming. Young men will hear the message that national progress and dignity are found in liberty, not tyranny and terror."

Kerry, too, envisions a freer and more democratic Middle East. But he flatly rejects the premise of viral democracy, particularly when the virus is introduced at gunpoint. "In this administration, the approach is that democracy is the automatic, easily embraced alternative to every ill in the region," he told me. Kerry disagreed. "You can't impose it on people," he said. "You have to bring them to it. You have to invite them to it. You have to nurture the process."

Those who know Kerry say this belief is in part a reaction to his own experience in Vietnam, where one understanding of the domino theory ("if Vietnam goes communist, all of Asia will fall") led to the death of 58,000 Americans, and another ("the South Vietnamese crave democracy") ran up against the realities of life in a poor, long-war-ravaged country. The people of Vietnam, Kerry found, were susceptible neither to the dogma of communism nor the persuasiveness of American "liberation." As the young Kerry said during his 1971 testimony to the Senate Foreign Relations Committee: "We found most people didn't even know the difference between communism and democracy. They only wanted to work in rice paddies without helicopters strafing them and bombs with napalm burning their villages and tearing their country apart. They wanted everything to do with the war, particularly with this foreign presence of the United States of America, to leave them alone in peace."

Biden, who is perhaps Kerry's closest friend in the Senate, suggests that Kerry sees Bush's advisers as beholden to the same grand and misguided theories. "John and I never believed that, if you were successful in Iraq, you'd have governments falling like dominoes in the Middle East," he told me. "The neo-cons of today are 'the best and the brightest' who brought us Vietnam. They have taken a construct that's flawed and applied it to a world that isn't relevant."

In fact, Kerry and his advisers contend that the occupation of Iraq is creating a reverse contagion in the region; they say the fighting—with its heavy civilian casualties and its pictures, beamed throughout the Arab world, of American aggression—has been a boon to Al Qaeda recruiters. They frequently cite a Pentagon memo, leaked to the media last year, in which Defense Secretary Donald Rumsfeld wondered whether Al Qaeda was recruiting new terrorists faster than the U.S. military could capture or kill them. "God help us if we damage the shrine in Najaf," Richard Holbrooke told me on a day when marines surrounded insurgent Shiites inside the shrine, "and we create a new group of Shiites who some years from now blow up the Statue of Liberty or something like that, all because we destroyed the holiest site in Shiism."

If forced democracy is ultimately Bush's panacea for the ills that haunt the world, as Kerry suggests it is, then Kerry's is diplomacy. Kerry mentions the importance of cooperating with the world community so often that some of his strongest supporters wish he would ease up a bit. ("When people hear multilateral, they think multi-*mush*," Biden despaired.) But multilateralism is not an abstraction to Kerry, whose father served as a career diplomat during the years after World War II. The only time I saw Kerry truly animated during two hours of conversation was when he talked about the ability of a president to build relationships with other leaders.

"We need to engage more directly and more respectfully with Islam, with the state of Islam, with religious leaders, mullahs, imams, clerics, in a way that proves this is not a clash with the British and the Americans and the old forces they remember from the colonial days," Kerry told me during a rare break from campaigning, in Seattle at the end of August. "And that's all about your diplomacy."

When I suggested that effecting such changes could take many years, Kerry shook his head vehemently and waved me off.

"Yeah, it is long-term, but it can be dramatically effective in the short term. It really can be. I promise you." He leaned his head back and slapped his thighs. "A new presidency with the right moves, the right language, the right outreach, the right initiatives, can dramatically alter the world's perception of us very, very quickly.

"I know Mubarak well enough to know what I think I could achieve in the messaging and in the press in Egypt," Kerry went on. "And, similarly, with Jordan and with King Abdullah, and what we can do in terms of transformation in the economics of the region by getting American businesspeople involved, getting some stability and really beginning to proactively move in those ways. We just haven't been doing any of this stuff. We've been stunningly disengaged, with the exception of Iraq.

"I mean, you ever hear anything about the 'road map' anymore?" he asked, referring to the international plan for phasing in peace between Israel and the Palestinians, which Kerry supports. "No. You ever hear anything about *anything* anymore? No. Do you hear anything about this greater Middle East initiative, the concepts or anything? No. I think we're fighting a very narrow, myopic kind of war."

It is not a coincidence that Kerry's greatest success in the Senate came not during his long run of investigations but in the realm of diplomacy. He and John McCain worked for several years to settle the controversy over P.O.W.-M.I.A.'s and to normalize relations with Vietnam—an achievement that Kerry's Senate colleagues consider his finest moment. "He should talk about it more," Bob Kerrey said. "He transformed the region." In the same way, John Kerry sees himself as a kind of ambassador-president, shuttling to world capitals and reintegrating America, by force of personality, into the world community.

He would begin, if sworn into office, by going immediately to the United Nations to deliver a speech recasting American foreign policy. Whereas Bush has branded North Korea "evil" and refuses to negotiate head on with its authoritarian regime, Kerry would open bilateral talks over its burgeoning nuclear program. Similarly, he has said he would rally other nations behind sanctions against Iran if that country refuses to abandon its nuclear ambitions. Kerry envisions appointing a top-level envoy to restart the Middle East peace process, and he's intent on getting India and Pakistan to adopt key provisions of the Nuclear Nonproliferation Treaty. (One place where Kerry vows to take a harder line than Bush is Pakistan, where Bush has embraced the military ruler Pervez Musharraf, and where Kerry sees a haven for chaos in the vast and lawless region on the border with Afghanistan.) In all of this, Kerry intends to use as leverage America's considerable capacity for economic aid; a Kerry adviser told me, only slightly in jest, that Kerry's most tempting fantasy is to attend the G-8 summit.

Kerry's view, that the 21st century will be defined by the organized world's struggle against agents of chaos and lawlessness, might be the beginning of a compelling vision. The idea that America and its allies, sharing resources and using the latest technologies, could track the movements of terrorists, seize their bank accounts and carry out targeted military strikes to eliminate them, seems more optimistic and more practical than the notion that the conventional armies of the United States will inevitably have to punish or even invade every Islamic country that might abet radicalism.

And yet, you can understand why Kerry has been so tentative in advancing this idea. It's comforting to think that Al Qaeda might be as easily marginalized as a bunch of drug-running thugs, that an "effective" assault on its bank accounts might cripple its twisted campaign against Americans. But Americans are frightened—an emotion that has benefited Bush, and one that he has done little to dissuade—and many of them perceive a far more existential threat to their lives than the one Kerry describes. In this climate, Kerry's rather dry recitations about money-laundering laws and intelligence-sharing agreements can sound oddly discordant. We are living at a time that feels historically consequential, where people seem to expect—and perhaps deserve—a theory of the world that matches the scope of their insecurity.

Theoretically, Kerry could still find a way to wrap his ideas into some bold and cohesive construct for the next half-century—a Kerry Doctrine, perhaps, or a campaign against chaos, rather than a war on terror—that people will understand and relate to. But he has always been a man who prides himself on appreciating the subtleties of public policy, and everything in his experience has conditioned him to avoid unsubtle constructs and grand designs. His aversion to Big Think has resulted in one of the campaign's oddities: it is Bush, the man vilified by liberals as intellectually vapid, who has emerged as the de facto visionary in the campaign, trying to impose some long-term thematic order on a dangerous and disorderly world, while Kerry carves the globe into a series of discrete problems with specific solutions.

When Kerry first told me that Sept. 11 had not changed him, I was surprised. I assumed everyone in America—and certainly in Washington—had been changed by that day. I assumed he was being overly cautious, afraid of providing his opponents with yet another cheap opportunity to call him a flip-flopper. What I came to understand was that, in fact, the attacks really had *not* changed the way Kerry viewed or talked about terrorism—which is exactly why he has come across, to some voters, as less of a leader than he could be. He may well have understood the threat from Al Qaeda long before the rest of us. And he may well be right, despite the ridicule from Cheney and others, when he says that a multinational, law-enforcement-like approach can be more effective in fighting terrorists. But his less lofty vision might have seemed more satisfying—and would have been easier to talk about in a political campaign—in a world where the twin towers still stood.

Female Matters
Mimi Swartz

Vogue | October 2004

In the runup to the 2004 presidential vote, most observers agreed that the election would hinge largely on which candidate's operation could generate the largest voter turnout. Aided by increasingly sophisticated voter profiles, both the Bush and Kerry campaigns made unprecedented efforts to target their candidates' message to specific demographic groups, in hopes of persuading likely-but-recalcitrant supporters to the polls. In this essay, Texas Monthly *executive editor Mimi Swartz examines how this campaign strategy is targeting America's women. . . .*

When I was young, my mother used to take me with her to the polls. There was always something magical and mysterious about Election Day, something both wildly public and devoutly private. We waited in long lines alongside cheerful neighbors for what seemed, to my five-year-old self, like hours. The voting booth was like a confessional: Even as a child, I couldn't venture with my mother into that solitary, solemn space. Instead, I watched her step in and pull the lever that drew the curtain around her, listened anxiously for the click, click, click of the levers as she pressed them, watched her calves beneath the drapes as she shifted her weight and tapped her toes, making her decisions. And then she emerged—somehow transformed, I thought. In the space of a few moments she communicated something that would stay with me for the rest of my life: It was my right and my obligation to step into the voting booth and make a difference.

I thought of that sweetly anachronistic scene the other day, as I came upon a few Web sites designed to encourage women to vote this November. At www.rockthevote.org, for instance, I could buy a GIVE A SH*T T-shirt, while at www.axisofeve.org I could choose between MY CHERRY FOR KERRY hot shorts or a LICK BUSH thong. With his new www.citizen change.org, P. Diddy was promising to make voting "sexy"—"the same way we make a Biggie album, a Sean John shirt, or a *Spiderman* movie hot, cool, and sexy." Then there's Christina Aguilera, with her mouth stylishly sewn shut—ONLY YOU CAN SILENCE YOURSELF—on a Times Square billboard. Laura Dawn, the event and cultural director of MoveOn.org, explained it all for me: "I understand why women don't vote. Who is more interesting to you, Hillary Clinton or Britney Spears? We need someone like Britney Spears saying it's cool to vote."

Welcome to the world of the 2004 election, in which the single women's vote—that's unmarried, divorced, and widowed women, not just Britney or Christina fans—is key. Ever since the 2000 election, when it was discovered that 22 million unmarried females stayed away from the polls, political experts have been trying to figure out how to get them back in time to reelect George Bush or send John Kerry to the White House. Their numbers represent an enormous bloc—the largest group of nonparticipating eligible voters—that could have changed the fate of the 2000 race, altered the current status of health-care, child-care, job-creation, and education legislation, shifted the tactics of the war on terror, and perhaps avoided entirely the very existence of the war in Iraq. With the 2004 presidential race, these women, who tend to be progressive, are even more crucial than before: Most people already know which presidential candidate they'll be supporting, so it will be turnout—as opposed to ideas—that will decide the race. "We are in the beg, borrow and plead era of voting," says Page Gardner, codirector of Women's Voices/Women Vote.

No one is entirely clear about how we got to this point. According to Michael Delli Carpini, a political scientist and dean of the Annenberg School of Communication at the University of Pennsylvania, the good news is that more women than men actually get themselves to the polls at election time. But voting has been dropping off among both sexes for the last four decades, thanks partly to the upheavals of the 1960s, Watergate and other government scandals of the 1970s, Ronald Reagan's government-is-the-problem-not-the-solution stance in the 1980s, and more scandals—

Whitewater, Monica, et cetera—leading to even greater voter disillusion-ment in the 1990s and beyond. Throughout this period the gender gap has been growing. In the 1960s, for instance, women were more likely to vote Republican; by the 1980s, they went for Jimmy Carter, and have stayed true to the Democrats ever since.

Gore's loss in 2000 prompted further research into the women who stayed home from the polls—the ones who most likely tossed the election to Bush. First of all, these nonvoting women are believed to be insecure: Unlike their male counterparts, they feel they have to be well informed to vote, and will stay away before they cast a vote they feel is foolish. Then there is the second-shift excuse: Women are too busy multitasking, holding down jobs (that, by the way, still pay them 80 cents for every dollar earned by a man), doing the grocery shopping, housework, and carpooling, as well as helping with homework; they don't have time to get to the polls. There is also a narcissism issue: Women—especially busy women—don't see what's in it for them to vote, particularly when the majority of the candi-dates are still white males who don't speak to their concerns. They don't particularly care that women fought long and hard to win the right to vote 84 years ago, and they don't believe their votes can make a difference. "We have not made the connection for them," says Marie C. Wilson, founder of the White House Project and author of *Closing the Leadership Gap: Why Women Can and Must Help Run the World.* "The same thing that applies to companies applies to countries. We have to show young women that there are opportunities."

With the 2004 presidential race looming, that's what politicians and myriad interest groups are trying to do, in what promises to be the strangest voter drive in American history. Expect to see more of John Kerry playing guitar at rock concerts; expect to see G.W.B. courting NASCAR belles. Expect Radical Cheerleaders, with pompoms and X-rated cheers, swearing that their movement is spreading "like Blue Bonnet margarine on vegan biscuits." Forget the Soccer Mom this time around—she votes. Can-didates are now going after Waitress Moms, Single Moms, Security Moms, Sexy Moms, Grandmoms, and Non-Moms with more incentives than com-peting cell-phone companies. "Women are always looking for twofers," notes pollster Celinda Lake, part of a group of Washington strategists who coined the term Soccer Mom in 1998.

• • •

When it comes to seducing 22 million women voters in 2004, then, panties and thongs are just the beginning. Political organizers know that women want it both ways: "We can take our husbands' names, we can be smart and powerful, but we also watch *The Bachelorette* and want to talk about what eye cream we're wearing," says Heather Lurie, cofounder of the Rocky Mountain Riveters, a group of politically active Colorado women who are determined to make politics "fun." Lurie hired a nonpartisan comedian for the group's kickoff event, because she believes the only way to bring about electoral change—and better lives for women—is to hide the ball. "We don't go around preaching democrat with a big D," she told me, since that doesn't increase membership or change minds. The more moderate Junior Leaguers she hopes to attract, she pointed out, "are educated and have incredible spending power. They can reach a different demographic. Everyone I know reads *The New York Times* and listens to NPR, and what good is that going to do?" A Houston chapter of Running in Heels, yet another organization devised to get out the women's vote, staged a Kerry-Oke in July. (The organization served Bushtinis—sour-apple martinis.) "We're doing Pilates Against Bush next," event organizer Sasha Vaikhman told me.

There's something simultaneously traditional and radical about these appeals—maybe they understand the schizophrenic nature of being female today; maybe candidates have just reached the desperation point. Instead of First Lady Bake-offs—remember Laura Bush's cowboy cookies and Tipper Gore's gingersnaps?—MoveOn.org staged a bake sale, raising $750,000 nationwide, thanks to participation by the likes of Al Franken and Janeane Garofalo. (Somehow, it's easier to imagine Teresa Heinz Kerry running the company that makes the cookies than baking them herself.) Next up is a virtual garage sale, and a Women's Day of Action, when women can go to hair salons and malls to shop, get pedicures, talk politics, and register to vote. "We're trying to do things all Americans have done," Laura Dawn explains.

For the same reason, the Riveters' Lurie provided her facialist with a T-shirt from Vote, Run, Lead, a nonpartisan women's voting organization. The esthetician has since become a registration powerhouse because of her captive audience. "She talks to ten people a day," Lurie told me. Other groups are trying voter registration at shopping malls: Research shows that, for the most part, politicians have to go to women; they don't have time to go to the politicians.

There are also new appeals to women's passion for self-improvement—a.k.a. their insecurities. One Colorado women's group took a page from the Bush family's ongoing literacy campaign and set up a political book club, sampling everything from Richard Clarke to David Brock. (I assume Republicans read Karen Hughes on the benefits of the commuter marriage.)

It's a political truism that voters usually get the campaigns, and the candidates, they deserve, and I've found myself wondering whether these tactics have to do with a lingering underestimation of women or our own inability to marshal their resources. Despite the fact that P. Diddy took the Declaration of Independence as a date to his July 4 White Party, the level of discourse and organization among African-American voters is much more canny and has been, historically, much more successful. Who babysits and drives women to the polls when they can't make it because of family obligations? Who chides them for taking their voting rights for granted? Who reminds them that the next president may be choosing two or three Supreme Court justices, who will be ruling on choice, Social Security and education? Women, like minorities, are traditionally more active in local politics than national, because they feel that they can make more of a difference—and be taken more seriously—on the city council or the school board. They need to be reminded, as many African-American and Hispanic males know, that all politics is local.

Maybe women need less Britney and more Dr. Laura, shaming them into acknowledging their power, and more political organizers to teach them how to mobilize it for the way they live now. The most sensible appeal I heard to increase the women's vote was to follow the lead of Oregon and expand voting by mail. Political research showed that many working women pay their bills late at night, after dinner has been cooked, the dishes done, homework is finished, and the kids are in bed. That's when they have time to think about politics and their civic duty.

"Don't talk a bunch of mush," Ann Richards recently implored the presidential candidates during the Democratic convention. "Women want to hear about what's going to make a difference in their lives." That's true. But men won't take us seriously until we show them we take ourselves seriously as well.

Permanent Fatal Errors

Louis Menand

The New Yorker | December 6, 2004

So, what really tipped the 2004 presidential election in George Bush's favor? The early analysis, based on one widely reported exit poll, was that "moral values" had decided the race—which fit in nicely with liberal Democrats' sense that the nation was being overrun by a sea of conservative fundamentalism. In this article, written as the post-election dust was beginning to settle, Louis Menand takes a closer look at the so-called "values poll" and other data, and concludes that the real deciding issue was . . . national security. As Menand notes, when it came down to the question of who could best protect the country from future attacks, the voters made a clear choice: They trusted the incumbent president far more than his untested challenger. . . .

"You can't imagine how much time it takes to lie on the floor in a fetal position," Mark Mellman explained to a gathering of political scientists and polling experts at Stanford a week after the Presidential election. Mellman is the C.E.O. of the Mellman Group and, until his services were rendered unnecessary by events, was the lead pollster for the Kerry campaign. He is a friendly and outspoken man, with the look of dishevelment that is associated with brainy enthusiasm, and it was entertaining to imagine him curled in a ball somewhere after November 2nd, trying to forget about a very bad night for John Kerry and for the art of polling.

One of the Bush campaign's leading pollsters was at the conference, too—Jan Van Lohuizen, the president of a group called Voter Consumer Research. Van Lohuizen is a figure of more business-like mien, a man whose reaction to disappointment would not, one feels, include lying on the floor. He and Mellman had been on the radio together at 7 P.M. that night of the election, a time when there was every indication, from the exit polls, that the Presidency was going to change hands. At Stanford, Mellman admitted to "the cardinal sin," as he put it, "of gloating, and gloating early and inappropriately," on the air, and he apologized to Van Lohuizen. Van Lohuizen was gracious, in the spirit not so much of a good winner as of a professional who has been there, too, and who fully expects to be there again, one day. The pollsters are like the pundits and the press: they are the survivors. Politicians come and go, but there is always another campaign.

"How did people decide for whom to vote?" was the question that the Stanford postmortem was organized to answer. There were, by November 9th, plenty of answers out there already, of course. Everybody had an opinion. You can't not have an opinion, and that's the problem. A consensus that George Bush won because voters cared about x easily turns into a consensus that voters were "sending a message" about x, and this determines the story line of the next four years. Ultimately, it can determine the three paragraphs on the election of 2004 in every American-history textbook of the future. But picking out the x, if there is an x, from the available reasons that Bush won and Kerry lost is a delicate piece of statistical calculation. This is why polling is an art.

Why did you order the cheeseburger? "Because I always order the cheeseburger" is an acceptable answer. "Because I felt like a change" is also acceptable. But those (or their electoral equivalents) are generally not considered good answers to the question "Why did you vote for John Kerry?" Most people feel that a civically responsible answer must name an issue. So they say something like "Because I am very concerned about the rising cost of health care." In fact, though, millions of people vote the way they do on the theory of "I always order the cheeseburger." This is not because of ignorance or indifference; on the contrary, many people who follow politics closely are partisans who choose the Republican or the Democrat no matter what. They have already picked the party, and they let the party pick the candidate. It's a reasonable and respectable labor-saving device.

And, in some elections, "I felt like a change" is the only reason many people have for voting against an incumbent. "Leadership, for a change" was a slogan that Bill Clinton campaigned on against George Bush in 1992. It worked, because Bush's approval rating went as low as thirty-three percent —about the same as Jimmy Carter's in 1980, when Carter lost to Ronald Reagan. The younger Bush's approval rating was fifty percent, which is low for an incumbent seeking reelection. But he was less vulnerable to a need-for-a-change strategy because this year, as Mellman explained at the

Stanford conference, voters reported that they wanted stability. Kerry therefore tried to work "change" into his message without using the actual word—for example, he called for a "new direction." Evidently, the voters were not fooled.

The potential story line that floated fastest to the surface after the election was that voters were sending a message about moral values. This is a little strange, because the "moral values" peg is entirely an artifact of the very exit polls that led Mellman to his brief and illusory moment of Election Night triumph. Those polls, as everyone knows, were a fiasco. Exit polls conducted by the National Election Pool (a consortium created by the networks, CNN, and the Associated Press to replace the service that was responsible for the disastrous miscalls of the *last* Presidential election) and the Los Angeles *Times*, along with election predictions by Zogby International, showed Kerry pulling away. CNN, on its Web site on Election Day, posted exit polls that, according to Steven Freeman, at the University of Pennsylvania, had Kerry winning Ohio by 4.2 percentage points (he lost by 2.5 points), Pennsylvania by 8.7 percentage points (he won by 2.2), and Minnesota by 9 points (he won by 3.5). At 5:30 P.M. on Election Day, Zogby's Web site had Kerry with a projected total of three hundred and eleven electoral votes, a blowout. (Kerry ended up with two hundred and fifty-two electoral votes to Bush's two hundred and eighty-six.) At 8 P.M., journalists were looking at national exit polls showing Kerry winning the popular vote by three points. And even after the polls had closed in Virginia, the networks designated the race there too close to call, based on the exit data. Bush won Virginia by nine points.

Traditionally, polls that ask people whom they just voted for have been regarded as about as sound as polls can get—which is why their failure this time gave so much anguish to Kerry supporters. People don't forget, in the few minutes after leaving the booth, whom they chose; they have little reason to lie; and their answers aren't affected by the I-was-at-Woodstock syndrome, which leads more people to claim, after they know the outcome, that they voted for the winner than actually did. But polls that ask people why they voted for a particular candidate have usually been regarded with a heavy drip of saline solution—not because people do not tell the truth but because they often don't know the truth. If a poll has trouble naming the winner within the margin of error, how reliable are its answers to the question why people voted the way they did?

The National Election Pool questionnaire asked people leaving the polls to pick "the ONE issue that mattered most in deciding how you voted for president." These were the reported results:

Education	4%
Taxes	5%
Health care	8%
Iraq	15%
Terrorism	19%
Economy/jobs	20%
Moral values	22%

Eighty percent of the respondents who picked "moral values" as the issue that was most important to them voted for Bush, but even the Bush pollster dismissed the significance of the poll. The "moral values" number, Van Lohuizen said at Stanford, is "entirely determined by what else is on the list." Voters weren't asked to name an issue that mattered to them; they were asked, in what is known in polling as a "closed-ended question," to pick one answer out of seven. "And, if you look at the list, there are a lot more places for a Kerry voter to park himself than for a Bush voter to park himself," Van Lohuizen said. "That's point No. 1. Point No. 2: if you give people a list of seven and you ask them what's their top concern and the highest number is twenty-two, that means there is no consensus. It means there was no one issue that drove the election."

The belief that the issue of "moral values" was somehow decisive is tied to the belief that a greater proportion of voters this year were highly religious. This, too, is a belief unsupported by the data. "As a conservative, you love to see the liberal media twinge and say, 'Oh, my God, it's these moral values,'" Van Lohuizen said. "It was an important factor, but I have seen no data that it was more important in '04 than it was in 2000 or '96. I've seen no data that, in the composition of the electorate, the religious vote was more heavily represented." More churchgoers turned out to vote in 2004 than in 2000, but only because more people turned out to vote.

According to a report on Beliefnet, a religious Web site, by Steven Waldman, the editor of the site, and John Green, a political scientist at the University of Akron, forty-three percent of Ohio voters in 2000 attended church once a week or more often. In 2004, the figure was forty percent. In

Florida in 2000, forty-one percent of voters were regular churchgoers, but only thirty-five percent were this year. Bush even seems to have won a greater percentage of voters who never attend church than he did in 2000. "Moral values" has been tracked as an issue in Presidential elections at least since 1992. Many voters care about moral values, but there is no reason to conclude that more voters care about them now than ever. At Stanford, Kathleen Frankovic, the director of surveys for CBS News, pointed out that in the Los Angeles *Times* exit poll voters were asked to identify, from a closed list, the issues that were most important to them. In 1996, the year Clinton was reelected, forty percent chose "moral/ethical values"; in 2000, thirty-five percent chose it. In 2004, it was back to forty percent. And a recent report from the Pew Research Center shows that on open-ended surveys, which allow respondents to name any issue that matters to them, items associated with moral values finish behind the economy and the war in Iraq.

The phrase "moral values" is open to interpretative license. Peace and social justice are moral values; they just happen not to be values associated with the Bush Administration. Most commentators assume that voters understood the phrase as code for two issues: gay marriage and abortion. So-called "marriage initiatives," designed to prevent same-sex marriages, were on the ballot in eleven states and carried easily in all of them, even Oregon, where fifty-two percent of the voters voted for Kerry and fifty-seven percent voted against gay marriage. (Kerry, after all, is not a supporter of gay marriage.) Still, there was agreement among the experts at Stanford that the presence of a marriage initiative on the ballot did not measurably increase turnout for Bush, and did not help him win states that he otherwise would have lost. If the National Election Pool's list had offered "gay marriage" instead of "moral values," it is hard to imagine that twenty-two percent of the respondents would have pointed to it—an assumption that seems to be confirmed by the Los Angeles *Times* exit poll, where voters were asked specifically about gay marriage and abortion. A smaller proportion of voters picked those as important issues than picked "moral values" on the National Election Pool questionnaire, and they split almost evenly between Bush and Kerry.

"Why did President Bush win this election?" Gary Langer, the director of polling at ABC News, said at the Stanford conference. "I would suggest that the answer can be expressed in a single phrase: 9/11." No one there disagreed.

"Fifty-four percent of voters on Election Day said that the country was safer now than it was before September 11, 2001," Langer pointed out. "And perhaps, I would suggest, more important, forty-nine percent of voters said they trusted only President Bush to handle terrorism, eighteen points more than said they trusted only John Kerry." He went on, "Among those who trust only Bush to handle terrorism, ninety-seven percent, quite logically, voted for him. Now, right there, if forty-nine percent of Americans trust only Bush to handle terrorism and ninety-seven percent of them voted for him, those are forty-eight of his total fifty-one percentage points in this election. Throw in a few more votes on ancillary issues and that's all she wrote." Langer thinks that a key statistic is the change in the votes of married women. Gore won the women's vote by eleven percent. Kerry won by only three percent, and he lost most of those votes among married women. Bush got forty-nine percent of the votes of married women in 2000; he got fifty-five percent this year. And when you ask married women whom they trust to keep the country safe from terrorists fifty-three percent say "only Bush." (The really salient demographic statistic from the election is one that most Democrats probably don't even want to think about: If white men could not vote, Kerry would have defeated Bush by seven million votes.)

Assuming that the election did come down to a referendum on terrorism, there was very little that a Democrat could have done to win it. Kerry could not change the subject; war and terrorism were on the news every day. According to Mellman, polls showed that although only thirty-three percent of voters thought that the invasion of Iraq was worth it, fifty-two percent thought that it was the right thing to do. Those are tough numbers from which to devise a campaign strategy. They are the numbers behind Kerry's notorious trouble in parsing the matter of his own position on the invasion—his attempt to criticize the outcome but not the decision. It's getting hard to remember now, when Iraq has become a violent and ungovernable mess, but the invasion of Iraq had overwhelming public approval, and people don't like to admit that they were wrong. Neither does the President. It's one of the attributes that voters seem to identify with.

Of course, it doesn't matter what the science of public opinion concludes. It only matters what the politicians conclude. If Democrats believe that the lesson of the election is that the Party needs to move to the right, then, if it moves, that will be the lesson. It might be wiser for the Democrats to chalk Bush's reelection up to 9/11 and stick to their positions. The

Democratic candidate did not lose votes in 2004: Kerry got five million more votes that Al Gore got in 2000, when Gore won a plurality. Unfortunately for the Democrats, Bush got nine million more votes than he did four years ago. But it wasn't because the country moved to the right. The issue that seems to have permitted an incumbent with an unimpressive approval rating to survive reelection was not an ideological one. The country did not change radically in the past four years. Circumstances did.

Part Two:
Politics in the Bush Era—
Four More Years

Breaking the Code

Nicholas Confessore

The New York Times Magazine | January 16, 2005

As far as economic policy is concerned, President George W. Bush's legacy is already clear: it will be defined by his unyielding push to lower the federal tax rate on individuals (especially those in the top income brackets) and on investment income. At the president's urging, Congress has passed a major tax cut every year since he took office. While the Democrats have tried to portray these cuts as payback for Bush's wealthy GOP supporters, his administration's tax policies are actually the culmination of a decades-long effort by a determined group of anti-tax crusaders—all united behind the belief that the American economy is being crippled by over-taxation of capital and its companion, bloated government.

With Bush and a Republican Congress in power, the anti-tax crowd finally has a political coalition willing to enact their agenda—at least in part. When it comes to cutting taxes, Bush and his Congressional allies have been terrific. The problem, of course, is that federal spending has continued to go up under the Republicans, even as tax revenues have fallen. As a result, the federal deficit has remained high—the red ink totaled $412 billion in fiscal year 2004, and is expected to top $300 billion in 2005. In this article, published two months after Bush's reelection, Nicholas Confessore catches up with some leading lights of the anti-tax movement to discover what their next move will be.

(Note: As this was being written in early June, the Administration announced that the Bush tax-reform commission referred to in Confessore's article would delay the release of its final report until autumn—virtually assuring that no tax-reform legislation will be passed in 2005.) . . .

One afternoon late last month, I paid a visit to the offices of Americans for Tax Reform, the conservative lobbying outfit headed by Grover Norquist. Though Norquist ranks among the Republican Party's leading operators, neither he nor his organization is quite yet a household name. Outside the Beltway, he is known mainly, if at all, for the cheerfully visceral quotations that regularly appear next to his name in newspaper articles. (Shortly after the GOP's Election Day victory, Norquist mused to *The Washington Post* that the city might become less bitter and fractious now that the Democrats had been more or less neutered. "Certain animals run around and are unpleasant," he noted, "but when they've been fixed, then they are happy and sedate.") Inside the Beltway, however, Norquist has made his mark as a political organizer. Each Wednesday morning, more than a hundred leading conservative activists, policy pundits, talk-show producers and journalists, joined by assorted Hill staff members and White House aides, gather in Americans for Tax Reform's conference room to discuss the issues of the day, from prescription drugs to school choice. Within Republican circles, Norquist's job is to organize other organizations, making sure the different branches of conservatism are moving in the same direction, at the same time, to the greatest extent possible. His particular genius is for persuading one organization to reach beyond its own agenda to help out another—for getting, say, the cultural traditionalists at the Eagle Forum to join the business libertarians at the Competitive Enterprise Institute in opposing fuel-economy standards for automobiles by convincing the traditionalists that, as Norquist once explained to me, "it's backdoor family planning. You can't have nine kids in the little teeny cars. And what are you going to do when you go on a family vacation?"

Taxes, though, are Norquist's first passion. A.T.R. was formed 20 years ago, at the Reagan administration's behest, to rally grass-roots conservative support for an ambitious bipartisan effort to reform the federal tax code, which would culminate in the Tax Reform Act of 1986. Norquist, then a 29-year-old Reagan acolyte and former speechwriter at the United States Chamber of Commerce, was brought on board as the group's executive director. He soon discovered that many conservatives were deeply skeptical of the legislation, which proposed to slice reams of special-interest tax credits, breaks and shelters out of the tax code in exchange for lower marginal rates across the board. They were attracted to the idea of more tax cuts, but suspected that they might later be double-crossed. "They said, 'We're going to get rid of these credits and deductions, we're going to broaden the base and then they're going to come back and raise the rates again, and we won't even have the deductions and credits anymore,'" Norquist recalled, sitting behind a massive desk, with a county-by-county map of the 2004 election results—a blur of Republican red—hanging nearby. "At which point, I said, 'Well, what if we made it difficult for them to raise rates?'"

Thus was born the Pledge. This was a promise, first circulated by

Norquist in 1985 and originally signed by more than 100 members of Congress, never to vote to raise tax rates. The Pledge helped deliver enough conservative votes to pass tax reform, but not enough to prevent future backsliding. Four years later, President George H.W. Bush, who had famously promised voters that there would be "no new taxes" on his watch, changed his mind. Faced with a swelling federal deficit, he proposed a budget deal that raised taxes overall and even added a new bracket for high-income earners, and he urged Republican members to support it in the name of paying down the debt.

Bush's betrayal—a seminal moment in Republican politics, and one that reverberates still—is immortalized in an enormous framed reproduction of an October 2, 1990, *Wall Street Journal* editorial, occupying most of one wall near the entrance to A.T.R.'s office suite. Titled "Honor Thy Pledge," the editorial listed the names of Republicans who took Norquist's oath and urged swift retribution on anyone who ended up voting with the president. More than 30 eventually did, providing the crucial margin for Bush's tax hikes. But the editorial isn't hanging there to commemorate failure: 1990 was the last year any GOP politician at the national level voted for any income-tax increase, period. "Had Bush broken his pledge and gotten reelected, it would have made the Pledge much less valuable, maybe completely worthless," Norquist told me. "But because the most famous pledge-taker-slash-pledge-breaker lost reelection, on that subject, it's had an effect."

In the years since Bush's defeat, Norquist's way of thinking about taxes—that they should be cut whenever and wherever possible—has become the central tenet of American conservatism. Currently, the Pledge has been signed by 222 members of the House and 46 Senators, which includes pretty much every Republican in both chambers. It has also been signed by Bush's son President George W. Bush, who has not only kept his pledge but also made cutting taxes the signal domestic accomplishment of his first term. Taxes are likely to be at the heart of Bush's second-term agenda, too: not long after Election Day, Bush announced that the tax code had become "complicated and outdated" and "a drag on our economy" and that it was time, once again, for tax reform. Earlier this year, Bush named members to a bipartisan commission to get the ball rolling. "All options," a Treasury Department official warned, "are on the table." Boilerplate as they may sound, those kinds of words can set Washington aflame like little else. Just as in 1986, the call for tax reform puts at risk hundreds of special provisions, affecting nearly every organized interest in town, from insurance companies to charities, from Wall Street banks to forklift manufacturers, from the biggest state in the union on down to little municipalities putting out tax-free bonds.

But the pressures Norquist and his allies have brought to bear on American politics over the last two decades make it unlikely that Bush's attempt at tax reform will much resemble the 1986 version. During the latter half of the 20th century, most Democrats and Republicans accepted—at least in theory—the notion that taxation should be as broad-based as possible; no one swathe of the public, and no one sector of the economy, should absorb too much of the cost of government, both because it was unfair and because it was inefficient. The 1986 act brought the federal tax code closer to that vision by cutting loopholes and, as a consequence, expanding the pool of taxpayers. But Republicans today have something else in mind. By their lights, the old consensus is not only outdated, but egregiously so, even offensively so. Bush's call for reform gives them a chance to replace it with something else.

And in many respects, the replacement is already well under way. After four rounds of largely Republican-inspired tax legislation, today's code is a profoundly different instrument than the one that existed when Bush first took office. And though the White House has never publicly laid out a common rationale for its policies, Bush's changes—which have cut income taxes on high earners, reduced rates on capital gains and dividend income, temporarily eliminated the estate tax and allowed businesses to write off the cost of new capital purchases more quickly—depart drastically from the old model of reform. Bush's cuts have greatly reduced the costs formerly borne by corporations and the wealthy, leaving the tax code considerably less progressive than it once was. Instead of getting rid of loopholes so that fewer businesses escape paying taxes, conservatives have essentially set out to universalize those loopholes, aiming for a day when corporations won't have to pay taxes at all. (According to a recent report from the Center for Tax Justice, a liberal watchdog group, 82 of America's largest corporations paid no income tax in one or more years of Bush's first term.) Bush's tax reform, in other words, is shaping up to be not merely a departure from the spirit of the 1986 reform—but a wholesale repudiation of it.

Though the end result was far from foreordained, the basic outlines of what would become the Tax Reform Act of 1986 began bubbling up on both sides of the aisle a couple of years into Reagan's first term. Liberal Democrats had long favored dumping corporate deductions and tax shelters for the wealthy; Republican supply-siders—the architects of Reagan's large 1981 tax reduction—were looking to push new cuts through Congress but needed to assuage deficit hawks in both parties who were concerned about the rising budget shortfall. Some of Reagan's political advisers had become concerned that loopholes for the wealthy might become a Democratic campaign issue in '84, while others had come to believe that narrow tax breaks weren't a very effective way to encourage growth in particular industries. Economists of all stripes agreed that the code had become so complicated by loopholes that it was sucking up potential growth. "Pre-1986, you could get a tax reduction for investing in tobacco farms and bull sperm and windmills and things like that," notes Stephen Moore, then a budget expert at the conservative Heritage Foundation and now a senior fellow at the Cato Institute. "The tax code looked like a piece of Swiss cheese."

But that wasn't an accident. During the '70s and early '80s, the Beltway lobbying industry, known colloquially as "K Street" after the downtown avenue populated by trade associations and corporate offices, metastasized into the Fifth Estate of American politics. Over the years, these lobbyists spent millions of dollars to persuade members of Congress to carve this or that break into the tax code, breaks that benefited thousands of well-connected companies and individuals. And they were a powerful force against reform. As the reporters Jeffrey H. Birnbaum and Alan Murray explained in their definitive 1987 account, *Showdown at Gucci Gulch*, "the groups with an interest in the existing tax system were well organized and ready to defend their breaks at a moment's notice; the populace who stood to benefit from lower rates was unorganized and diffuse." In 1985, the year tax reform began to be seriously considered in Washington, corporate PACs substantially increased the amount of money they pumped into House and Senate coffers—cash that exerted a powerful effect on rank-and-file members of Congress. Only by working in concert, from a shared sense of what reform should look like, could Democratic and Republican tax reformers keep a deal from being scuttled.

In policy terms, that required the '86 effort to be a compromise between two groups that had vastly different visions of what an ideal tax system would look like. Ultimately, each side achieved some of its goals: liberal reformists got more corporations and high earners back on the books, while conservatives got lower marginal tax rates. "Any time you change the tax code, it's obviously going to be controversial," says Ronald Pearlman, a Georgetown University law professor who helped create the Reagan administration's initial package of reform proposals. "And it's nice to be able to say you've got bipartisan support for big, gutsy changes."

The last four years in Washington have upended most of the political realities that fostered the bipartisan results of 1986. The most visible change is that Washington is no longer a functionally bipartisan town. Three successive electoral defeats have rendered the Democrats, once Washington's entrenched ruling class, a beleaguered opposition party. Significantly, Republicans have not only widened their hold on power but also tightened it. In the ten years since the GOP takeover of Congress, the House, in particular, has become progressively more centralized and top down than it was during the era of Democratic control. Important legislation tends to emerge from the leadership offices and be put to up-or-down votes; rank-and-file Republicans play a diminished role in policy making, and the Democrats next to no role at all. In November, Representative J. Dennis Hastert, the House speaker, announced that he wouldn't allow votes on any bills that lacked majority support among the Republican caucus, whether or not measures enjoyed majority support among the country's elected representatives as a whole.

As Bush's second term takes shape, the GOP has little incentive to broker compromises, and by all appearances, not much interest either. That means that to a degree unimagined in the '80s, tax reform under Bush can be a discussion within the Republican Party, among people who share a basic sense of how the tax code needs to change. The various constituent parts of the conservative coalition, of course, have multiple stakes in the broader agenda of tax cutting. Large industrial concerns might be most interested in lowering the tax bill on purchases of equipment; rich party donors would like to see the top marginal tax rates reduced; and social conservatives have rallied around calls for permanently eliminating the so-called marriage penalty. The key visionaries of conservative-style tax reform, however, are a vanguard of anti-tax activists, conservative economists and a handful of Republican politicians who have made taxes their pet issue. Like all conservatives, they think that the government is too big and that taxes ought to be lower and flatter. But this group has also come to share a few articles of faith about the relationship between taxes and growth. One is that for years the American economy has been enormously handicapped by excessive taxation on savings and investment; because people and businesses are discouraged from saving, the theory goes, there is a pervasive shortage of capital for future investments. Another belief is that lifting those burdens would create a permanent increase in most Americans' standards of living. Still another belief is that cutting all those taxes won't worsen the deficit, because the growth the cuts will unleash would produce more than enough income—and, therefore, tax revenue—to make up the difference.

Most economists typically find this line of argument questionable. (When rates on savings and investments were cut back beginning in the '70s, they note, the savings rate actually went down, indicating that people's propensity to save probably isn't greatly affected by changes in marginal tax rates.) So Bush's proposals are unlikely to win the kind of expert consensus that the 1986 tax reform did. But if the administration can count on much more resistance to its vision from professional economists, it can count on far less from the constituency that was once the most formidable obstacle to fundamental reform of the tax code: K Street. In part, this is a consequence of the broader power shift in Washington. When the parties shared power, business lobbyists could bid Democrats and Republicans against one another. (Reagan's 1981 tax cut became a deficit exploder in part because Congressional Democrats, eager to win back business support following the disastrous 1980 election, were competing against their Republican counterparts to see who could open more corporate loopholes in the tax code.) With Democrats more or less out of the picture, lobbyists must rely far more heavily on the GOP to look after its interests—and that gives Republican leaders more leverage over K Street than vice versa.

Thanks to this arrangement, Bush's first three tax bills were fairly "clean" ones, containing relatively few special-interest breaks narrowly benefiting a given industry or corporation. That doesn't mean K Street hasn't done well under Republican rule. Bush's fourth tax cut—a bill originally intended to fix an existing tax provision deemed illegal by the World Trade Association and passed with little public notice shortly before Election Day—was packed

with billions of dollars' worth of corporate giveaways, most of it to the manufacturing sector. But it does mean that the party can compel business
interests to delay narrow gratification—special-interest loopholes that
arouse public ire and inspire a political response—in support of a broader
and more ambitious ideological agenda that will pay dividends down the
line. "As long as we have the annual tax cut, all the business guys are in
line," Norquist explained to me, noting that business trade associations like
the National Association of Manufacturers helped lobby for Bush's 2001
cut, even though it did nothing to reduce corporate rates. Norquist described
his pitch to K Street this way: "This year, we're doing a tax cut. You want to
help us with this year, you're at the front of the line for next. You didn't get
in this year, you can get in line for next year. But we're going to be doing a
tax cut, however small, because we can go as small as we have to to get a tax
cut every year. That is what we did for the last four years. That is what we
are going to do for the next four years."

Just as important as the sequencing of Bush's tax cuts has been the substance of them, which provides a hint of where tax reform is likely to go.
In theoretical terms, Bush's cuts have brought the United States tax code
closer to a system under which income from savings and investments
aren't taxed at all and revenues would be raised exclusively from taxes on
labor. The consequence of those policies is that a greater proportion of tax
revenues now come from what the middle class earns and a smaller proportion from what the wealthy earn. Whatever changes the Bush administration pursues, there is every reason to believe it will aim to move further
in that direction. "I think Bush does have a master plan on tax policy,"
Stephen Moore says. "The goal is to eliminate all taxes on savings and
investment. That means no capital-gains tax, no dividends tax, no estate
tax, no tax on interest."

How you view this arrangement depends a lot on whether you buy the
assumption that letting the wealthy off the hook will eventually benefit
everyone else. Early one recent Saturday morning, I paid a visit to John
Podesta, the last chief of staff to serve under Clinton, at his home in Washington. He greeted me at the door in sweat pants and a T-shirt, and we sat
down at his kitchen table to talk taxes. Podesta has a lean, shrewd face, a
twinkle in his eye and a reputation as one of the party's canniest operatives;

these days, he heads the Center for American Progress, which he founded a little more than a year ago to incubate new policies and approaches among left-of-center types.

Podesta has little faith in the conservatives' trickle-down approach. He also says it is bad economic policy—"fatally flawed," as he put it. "We're already seeing the current account deficit increase by $600 billion a year," he continued. "People are mortgaged to the hilt. The middle class is now being fundamentally squeezed. They've gotten no benefit from the tax reduction. GDP growth is going almost all to corporate profits. And we're creating an overall economic circumstance in which the dollar is certain to drop, interest rates are certain to rise and growth over the long term looks kind of sketchy."

To understand why the GOP has pursued such a policy, Podesta argues, you have to look at the political dividends, not the economic ones. "What are the structural elements of what they are trying to do with the tax code?" he began, busying himself at a small coffee machine. "I would say there are three. One is to eliminate taxation on wealth and investment. Second is to create a revenue stream that aims at a government the size of which we haven't seen almost since before the Depression." Already, he points out, the government takes in far less than it spends, forcing the Bush administration to borrow billions of dollars to cover the revenue lost from cutting taxes. "Three is that if you build in taxation only on wage income, you have massive resistance by the middle class to letting those taxes rise. So you've kind of locked in three structural components that end up being highly beneficial to wealthy people, and I think, from a conservative governance point of view, create not just restraint on the growth of government, but essentially pressure to downsize the government."

Podesta's analysis suggests that conservative tax reformers are in something of a bind: telling middle-class voters you want them to pay for more of the government so that they will want to shrink it is not a very good way to win their votes. Conservatives insist, however, that their plans not only won't deepen the deficit; they won't increase the load on the middle class either. Not long ago, I spoke with South Carolina's new Republican senator, James DeMint, who over the past few years made a name for himself on tax issues in the House. DeMint's campaign Web site included pictures of him standing next to a tall stack of I.R.S. regulations and displayed statistics like the number of pages in the tax code (45,622) and the number of hours Americans spend each year filling out tax returns (6.1 billion), sure to ruffle taxpayers' feathers. Like many conservatives, he says that the middle class is already paying for most of the government—they just haven't figured it out yet. "People don't understand the cost of government," he told me.

DeMint says he believes that taxes paid by corporations and wealthy investors tend to end up costing middle- and working-class people money, in the form of higher prices at the cash register or the lost jobs that result when rich people have to pay the estate tax instead of investing in, say, steel factories. Taxes on capital, from this point of view, are inevitably self-defeating: they are simply passed along to the rest of us, along with the accountant's bill. But because average workers pay less in "visible" taxes than corporations and the rich, they tend to think they're getting a good deal out of the federal government. "They're paying a disproportionate share of their income in taxes, and they don't know it," DeMint said. "So, politically, they're not activated to change it, because they can't see the taxes. They don't have that sense of urgency."

DeMint advocates scrapping the entire tax code, including income taxes and taxes on wealth, and replacing it with a flat national sales tax. By his reasoning, that would convert all the hidden taxes embedded in the price of goods and services into one tax that is printed at the bottom of a cash-register receipt. Middle-class people wouldn't pay any more in federal taxes than they're effectively paying now, and they would end up economic winners, since the simpler tax system that resulted would be less of a drag on the economy. And once people were paying all their taxes up front, and could see how expensive the government really was, they would be much more inclined to demand huge cuts in spending than they are today. "The intent here is not to shift the tax burden to the poor," he said, "but to allow every American to see the real cost of government." Left unsaid, of course, is the alternative: if middle-class taxpayers wanted to keep the same size government that exists today, they would have to pay for it up front.

But if you don't share the conservatives' assumption that the middle class ends up footing the bill for onerous taxes on capital, a new flat sales tax would—as Bush's previous cuts already do—simply shift even more of the burden of taxation from businesses and the wealthy over to the middle and working classes. "Any responsible person advocating tax reform has to admit the following: A reform that is revenue-neutral has losers," said Gene

Sperling, a leading Democratic budget expert who served as a top economic adviser for John Kerry during the 2004 presidential campaign. "There's a basic math to that. Every Republican flat-tax proposal lowers the rate on people at the top. Now, if you're raising less revenue from the most well-off, one of two things are going to happen. You're either going to raise more revenue from the middle class, or you're going to pass on more debt to our children. The only argument against that is supply-side magic—that somehow, lowering taxes will generate more revenue so there's a free lunch for everyone."

When I noted that Republicans seem much more energetic about tax reform than Democrats, Sperling got a little exasperated. "It's not that Republicans are so much more noble," he said. "The usual dialogue that happens on tax reform is, people love the idea of reducing deductions and lowering rates in theory. When they get to the specifics, they realize that they have to get rid of very popular deductions that people know well for the possible benefits of a system they don't know." For example, proposals for replacing the income tax with a tax on consumed income—that is, the income people use to buy things—have circulated among left-of-center tax experts for years. DeMint's sales tax is one version of a consumption tax. But, Sperling argues, it's a lot harder to design a version that is actually revenue-neutral, progressive in structure and politically viable: "First, you're getting rid of popular breaks like the mortgage deduction, and second, by the time time you've finished exempting food, clothing and so forth, the new tax has gotten pretty high." And unlike Republicans, he maintains, Democrats aren't willing to pretend that there can be tax reform without any losers. (Later this month, Podesta's policy institute will release a detailed plan that eliminates loopholes, cuts taxes on the middle class and creates more savings incentives for those without much wealth income— but finances it mostly by reversing Bush's rate cuts on the rich, who, of course, would be the losers should Podesta's plan come to pass.)

So what will Bush propose? The president did cause a minor stir during the campaign in the summer when he mentioned that a national sales tax was "the kind of interesting idea that we ought to explore seriously." But he has since retreated into anodyne rhetoric about simplifying the code and promoting savings and investment.

In part that's because a sales tax is indeed controversial; DeMint's Democratic opponent temporarily erased a double-digit deficit in the polls by hammering him on the sales tax, though DeMint did win in the end. But it is also because, while Republicans generally know what direction they want to move in, they don't agree on exactly how to get there. DeMint's is only one of several Republican tax-reform plans that have percolated through Washington in recent years. There are other sales-tax proposals, plus plans that put a flat tax on all forms of income or institute a European-style value-added tax (V.A.T.), basically a sales tax levied at each stage of production.

In theory, the members of Bush's tax commission are supposed to approach their efforts with an open mind. In practice, its purpose is to test the political waters, to see which version of conservative tax reform would be most palatable to the public and how far it can be pushed. "It'll come out with three or four proposals, which are already written, and already on people's desks," Grover Norquist told me. "So this is not a commission to invent something, or several somethings. This is a commission to discuss several somethings. Poke 'em, bring 'em around the country, test-fly them, run 'em up the flagpole, see who shoots at it, see who salutes." Norquist argues that much as Bush's 2001 Social Security commission helped detoxify the argument over whether to privatize that program, the tax commission will make it safer to propose new ideas, even radical ones. Given the ultimate end goals of conservative tax reformers, this is no small concern: as a confidential 2002 memo prepared by the Treasury Department notes: "Any reform is likely to have vocal losers and largely silent winners. In other countries, the adoption of a consumption tax has led to election losses for the incumbent party."

For now, the Bush administration appears to be heeding that warning. After floating a few provocative ideas in the press last year—eliminating the deductions for mortgages and state and local taxes, benefits enjoyed disproportionately by ordinary workers and families—White House officials signaled that they were more likely to pursue the kind of incremental changes Bush has already shown a taste for when debate commences in earnest. "We don't have to decide whether we want a flat tax, or a V.A.T. or a retail sales tax," Norquist said. "Because there are a dozen things you have to do that would get you to the point which would get you to one of those three."

But as Bush's first four years have made clear, incremental doesn't equal inconsequential. During his first term, the president floated the idea of large tax-free savings accounts, sort of like supersize I.R.A.s, in which people who already have lots of money to save—that is, high earners— could shelter large amounts of income. Add in further cuts in taxes on capital gains and dividends, elimination of the estate tax and a move to make Bush's earlier income-tax reductions permanent, and even without big all-at-once tax reform, conservatives will come pretty close to legislating a new contract between the government and its citizens, one that has the power to change politics profoundly.

"Here's the danger," Norquist said. "They'll say, 'Let's wait for tax reform,' which will be this sort of angels-dancing-on-the-head-of-a-pin argument. That may never be real. There may never be something that everyone agrees is tax reform. What was it—Zeno's paradox, where you never quite get where you're going?

"You keep taking half-steps, eventually you're pretty darn close," he went on to say. "I'll take three half-steps and call it a day."

Is Grover Over?
Daniel Franklin and A. G. Newmyer III

The Washington Monthly | March 2005

While Grover Norquist and the rest of the pro–tax cut crowd love to tout the idea of drastically scaling back government (see "Breaking the Code," p. 55), the federal budget has continued to grow every year, even with Republican George W. Bush in the White House and the GOP in control of both houses of Congress. Clearly, government isn't going anywhere soon—and for a simple reason: people want and need government services and, ultimately, will elect the politicians who can deliver them. And because these services cost money, there's a limit on how far taxes can be cut without causing serious disruptions.

This truth is felt most keenly on the state level. Since (unlike the federal government) states are required to balance their budget each year, any shortfalls in tax revenue translate directly into budget cuts. In this article, Daniel Franklin and

A. G. Newmyer III report on how severe budget crunches are leading a number of prominent Republican governors to call for tax increases—and ask whether this trend signals the beginning of the end of the anti-tax movement. . . .

If ever two men seemed to share one political soul, surely they were Grover Norquist and Mitch Daniels. From his perch as president of Americans for Tax Reform, Norquist was the architect of President Bush's strategy to cut taxes every year and has elicited signed promises from virtually every congressional Republican never to vote for a tax hike. Norquist once famously boasted that he hoped to "reduce [government] to the size where I can drag it into the bathroom and drown it in the bathtub." During Bush's first term, it was Daniels, the White House budget director, who began running the water. During his time in the White House, Daniels conceded nothing in arguing for the president's tax cuts, even going so far as suggesting that the president's trillion-dollar tax cut represented "our best chance of another unexpected surplus." So if the smile on Norquist's face seemed extra-wide on Election Day, even considering the Republicans' reinforced grip on Washington power, it might have had something to do with Daniels's election as governor of Indiana. Daniels was bringing Grover's jihad back to the Heartland.

Where he promptly dropped it. Daniels had campaigned touting citations from Norquist's ATR and other anti-tax groups. But eight short days after settling into the Indiana Statehouse, Daniels proposed a budget that sought to close a $600 million budget gap by socking high-income Hoosiers with a 29-percent increase in income tax. Norquist quickly accused his old cohort of "betraying" taxpayers with his budget proposal. "This is the fastest any governor claiming to be a Reagan Republican has folded under the pressure of the big-spending interests," Norquist said. Daniels was stung. "Two years ago, Grover was giving me the Hero of the American Taxpayer Award," Daniels lamented to the *Indianapolis Star*. "I'm the same guy I was then."

To bring pressure on the apostate, Norquist publicly and negatively compared him to other governors who he said hewed more closely to the doctrine that taxes can go in only one direction: down. "On behalf of Indiana's families and businesses," Norquist wrote Indiana state legislators, "I urge you to prevent Gov. Daniels from closing Indiana for business, and turn to people like [Texas] Gov. Rick Perry . . . for alternative solutions." But just four days later, it was Perry's turn to break Norquist's heart. Introducing a new tax program to the Texas Association of Businesses, Perry said Texas had a "once in a generation opportunity . . . to put in place an educational system to really impact our children and our children's children."

Poor Grover. Nearly everywhere he looks, it seems, a Republican governor or legislature is finding the seductions of tax hikes too powerful to resist in the face of reduced federal support and soaring education and health-care costs. Anti-tax groups such as ATR, the Club for Growth, Americans for Prosperity, and FreedomWorks seem to have feet-on-the-desk privileges in the White House and Republican Congress. For a time, they appeared to have even more pull in the states, where 1,200 of 7,400 state legislators have signed Norquist's pledge never to vote for a tax increase. Anti-tax advocates are quick to threaten political death to any Republican who strays from the no-tax gospel. But with the red ink still flowing, even after collectively closing more than $200 billion in budget shortfalls over the last three years, cracks are forming within the no-tax coalition. Governors are finding that they can't cut more without endangering programs that hit people where they live—such programs as road construction, nursing home assistance, and reading, writing and arithmetic lessons. Surprisingly, legislatures are going along. Indeed, the day after Norquist announced his opposition to Daniels's budget plan, the Republican chairmen of the Indiana House Ways and Means and Senate Budget committees admitted that they didn't consider the no-tax pledges they had given the ATR binding because they signed them years before they acquired their current budget responsibilities. Another Republican Hoosier lawmaker complained to the *Indianapolis Star*, "I knew it [ATR's no-tax pledge] was like a marriage when I signed it, but now I want a divorce."

It was not always thus. In the early '90s, state Republican parties rode the anti-tax backlash to power, going from controlling five statehouses in 1992 to 20 today. (Democrats and Republicans split control of ten others.) A big reason why was the fundraising and organizational help offered from national anti-tax groups. "You cannot discount the impact of Grover Norquist and Americans for Tax Reform and the Club for Growth," says Bill Pound, executive director of the National Conference of State Legislatures, the main umbrella group for state lawmakers. "To their credit, they have had considerable effect." And indeed, many a Republican statehouse still keeps a light on for Norquist and his Washington friends. ATR and others have helped beat back major tax increase proposals from Alabama and Arkansas to Oregon and Washington in recent years.

Lost among press stories heralding the Republicans' victories in the presidential and congressional elections, however, is evidence that the tide may be turning. Voters in November rejected every tax-limitation measure on state ballots, including a Maine property tax initiative that was the most ambitious of its kind in 20 years. Voters in several other states, meanwhile, approved tax increases to pay for specific programs such as schools, roads and mental health. States have not exactly gone on a spending spree—they've cut spending much more than they've raised taxes over their last few years of budget difficulties—but because they are under so much pressure, they are increasingly resistant to the ministrations of Norquist and others who are telling them to cut taxes even more.

No state demonstrates the rise and wobble of the anti-tax movement better than Colorado. In 1992, at the instigation of Douglas Bruce, now a county commissioner in Colorado Springs, Colorado voters passed a referendum known as the Taxpayers Bill of Rights, or TABOR, which attached an amendment to the state constitution that required any tax increase to be approved by a vote of the people and limits state spending increases to inflation, with adjustments made for population growth. Any amount that the state collects above its spending limit has to be returned as a tax refund, unless the public specifically votes to allow the state to keep the money. So far, no Colorado official has even tried to bring the question to a vote. "It sounds good, so it's hard to fight politically," says Brad Young, the former Republican chairman of Colorado's joint budget committee.

TABOR has completely warped Colorado politics ever since. One of the original supporters was a little-known state representative from Aurora named Bill Owens. Six years later, Owens was elected to be Colorado's first Republican governor in 24 years. It wasn't long before national Republicans began to notice. *National Review* named him "America's Best Governor" in 2002 and admiringly listed his government-cutting bona fides. Anti-tax advocates began touting TABOR as a national model and Owens as a potential presidential candidate for 2008.

But while Colorado has been terrific for TABOR, TABOR has been a nightmare for Colorado, and for Colorado Republicans in particular. The state budget was fine as long as the state's economy was growing, and bills could be pushed into the following year. Once things slowed down, retrenchment became a serious business just as health care and education expenses began to shoot upwards. Thanks to TABOR, the state can't increase its spending on roads and other expenditures it's been putting off. Now, Governor Owens himself has proposed a ballot measure to curtail some of the law's limits.

Business is the chisel driving a crack between moderate Republicans and the anti-tax fanatics. Although there is no group in Washington more loyal to the GOP's anti-tax doctrine than the Chamber of Commerce, in the states, reality often trumps ideology. "For businesses to be successful, you need roads and you need higher education, both of which have gotten worse under TABOR and will continue to get worse," says Tom Clark of the Denver Metro Chamber of Commerce, who notes that higher education has shrunk from 25 percent of the state budget in 1995 to about 10 percent today. "I'm a Republican," Clark says, "but I made the decision not to give any money to the state party."

Throughout the state, moderate businessmen such as Clark kept their political checkbooks closed to many Republicans last year. Several state-house incumbents who might otherwise have counted on huge campaign spending advantages over Democratic challengers instead faced something approaching parity. A tightly organized state Democratic Party was able to take advantage, knocking off enough Republican incumbents to gain control of the Colorado legislature for the first time in 40 years. Democratic leaders in the state legislature are now reaching out to moderate Republicans to make changes to TABOR. As for Owens, he's term-limited and preparing to begin his last two years as governor. With a reinvigorated Democratic majority in the statehouse and a conservative base disappointed with his concessions to budget realities, he's quacking lamely. TABOR is at no risk of being jettisoned altogether, but its reputation as the third rail of Colorado politics has taken a permanent hit, as have Owens's hopes for competing in the GOP presidential primary 2008.

The fight now moves to Virginia, where, last year, business groups helped enact the state's largest tax increase since 1966. Democratic Governor Mark Warner conceded he might be "a lunatic" for trying to reform his state's tax system. He had run on a no-tax pledge, but recanted after finding that the state's fiscal hole was deeper than he could fill. He spent his first two years in office slicing spending by $6 billion, but finally concluded that the state would continue to bleed red even if the economy grew by higher than historic rates. The state would be facing deficits through 2010, just funding current programs. So Warner proposed raising taxes by $1.1 billion by offering tax breaks to most people but raising a number of rates, such as sales and cigarette taxes, and closing up some of the most gaping loopholes. Republican lawmakers began sharpening their knives until they realized that many of their constituents, business groups among them, were squarely behind the Democratic governor. Over the howls from national anti-tax groups, Virginia Republicans actually outdid the governor's tax hike, increasing it by an additional $700 million, fully two-thirds larger than Warner's proposal.

Norquist and the Club for Growth have vowed to defeat dozens of Republican legislators who supported the tax hike, dubbing them "Virginia's Least Wanted." "We had a bunch of worthless Republicans in the Senate who have been there forever and don't have any core free market beliefs," complained Club for Growth then-President Stephen Moore in an online chat. "They sold us out and then enough Benedict Arnold Republicans in the House went along. The good news is that these Republicans are through politically—we will be sure of that."

Two years ago, anti-tax groups made good on earlier threats to target legislators who referred regional sales tax hikes to voters, unseating the House transportation committee chair. But there is a different mood in Richmond. John Chichester, the Republican president pro tempore of the Virginia Senate who steered the tax hike through as finance chairman, calls Norquist and Moore "generals without armies. . . . The Norquist crowd—if they had a flame burning someplace, it's dimming now. The shrillness and strident rhetoric probably did their cause more harm than good."

As in Colorado, business groups have already come to the financial and organizational aid of the apostates facing challengers in this June's primaries. "The 17 members of the Republican House majority who voted for the modest tax increases demonstrated statesmanship and political courage in the old-fashioned sense," says Hugh Keogh, president of the Virginia Chamber of Commerce. "We'll do whatever seems to make sense to help encourage their reelection."

Given that kind of support from business interests, which have formed a new PAC specifically designed to help Republican lawmakers who supported Warner's tax increases, coupled with the fact that the moderate Republicans are mostly well established and well-liked in their districts—it may be difficult for Norquist and Moore to dislodge very many of them. "No doubt, Norquist and his allies can bring some money in on the other side," says University of Virginia political scientist Larry Sabato. "But to beat the legislators, he'll have to find strong opponents, always tough with established incumbents; catch the incumbents napping, which they aren't; and significantly outspend them, which I doubt he can do. In some competitive districts, Norquist's efforts might elect Democrats in the fall."

It is a bizarre notion when set against Norquist's outsized reputation as the preeminent Washington conservative power broker. But with Colorado looking shaky for Republicans and Daniels launching his administration with a direct slap to the anti-tax crowd, Virginia's statewide elections later this year loom large. If "Virginia's Least Wanted" survive their primary challenges or Democrats pick up seats in November's statewide election, Norquist and the anti-tax movement's threats could carry significantly less sting in the 2006 midterms nationwide. Grover is a long way from being politically neutered, to be sure. But it is in the nation's capital, rather than the states, that he continues to find his soulmates. From statehouse Republicans, such as his former friend Daniels, Norquist keeps hearing heresies. "Many other states have cut education spending—I didn't want to do that," Daniels said. "Many have cut higher education spending—I didn't want to do that." But weep not for Norquist and Daniels. They'll always have Washington.

Blowing Up the Senate
Jeffrey Toobin

The New Yorker | March 7, 2005

One important function of the U.S. Senate is to vote on whether or not to confirm the president's various nominees to vacant seats on the nation's federal courts. And while most judicial nominees sail through the confirmation process, both major political parties have a tradition of blocking a small percentage of nominees put forth by a president from the opposing party—those who, in their view, are just too politically unpalatable (or "extreme," to use the current term of choice) to allow onto the federal bench.

During the six years that the Republicans controlled the Senate during Bill Clinton's presidency, they made sure especially undesirable nominees never made it out of the Judicial Committee. With George W. Bush in the White House and the Senate still in GOP hands, the minority Democrats turned to a new strategy, employing a filibuster—which takes sixty votes to break, five more than the number of Republican senators—to prevent the Senate from ever voting on ten of Bush's most conservative appellate-court nominees. As Jeffrey Toobin chronicles here, Bill Frist and the GOP leadership responded by plotting a rule change that would end judicial filibusters once and for all—ensuring every judicial nominee (including future Supreme Court nominees) an up-and-down vote, but significantly altering the Senate's carefully-balanced power structure in the process.

In May of 2005, two months after this article was published, the filibuster issue finally came to a head when Bush renominated three judges, Priscilla Owens, Janice Rogers Brown, and William Pryor Jr., all of whom had previously been filibustered by the Democrats, and the Senate leadership once again attempted to bring them to a vote. At the eleventh hour, a showdown over the proposed rule change was averted when fourteen Senators—seven Republicans and seven Democrats, enough to break any filibuster—forged a compromise. The "Gang of 14" agreed to allow a vote on the three nominees, and also pledged that, in the future, the minority Democrats would resort to a judicial filibuster only "under extraordinary circumstances." Just what those circumstances might be, no one was saying. . . .

Most popular histories of Congress include an exchange, very likely apocryphal, in which Washington and Jefferson discuss the difference between the House and the Senate. "Why did you pour that coffee into your saucer?" Washington asks. "To cool it," Jefferson replies. "Even so," Washington says, "we pour legislation into the senatorial saucer to cool it." For Joseph Biden, the Delaware Democrat and a senator since 1973, the Senate remains a place where "you can always slow things down and make sure that a minority gets a voice," he said recently. And, he added, "the chance to filibuster"—using extended debate in order to block legislation—"is what makes the difference between this body and the other one." It takes three-fifths of the Senate—or sixty senators—to break a filibuster. (The cloture rule, as it is known, has been in effect since 1917; before 1975, it took a two-thirds vote to end a debate.) But the filibuster rule may soon be altered in a dramatic way, and the Senate itself may change along with it.

The precipitating factor is a continuing controversy over President Bush's judicial selections. Although more than two hundred of Bush's nominees were approved by the Senate in the past four years, Democrats used the filibuster to stop ten appellate-court choices. As a result, some Republicans are pushing to alter the Senate's rules so that a simple majority could cut off debate on judicial nominees. With the Senate now split fifty-five to forty-four (with one independent) in favor of the Republicans, the change could render the Democrats almost powerless to stop Bush's choices, including nominees to the United States Supreme Court. The magnitude of this transformation of the rules is suggested by the nickname it has acquired within the Senate: the "nuclear option."

The man at the center of the controversy over judicial nominations is Senator Arlen Specter, who also, as it happens, reflects the broader transformation of the Senate itself. Specter, of Pennsylvania, was elected in 1980. These days, in his office overlooking the Supreme Court, he surveys, not happily, the current state of his party—especially the disappearance of moderates like him. "We had a lot of senators," he said. "We could go on and on and on," and he named, as examples of this group, Bob Packwood, Mark Hatfield, Lowell Weicker, Charles Mathias, and John Heinz. "And we don't have them now. So it's not good for the Party, and it's not good for the country. It's not good for the Party because you need balance. You need to be a national party." Since 1980, the year of the Ronald Reagan landslide, moderate Republicans have been a vanishing species.

Specter's election, last year, to his fifth term showed how estranged he had grown from much of his own party. In an abrasive Republican primary, one in which Bush campaigned for him, Specter barely defeated a conservative challenger; but he won by eleven percent in the general election, in a state carried by John Kerry. On November 3rd, the day after the election, a reporter asked Specter about possible Supreme Court nominees, an issue that had fresh importance because Specter, a longtime member of the Senate Judiciary Committee, was finally in line to become its chairman and thus the steward of Bush's judicial appointments. Repeating a view that he had expressed many times, Specter said that he regarded the protection of abortion rights, established by Roe v. Wade, as "inviolate," and he suggested that "nobody can be confirmed today" who disagrees with that opinion. Virtually overnight, the conservative groups that had supported the primary challenge against Specter, such as Focus on the Family, demanded that he be denied the chairmanship.

The criticism had a personal dimension, too. Charm has played little role in Specter's political career; he has an air of superiority that hovers just short of a perpetual sneer, which he isn't afraid to inflict on senatorial colleagues or on his staff. (To see Specter walk through his office, where I met with him recently, is to watch his underlings cower.) His abundant self-confidence was first on view during his days as a staff lawyer on the Warren Commission, where he championed the "single-bullet theory" for the assassination of John F. Kennedy. (The theory—upon which the possibility of a lone gunman depends—supposes that one bullet struck President Kennedy before travelling onward to inflict multiple wounds on Governor John Connally.) During his tenure on the Judiciary Committee, Specter has been at the center of several major battles. In 1987, he voted against President Reagan's nomination of Robert Bork to the Supreme Court; four years later, though, he was one of Clarence Thomas's principal supporters, and at one point accused Anita Hill of committing perjury during her testimony.

Not surprisingly, more than a few people, especially in the conservative base of the Republican Party, enjoyed the thought of making Specter's life uncomfortable. On November 17th, he was forced to ask his colleagues for the Judiciary chairmanship. After separate meetings with the Senate leadership and with other Republicans on the Judiciary Committee, Specter was told that he could assume the chairmanship—on several conditions. At a press conference the next day, Specter made those conditions public. Introduced by Orrin Hatch, of Utah, who was barred by term limits from continuing as Judiciary chairman, Specter recited the provisions of the deal. "I have not and would not use a litmus test to deny confirmation to pro-life nominees," Specter said, in the weary monotone of a Soviet prisoner forced to confess his ideological errors. "I have voted for all of President Bush's judicial nominees in committee and on the floor, and I have no reason to believe that I'll be unable to support any individual President Bush finds worthy of nomination."

I had been in Specter's office the previous day and had asked him whether he supported the change in the filibuster rule. He was noncommittal, saying, "If the Republican caucus decides to consider it, I'll give it some serious thought." Overnight, apparently, he had. At the press conference, Specter said he would use his "best efforts to stop any future filibusters. . . . If a rule change is necessary to avoid filibusters, there are relevant recent precedents to secure rule changes with fifty-one votes."

On the Judiciary Committee, the chairman remains on a kind of extended probation. "Everyone who pays attention knows that Senator Specter comes from a state and a segment of the Party that are to the left of the President and the Republican caucus," John Cornyn, a conservative first-term senator from Texas, said. (In his outer office, Specter has three photographs of himself with Bill Clinton, while the television in Cornyn's space is tuned to Fox News.) "People are looking very closely to see what he is really going to do. I have been pretty pleased from what I've seen of Senator Specter's performance so far."

The controversy effectively neutralized Specter as a possible impediment to Bush's judicial nominees; the rules of the Senate remained another obstacle. A vote of two-thirds of the Senate is required to end a filibuster against a rules change. But, as one delves into those rules, they look less like fixed laws and more like accommodations of a shifting power structure.

Changing the Senate's rules on judicial filibustering was first addressed in 2003, during the successful Democratic filibuster against Miguel Estrada, whom Bush had nominated to the United States Court of Appeals for the District of Columbia Circuit. Ted Stevens, a Republican Senate veteran from Alaska, was complaining in the cloakroom that the Democratic tactic should simply be declared out of order, and, soon enough, a group of Republican aides began to talk about changing the rules. It was understood at once that such a change would be explosive; Senator Trent Lott, the former Majority Leader, came up with "nuclear option," and the term stuck.

This cloakroom conversation has evolved into a full-fledged proposal, complete with an intellectual pedigree. Several Republican senators told me that they had spent part of the Christmas recess reading the draft of a law-review article co-written by Martin B. Gold, an expert on Senate procedures, who served as an aide to Bill Frist after he became Majority

Leader. The article, "The Constitutional Option to Change Senate Rules and Procedures: A Majoritarian Means to Overcome the Filibuster," which was recently published by the *Harvard Journal of Law & Public Policy*, is a step-by-step guide to changing the Senate rules.

According to Gold's scenario, in an extended debate over a judicial nominee a senator could raise a point of order that "any further debate is dilatory and not in order." If the Presiding Officer of the Senate—Vice-President Dick Cheney—sustained the point of order, Gold wrote, "he would set a new, binding Senate precedent allowing Senators to cut off debate." Democrats could challenge the Vice-President, but it takes only a majority vote to sustain a ruling by the Presiding Officer. The Republicans, with their majority, could both cut off debate on a nominee and establish a precedent that would apply to all future judicial nominations. (A legal challenge by Democrats would almost surely fail, because courts generally defer to the other branches of government on matters concerning their internal operations.) Henceforth, then, filibusters on judges would be impossible.

Republicans have started to call the tactic the "constitutional option." In part, this is simply marketing, but the name also reflects the opinion of Orrin Hatch, among others, that the Republicans' action has a basis in the Constitution, as well as in the Senate rules. With nearly three decades in the Senate, Hatch, who is seventy, may be the nation's best-known Utahan, even though his Midwestern accent betrays his roots, in Pittsburgh. He was for many years rumored to be a possible Republican appointee to the Supreme Court, and has become instead the unofficial lead constitutional lawyer for Senate Republicans. "The Founding Fathers knew how to create a supermajority requirement when they wanted to," he told me. "They did it with amending the Constitution, they did it with ratifying treaties, which both require two-thirds of the Senate. And just a few lines below that they said 'advice and consent' on judges—no supermajority requirement. By using filibusters on the judges, the Democrats have essentially imposed a supermajority requirement, and we are entitled to stop them. This would not affect filibusters on legislation, which could still take place." Charles Grassley, an Iowa Republican, who also supports the change, said, "Filibusters are designed so that the minority can bring about compromise on legislation. You can always change the words of a bill or the dollars involved. But you can't compromise a Presidential nomination. It's yes or no. So filibusters on nominations are an abuse of our function under the Constitution to advise and consent."

Hatch didn't want to wait until the next filibuster to change the rules. "I have recommended that we go to the constitutional option early in the game," he said. "The worst way to do it is during a Supreme Court nomination, and then it becomes all politics. Let's do it now."

The escalation in parliamentary warfare began during Bush's first term, when Democrats took an uncharacteristically aggressive tack in opposing some of his nominees to the federal appellate courts. "The standard that was used before—it's likely it will be used again—was that if the Democrats on the Judiciary Committee vote unanimously against a nominee, then the recommendation to the caucus will be to oppose the nominee, including through the use of the filibuster," Richard Durbin, the Illinois senator and assistant Majority Leader, said. "That is what led to the ten who were not confirmed." These filibusters were especially controversial because Senate Republicans certainly would have confirmed the nominees if they had received a straight up-or-down vote. "Every one of these nominees had a majority," Hatch said. "This has caused a tremendous amount of angst."

The Democratic judicial filibusters of the past several years lacked any of the accoutrements of the great marathons of the Senate's past—no men in suits dozing on cots in the cloakrooms, no recitations of poetry (or recipes) to pass the hours in debate. (In 1957, Strom Thurmond gave the longest speech in Senate history—twenty-four hours and eighteen minutes, as part of his unsuccessful effort to stop the passage of the Civil Rights Act.) During the past two years, Democrats simply announced that they planned to filibuster against certain nominees, and the Republicans agreed to move on to other business. According to one Republican Senate aide, "The Democrats could keep one or two of their people on the floor, talking all night, and they could request a quorum anytime they wanted. We'd have to keep fifty-one of our people there all night, and our people wouldn't do it. Some of them are old. Some are sick. And it wouldn't break the filibuster anyway. That's why the filibuster is so effective."

Republicans claimed that the use of the filibuster against judicial nominees who had majority support on the floor was unprecedented—a charge that had some elements of truth. Before 2000, there had been a handful of filibusters on judicial nominees, but only in extraordinary circumstances. In 1968, Republicans used one to head off Lyndon Johnson's nomination of

Abe Fortas as Chief Justice, although Fortas might not have been con-firmed anyway. Other kinds of obstruction, however, have become increas-ingly common. Republicans controlled the Senate for six of President Clinton's eight years in office, and during that time the Judiciary Com-mittee blocked more than sixty of his judicial nominees from reaching the floor, where many of them would have been confirmed. A substantial number of these nominees never made it out of committee. "The Republi-cans did plenty of obstruction of Clinton's judicial nominees in the nine-teen-nineties, but they did it in a different way," Sarah Binder, a professor at George Washington University and the co-author of a book on filibus-tering, said. "The Republicans just didn't need filibusters."

Democrats assert that, by confirming more than two hundred of Bush's nominees, they have produced for this President a better per-term average of confirmations than those for Presidents Clinton, Reagan, or George H. W. Bush. Hatch called Democratic complaints "total bullcorn," and went on, "Ronald Reagan was the all-time confirmation champion, with three hundred and eighty-two federal judges. He had six years of a Republican Senate to help him. Guess how many Bill Clinton had with only two years of a Democratic Senate? Three hundred and seventy-seven. Not bad at all. I always gave their nominees a fair shake."

Both parties, in any case, have continued to ratchet up the partisanship. "Let me tell you how we did it in the Reagan Administration," Biden, who chaired the Judiciary Committee for several of those years, said. "They came to me and told me whom they were going to nominate, and I'd say, 'You're going to have a problem with this one or that one'—maybe a dozen out of the hundreds of judges that Reagan appointed. And I'd say, 'If you want to push that guy, all the others will wait in line behind him.' And the problems generally were removed. We did business that way for years, and it worked. Now this crowd wants to shove everything down our throats. They don't pull back on anybody. So we escalated with the filibusters. And they escalate with the nuclear option."

The decision of whether, and when, to push the rules change will rest largely with Bill Frist, the Republican leader. Most Majority Leaders tend to be long-serving Senate insiders, but Frist, a heart surgeon from Nashville, is only in his second term. (The job became available when Trent Lott had to step down, in December, 2002, because he made favorable comments about the 1948 Presidential campaign of the segregationist Strom Thurmond.) Frist has announced that he plans to leave the Senate in 2006, presumably to begin a run for President in 2008. "He believes that there is no issue that is more closely identified with him personally than judicial filibusters," a Frist aide told me.

Frist has been moving toward a showdown with Democrats over the issue. In May, 2003, Frist and Senator Zell Miller, a conservative Georgia Democrat, proposed a compromise of sorts, in which debate on judges could be ended on a sliding scale: the first attempt would require sixty votes, then fifty-seven, and so on until a simple majority would suffice. (Democrats threatened to filibuster the proposal, effectively killing it.) Then, on November 12, 2004, Frist gave an uncharacteristically fiery speech to the Federalist Society, the conservative lawyers' organization, denouncing judicial filibusters. "This filibuster is nothing less than a formula for tyranny by the minority," Frist said. On January 4th, in a speech on the Senate floor, Frist declared that he would bring one of the President's judicial nominees to the floor sometime in February, and he would see to it that there was an up-or-down vote. Frist also said that he does "not acquiesce to carrying over all the rules from the last Congress." Frist was taunting the Democrats, saying, "Some, I know, have suggested that the filibusters of the last Congress are reason enough to offer a procedural change today, right here and right now, but at this moment I do not choose that path." Bush gave an implicit endorsement to the change in his State of the Union address, insisting, to huge applause on the GOP side of the chamber, "Every judicial nominee deserves an up-or-down vote."

Frist has the sympathetic half smile of a doctor making a house call. In his splendid Senate office, he conveys earnestness more than passion. "I'm here for twelve years in the Senate, and I'm sticking to that," he told me. "And the time limit has made me focus on the big things, the big core values, while I'm here. To me, it is crystal clear that the change in the Democrats' behavior, the use of the filibuster the way they have, is an affront to the advise-and-consent power of our Constitution."

Frist has a strong political motive to embrace the change. His allies believe that in 2008 Republican-primary voters will reward him both for defying Senate Democrats and for confirming some conservative judges. "Frist knows he is seen as a bit of a compromiser," his aide said. "He understands that this will nail it down with the base. Frist is not an institutional 'Senate guy.' He has no illusion about the Senate being the world's greatest deliberative body. To him, it's a place to get things done."

Frist's enthusiasm may not be enough to get the fifty Republican votes he needs to change the rules. On February 10th, Frist told the Washington *Times* that he had fifty-one votes, but a few days later, to me, he said, "I'm not going to talk about vote counts." Senator John McCain, of Arizona, seems likely to oppose the idea. "We Republicans are not blameless here," McCain told me. "For all intents and purposes, we filibustered Clinton's judges, by not letting them out of committee. Making this change would put us on a slippery slope to getting rid of the filibuster altogether. It's not called 'nuclear' for nothing." Several other Republican senators also expressed reservations about the idea, often using similar language. Chuck Hagel, from Nebraska, said that he was undecided, and added, "I think the judges deserve up-or-down votes, but the filibuster is an important tool for the minority in the Senate." Susan Collins, a moderate from Maine, who is also undecided, said, "It's wrong for the Democrats to filibuster judges, but I'm concerned about the effect on the work of the Senate if the constitutional, a.k.a. nuclear, option is pursued." John Sununu, a first-termer from New Hampshire, and Lamar Alexander, Frist's junior colleague from Tennessee, have not made up their minds, either. Even Lindsey Graham, a Republican from South Carolina who supports the rules change, seemed to speak for many when he said, "Nobody wants to blow the place up."

That—or something close to it—is what Democrats are threatening. "On both sides of the aisle, even among a good number of Republicans who are quite conservative, they know the nuclear option dramatically changes this place," said Charles Schumer, the New York Democrat, who has been a leader for his party on judicial confirmations. "It makes the Senate into the House of Representatives. We are no longer the cooling saucer. The whole idea of the Senate is you need a greater degree of bipartisanship, comity, than in the House. And there are many conservative senators, particularly the ones who've been around a long time, who will not change that." As Richard Durbin put it, "Several of the Republican members have been in the minority, and they know they will not be in the majority forever. They don't want to do this to the institution." But on every important vote of the past four years the Republicans have ultimately rallied to support the President.

The possibility of a Democratic retaliation—the Party's own attempt at all-out war—is real. Even without the filibuster, Senate rules give a minority the chance to make life miserable for the majority. A single member can gum up the legislative machinery, as Tom Daschle, the South Dakota Democrat, who was his party's leader for a decade in the Senate, explained. "The Senate runs on 'unanimous consent,'" Daschle said. "It takes unanimous consent to stop the reading of bills, the reading of every amendment. On any given day, there are fifteen or twenty nominations and a half-dozen bills that have been signed off for unanimous consent. The vast work of the Senate is done that way. But any individual senator can insist that every bill be read, every vote be taken, and bring the whole place to a stop." Daschle also doubted that the limitations on filibustering would in the future be applied only to judicial nominations. "Within ten years, there'd be rules that you can't filibuster tax cuts," he said.

Last November, Daschle became the first party leader in a half century to be defeated for reelection. In a strongly Republican state, he lost a close race to John Thune, a telegenic former congressman, who made effective use of the fact that Daschle had once referred to himself as a District of Columbia resident. But another of Thune's arguments was that Daschle had become the "obstructionist-in-chief." Daschle's defeat may make a strategy based on tying up the Senate appear less than promising for the Democrats.

Specter has done his best to try to avoid a confrontation. He plans to bring up some of Bush's less controversial judicial nominees first, in an attempt to build momentum for compromise. But on February 14th Bush formally resubmitted to the Senate seven nominees whom the Democrats had filibustered in the previous two years. The confrontation may be delayed, but now, clearly, it can't be avoided. Specter's appetite for a fight may be lessened for personal reasons. On February 16th, he announced that he had Hodgkin's disease. Last week, Specter told the *Washington Post*, "If we go to the nuclear option . . . the Senate will be in turmoil and the Judiciary Committee will be hell."

One day outside the Senate chamber, I saw John Warner in an uncharacteristic pose for a politician. He had squeezed himself up against one of the old stone walls in an attempt to remain out of camera range while another senator talked to the press. In the first few years following his election in

1978, Warner was known more for being Elizabeth Taylor's sixth husband than for any legislative achievements. (The marriage lasted from 1976 to 1982.) But Warner, who is now seventy-eight, patiently moved up through the ranks, and today chairs the Armed Services Committee and is an important source of institutional memory for the Senate. "When I came to the Senate, I studied the history of the filibuster," he told me, "and unlimited debate has been an essential part of what we do since the inception of the body. Of course, the Democrats have pushed too hard and stopped too many judges, and I still don't know what I'll do if this thing comes up for a vote. I'm worried about it, and I'm worried about what's happening to the Senate. You see, I'm a traditionalist. That's my party."

Bush's War on the Press
Eric Alterman

The Nation | May 9, 2005

Every White House tries to exert influence over the media, both by limiting reporters' access to information and by courting journalists and actively promoting the administration's own perspective on current affairs. In this essay, however, Eric Alterman argues that the Bush administration has taken the concept of "managing" the press to an entirely new level. Not only is information hard to come by and access to White House officials tightly controlled, but the Administration has also created its own, semi-covert media operation. In the past year, it was discovered that several nationally-known journalists had quietly been put on the executive branch payroll as public relations consultants. More titillating still was the mid-winter revelation that a former male prostitute working under a pseudonym had been hanging out at White House press conferences for the past two years; his job apparently was to throw softball questions to Bush press secretary Scott McClellan, and even the president himself, as needed.

Fairly lurid stuff. But Alterman makes the case that these mini-scandals are really just a small part of a much broader effort by the White House—and conservatives in general—to "undermine journalists' ability . . . to hold power accountable." And as our independent news media goes, Alterman warns, so goes our democracy. . . .

Journalists, George Bernard Shaw once said, "are unable, seemingly, to discriminate between a bicycle accident and the collapse of civilization." How odd, given the profession's unequaled reputation for narcissism, that Shaw's observation holds true even when the collapsing "civilization" is their own.

Make no mistake: The Bush Administration and its ideological allies are employing every means available to undermine journalists' ability to exercise their First Amendment function to hold power accountable. In fact, the Administration recognizes no such constitutional role for the press. White House Chief of Staff Andrew Card has insisted that the media "don't represent the public any more than other people do. . . . I don't believe you have a check-and-balance function."

Bush himself, on more than one occasion, has told reporters he does not read their work and prefers to live inside the information bubble blown by his loyal minions. Vice President Cheney feels free to kick the *New York Times* off his press plane, and John Ashcroft can refuse to speak with any print reporters during his Patriot-Act-a-palooza publicity tour, just to compliant local TV. As an unnamed Bush official told reporter Ron Suskind, "We're an empire now, and when we act, we create our own reality. And while you're studying that reality—judiciously, as you will—we'll act again, creating other new realities, which you can study too, and that's how things will sort out. We're history's actors . . . and you, all of you, will be left to just study what we do." For those who didn't like it, another Bush adviser explained, "Let me clue you in. We don't care. You see, you're outnumbered two to one by folks in the big, wide middle of America, busy working people who don't read the *New York Times* or *Washington Post* or the *L.A. Times*."

But the White House and its supporters are doing more than just talking trash—when they talk at all. They are taking aggressive action: preventing journalists from doing their job by withholding routine information; deliberately releasing deceptive information on a regular basis; bribing friendly journalists to report the news in a favorable context; producing their own "news reports" and distributing these free of charge to resource-starved broadcasters; creating and crediting their own political activists as "journalists" working for partisan operations masquerading as news organizations. In addition, an Administration-appointed special prosecutor, U.S. Attorney Patrick Fitzgerald, is now threatening two journalists with jail for refusing to disclose the nature of conversations they had regarding stories they never wrote, opening up a new frontier of potential prosecution. All this has come in the wake of a decades-long effort by the right and its corporate allies to subvert journalists' ability to report fairly on power and its abuse by attaching the label "liberal bias" to even the most routine forms of information gathering and reportage (for a transparent example in today's papers, see under "DeLay, Tom"). Some of these tactics have been used by previous administrations too, but the Bush team and its supporters have invested in and deployed them to a degree that marks a categorical shift from the past.

Many of these lines of attack on the press might at first appear to have little in common. What does an increase in official secrecy have to do with payments to pundits, or the broadcast of official video news releases, or the presence of a right-wing charlatan in the White House press room pretending to be a reporter and serving up softball questions to the President in prime time? And how is any of this connected to the Administration's willingness to mislead the nation on everything from stem cells to Social Security?

The right wing's media "decertification" effort, as the journalism scholar and blogger Jay Rosen calls it, has its roots in forty years of conservative fury at the consistent condescension it experienced from the once-liberal élite media and the cosmopolitan establishment for whom its members have spoken. Fueled by this sense of outrage, the right launched a multi-faceted effort to fight back with institutions of its own, including think tanks, advocacy organizations, media pressure groups, church groups, big-business lobbies and, eventually, its own television, talk-radio, cable and radio networks (to be augmented, later, by a vast array of Internet sites). Today this triumphant movement has captured not only much of the media and the public discourse on ideas but both the presidency and Congress (and soon, undoubtedly, the Supreme Court as well); it can wage its war on so many fronts simultaneously that it becomes nearly impossible to see that almost all these efforts are aimed at a single goal: the destruction of democratic accountability and the media's role in insuring it.

The Bush attack on the press has three primary components—Secrecy, Lies and Fake News. Consider these examples:

Secrecy

All presidents try to keep secrets; it comes with the job description. Following 9/11, the need for secrecy increased significantly. Bush, however, has taken advantage of this new environment to shut down the natural flow of information between the governing and the governed in ways that have little or nothing to do with the terrorist threat. As Charles Lewis of the Center for Public Integrity points out, "The country has seen a historic, regressive shift in public accountability. Open-records laws nationwide have been rolled back more than 300 times—all in the name of national security." Federation of American Scientists secrecy specialist Steven Aftergood adds, "Since President George W. Bush entered office, the pace of classification activity has increased by 75 percent. . . . His Information Security Oversight Office oversees the classification system and recorded a rise from 9 million classification actions in fiscal year 2001 to 16 million in fiscal year 2004."

Some of these efforts may be justified as prudent preparation in the face of genuine threats, but this is hard to credit, given the contempt the Administration has demonstrated for the public's right to information in non-security-related matters. Upon entering office, Bush attempted to shield his Texas gubernatorial records by shuttling them into his father's presidential library. That was followed by an executive fiat designed to hide his father's presidential records, as well as those of the Reagan/Bush Administration, by blocking the scheduled release of documents under the Presidential Records Act of 1978 and issuing a replacement presidential order that allowed not only presidents but also their wives and children to keep their records secret. (The records had already been scrubbed for national security implications.)

In the aftermath of 9/11, Administration efforts to prevent accountability accelerated to warp speed. Attorney General Ashcroft reversed a Clinton Administration-issued policy governing FOIA requests that allowed documents to be withheld only when "foreseeable harm" would likely result, to one in which merely a "sound legal basis" could be found. And that was just the beginning. Even when documents were not withheld de jure, Administration officials often withheld them de facto. When People for the American Way sought documents on prisoners' cases being litigated in secret, the Justice Department required it to pay $373,000 in search fees before officials would even look. "It's become much, much harder to get responses to FOIA requests, and it's taking much, much longer," David Schulz, the attorney who helps the Associated Press with FOIA requests, explained to a reporter. "Agencies seem to view their role as coming up with techniques to keep information secret rather than the other way around. That's completely contrary to the goal of the act."

In addition, as Aftergood notes, "an even more aggressive form of government information control has gone unenumerated and often unrecognized in the Bush era, as government agencies have restricted access to unclassified information in libraries, archives, websites and official databases." These sources were once freely available but are now being withdrawn from view under the classification "sensitive but unclassified" or "for official use only." They include: the Pentagon telephone directory, the Los Alamos technical report library, historical records at the National Archives and the Energy Department intelligence budget, among many others. Even more alarming is the web of secrecy surrounding the operations of what has become the equivalent of a police state at Guantánamo Bay and other military prisons around the world, where the accused are routinely denied due process and traditional rules of evidence are deemed irrelevant. Exactly two members of Congress, both sworn to secrecy, are being briefed by the CIA on these programs. The rest of Congress, the media and the public are given no information to judge the legality, morality or effectiveness of these extralegal machinations, some of which have already resulted in officially sanctioned torture and possibly even murder.

Lies

The issue of "lies" has been the most consistently clouded by the Administration's supporters in the conservative media, who refuse to report facts when they conflict with White House spin. It's true, as I show in my book *When Presidents Lie: A History of Official Deception and Its Consequences*, that many presidents have demonstrated an almost allergic reaction to accuracy. Still, the Bush Administration manages to set a new standard here as well, reducing reality to a series of inconvenient obstacles to be ignored in favor of ideological prejudices and political imperatives—and it has done so virtually across the entire executive branch. As Michael Kinsley noted way back in April 2002, "What's going on here is something like lying by reflex. . . . Bush II administration lies are often so laughably obvious that you wonder why they bother. Until you realize: They haven't bothered. If telling the truth was less bother, they'd try that too."

Rather than regurgitate that fruitless debate over the war—the deliberate untruths told by the Administration have been delineated ad nauseam—consider just two recent examples of its deception on matters relating to scientific and medical evidence:

- Mercury emissions: When the EPA unveiled a rule to limit mercury emissions from power plants, Bush officials argued that anything more stringent than the EPA's proposed regulations would cost the industry far in excess of any conceivable benefit to public health. They hid the fact, however, that a Harvard study paid for by the EPA, co-written by an EPA scientist and peer-reviewed by two other EPA scientists, found exactly the opposite, estimating health benefits 100 times as great as the EPA did. Even more shocking, according to a GAO investigation, the EPA had failed to "quantify the human health benefits of decreased exposure to mercury, such as reduced incidence of developmental delays, learning disabilities, and neurological disorders."

- Nuclear materials: The *Los Angeles Times* recently reported that government scientists apparently submitted phony data to demonstrate that a proposed nuclear waste dump in Nevada's Yucca Mountain would be safe. As with the EPA and mercury emissions, the Interior Department found unsatisfactory the results of a study from the Los Alamos National Laboratory concluding that rainwater moved through the mountain sufficiently quickly for radioactive isotopes to penetrate the ground in a few decades, so it just pretended it hadn't happened.

In these two emblematic cases, as it has done so many times before, the Administration simply issued its own pronouncements, ignored reality and went its merry way, damn the consequences both for the reality of its policies and for its own credibility. Those found guilty of deception did not mind the one-day story that would result demonstrating them to be liars any more than Vice President Cheney minded the fact that a videotape existed of him claiming on *Meet the Press* that the alleged Prague meeting between Mohammed Atta and an Iraqi intelligence official had been "pretty well confirmed" when he twice insisted, also on videotape, that he "never said that." And the political calculation turned out to be a good one.

It was left to *The Daily Show* to run the two tapes of Cheney together. Reporters may have been angry at being lied to, but they returned the next day to swallow some more.

Fake News

The Bush Administration has invested untold millions in video "news releases" that disguise themselves as genuine news reports and are frequently broadcast by irresponsible local news programs. In three separate opinions in the past year, the Congressional Government Accountability Office held that government-made news segments may constitute improper "covert propaganda" even if their origin is made clear to television stations. Yet the Administration has rejected these rulings, fortified by a Justice Department opinion that insists that the reports are purely informational. Of course, the Administration's idea of "purely informational" is sufficiently elastic to stretch all the way from the White House to Ahmad Chalabi's house. As the *New York Times* reported, a "jubilant" Iraqi-American chanting "Thank you, Bush. Thank you, USA" is deemed to fall into this category, as is a report of "another success" in the Administration's "drive to strengthen aviation security" in which the "reporter" called the effort "one of the most remarkable campaigns in aviation history." A third segment, broadcast in January, described the Administration's commitment to opening markets for American farmers. The reports are clearly designed to simulate legitimate news programming. A now-infamous report narrated by PR flack Karen Ryan for the Department of Health and Human Services praising the benefits of the new Medicare bill imitated a real news report by having her sign off as "Karen Ryan, reporting" and by not identifying the story's source. The Clinton Administration made use of video "news releases" as well, but now the government's investment in them appears to have nearly doubled, as has its brazenness.

These phony news reports have much in common with stage-managed "public" presidential events that bar all potential dissenters and script virtually every utterance. In March, for instance, three people found themselves kicked out of a Bush Social Security event because of a bumper sticker on their car in the parking lot that read "No More Blood for Oil." White House press secretary Scott McClellan said a volunteer asked the three to leave "out of concern they might try to disrupt the event," but, of course, no evidence of any potential disruption could be found save the "thought crime" of coming to the event with an antiwar bumper sticker on a car. This was not, recall, a Bush/Cheney '04 campaign event but a presidential forum to discuss the future of Social Security. (Previously citizens had been kept out of Bush events because of clothing deemed inappropriate or for reasons unexplained, as when most of a group of forty-two, barred from an event in Fargo, North Dakota, later discovered that what they had in common was membership on a Howard Dean meetup.com list.)

In addition to creating its own mediated version of reality, the Administration has also invested considerable resources in corrupting members of the media with cash payments, in what George Miller, ranking Democrat on the Committee on Education and the Workforce, has termed a "potentially criminal mismanagement of expensive contracts." These include hundreds of thousands of dollars in payments to right-wing pundits Armstrong Williams ($240,000), Maggie Gallagher ($21,000) and Michael McManus ($10,000), the conservative author of the syndicated column "Ethics & Religion," who, like Gallagher, was paid to help promote a marriage initiative. And yet the resulting scandal has benefited the Administration's war on the press by damaging journalism's public image and reinforcing the false belief that everyone in the media is somehow "on the take."

Undoubtedly the Administration's most bizarre effort to manipulate the media was its embrace of former gay prostitute James Guckert, a.k.a Jeff Gannon, who showed up at the White House under a phony name and worked for a right-wing shell operation that acted less like a news organization than an arm of the Republican National Committee, publishing articles like "Kerry Could Become First Gay President." Gannon's ostensible employer, Talon News Service, employed an editor in chief, Bobby Eberle, who served as a delegate to the 1996, 1998 and 2000 Texas Republican Conventions and to the 2000 Republican National Convention and enjoyed many direct connections to Republican and right-wing organizations. Press secretary McClellan would often call on Gannon when he wanted to extricate himself from a particularly effective line of questioning. The words "Go ahead, Jeff," signaled that the press corps could be getting into an area that might embarrass the White House—or could be discovering a nugget of genuine news. Gannon's ploy might have continued indefinitely had the President not helped make him famous by calling on him at a January 26 [2005] news conference in order to be served up a softball that mocked Democrats for being "divorced from reality." Once exposed,

Gannon resigned and Talon folded up shop like a rolled-up CIA cover-op. As James Pinkerton, an official in both the Reagan and Bush I White House, admitted on Fox News, getting the kind of clearance Gannon did in this security atmosphere must have required "an incredible amount of intervention from somebody high up in the White House," that it had to be "conscious" and that "some investigation should proceed, and they should find that out." As Frank Rich observed, "Given an all-Republican government, the only investigation possible will have to come from the press."

Perhaps the most disturbing aspect of this war against the media has been the fact that members of the media have largely behaved as if it is just business as usual. In fact, much of the success of the effort derives from the cooperation, both implicit and explicit, of the press. No one, after all, forces local TV stations to run official propaganda videos in lieu of their own programming, or without identifying them as such, and no one forces CNN Newsource, among others, to distribute them. And why did the curious mystery of "Gannon," despite its obvious newsworthiness—and sex appeal—receive so little critical coverage and virtually no outrage in the mainstream press? (*Washington Post* media critic and CNN talking head Howard Kurtz even went so far as to blame the scandal on "these liberal bloggers, [who] have started investigating his personal life in an effort to discredit him," and the National Press Club invited Gannon to be an honored guest on a panel on blogging and journalistic credibility.) Mike McCurry, White House press secretary under Bill Clinton, says he marvels at the willingness of the press corps to swallow the various humiliations offered them by Bush & Co. He told a recent gathering of Washington reporters and editors, "I used to think that if I ever tried to control the message as effectively as the current White House did, that I would have been run out of the White House press briefing room. But clearly I misjudged the temperament that exists."

The media's failure to resist this assault is perhaps understandable. Members of the profession are under siege from so many directions simultaneously they may feel they can hardly keep up with each incoming salvo. Not only is much of the traditional media controlled by multinational corporations that view their operations not as a public trust but as profit centers to be squeezed, but newspapers are facing an alarming decline in readership (and more than a few are admitting to having padded those numbers all along). Broadcast news has been steadily losing audience share for decades. In a vicious cycle, the results of such declines are more declines, as resources are cut to match reduced profits and pressure escalates from above to do more with less. Meanwhile, more and more "news" programs are succumbing to the tabloid temptation, and the lowering of quality has been accompanied by a proliferation of factual errors, plagiarism and outright fiction proffered as reportage, further undermining public respect for the field. As Philip Meyer recently wrote in the *Columbia Journalism Review*, there is a sense that journalism itself "is being phased out. Our once noble calling is increasingly difficult to distinguish from things that look like journalism but are primarily advertising, press agentry, or entertainment." Throw in the nonstop ideological assault from the self-intoxicated section of the (mostly conservative) blogosphere, from (even more conservative) talk-radio and cable loudmouths like Limbaugh and O'Reilly, plus the fact that members of generations X and Y seem more likely to commit acts of terrorism than pick up a newspaper or watch a news broadcast, and it seems almost a luxury to worry about the Bush Administration's attack as well.

Another reason for the press's complacency is that many of these tactics are nothing new. Reporters have always engaged in a complex push-me/pull-you relationship with the President, alternately sucking up and pulling down as the political tides rose and fell. More than thirty years ago, Daniel Patrick Moynihan observed in *Commentary* that "in most essential encounters between the Presidency and the press, the advantage is with the former. The President has a near limitless capacity to 'make' news which must be reported. . . . The President also has considerable capacity to reward friends and punish enemies in the press corps. . . . Finally, a President who wishes can carry off formidable deceptions." What's unprecedented is the degree to which this Administration has employed these efforts to undermine the journalist's democratic function.

His formidable deceptions notwithstanding, George W. Bush has charmed many in the press personally, and his Administration, in the person of Karl Rove, has impressed them with its political perspicacity. Media insiders believe Bush/Rove to be a tougher political combination than most but have trouble believing they are seeking to effect a fundamental transformation in press-presidential relations. Media insiders appear to like

Bush a great deal more than the public does and frequently overestimate his popularity (in fact, in early April, Bush's approval rating had fallen to the lowest level of any president since World War II at this point in his second term, according to the Gallup organization).

What's more, for journalists to admit they are being deceived, or even manipulated, contradicts their sense of self-importance as "players" in a perpetual game of good governance. To read ABC News's "The Note"—which has developed into a kind of *Pravda* for the "Gang of 500" who cover national politics every day—is to enter a world in which the President and his advisers are treated in a manner not unlike the way *US Weekly* treats "Brad and Jen." Its affectionate tone speaks, too, to Washington reporters' coziness with the subjects they're ostensibly covering, their sources. McCurry notes that unnamed sources are such a problem today in part because reporters are frequently more eager to grant anonymity than officials are to demand it. "I have had probably thousands of conversations with reporters in twenty-five years as a press secretary, and I'd say 80 percent of the time I am offered anonymity and background rather than asking for it. I rarely have to ask for it and don't ask for it because I prefer to keep on the record as often as I can."

While individual reporters and even news organizations are undoubtedly vulnerable to White House retaliation if they refuse to play ball—former White House officials spoke openly of their desire to punish CBS and Dan Rather—if these organizations were to unite on behalf of their constitutional charge and collective dignity, they would likely find a White House that knows when it's beaten. Alas, reporters, like Democrats and cats, are maddeningly hard to organize. When some recently tried to map out a collective response to the White House's secrecy obsession, it got few takers. Knight-Ridder reporter Ron Hutcheson, president of the White House Correspondents' Association, walked out of an anonymous briefing last term to be followed by exactly no one. Len Downie, executive editor of the *Washington Post*, has ruled out the possibility of participation in any such action. "We just don't believe in unified action," he explained in a note to former *Post* ombudsman Geneva Overholser, "and would find a discussion aimed at reaching agreement with others on 'practicable steps' or even agreement on when not to agree to various ground rules uncomfortable and unworkable."

The net result of this one-sided battle is the de jure destruction of the balance that has characterized the American political system since the modern, nonpartisan media began to emerge a century ago. And unless journalists find a way to fight back for the honor, dignity and, ultimately, effectiveness of their profession, the press's role in American democracy and society will continue to diminish accordingly, to the disadvantage of all our citizens. Bush adviser Karen Hughes has explained, "We don't see there being any penalty from the voters for ignoring the mainstream press." And there's been none to date. Speaking to *Salon*'s Eric Boehlert, Ron Suskind outlined what he sees as the ultimate aim of the Administration upon which he has reported so effectively. "Republicans have a clear, agreed-upon plan how to diminish the mainstream press," he warns. "For them, essentially the way to handle the press is the same as how to handle the federal government; you starve the beast. When it's in a weakened and under-nourished condition, then you're able to effect a variety of subtle partisan and political attacks."

"Two cheers for democracy," wrote E.M. Forster, "one because it admits variety and two because it permits criticism." But the aim of the Bush offensive against the press is to do just the opposite; to insure, as far as possible, that only one voice is heard and that no criticism is sanctioned. The press may be the battleground, but the target is democracy itself.

Alan Greenspan Takes a Bath
Wil S. Hylton

GQ | April 2005

The concept of an independent national bank—whose chairman is appointed by the president, and then left alone for the rest of his term to tinker with the national treasury's lending rates as he and his team see fit—is one of the key developments in modern economic history. Shielding this central bank from political influence is considered essential, since national leaders, left to their own devices, tend to favor cutting interest rates—which can boost the economy, but which invariably leads to spiraling inflation when done inexpertly. Hard experience has proven the value of having an independent conductor (one who can't be fired

at the drop of a recessional hat) at the helm of the nation's money supply, keeping
one foot poised on the brakes and the other on the accelerator.

For the past eighteen years, America's conductor has been the estimable
chairman of the U.S. Federal Reserve, Alan Greenspan, known for his trademark
thick glasses, his professorial air, and his reputation as a financial genius. Who
would have guessed that now, after presiding over nearly two decades of unprece-
dented growth and on the verge of retirement, Greenspan's sterling reputation
would suddenly be threatened? The tarnish can be traced to the intellectual gym-
nastics he went through to endorse the Bush White House's tax-cut policy back in
2001 (when the federal budget briefly showed a surplus).

In this article, Wil S. Hylton ponders the Maestro's legacy in light of the Bush tax
cuts and the ballooning federal budget deficits that have followed. In the process,
he explores the high-level political horse trading that goes on behind the scenes
between the Fed and the White House—and reveals that Greenspan may be the
most talented and powerful horse trader of them all. . . .

The last time Alan Greenspan spoke openly to the press was in 1987, soon
after he was appointed chairman of the Federal Reserve. Ever since, when
Greenspan speaks to reporters, he keeps it off the record and behind closed
doors. Typically, he will escort the writer into a conference room down the
hall from his office, where he holds forth on all the major issues of the day,
from budget deficits to interest rates to the scourge of spin, until he can
politely excuse himself and return to work, having made his opinions clear
while offering none of them for quotation. With Greenspan, this is the one-
two punch: He leaves his mark, not his fingerprints.

Over the past thirty-eight years, Greenspan has mastered this form of
political aikido, and not only with the press. Having served six presidents
in four different jobs, he has become one of the most entrenched, powerful
figures in Washington, yet he remains one of the most opaque. Even when
he does speak publicly, he says very little: Twice a year, he emerges from the
labyrinth of the Federal Reserve building on C Street and, with his trademark scowl, shuffles down the aisles of Congress to testify about the Fed,
the economy, the dollar . . . but most of the time, nobody can figure out
what, exactly, he is saying.

"Financial capital raised in markets or generated from internal cash
flow from existing plant and equipment must be continuously directed by

firms," he will say to a chamber of bewildered senators. "The corporate securities that displace treasury securities in the Social Security trust funds must be exactly offset by the mirror-image displacement of corporate securities by government securities in private portfolios."

In certain parts of Washington, parsing the Fed chairman's language—known as "Greenspeak"—has become a sort of parlor game. But according to people close to Greenspan, that's a waste of time. There is nothing to figure out, they say, because Greenspan isn't saying anything. As his friend of fifty years, Charles Brunie, recalls, "Before he took office, he said, 'If ever you think you understand me, you will be mistaken, because I plan to obfuscate.' I remember the word obfuscate." Or as Greenspan's tennis partner and former Clinton aide, Gene Sperling, explains, "When he's sending a vague or mixed signal, it is by design." Or as Greenspan's old friend, the economist Milton Friedman, puts it, "I don't think it's an accident, whether he's ambiguous or not." According to sources at the Fed, Greenspan even takes pleasure in his obfuscation. Sometimes he will return from one of his speeches before Congress and order a video of his testimony, marveling out loud as he watches: "What in the world does *that* mean?" Obstruction, then, is the name of the game.

Partly, this is because Greenspan can get away with it. As chairman of the Fed, he is virtually untouchable. He is not elected by voters and not controlled by any branch of government. By law, he sets his own budget. By mandate, he and the six other Fed governors have final authority over monetary policy. And by custom, Greenspan can overrule the other governors, which means that he controls a critical portion of the world's money supply all by himself. He is even immune to most criticism. "The Federal Reserve has a compact with the rest of the government that it doesn't get criticized," says the economist and historian James Galbraith. "The Fed gets examined by Congress usually in a very deferential way, and the White House follows a policy of keeping its trap shut." So if Greenspan wants to keep his opinions to himself or speak gibberish to the world, well, there isn't anybody who can stop him.

But the real reason Greenspan holds his cards so tight is because secrecy only adds to his power. Within the government, he may be sovereign, but outside, his influence is less concrete. On his own, he administers only two short-term interest rates: the discount rate, which applies to loans from the Fed to banks, and the federal-funds rate, which applies to overnight loans between banks. Neither of these rates has a tremendous impact on the economy in and of itself. What makes them so influential is the fact that nearly every bank in America bases its interest rate on the Fed's. So if Greenspan raises the federal-funds rate by one percentage point, mortgage rates and business loans will usually rise a point, too; if he brings the funds rate down, banks will lower their rates, which floods the market with borrowed money and gives the economy a boost. This is purely a matter of convention—and nothing in the law requires lenders to follow Greenspan so closely, but the fact that they do gives him a reach into the economy that far exceeds his institutional power. That's why it's helpful for him to cultivate an air of mystery and authority, to seem beyond the comprehension of the masses. At the Fed, reputation is everything.

What is remarkable about Greenspan is not how well he has mastered this bit of image broadcasting, becoming the most exalted Fed chairman in history, earning the nickname Maestro and a renown that borders on celebrity. It is not even the great skill with which he has used his fame for influence, overseeing one of the longest periods of growth in American history, doubling the size of the economy, and keeping inflation almost nonexistent. What is *most* remarkable about Greenspan is that none of this has been enough for him. Over the past two decades, as he has elevated his prestige and power in the market, he has also managed to extend his reach even further—beyond monetary policy altogether and into the realm of politics. According to members of the last three administrations, Greenspan's veil of secrecy has done more than boost his reputation; it has concealed a long legacy of political activism—the secret meetings he holds with presidents and the secret deals he offers them, using his leverage at the Fed to influence public policy. When you pull back the curtain on Chairman Greenspan, you find a very different man than the neutral academic who speaks in koans to Congress. You find a man who is regarded at the highest levels of government as a shrewd political negotiator, a man who spent the first half of his career as a partisan operative and has only become more political with time—who was handed his job by political allies in exchange for political loyalty and has used that job for political cover while pursuing a political agenda. You find a man who has pushed and pulled the levers of government longer than almost anyone else in Washington. The question is: For what?

• • •

Up close, Greenspan is a lumbering man, thick like a wrestler, with a low center of gravity and a broad frame. At 79, he shuffles when he walks, and his round shoulders bowl forward under the weight of time. His back, never strong, has only barely brought him through the years; the long, hot bath he takes every morning, opening his spine with the fan on high and the light streaming through the bathroom window just right, the extended spells lying on his office floor to align his vertebrae—they do little to mitigate his pain. He is an old man now, and he looks the part, with loose skin and a gravelly voice that rolls away in whispers. But Greenspan's mind has lost nothing to the years. When he speaks, his eyes scour the room as if searching for details, darting across the landscape of his imagination for some apt example or metaphor. On the surface he may be fading, but he is a man of interiors.

One of the first things you notice when you probe that interior, when you speak to the people who have known him and have worked with him throughout his career, is his disdain for politicians. It is not that Greenspan *dislikes* the six presidents he has served; it's that he has known them all too well. He has seen average men of average intellect enchant the nation with average ideas, and the temptation to influence them has been too great to resist.

"I was playing tennis with Alan one time," says his friend Charles Brunie, the founder of Oppenheimer Capital. "It was January '85. We were waiting for a court, and I had just been down to Reagan's second inauguration with a group called Citizens for America—it was the only group that Reagan saw the week of the inauguration, I'm told. Anyway, I told Alan that I had asked Reagan, 'Mr. President, if you've promised not to cut Social Security benefits, why don't you tax them?' and Reagan's reply was, 'Well, they've already been taxed on the income tax, and when they invest they get taxed on the dividends, and I don't think it's morally right to tax them a third time on the same money.' But Alan said, 'Oh, Chuck, that couldn't have been President Reagan. That was Don Regan.' I said, 'Alan, I've known Reagan for twenty years! I was standing *twelve feet* from him. It was Reagan.' But Alan said, 'No, no, it couldn't have been Reagan. He wouldn't have understood that.' "

Or the time Greenspan and Brunie were out to dinner with Milton Friedman. "I asked the two geniuses," recalls Brunie, " 'Of all the politicians you have known, how would you rank their intellectual ability?' And

Milton said, 'Well, on a Bo Derek scale, Bob Taft was a nine and a half, Nixon was a nine, and Reagan's a seven—'and Alan interrupted, 'No, no, Milton. Reagan's not a seven. He's a four!' Milton said, 'Alan, what do you mean by four?' Alan said, 'Well, Gerry Ford's a four.' And Milton said, 'I don't know what that means.' And Alan said, 'Well, if you gave Gerry Ford a series of data, no matter what the series was, he could not develop a concept. And Reagan is the same.' "

Anyway, not to pick on Reagan and Ford. They're just the obvious examples, but it's no better now. The debates last fall almost *killed* him, seeing Bush and Kerry stand on stage and just *shatter* and *destroy* the facts. Watching, Greenspan could feel his whole body tighten up; he was complaining about it for weeks, to anyone who would listen. Is there no room for accuracy anymore? No place for facts? This is what drives him, what makes it almost impossible *not* to meddle. Twelve hours a day, he sits alone in his office, burying himself in data, in the bland, unglamorous world of figures, while these shiny politicians clog the airwaves with their empty rhetoric and drivel. Day by day, he hunches over his keyboard, poring over the economic reports and financial analyses, the statistics and charts and graphs, the GDP figures and quarterly records and lending patterns, soaking it in, processing it, while the politicians outside hem and haw and rack up deficits like drunken sailors. It is impossible *not* to notice what they're doing. Impossible *not* to recognize that they are out of control, steering the economy toward ruin. He cannot say that publicly. That is a line that he will not cross. Publicly, he is diplomatic and vague, as inscrutable as ever. Fiscal policy is not his jurisdiction; budgets are not his domain. But privately, how can he ignore these things? Privately, he tells his friends that the deficit is a crisis on wings. There is no more room for excuses. No more pinning the blame on war and recession. There are only three options now: to cut spending, raise taxes, or both. Yes, it has come to that, to the point where he, Alan Greenspan, would rather see higher taxes than a higher deficit.

"He has said that he would recommend higher taxes to cut the size of the deficit," says Milton Friedman. "Several times he has said that. While he prefers to lower spending as a way of reducing the deficit, he would prefer higher taxes to no reduction at all."

And yet nothing happens. Spending rises, revenue drops, and the gap yawns wider. This year the deficit is projected at $427 billion, higher than ever, breaking last year's record of $412 billion. The government is now losing more than *a billion dollars a day*, and they don't even seem to care. They call this budget "austere." Dick Cheney calls it "the tightest budget." These are *conservatives?*

It was not like this with Bill Clinton. Greenspan will say that for Clinton, and for Larry Summers, Bob Rubin, Lloyd Bentsen . . . the whole Clinton roster. He could talk to those guys. He and his wife, Andrea Mitchell of NBC, still see them socially. Hell, he even hired some of their staff members in 2000, the biggest compliment of all. Those guys balanced budgets. They were disciplined, smart, responsible. They were conservative! They built a surplus, not a deficit. Where is the surplus now?

Now he faces his last year in office, the final 250 federal workdays before it all comes to an end, and what does he leave behind? If he had retired five years ago, he would have walked away from a pristine record— unprecedented growth, a strong dollar, and a balanced budget four years running. That was a legacy to go home on, the fruit of thirteen years of cajoling politicians, coaxing fiscal policy, and, yes, reaching outside the limits of his own office. But now there is a great red abyss where the surplus lay, and on January 31 of next year, when he snaps shut the brass fasteners of his leather briefcase to make his final journey home, after eighteen years, five months, and twenty-one days in this office, he will walk away from that abyss forever. He will leave behind a falling dollar, an exploding deficit, and a looming financial crisis. Can you imagine how that feels?

There is a story he tells. When he was a kid growing up in Washington Heights on the northwest corner of Manhattan, the son of a stockbroker and a furniture saleswoman, this tall, rangy kid with a passion for baseball and a taste for jazz, there was a kid down the street named Stan Getz, and both of them had saxophones. Stan was 15, he was 16, and man, they would wail together. Or anyway, Stan would wail and he would try. Seemed like there was nothing he could do, no amount of practice or passion, nothing to catch up to little Stan Getz. Day by day, it just got worse, getting washed by this kid down the block. And do you want to know what it's like for him now, to spend the last ten months of a thirty-eight-year career watching politicians destroy his life's work? It's like being Stan Getz and trying to play with Alan Greenspan.

• • •

From the beginning, his relationship to the party was tenuous. He was not so much a Republican as he was a non-Democrat. He had spent the 1950s and 1960s figuring this out in the living room of the philosopher and novelist Ayn Rand, dissecting the principles of free-market theory and railing against government regulation. Rand was the founder of a philosophy called objectivism, which held individualism as the highest ideal and championed the free market. To Rand, the market was not merely an economic system; it was a social contract. People formed relationships in the economy—as colleagues, customers, and employers. To allow government regulation of those relationships would not just be inefficient. It would be wrong.

For Greenspan, discovering Rand was like finding a chorus to back his favorite song. Ever since he had given up jazz to study economics in the 1940s, he had been a proponent of the free market and had made good money putting his ideas to work as an economic consultant in New York. But in Rand he found a new perspective: The market was also moral.

In the world of economics, Rand's laissez-faire ideas fell under the category of market liberalism, in the sense that the market should be liberated from the government, but in the world of politics, the same ideas landed on the opposite end of the spectrum, in the far extreme of conservatism. When Greenspan merged his economics with Rand, he chose his politics, too.

If it is tempting for Greenspan's allies to downplay his connection to Ayn Rand—who is widely regarded as an extremist, even by conservatives—or chalk their friendship up to youthful enthusiasm, it should be noted that Greenspan was a fervent acolyte of Rand for nearly thirty years, well beyond his youth. In fact, as late as 1966, the 40-year-old economist published an essay titled "Gold and Economic Freedom" in one of Rand's journals, in which he denounced government regulation, arguing for the elimination of taxes, the end of what he called "the welfare state," and the abolition of the Federal Reserve as we know it.

"Stripped of its academic jargon," Greenspan wrote, "the welfare state is nothing more than a mechanism by which governments confiscate the wealth of the productive members of a society to support a wide variety of welfare schemes. A substantial part of the confiscation is effected by taxation."

Barely two years later, Greenspan went to work for Richard Nixon. His friend Lenny Garment had taken a job in Nixon's presidential campaign and invited Greenspan to meet the candidate. It didn't take long for Greenspan to impress Nixon with his intellect. According to someone who was present during their first meeting, Greenspan dominated the conversation, regaling Nixon with ideas about reducing government and restraining the budget, and by the time the two men parted company, Nixon knew he wanted Greenspan on board. In fact, within only a few weeks, Greenspan had become Nixon's domestic-policy coordinator, spending a portion of each day combing through newspaper editorials and policy papers, looking for ways to infuse the campaign with his own values. Each evening, he would prepare a stack of paperwork to be sent to Nixon's plane or hotel room, and Nixon would sort through the material and incorporate it into his platform.

According to Nixon's research coordinator that year, Marty Anderson, Greenspan applied his conservative principles to anything and everything he saw. "He was involved in everything," says Anderson. "Energy, agriculture, across the board. Every single piece of policy that a president deals with." In addition, says Anderson, Greenspan became closely involved in campaign strategy. "He had one of the few powerful computers in New York City, and he did some very interesting analyses of electoral votes. He did a lot of political things. Alan Greenspan is a very good politician."

Nixon's foreign-policy coordinator, Dick Allen, remembers Greenspan the same way. "In terms of raw influence," says Allen, "he was a resource that was matched by almost no other. The guy has a concept of how the world should be organized, and he pursues it relentlessly."

One of Greenspan's top priorities that year was to get Nixon to endorse an all-volunteer army, a radical idea at the time. To Greenspan, the draft was just another form of government intrusion and should be abolished. When Nixon adopted the policy—remember, this was at the height of the Vietnam War—his numbers went up. As Greenspan's friend Charles Brunie remembers, Nixon never forgot whom to thank.

"In December 1968, I was sitting in the Barcalounger in Alan's office, and I heard him on the phone," says Brunie. "He was very deferential, and I said, 'That doesn't sound like Alan.' When he got off, he came out, and he took those thick glasses off so I could see his eyes were kind of bugged out, and I said, 'Alan, may I ask who that was?' He said, 'That was the president-elect. It was Nixon.' And I said, 'May I ask what the conversation was about?' He said, 'Well, he offered me any job I wanted in Washington.' I said, 'Really? Why did he do that?' He said, 'I wrote the speech for him in favor of the volunteer army, and the president said that was the margin of victory.'"

Greenspan turned the president down—not for lack of interest, he told friends, but because he sensed that Nixon was intimidated by him, and it seemed unlikely that they would work well together. But when Nixon's presidency began to collapse in the summer of 1974, Greenspan saw an opportunity. Hurrying back to Washington, he arrived at Vice President Ford's office, uninvited and unannounced.

"I got word from my secretary that Alan Greenspan was there and he wanted to talk to me," recalls Ford, who had no relationship with Greenspan at the time but knew him by reputation. "I said I'd be glad to see him, and he came in. He said, 'Mr. Vice President, you're probably going to be president in a couple of days, and if you are, I'd like to be on your team.' Well, I told him that I couldn't predict whether I was going to be president at all, but if I was, I would like to have him on my team."

It was only a matter of days before Nixon resigned, and Ford named Greenspan to the Council of Economic Advisers. At the swearing-in ceremony, his mother stood on one side. On the other: Ayn Rand.

From the outset, Greenspan made the most of his access to the White House and its occupants. In the evenings, he would stretch out on the floor of chief of staff Dick Cheney's office in the West Wing, resting his bad back and watching the news with Cheney's assistant, David Gergen, while in Cabinet meetings he would frequently take a seat beside OMB deputy director Paul O'Neill or defense secretary Don Rumsfeld, chiming in on virtually any issue that caught his attention. Technically, he was the president's economist, but as his friendships within the Ford administration grew, he found that his ideas were welcome on other subjects, too—indeed, on any subject at all.

"I can assure you," says Ford, "at Cabinet meetings, Alan expressed himself on any subject he had strong feelings about."

Greenspan soon became involved in Ford's 1976 reelection campaign, too, reprising the role he had played for Nixon eight years earlier. Still technically chairman of the economic council, he began to spend a large portion of his time on the road with the campaign, advising on both policy and strategy. Ford had fallen thirty points behind Jimmy Carter by August of 1976, and Greenspan was part of the élite circle of aides assigned to put the president back into the race. Touring the country with Jim Baker, Dick Cheney, and Ford, Greenspan was involved in virtually every aspect of the campaign. "He was the substance guy on economic stuff," says a source from the campaign, "But there was also a feeling that he understood the politics. That's why he was on the plane."

In the end, Ford rose from the ashes to make the 1976 presidential race the second-closest of the twentieth century—but it wasn't enough. In January of 1977, Ford went home to California, and Greenspan returned to his consulting practice in New York. It wasn't long, though, before Greenspan found a new route to power. As the 1980 presidential race approached and Ronald Reagan seemed poised for the Republican nomination, Greenspan became an informal adviser to Reagan, but he also engaged in a secret dialogue with Henry Kissinger to return Gerald Ford to office. To this day, opinion varies on who conceived the idea for Reagan to nominate Ford as his running mate, but it was Greenspan and Kissinger who almost made it happen.

On the night of July 16, 1980, with the Republican convention in full swing in Detroit, Reagan's vice presidential slot was still open. Taking a suite on the seventieth floor of the Detroit Plaza Hotel, just one floor above Reagan's suite, Ford, Kissinger, and Greenspan began a series of secret meetings with the Reagan campaign to establish a "copresidency" between Reagan and Ford. Some on the Reagan team were shocked to arrive at the hotel and discover what was happening.

"I walked into Reagan's suite at about five thirty," remembers Dick Allen, Reagan's foreign-policy adviser. "I asked, 'Is there anything I can do for you?' and Reagan said, 'Well, Dick, what do you think about the deal?' I asked what the deal was. He told me, and I said, 'That's the dumbest idea I've ever heard.' "

According to Allen, the deal was not so much a partnership as a trade. Ford would bring experience and credibility to the ticket, and in return Reagan would surrender an unprecedented amount of control. According to sources present that night, Ford would dictate several Cabinet choices. "Reagan said, 'Ford wants Kissinger as secretary of state and Greenspan at treasury,' " remembers Allen.

But that was just the beginning. In addition to naming Kissinger and Greenspan to the Cabinet, the deal would also give them expanded authority—especially Greenspan. "The idea was that the secretary of the treasury would have a major part in the whole development of domestic policy," says former attorney general Ed Meese, who handled the negotiations for Reagan. "It would have been more than just the usual secretary of the treasury as one of the Cabinet people." He pauses. "I'm not sure how that came out of the discussions."

The Reagan and Ford camps haggled over the details for hours, trying to make it work, but in the end they could not reach an agreement. According to Allen, Reagan was willing to make concessions to Ford, but the addition of Kissinger and Greenspan killed the deal. Just before midnight, Reagan placed a call to George H. W. Bush's hotel room and asked him to join his ticket instead. The Bush presidencies were born.

Ford insists that he wasn't disappointed by the decision, mostly because he wasn't all that interested in the deal. "I never thought it was practical," he says. The day after the nomination, he returned to California and a peaceful retirement. Greenspan and Kissinger went home to New York—to the political wilderness again.

In theory, the Federal Reserve is not an obvious outpost for political ambition. The chairman of the Fed is almost entirely cut off from politics. That is the trade he must make for the job. In exchange for his own sovereignty, he cannot meddle in the sovereignty of others. That means he has no say on Social Security reform or the Medicare crisis, no role in the budget, no input on the national debt or spending priorities. These are political and fiscal issues. His turf is monetary policy alone. He may have great insight and wisdom about other matters, but he cannot interfere with them. This may seem restrictive, but it is the economic version of the separation of powers—a barrier not only to protect the White House but also to protect the independence of the Fed.

Naturally, that barrier has had all the stopping power of a sieve. Over the years, the temptation to meddle has proven too great for most presidents to resist. Eager to lower interest rates and boost the economy, they have found ways to pressure the Fed, sometimes through friendly overtures and sometimes through outright bullying. "Back in Kennedy's time," says James Galbraith, who knew Kennedy personally and served as the executive director of the Joint Economic Committee, "if they wanted the interest rate to come down, [White House economist] Walter Heller would call up [Fed chairman] Willam McChesney Martin and schedule a meeting. As the meeting date approached, the interest rate would come down. Heller said, 'We never had to actually hold meetings. We just scheduled them.'"

What sets Greenspan apart from his predecessors is that he has turned the tables on the White House. When it comes to political pressure, he gives more than he receives. "The Federal Reserve now has the upper hand," says Galbraith. "Greenspan has abused his position in that respect."

Because of Greenspan's conservative background, this may seem advantageous to the Republican party. It certainly was intended to be. After all, party loyalty was one of the primary reasons Greenspan was selected for the job in 1987. After the failed attempt to conjoin Reagan and Ford in 1980, Greenspan returned to his consulting firm in New York, but he kept a close relationship with Jim Baker, his old friend from the Ford administration. Baker had joined the Reagan administration as chief of staff, then as treasury secretary, and would frequently call Greenspan in New York to run ideas by him. By the time Paul Volcker's term expired as Fed chair, in August 1987, Baker had just the man to replace him—not only because he trusted Greenspan's economic ideas, but because he trusted his politics, too.

"The feeling on our part," says Baker, "was that a president is entitled at some point in his presidency to have his own chairman of the Federal Reserve. And there wasn't anybody else in America that I thought, or that we thought, would be suitable."

But Baker was wrong about Greenspan in one respect. Despite his nearly twenty years of partisan work, Greenspan's loyalty had never been to the Republican Party. It was to conservatism itself. This was a critical difference. When Greenspan looked at the legacy of Reaganomics, he did not see conservative policy. In the course of eight years, Reagan had almost tripled the national debt, from $930 billion to $2.6 trillion. The federal budget had been in the red for an average of $209 billion each year. Some economists were finding ways to justify these deficits, but Greenspan was not among them. Spending more than you earn, whether you're a government, a business, or an individual, is a path to ruin, he felt. An ever increasing portion of income must be diverted to interest payments, and the cycle of debt can become inescapable. To Greenspan, it was especially irresponsible to slash taxes when spending was rising. He was no advocate of taxes, but as long as there was high government spending, taxes were a necessary evil: The only thing worse than tax-and-spend was spend-and-don't-tax.

By the time Greenspan closed up his consulting business in Manhattan and settled into the Fed chairmanship, Reagan's presidency was in its final eighteen months, too late for radical change. But almost from the moment Reagan's successor, George H. W. Bush, assumed office in 1989, bringing Baker and Dick Cheney and several of Greenspan's allies with him, Greenspan set out to correct the fiscal course of Reaganomics. Technically, this was none of his concern. As a citizen, he had the right to his opinions, and as Fed chairman, he even had a right to consider the deficit in assigning interest rates. But he had no right to influence the budget directly.

According to sources from the Bush Cabinet, that didn't stop Greenspan. He offered the president a deal: If Bush would persuade Congress to raise taxes and tackle the deficit, violating his 1988 campaign promise—"Read my lips, no new taxes"—Greenspan would cut the interest rate and boost the economy in time for the 1992 campaign.

For years, stories about that deal have circulated in political circles, but they can be difficult to pin down. Greenspan has denied any quid pro quo with the forty-first president, and although Bush has offered comments that seem to allude to a trade—"I reappointed him, and he disappointed me," he told an interviewer in 1998—nobody has ever gone on the record to verify it. This makes the subject somewhat difficult to report. In the course of numerous interviews about Greenspan with Bush appointees, I heard the rumor many times, but no one would go on the record—until I called Nicholas Brady.

Bush's treasury secretary from 1989 to 1993, Brady is known for his brash and blunt style, and I heard from sources that he felt Greenspan had broken the deal—doing too little, too late, to boost the economy. I wanted to hear that from Brady myself—not only to understand why he might think Greenspan had burned him, but also whether the "deal" had really been explicit. It is one thing to send out signals to the White House; it is something else to make a trade. Reaching Brady proved difficult. I called him more than a dozen times last winter, and his secretary told me repeatedly to call back later. But when I finally reached him, Brady didn't hesitate to talk.

I asked about the deal—if he had been disappointed by Greenspan as Bush had been.

"It was *very* frustrating," Brady said. "There was an agreement that if the president would tackle the fiscal policy, he would lower interest rates. . . . He just plain didn't do what he said he was going to do."

I asked Brady why he thought Greenspan hadn't followed through, and he said, "I have no idea. Particularly since that was the agreement."

"How clear was the agreement?" I asked. "Are you sure that he under-stood the agreement?"

"He's a smart guy," says Brady. "Was it signed in blood? No. Was it dis-cussed thoroughly? Absolutely."

"Are you surprised at how long he's made it, if he doesn't honor these agreements?"

"That's not my job," Brady snapped.

"Okay, well, I appreciate it," I said.

"Righto," Brady said.

A few hours later, Brady called me back.

"Lookit," he said, "would you send me the quotes that you're going to use of mine, because you got going pretty aggressively. I don't mean I won't say what I said, but I want to see what I said before I'm quoted."

"I can talk to you about what you said," I told him, "but we don't read back quotes. It's the first thing you learn in journalism."

"I was in the government for four and a half years," he barked. "I think I understand the system. But I mean, you know, you might as well get it right, because if you get it wrong, I'm going to write a letter to the editor, stuff like that."

I offered to give Brady the gist of his comments to think about, but he interrupted me: "I'm not interested in the *gist*. I'm interested in specifically what I said."

"Are you backing off from the interview?" I asked.

"I'm not backing off from the interview, I'm backing off from your inter-pretation of the interview."

"Well, unfortunately, after you do an interview, it's not protocol to go back and take it back," I said.

"Unless it's inaccurate."

"The accuracy is in the transcript," I told him.

A few hours later, I got another call from Brady's secretary, asking for my mailing address; then, that afternoon, I got a third call from Brady, then another, into the evening and through the next day, trying to remember exactly what he'd said and then back off from it.

Finally, I arrived at work one morning and found this message on my answering machine: "Wil, this is Nick Brady. I gather you're not willing to send me the transcript of my conversation with you. In that case, I would like to withdraw the interview."

Clearly, Brady was having second thoughts. However important his story was, it seemed obvious that he expected to pay a price for telling it, for implicating Greenspan in an ethical breach and possibly a quid pro quo. But Brady's story wasn't unique. I had also heard, from former Clinton adviser Dick Morris, about a quid pro quo between Greenspan and Bill Clinton in 1993. Again, the issue was taxes. In 1993, a few months after entering office, Clinton proposed that the federal income tax should become more progressive, putting more burden on the rich. He wanted to raise the upper tax bracket from 31 percent to 38 percent for people making more than $200,000 per year. To Clinton, this was only fair, an equalizing measure. But to Greenspan, it would have been the essence of unfairness, just the kind of policy that he had described in 1966 as "the welfare state," in which "governments confiscate the wealth of the productive members of society." According to Morris, Greenspan and Clinton "made, together, an explicit or de facto deal." If Clinton would raise revenue through a different tax—one that affected everybody, not just the rich—Greenspan would cut the interest rate and give the economy a boost.

As Morris remembers, Clinton felt compelled. "Clinton told me that the top-bracket increase would not appease Greenspan," says Morris. "*Greenspan* was the word that he used. He said, 'Greenspan wants to force me into raising a broad-based tax, because only my political blood will appease him.'

"I think [Clinton] felt that the top priority was to do whatever he had to do to bring the short-term rates down through Greenspan, and unless he incurred political harm, he wouldn't be able to do that."

Morris adds, "You figure out what Greenspan wants, and then you get it to him."

By the time George W. Bush assumed the presidency in 2001, Greenspan's political power had reached its apogee. Under a Democrat, the budget was balanced, the economy was strong, and interest rates were low. Whatever Greenspan's personal history, it was clear he was not merely partisan any longer. If anything, being at the Fed had freed him of that burden. No longer bound to either party, he could foist his will on both. He could punish the first Bush administration for Reagan's deficits and reward Clinton for the surplus. He had overstepped the bounds of his position, sure, but in doing so, he had set the stage for an unprecedented level of growth. Nobody—certainly not the Democrats—was prepared to challenge his back-door influence. Not when they could take credit themselves.

But George W. Bush was well aware of Greenspan's power, and when he picked his new treasury secretary, he had Greenspan in mind. Paul O'Neill's relaationship with Greenspan extended back to the Ford administration, and Bush knew from his father's experience that a strong connection to the Fed would be a political asset. Among other things, Bush hoped that Greenspan would support his radical tax-cut proposal. During the campaign, Bush had promised to return the budget surplus to taxpayers, and he wanted Greenspan to support the idea. Even before O'Neill was confirmed, he began to meet with Greenspan, selling him on the policy. Politically, Greenspan agreed with Bush: It was better to return the tax revenue than to increase spending. But he also felt that the tax cuts should occur only if the budget surplus remained. If the surplus turned into a deficit, there would be no money to return. On this condition, Greenspan signed on. Speaking to Congress in January 2001, he said, "Tax reduction appears required."

Nothing could have surprised Clinton's economic team more. Not only had Greenspan gone public with his support, but his support seemed to contradict his own principles. The deficit might be gone, but the national debt was still enormous. Based on everything they knew about Greenspan, it was stunning that he would endorse tax cuts rather than paying down the debt.

"When he made those statements in January 2001, I was confident that it had been misreported," says Jeffrey Frankel, who served on Clinton's Council of Economic Advisers from 1996 to 1999. "It was so obviously supporting the administration tax cuts and what I would have thought he, Greenspan, would view as fiscal irresponsibility that I initially asserted confidently—in public—the he couldn't really have said those things. And of course, he did!"

Greenspan's support for the tax cuts had been conditional—no surplus, no tax cut—but when O'Neill tried to hold Bush to the agreement, he was thwarted at every turn. As O'Neill told the writer Ron Suskind in the book *The Price of Loyalty*, Bush said, "I won't negotiate with myself." In the end, Greenspan's deal was not honored.

As the surplus turned to deficit, O'Neill left the administration in anger and went public about the broken deal with Greenspan, but Greenspan has remained quiet. In a rare slip during a speech that he gave in London this

February—in perhaps the greatest-ever example of damning with faint praise—he said, "The voice of fiscal restraint, barely audible a year ago, has at least partially regained volume." Two weeks later, he told the Senate Banking Committee that it has become "imperative to restore fiscal discipline." But so far, that's been it.

In one sense, as Greenspan winds down his final year in office, he seems beaten at his own political games, a victim of one of his games gone bad. But in another sense, he has more power now than ever. For the first time in eighteen years, there is nothing left to lose, no reappointment looming over his head, no political allies to defend. The only thing left to protect is his legacy—but to do so, he may have to speak.

Every morning, Greenspan rises from bed at 5:30 A.M. and feels the rush of his mind coming awake with the rising sun. He has no need for coffee or tea. As far as he can tell, within two minutes of waking up his mind is at full capacity, and the rest of the day is a steady decline from there. By 8 P.M., when he leaves his office to return home, his IQ will have dropped some twenty points and the answers will not come so quickly. Morning, then, is his finest hour, and Greenspan doesn't want to waste it.

That means he can't go in to work or speak to his friends and family. To squander his best moments on human interaction and bureaucratic management would be, to him, a mistake. Instead, Greenspan heads straight to the bathroom, turns on a large fan to create a blast of white noise that blocks out sound, draws a hot bath, strips off his clothes, and settles into the water for at least an hour and sometimes two, until the skin of his body has begun to pucker and prune and he has drained his best ideas onto the notepad beside the tub.

Most of the time, what Greenspan writes in the tub are speeches and public testimony. It is important to use the right kind of pads and pens for this; often, while writing, the pad will slip from his grasp into the water, and if he has used the wrong type of pen—say, a fountain pen—the ink will bleed from the paper and his ideas will be lost forever. If he uses the right pen, like a Bic, he will be able to pluck the paper back out of the water without damage, stuff the pad into his briefcase, and deliver the pages to his secretary to hang dry and transcribe.

By then, he will have found just the right combination of words so that later in the day, or later in the week, when he ambles down the aisles of Congress to deliver another one of his reports, his message will be exactly as he intends—as clear or as confusing. Which it will be, only he knows. Greenspan has a choice: He can meddle in politics one more time, speaking out against the deficits and fighting for fiscal responsibility, or he can remain quiet and protect his old friends, leaving his principles behind.

National Conversation:
Social Security Reform

Personal Dispute: Why Democrats Oppose Bush

N. Gregory Mankiw

The New Republic | March 21, 2005

"I earned capital in the campaign, political capital, and now I intend to spend it," said President Bush, two days after his reelection. His top domestic priority was to remake Social Security by carving out personal investment accounts that would let people invest a portion of the money they paid into Social Security taxes in their own portfolios, which they could draw on once they retired. The president spent the spring of 2005 barnstorming the country to sell his proposals. And yet, as of this writing, the chances of any Social Security legislation making it through Congress this year are slim to none, and the president's approval rating on the issue is hovering in the 30 percent range.

What happened? For one thing, Bush may have been too successful at drumming home the fact that, sometime around 2018, the Social Security fund will begin paying out more than it's taking in. To many conservatives, the idea of accounts that are "owned" by individuals and that put Social Security monies to work as investment capital (rather than using them to make transfer payments), thus reducing the government's financial obligations to future generations, is a no-brainer. But whatever the advantages of personal accounts may be, they have one huge drawback: by Bush's own admission, they do nothing to shore up Social Security's solvency over the next two decades—the very thing the president has been raising the alarm about. Backed by public opinion, the Democrats—who have the ability to block any proposed legislation through a filibuster—have insisted they will only address the funding problem, and will have nothing to do with private accounts. As a result, the Republicans, leery of leaving themselves exposed on the issue in the 2006 elections, have put Social Security reform on the slow track.

In this essay, N. Gregory Mankiw, a former Bush economic adviser, makes a strong case for the advantages of personal accounts, suggesting (as the title implies) that critics of the accounts are motivated in part by animosity toward the president. . . .

Harvard University is, by some measures, one of the most left-wing institutions on the face of the earth. So you may be surprised to hear that it has endorsed George W. Bush's proposal for Social Security reform. Literally, of course, that is not true. But the retirement plan Harvard has set up for faculty members like me bears a striking resemblance to what the Social Security system would become under the president's proposed changes.

Harvard's retirement plan is essentially the nonprofit sector's version of a 401(k). Each year, the university puts a certain percentage of my income into my retirement account. I then invest this money in low-cost mutual funds, which hold a diversified portfolio of stocks and bonds. I can choose a safer portfolio with a lower expected return or a riskier portfolio with a higher expected return. The money is mine, even if I decide to leave the university. If I die, I can leave it to my kids. When I retire, I can use it to buy an annuity to ensure a stream of income for the rest of my life.

Under Bush's proposal, you would have the option of diverting some of your payroll taxes into a personal retirement account. You would invest this money in low-cost mutual funds, which would hold a diversified portfolio of stocks and bonds. You could choose a safer portfolio with a lower expected return or a riskier portfolio with a higher expected return. The money would be yours, no matter how many times you changed jobs. If you died before collecting any money, you could leave your account to your kids. When you retired, you could use it to buy an annuity to ensure a stream of income for the rest of your life.

Historically, Social Security has been a defined-benefit system. You put money in when you are working, the government promises you an income when you retire, and, in the meantime, the feds take care of everything. Bush is proposing that Social Security gradually evolve into a defined-contribution system, where money is put in your account and then you watch over your own retirement assets.

I am perfectly happy with Harvard's retirement plan. I have the sense that my colleagues at Harvard are happy with it as well, as are millions of other workers who have similar arrangements. This raises the question: If the liberal Harvard faculty is content with the defined-contribution structure for their private retirement income, why are liberals in Congress (and the liberal *New Republic,* for that matter) so appalled that Bush would propose moving the public retirement system in the same direction?

As far as I can tell, there are three reasons. The first is that the president proposed it, and some Democrats will oppose anything he advances. Many hope that Social Security reform will do to Republicans what Hillarycare did to Democrats: hand the president a defeat so humiliating that it would undercut his ability to set the domestic policy agenda. It is not hard to imagine that this outcome would affect midterm elections and perhaps even alter the balance of power in Congress.

The second reason the left hates personal accounts is that, over the long term, they could destroy one of its favorite battle cries: the alleged conflict between evil capitalists and oppressed workers. ("Workers of the world unite; you have nothing to lose but your chains.") No ambitious political figure today would be stupid enough to quote Marx, but let's face it, much of the left's rhetoric is a less elegant paraphrase of his worldview.

Social Security reform could put a stake through the heart of this populism once and for all. After workers develop an equity stake in corporate America, they will start watching CNBC and the *Nightly Business Report*. Their view of how they relate to the economy will fundamentally change. Bush understands this, and it is one reason he talks about an "ownership society." Democratic leaders understand it as well. Their biggest fear is that a nation of stockholders could easily morph into a nation of Republicans.

The third reason for the left's opposition to personal accounts is simple paternalism. Liberal critics of the Bush plan may be willing to accept that Harvard professors are capable of investing sensibly for their own retirement, but they are not ready to trust the general public to do the same. Compared with Republicans, Democrats are more averse to an economic system in which people play a larger role in taking care of themselves. To be sure, the paternalists raise a valid concern—some segments of the population are not economically sophisticated—but this is not so much an argument against personal accounts as a reason why we need to get the details right. Any reform should include some restrictions to protect people from themselves. There should be limits on how much risk people can take in their portfolios, especially as they approach retirement. There should be requirements that people annuitize enough of their accumulation upon retirement to ensure they are kept out of poverty for the rest of their lives.

Of course, when Democrats speak publicly, they are rarely this frank. They will not readily admit to political opportunism, to opposing the spread of stock ownership, or to distrusting the public with its own money.

So, instead, they raise two canards—one involving the deficit, the other involving risk.

Opponents of Bush's proposal say that funding personal accounts will require irresponsibly large increases in the budget deficit. This argument, however, is mostly fatuous. For one thing, the president is proposing to phase in the new system gradually. Eventually, everyone would be able to place 4 percent of their wages (up to the maximum of taxable earnings, which today is about $90,000) into a personal account. But, initially, the contribution would be capped at $1,000 per year, precisely to calm fears about the short-run budget impact.

More important, under the president's proposed policy, the long-run impact of personal accounts on the government's finances is approximately zero. When a person signs up for a voluntary personal account, the government puts, say, $1,000 in his or her account. In exchange, that person agrees to receive lower benefits from the traditional defined-benefit system, by an amount equal to $1,000 in present value. The initial payment into the account requires $1,000 in extra government borrowing, but that debt is offset by a reduction in the government's liability to pay future Social Security benefits.

All economists will tell you that the government faces a budget constraint that is expressed in terms of the present value of current and future cash flows. If a worker takes more out of the system today and agrees to take less out in the future—and those two changes balance in present value—then the government's finances are neither better nor worse than they were before. Higher budget deficits in the near term are balanced by smaller deficits or larger surpluses further out. In essence, the establishment of personal accounts recognizes an existing liability rather than creating a new one.

Some economists go so far as to suggest that the borrowing to finance personal accounts is an advantage of the proposed reform. One problem with traditional Social Security is that liabilities are implicit and, therefore, easy to ignore. Politicians have found promising higher benefits too attractive, because the cost of those benefits has been too well-hidden. Indeed, the funding shortfalls now facing Social Security are like those many companies face with defined-benefit pension plans. Recognizing these problems, younger businesses are more likely to set up defined-contribution plans like Harvard's. A defined-contribution system is more transparent—the worker knows what he is getting, and the employer knows what he is paying. Greater transparency should also be a goal for the federal government's finances.

The second canard raised by critics of the president's proposal is the claim that it would leave retirees of the future facing too much risk. They argue that personal accounts would leave the safety net for the elderly with too many holes. The most obvious response is that the proposed personal accounts are voluntary. If you want to stay in a traditional defined-benefit plan, just don't opt in. And, even if you opt in but then want a low-risk retirement income, you can invest in inflation-indexed Treasury bonds.

Most financial planners, however, recommend that everyone invest at least a portion of their retirement resources in equities. Sure, this means higher risk, but the risk is compensated for by a higher possible return. Harvard faculty can decide for themselves how much risk they are willing to bear. Personal accounts in Social Security would expand the number of Americans given this choice.

One important risk that reform could reduce is the uncertainty about future benefits that arises from the vagaries of the political process—a type of risk that does not yield a higher return. Proponents of the current system like to say that it offers a guaranteed retirement benefit. But how guaranteed is that benefit when the system is so vastly underfunded? President Clinton talked about the "fiscal crisis in Social Security" in 1998, but no changes in the system were enacted. (Reliable sources tell me that Clinton's inaction on Social Security was in part a payoff to the left wing of his party for its support during impeachment.) Now, seven years later, Bush is trying to address the problem, but many in Congress want to kick the problem down the road yet again. In light of the political uncertainty, it is preposterous to view the current system as low-risk.

But, if personal accounts are not the irresponsible budget-busters that the left claims, nor are they the free lunch that some on the right seem to believe. The simple demographic facts are that Americans are having fewer children and living longer. As a result, the ratio of workers to retirees has fallen from 16 to one in 1950 to 3.3 to one today, and it is expected to continue to fall. Clearly, in retrospect, it was insane to set up a retirement system with a fixed retirement age (which now is slated to rise very slowly). Imagine if, instead, Franklin Roosevelt had set up a Social Security system in which the youngest 90 percent of the population agreed to support the oldest 10 percent—and those percentages were fixed over time. Such a system would have been better able to withstand changes in demography.

Unfortunately, that is not the system we inherited. The current system has a path of projected revenue and a path of promised benefits that do not line up. It will start running deficits around 2018, and those deficits will grow larger indefinitely. Under current law, when the trust fund runs out around 2042, benefits will be cut automatically by about 25 percent for everyone, including those already retired. At that point, there will be a battle among the generations—the outcome of which is anyone's guess. Those interested in semantic games can argue about whether this situation is really a crisis, as Clinton and Bush have called it, or simply a problem. But there is little doubt that the aging of the population has put the federal budget on an unsustainable path, and the sooner we act, the better.

Bush made clear in this year's State of the Union speech that personal accounts by themselves will not solve the funding problem. The solution will have to include some combination of slowing the growth of benefits, increasing the age of eligibility for benefits, or raising taxes. The president has rejected increasing the payroll tax rate, but he has left on the table raising the cap on taxable payroll. I have met no Republicans who like this idea, but it may be the price of convincing a few moderate Senate Democrats to support change.

Some have asked, if personal accounts will not fill the shortfall in Social Security's finances, why talk about them? The answer is that, once major Social Security reform is on the table, we should take the opportunity to improve the system in any way we consider prudent. When you bring your car into the shop for a new muffler, you shouldn't complain if your mechanic points out that your brakes are shot. Once you have brought the car in, you should want to fix all the problems that need fixing.

The same principle holds for public policy. We need to fix Social Security's funding problem, and that will require hard choices. But we should also make it a better system for future generations. Moving the system gradually from defined-benefit to defined-contribution would be a good step, giving people more choices and the government greater transparency. The funding problem is the catalyst for reform, but the nation should take this opportunity to give all Americans a retirement system as reliable as the one Harvard gives its faculty.

Blocking Move: A Principled Case for Obstruction
Jonathan Chait

The New Republic | March 21, 2005

One of the reasons Democrats have been so adamant in opposing Bush's plan to partially privatize Social Security is their widely-shared suspicion that personal accounts are just a stepping stone toward the conservative goal of eliminating Social Security altogether. Where did the Dems ever get this idea? As Jonathan Chait observes in this essay, which ran in the same issue of the New Republic *as the preceding selection, it's what Republicans themselves have been advocating loudly for years. . . .*

At a town-hall meeting last month in Philadelphia, Rick Santorum, the stalwart conservative senator from Pennsylvania, was pitching President Bush's plan to privatize Social Security, speaking the reassuringly nonideological language of insolvency dates and rates of return. It fell to a sympathetic college student in the audience, blessedly unversed in the arts of message discipline, to state what conservatives truly think—and have always thought—about Social Security. "I want to know what problem everybody has with taking care of themselves," she said. At a similar event, College Republicans chanted, "Hey hey, ho ho, Social Security has got to go."

Out of the mouths of babes came a pair of remarkably succinct statements about what is at stake as the Bush administration sets about privatizing Social Security: Should Social Security remain in something like its present form, as a social guarantee to retirees, widows, and disabled workers? Or should it be dismantled and replaced with a system in which everybody takes care of themselves?

What was clarified at those events has, alas, been obscured in Washington. The consensus among the capital's chattering classes holds that the Social Security debate primarily concerns the program's solvency. Therefore, the questions center around political courage, and the greatest threat is that the parties will not agree on a solution. This consensus is wrong in every particular. In truth, the debate is fundamentally ideological. It does not lend itself to compromise. Despite conservatives' insistence that Social Security faces a "crisis," in reality, the fiscal threat is distant and manageable, while the political threat is immediate and dire. It follows from all this that those who believe in Social Security should make it their highest priority to drive a stake through privatization.

To the Washington establishment, the suggestion that conservatives essentially want to do away with Social Security is something close to a lunatic conspiracy theory. When a guest on *Meet the Press* suggested as much, Tim Russert replied incredulously, "So you're suggesting that private personal accounts are a secret plan to get rid of Social Security?"

In fact, the plan hasn't been secret very long. Conservatives always saw the program as an indefensible infringement upon freedom. Alf Landon, the 1936 Republican presidential nominee, called Social Security a "cruel hoax." More than 40 years ago, Milton Friedman wanted to let workers opt out of it, and Barry Goldwater said, "Perhaps Social Security should be abolished." That view, however, has never proved popular. And so conservatives hit upon the tactic of phasing out the program by transforming it into a system of private accounts. Privatization activist Peter Ferrara was quite open about this point in a recent interview with Steven Thomma of Knight-Ridder. "A lot of conservatives thought Social Security was an unjustified invasion into the private sector," he said. "But they weren't getting anywhere, because that was all negative politics. . . . Personal accounts would work because that's positive politics."

Still, as long as they remained confined to the political fringe, advocates of privatization nonetheless confessed their abiding hostility to Social Security itself. Ferrara's 1980 book *Social Security: The Inherent Contradiction*, which first laid out a privatization plan in detail, asserts that "social security uses simple force and coercion to compel individuals to participate in a program that seizes control of a portion of their incomes."

In 1983, a paper in the *Cato Journal* called for privatization advocates to wage "guerrilla warfare against both the current Social Security system and the coalition that supports it." And a 1998 book by Ferrara and Michael Tanner of the Cato Institute, *A New Deal for Social Security*, concedes its preference to abolish the program. Ferrara and Tanner write, "[I]n an ideal world, each of us would be free to make our own decisions over how to provide for our retirement—how much and when to save."

Today the privatizers have gotten closer to their wish than ever before. Bush has raided the libertarian Cato Institute to stock his staff of Social Security advisers. And he has closely followed the "guerrilla warfare" strategy laid out more than two decades ago by unabashed foes of Social Security. Yet, when the president invokes Franklin Roosevelt, as he does every time he talks about Social Security, it is to praise the New Dealer and his works. In his State of the Union address, Bush called Social Security "one of America's most important institutions, a symbol of the trust between generations" and "a great moral success." Of course, Bush and his allies have not abandoned their fundamental hostility to Social Security. They've merely learned to bury it beneath a pile of disingenuous rhetoric. And that is why Democrats must not be afraid to block the president's plan.

One window into Bush's ideological disposition is his constant refrain that private accounts would offer "a better rate of return on your money than that which the Social Security system gets." On a technical level, that's a deeply misleading claim. One reason is a theoretical concept called "legacy debt." Social Security started paying out retirement benefits almost immediately after it came into existence, which meant that the early generations of beneficiaries collected benefits while paying little or nothing into the system. This created the legacy debt. Every subsequent generation, whose taxes support previous generations, must bear a higher tax burden to compensate for the first generation's free ride. That's the cost of the legacy debt, and it's why Social Security will *always* earn a below-market rate of return.

Now, any generation could decide to stop paying into the system and keep their contributions in private accounts for their own retirement. These private accounts would appear to earn a higher rate of return going forward—but only if you ignore the cost of trillions of dollars that must then be borrowed to pay off current Social Security obligations. When these transition costs are factored in, private accounts don't earn a market rate of return either.

On a deeper level, though, Bush's line of reasoning is illuminative. Privatizers portray Social Security as a kind of low-performing 401(k) plan. But the program was never intended as a personal retirement plan. It's a form of social insurance, designed to spread risks throughout the population. One such risk is that you get sick or hurt and can't work anymore; 11.5 percent of Social Security benefits go to disabled workers (which is another reason why retirees get a lower rate of return).

Another risk is that your income will decline, perhaps because economic changes make your skills less valuable. (Today, for example, steelworkers could be made redundant by productivity increases. Perhaps in 30 years it will be accountants or software engineers whose work was outsourced overseas.) That's why Social Security gives low-earning retirees a greater return on their taxes than high-income retirees. Still another risk is that you'll live a very long time and exhaust your savings, which is why old-age benefits are indexed to inflation and last for a lifetime.

A system of individual accounts would concentrate all these risks on the shoulders of the individual. The inherent risks of investing have captured the most attention. Obviously, if you invest poorly—or even retire at the end of a market slump—you may get a nasty surprise at retirement. (Gary Burtless of the Brookings Institution studied what would have happened historically if workers had invested two percentage points of their Social Security taxes in stocks. Those retiring at the end of a slump would have less than half the income of their more fortunate counterparts who cashed in a few years earlier.) But the risks of replacing social insurance pose an even harsher dilemma. If you suffer a career-ending disability before you've put aside enough in your account, if you find yourself at the low end of the income scale, or if you live longer than you had made contingencies for, you would be out of luck. Social Security doesn't make anybody a millionaire, but it offers everyone the assurance against suffering too much from outrageous fortune. A privatized system would invert that premise.

Privatization advocates insist that the changing economy has rendered social insurance obsolete. "The economy is changing, the world is changing," asserted Bush during last year's campaign. "In our parents' generation, moms usually stayed home while fathers worked for one company until retirement. The company provided health care and training and a pension."

Bush is right about the changes. As Yale political scientist Jacob S. Hacker has noted, this generation of workers faces much greater income variability than the previous generation. Rather than slow, steady pay increases and lifetime employment, workers change jobs and see their incomes fluctuate dramatically. One of the most potent changes has come in company pensions. Forty years ago, most pensions gave workers a fixed benefit. Today, most pension benefits are tied, at least in part, to stock-market performance.

But Bush has the implications of this change exactly backward. Because workers face higher risk in the economy today, social insurance that eliminates risk makes *more* sense, not less. Privatized Social Security might have made some sense 40 years ago for workers who stayed at one company their whole career and retired to a guaranteed pension. Why not let them take some risks with their public pension? But it utterly fails to meet the needs of the present day. The last thing you want is for your 401(k) and your Social Security to drop simultaneously during a market decline shortly before you retire. If workers are going to take on greater risk in a more dynamic economy, a risk-free bedrock of social insurance offers the perfect complement.

To this, Bush's allies would no doubt reply that they only intend to privatize the system in part. They would leave a minimum guaranteed benefit in place, along with survivors' benefits. What they rarely acknowledge is that partial privatization is designed to lead to full privatization.

Bush, in a rare moment of wandering off-message, actually admitted this once. Shortly after announcing his support for private accounts in 2000, he was asked about transitioning to a fully private system at a question-and-answer session, and he replied, "It's going to take a while to transition to a system where personal savings accounts are the predominant part of the investment vehicle. . . . This is a step toward a completely different world, and an important step."

How will this work? Conservatives believe, not without reason, that private accounts will offer an invidious comparison to traditional Social Security. Workers will note that the taxes they send off to the traditional program disappear, while the money in their own accounts grows before their eyes. The private accounts will, in most cases, also appear to provide a higher rate of return. As noted above, the comparison is deceptive— traditional Social Security will be bearing the weight of the legacy debt, disability benefits, and, for affluent workers, redistribution to those earning less. But the comparison will create a constituency clamoring for expansion. Conservatives once proclaimed this unabashedly. The 1983 *Cato Journal* paper, which advocated what it called a "Leninist Strategy" for undermining Social Security, argued, "This mechanism for demonstrating the individual gains and losses that occur under Social Security is a key step in weakening public support for our present system."

Today's privatizers offer assurances that private accounts will be strictly limited and regulated. But those promises can't easily be reconciled with one of their key selling points—namely that workers would own them. "Under a privatized Social Security system, workers would have full property rights in their retirement accounts," writes *Cato*'s Tanner. "They would own the money in them, the same way people own their IRA's or 401(k) plans." The comparison with IRAs and 401(k) accounts is instructive. These, like the proposed Social Security accounts, were created for the very narrow purpose of retirement savings. But their owners saw them as their own property and demanded the right to use them for children's educations, buying homes, and other purposes. Congress has steadily acceded to those demands, and the Bush administration has already proposed expanding IRAs into all-purpose tax shelters with even fewer restrictions.

As conservatives well understand, once a group of voters has been given a property right by Washington, they will never allow it to be taken away. The individual rights will be a ratchet, one that can be expanded but never contracted. The pressure for expansion would be especially strong during extended bull market runs, such as during the late '90s, when the public (and even some economists) tends to delude itself into thinking that stocks will rise forever. This is why conservatives are so insistent upon establishing individual accounts. They have uncharacteristically volunteered compromises—even offering to violate their theological opposition to tax hikes—in order to insert their opening wedge. Privatizers understand full well that any concessions they make can be legislated away in the future, while private accounts cannot.

In light of all this, it should be clear how critical it is to block private accounts. And it's curious, if not outright bizarre, that so many of those who do not share the privatizers' basic hostility to Social Security nonetheless urge the Democrats to compromise with them. Suppose a group of peaceniks, concluding that their long quest to slash defense spending has failed, decided to overhaul the Pentagon. They have the explicit goal of transforming the military into a shriveled force incapable of projecting power overseas, but they sell their plan as a solution to wasteful defense procurement. Of course, they wouldn't receive a serious hearing, just as Social Security privatization didn't two decades ago. But imagine that they patiently advocated their case, and, in due time, very liberal Democrats came to control the White House and Congress and put their brand of military "reform" on the national agenda. Would moderate conservatives feel the need to strike a deal? Would their failure to do so reflect a shameful lack of response to the (very real) problem of Pentagon waste? Probably —hopefully—not.

Why, then, is privatizing Social Security widely seen not as a contest of diametrical philosophies but as fertile ground for compromise? (As Joe Lieberman said on CNN last Sunday, "So, at some point, we've got to stop criticizing each other and sit at the table and work out this problem.") One reason is that the culture of Washington celebrates consensus. Refusing to compromise is considered unseemly. Republicans have played to this sentiment by accusing Democrats of opposing Bush merely for the sake of denying him a victory. The press has proved receptive to this line of attack. "So the Democratic position," PBS anchorman Jim Lehrer asked Senate Minority Leader Harry Reid last month, "is that there is no crisis and nothing needs to be done at all to the Social Security program right now?"

Republicans like to point out that none other than Bill Clinton called Social Security's financing a "crisis" in the late '90s. Indeed, it seemed that way at the time. But it has become less and less clear that Social Security actually will become insolvent. In 1997, the Social Security actuaries projected that the Trust Fund would run out in 2027. But every year since, even after the economic slowdown of 2001, faster growth has pushed that date back. Today, the actuaries project the Trust Fund will run out in 2042. It's now within the realm of possibility that the date of insolvency will be pushed back indefinitely. Quite possibly, in other words, little or nothing will need to be done to save Social Security. More likely, the benefit cuts or tax hikes required to keep it in the black will be less severe than currently projected.

Cutting the guaranteed benefit is the politically dicey part of reforming Social Security, and privatizers argue that establishing individual accounts will make such cuts easier. As an administration Social Security strategist put it, "You've got the bitter medicine of changing the indexing [which will reduce benefits], but, to go along with that, you've got the sweetener of the accounts." But, in reality, individual accounts make benefit reductions more painful by forcing deeper cuts than would otherwise be necessary. And, of course, the deeper the cut, the harder it is to enact.

Given that his own supposed solution will make it harder to shore up Social Security, Bush's claims to be motivated by a desire to save the program are patently disingenuous. Bush has argued that the true Social Security crisis will occur not when the Trust Fund runs out in 2042, but in 2018, when Social Security benefits outstrip tax revenues, forcing the program to cash in its Treasury bonds. What emergency will happen in 2018? The federal government will have to run deficits. But, of course, the government is already running large deficits right now, and Bush hardly regards that as a "crisis." If Bush wanted to control entitlement spending, he'd look to save Medicare, whose long-term deficit is seven times that of Social Security.

The only way to make sense of Bush's behavior is to understand that his professed concern for Social Security's solvency is a pretext. He wants to use this moment of maximal Republican power to put his ideological imprint on any change to the system. From a fiscal standpoint, repairing Social Security now as opposed to five or ten years from now makes almost no difference. The true basis for Bush's urgency is that Republicans may not control Washington in five or ten years. For ideological conservatives, this is a pressing reason to act now. For the rest of us, it isn't.

Bush has tried to pressure Democrats by accusing them of putting their heads in the sand by not putting forth a detailed plan to save Social Security. Amazingly, mainstream pundits have endlessly repeated this vacuous talking point, seemingly oblivious to the fact that Bush has no detailed plan, either. Bush has put forth some general principles. Democrats have also put forth general principles. (In a press conference, Democratic leaders indicated their preference for a bipartisan solution, mixing benefit cuts and tax hikes, similar to what a commission chaired by Alan Greenspan produced two decades ago.) Sure, Bush has focused more on the need for change and Democrats on the dangers of the wrong kind of change. But that's because Bush can be sure any plan that passes soon will meet his approval. Democrats, obviously, have no such confidence.

Bush and his allies have accused Democrats of opposing his agenda out of pure partisan interest. They have also warned that the public will blame Democrats if they block reform. Both these arguments happen to be wrong. Not only are there sound, substantive reasons for defeating privatization, polls show around 70 percent of the public opposes replacing part of a guaranteed benefit with an individual account. The minority party will not be blamed for failing to implement wildly unpopular changes.

The fear peddled by the administration that fiscal calamity will ensue if we do nothing is also groundless. What's so bad about waiting until the last minute? In 1983, Congress waited until the very eve of insolvency to act, and a very responsible bipartisan solution emerged. If we do nothing until 2042, and insolvency actually does loom then, the same thing would no doubt happen again.

There are other principled reasons for postponing a Social Security fix. Waiting too long may not be ideal, but acting too soon carries its own risks. Long-term projections are highly unreliable. The further in advance of the problem we act, the less reliable our guess. Also, acting now to "save" Social Security would consume scarce resources that may be needed to solve larger problems. Some moderates have suggested cutting a Social Security deal that includes a tax hike. But balancing the general operating budget and saving Medicare and Medicaid will probably require tax hikes, too. These twin problems—the deficit and health care—dwarf Social Security's future insolvency. Pouring resources into saving Social Security now is like driving a fire truck past the blazing inferno to fireproof the house across town.

Some liberals are naturally attracted to the prospect of offering subsidized savings accounts to help workers who have never had the chance to save money and build wealth. It's an attractive goal. (Though whether it's a compelling use of public funds given our desperate fiscal straits is open to dispute.) The key obstacle is that Bush supports those accounts only as a bludgeon against Social Security. If a given bill doesn't sow the seeds of the program's demise, Bush almost certainly won't sign it.

Likewise, he will have little incentive to sign a bill that merely eliminated the program's future deficit, because doing so would deprive him of his strongest pretext for privatization. The key point Democrats should understand is that, while it may be tactically useful to favor an alternative to privatization, no decent alternative is going to be signed into law under this president. There will be plenty of time in the future for shoring up Social Security or adding spiffy new savings vehicles. In the meantime, the crown jewel of the New Deal faces an existential threat. Defeating that threat is the task to which we must presently address ourselves.

King Karl
John Heilemann

New York magazine | April 4, 2005

The American public's apparent rejection of President Bush's plan to partially privatize Social Security—at least for now—seems to be, at first glance, a clear win for the Democrats. In this column, however, John Heilemann suggests that the whole Social Security debate may simply be a diversionary tactic, intended to keep the liberal opposition preoccupied while Bush and the Republican Congress quietly pursue the rest of their agenda. Heilemann detects Karl Rove's political calculus at work in both the Social Security fight and the Republicans' rush to weigh in on the fate of the unfortunate Terri Schiavo (see "Backward Christian Soldiers," p. 265, and "How Liberalism Failed Terri Schiavo," p. 268). In each case, he notes, Bush and the GOP were able to score big points with their core supporters and control the political discourse, all with little risk to themselves. If the Bush administration's Social Security initiative stalls (as appears to be the case) the Republicans can simply blame the "obstructionist" Democrats in Congress. Meanwhile, the issue has been put squarely on the table—to be revisited at some future date. . . .

Along the spectrum of public-policy concerns, it's hard to imagine two issues farther apart than Terri Schiavo and Social Security: The first is visceral, emotional, prone to craven and witless grandstanding; the second, so

arid and bloodless it's prone to inducing narcolepsy. But as political matters, the Schiavo imbroglio and Social Security share two things in
common. On both, the distinctive mark of Karl Rove is scrawled with a
flourish in Day-Glo. And on both, in the realm of public opinion, the
Republican Party is getting its ass kicked from here to Sunday.

The numbers are pretty striking. On Social Security, polls show support
for George W. Bush's position mired at under 40 percent, with 58 percent
of Americans saying that the more they learn about his plan the less they
like it. Meanwhile, an ABC poll last week reported that, by a 63 to 28 percent margin, the public favors the removal of Schiavo's feeding tube—and
that even Evangelicals are split down the middle on the question.

Not surprisingly, the Democratic reaction has been unalloyed glee—not
least at the implication that Bush's strategic supremo and deputy chief of
staff may be fallible after all. Democrats in Congress charge that the Rove-
ified Republicans' Schiavo intervention unmasks the GOP as the party of
big and intrusive government, while liberal strategists claim that the
parade of blunders on Social Security suggests that the Administration's
balding boy wonder has lost his populist touch. As New Democrat Network
president Simon Rosenberg said to me the other day, "This is one of those
times when you have to conclude that Rove isn't as smart as people say."

The Democrats' jubilation is understandable, and even justified. But I
also suspect it may turn out to be premature. Both Schiavo and Social
Security are, for Rove, parts of a bigger puzzle: how to cement the fractious
Republican coalition into a stable governing majority, one that advances
the cause of a historic partisan realignment. Solving that puzzle inevitably
poses knotty political challenges. But let's remember, they're the sort of
challenges Democrats can only wish they had.

Not long ago, I had a chance to see Rove speak to an audience of conservative activists down in Washington. The speech was as revealing for what
it left out as for what it included. Not once did Rove proclaim the importance of reducing the size and sphere of Washington's purview. Not once
did he echo Ronald Reagan's famous line—which codified a fundamental
verity of modern Republicanism—that "government isn't the solution to
our problems; government is our problem." Instead, Rove rejected the
party's "reactionary" and "pessimistic" past, in which it stood idly by while

"liberals were setting the pace of change and had the visionary goals." Now, he went on, the GOP has seized the "mantle of idealism," dedicating itself to "putting government on the side of progress and reform, modernization and greater freedom."

Here in Blue America, Rove is typically caricatured as an ideologue, a hard-right-winger of the Cheney-Ashcroft genre. But as those who've closely followed his career will tell you, he is in fact a pragmatist, an apostle of patronage with a keen sense of factional politics and the spoils system. (In his formative years, he was, after all, a direct-mail marketer.) His strategy is to cast Republicans as the party of the future—or, as the Clinton campaign once expressed it, of "change versus more of the same"—while dispensing largesse to reward core constituencies and buy off marginal ones.

Examples of Rove's Tip O'Neill–esque tactics during Bush's first term are abundant. Together they compose the Administration's embrace of big-government conservatism: tax cuts for the rich; subsidies for farmers, tariffs for the steel, shrimp, and lumber industries; the gargantuan Medicare prescription-drug entitlement for the drug companies and the elderly.

Given the zero-sum dynamics of Social Security, Rove's encouragement of Bush to focus on it this year seems mystifying at first. Certainly it hasn't worked out too well so far. "The discussion didn't get off to a good start for them," the Republican pollster Frank Luntz told me, "and there's no indication it's going to get better anytime soon." Free Enterprise Fund head Stephen Moore added, "We thought the stars were in alignment, but it's looking like we may have got our astronomy wrong."

Yet as ugly as the Social Security debate has been for Bush and the GOP, it has served—perhaps intentionally—one salutary purpose: distracting Democrats while Republicans legislate, with ungodly brio, the rest of their agenda. Class-action reform, the bankruptcy bill, drilling for oil in the Alaskan wilderness: Republicans are teeing up pet legislation and knocking it down the fairway like Tiger Woods with a brisk wind at his back. "Without Social Security," Grover Norquist, a Rove confidant and head of Americans for Tax Reform, told me, "this other stuff would've been the front line of battle. Instead, Democrats are holding us up on Social Security, while we get everything else we want done."

Like Moore, Norquist concedes that Social Security reform (at least any version featuring private accounts) is unlikely to be passed this year. But this, he contends, would hardly be catastrophic for Republicans—and he has a point. "On Social Security, we're playing on our field," Norquist says. "What would a Democratic win be? The status quo! Not exactly exciting for the party of progressivism."

More important, although Democrats, in my view, have been right as a matter both of principle and politics to fight Bush on Social Security, their stance leaves them open to attack. "Democrats did something really stupid by saying there's not a problem," argues Luntz. "They damaged their credibility and made themselves the party of No." Or, as Rove put it in his speech, "they're attempting to block reform," he said. "The risk is that they'll appear to be obstructionist, oppositional, and wedded to the past instead of the future—and that's not a good place to be in American politics."

To Rove's constituency-centric way of thinking, Social Security reform is a way of satisfying the party's laissez-faire purists. It's also a way of reaching out to young voters, especially in the West. And while failure would be a setback for Bush, the damage, I think, would be less dramatic than people now assume. As long as the economy is humming and foreign policy ticking along, the main threat to Bush, lame-duckism, will be minimized by the desire of congressional Republicans, especially those planning a presidential run, to stay on his good side—and also on Rove's. Indeed, that Rove has left open the possibility of his involvement in 2008 benefits Bush mightily. "The Rove primary," one Hill Republican says, "is very much under way up here."

The truth of that should be blindingly obvious to anyone who caught a nauseating glimpse of Senate Majority Leader Bill Frist's performance in the Schiavo affair. In Washington, Frist is universally seen as a wholly owned subsidiary of Rove's White House operation. In the Schiavo controversy, both men saw an opportunity to score points with the religious right—causing Frist, a licensed physician, mind you, to diagnose Schiavo by a videotape, a detour into telemedicine that would have been funny if it weren't so sad, and Rove to advise Bush to fly back to Washington to play his role in the *theatre macabre*.

For Rove, the need to throw a bone to Christian conservatives has been apparent since January, when he received a letter from a clutch of A-list Evangelicals (James Dobson, Donald Wildmon, etc.) complaining about the energy Bush was devoting to . . . Social Security. "Is he prepared to spend significant political capital on privatization but reluctant to devote the same energy to preserving traditional marriage?" the letter asked pointedly.

Compared with gay marriage, the Schiavo affair offered Rove a fairly simple means of showing fealty to the religious right. It also fit snugly into a larger political schema. That the courts (bound by, you know, the rule of law) would refuse to restore Schiavo's feeding tube was all but inevitable. And that, in turn, was bound to feed the ire of the right toward "liberal judges," thus stoking the flames in the looming battle in the Senate over the so-called nuclear option to stop Democratic judicial filibusters—which Rove badly wants to detonate.

The alleged risks to Republicans of cozying up excessively to the Christian right are so well rehearsed it hurts my head to list them here: the alienation of swing voters, intra-party fratricide between social conservatives and libertarians, blah blah blah. The problem with this analysis can be simply stated: the 2004 election, in which swing voters all but disappeared, and Evangelicals, though far from delivering the White House to Bush, surely didn't do him any harm.

For more than a decade, wishful liberals have forecast the impending collapse of the Republican coalition thanks to its internal conflicts. (I myself once wrote a long piece titled, ahem, "The GOP Big Tent Is Full of Holes.") What all of us seem to forget is that tensions and strains are an inevitable feature within any majority political party. We forget that, for several decades, Democrats somehow found room to accommodate ideologies ranging from northern quasi-socialist to southern segregationist. The accommodation wasn't always pretty, but neither was it terminally unstable.

In keeping the various breeds of elephant inside the Republican tent, Rove has his hands full. But while he may not qualify as a political Einstein—his tactics often crude (and even thuggish), his strategies susceptible to overreach—there's no gainsaying his achievements or overstating his ambitions. Today Rove (whom Bush has dubbed "The Architect") wields more power than any party operative since his hero Mark Hanna a century ago. If the GOP gains further ground in 2006, Rove's influence will only grow. And if a Rove-guided Republican takes the White House in 2008 . . . well, maybe we better not go there. The Rove primary is unsettling enough; a Grand Rove Party would border on terrifying.

**Part Three:
The Democrats Look
to 2006 . . . and Beyond**

What's the Matter with Liberals?
Thomas Frank

from *What's the Matter With Kansas?* as it appeared in *The New York Review of Books* | May 12, 2005

As the Democrats plot their strategy to regain the White House in 2008, one of the questions bedeviling the party is why so many low-to-middle income people vote Republican, even though GOP economic policies tend to favor the wealthier segments of U.S. society. In his best-selling book What's the Matter with Kansas?, *Thomas Frank theorized that many average Americans are turned off by the perceived arrogance of liberals, and feel much more comfortable with the populist, values-oriented rhetoric employed by conservative politicians. In this post-election essay (which appears, in slightly modified form, as a new afterword to the paperback version of Frank's book), he describes how the Republicans exploited this same phenomenon to a "T" in the 2004 election, painting John Kerry as an effete liberal who was out of touch with the common man (as Frank notes, Kerry's patrician demeanor made this all too easy)—and muses on why the Democrats just can't seem to shake their off-putting elitist image. . . .*

1.

For more than thirty-five years, American politics has followed a populist pattern as predictable as a Punch and Judy show and as conducive to enlightened statesmanship as the cycles of a noisy washing machine. The antagonists of this familiar melodrama are instantly recognizable: the average American, humble, long-suffering, working hard, and paying his taxes; and the liberal elite, the know-it-alls of Manhattan and Malibu, sipping their lattes as they lord it over the peasantry with their fancy college degrees and their friends in the judiciary.

Conservatives generally regard class as an unacceptable topic when the subject is economics—trade, deregulation, shifting the tax burden, expressing worshipful awe for the microchip, etc. But define politics as culture, and class instantly becomes for them the very blood and bone of public discourse. Indeed, from George Wallace to George W. Bush, a class-based backlash against the perceived arrogance of liberalism has been one of their most powerful weapons. Workerist in its rhetoric but royalist in its economic effects, this backlash is in no way embarrassed by its contradictions. It understands itself as an uprising of the little people even when its leaders, in control of all three branches of government, cut taxes on stock dividends and turn the screws on the bankrupt. It mobilizes angry voters by the millions, despite the patent unwinnability of many of its crusades. And from the busing riots of the Seventies to the culture wars of our own time, the backlash has been ignored, downplayed, or misunderstood by liberals.

The 2004 presidential campaign provides a near-perfect demonstration of the persistent power of backlash—as well as another disheartening example of liberalism's continuing inability to confront it in an effective manner. So perfect, in fact, that it deserves to be studied by political enthusiasts for decades to come, in the manner that West Point cadets study remarkable infantry exploits and MBAs study branding campaigns that conjured up billions out of nothing but a catchy jingle.

With his aristocratic manner and his much-remarked personal fortune, the Democratic candidate, John Kerry, made an almost perfect villain for the backlash pantomime. Indeed, he had been one of its targets since his earliest days in politics. In the 1972 proto-backlash manifesto, *The Rise of the Unmeltable Ethnics,* Michael Novak interpreted that year's TV showdown between Kerry and his fellow naval officer John O'Neill as a skirmish in this then-novel form of inverted class war. While the two men seemed to be debating issues related to the Vietnam War, and while Kerry was on the left and thus, theoretically at least, an ally of working people, Novak believed he saw the brutal social truth beneath it all:

> Comparison was immediately drawn between Kerry's Yale pedigree, good looks, smooth speech, powerful connections, and the limited resources, plainness of manner, ordinariness of O'Neill. Class resentment was tangible.[1]

Class resentment was more than just "tangible" in 1972 when Kerry ran for Congress in the area around the crumbling Massachusetts industrial cities of Lowell and Lawrence: the Democrat was snob-baited for days on page one of the local newspaper, mocked for his Yale education, his celebrity supporters, and, of course, his money. An advertisement placed by his Republican opponent asked:

> What do Otto Preminger of Hollywood and Louis Biron of Lowell have in common? This year they're influencing a congressional race. Otto Preminger contributed $1,000 to John Forbes Kerry. Louis Biron gave $15 to Paul Cronin.[2]

From the dying Massachusetts mill towns of 1972 to the dying Ohio steel towns of 2004, the backlash response to John Kerry would remain remarkably consistent. To judge by the candidate's actions, though, it was as if none of it had ever happened. Kerry had been hounded his entire career for being a snooty, distant aristocrat, but like so many of his Democratic colleagues, he seemed to take little notice.

For the 2004 campaign, Kerry moved to the center, following the well-worn path of the corporate Democrats before him, downplaying any "liberal" economic positions that might cost him among the funders and affirming his support for the Iraq invasion even after the official justifications for that exercise had been utterly discredited. Kerry's pallid strategy offered little to motivate the party's traditional liberal and working-class base, but revulsion against Bush was assumed to be reason enough to get out and vote. And besides, such an approach was supposed to protect the Democrat from the inevitable charges of insufficient toughness.

A newcomer to American politics, after observing this strategy in action in 2004, would have been justified in believing that the Democrats were the party in power, so complacent did they seem and so unwilling were they to criticize the actual occupant of the White House. Republicans, meanwhile, were playing another game entirely. The hallmark of a "backlash conservative" is that he or she approaches politics not as a defender of the existing order or as a genteel aristocrat but as an average working person offended by the arrogance of the (liberal) upper class. The sensibility was perfectly caught during the campaign by onetime Republican presidential candidate Gary Bauer, who explained it to *The New York Times* like this: "Joe Six-Pack doesn't understand why the world and his culture are changing and why he doesn't have a say in it."[3] These are powerful words, the sort of phrase that could once have been a slogan of the fighting, egalitarian left. Today, though, it was conservatives who claimed to be fighting for the little guy, assailing the powerful, and shrieking in outrage at the direction in which the world is irresistibly sliding.

The only centrism to be seen on the Republican side was the parade of GOP moderates across the stage of Madison Square Garden, an exercise clearly intended more to pacify and reassure the press than to win over actual voters. When the cameras were off, it was a completely different affair: what Karl Rove called a "mobilization election" in which victory would go to the party that best rallied its faithful. What this meant in practice was backlash all the way: an appeal to class resentment and cultural dread that was unprecedented in its breadth; ingenious state-level ballot initiatives on "values" questions that would energize voters; massive church-based get-out-the-vote efforts; and paranoid suggestions from all sides inviting voters to believe the worst about those tyrannical liberal snobs.

Senator Sam Brownback's activities at the Republican convention offer us a glimpse of this strategy in microcosm. In his speech before the assembled delegates and the eyes of the world, the godly Kansan came off as a thoughtful, caring Republican who wanted only to heal the sick and halt religious persecution overseas; when he spoke at a private meeting of evangelical Christians, however, he took on the tone of affronted middle-American victimhood, complaining to a roomful of Christian conservatives that "the press beats up on you like there's something wrong with faith, family and freedom" and exhorting them to "win this culture war."[4] For the conservative rank and file, this election was to be the culture-war Armageddon, and they were battling for the Lord.

Residents of West Virginia and Arkansas received mailings from the Republican National Committee warning that liberals would ban the Bible if they got the chance. In numerous other states, voters were energized by ballot initiatives proposing constitutional amendments reacting to the illusory threat of gay marriage, an institution that was already illegal almost everywhere, but that conservative activists nonetheless decried as a mortal, immediate menace to civilization itself. James Dobson, chairman of Focus on the Family, endorsed a presidential candidate for the first time ever and, proclaiming that "everything we hold dear is on the line" because of the threat of gay marriage, addressed gargantuan political rallies of evangelical Christians around the country.

Even the College Republicans got into the act, blanketing the land with letters exhorting recipients to send in $1,000 and a flag pin so that the President would know that "there are millions who are giving him the shield of God to protect him in the difficult days ahead." Meanwhile, an outfit called the American Veterans in Domestic Defense (AVIDD)[5] acquired the Ten Commandments monument that had been removed from the Alabama Supreme Court building the previous fall and hauled it around the country so that this holy relic, this physical reminder of the tyranny of liberalism, could strike fear into the hearts of the godless and stoke the flames of anger among the righteous and the persecuted.

In addition to these culture-war novelties, voters were also treated to a return engagement of the oldest backlash set-piece of them all: the treason of the rich kids during the Vietnam War.[6] Calling themselves the Swift Boat Veterans for Truth, a group of Kerry's former comrades-in-arms stepped forward to declare that the candidate was a liar who did not deserve the medals he had won in combat and that his later activities as an antiwar leader amounted to a betrayal of the men he served with in Southeast Asia. It didn't matter that the accusations angrily advanced by the "Swifties" (as they are fondly known on the right) crumbled under the slightest scrutiny, just as it didn't matter that the principal members of the Bush administration had actively avoided service in Vietnam while Kerry had volunteered for it, and just as it didn't matter that the Pentagon under Defense Secretary Donald Rumsfeld had botched the nation's current military effort and even sent insufficiently armored soldiers into action. The backlash narrative is more powerful than mere facts, and according to this central mythology conservatives are always hardworking patriots who love their country and are persecuted for it, while liberals, who are either high-born weaklings or eggheads hypnotized by some fancy idea, are always ready to sell their nation out at a moment's notice.[7]

Much has been made in the months since the election of the national security issue and the role of fear in the Republican triumph, with some using the point to demand even more hawkish Democratic candidates in the future and others to underscore the Bush administration's scurrility in whipping up unreasonable public alarm since September 11. It is important to remember when discussing these issues, however, that much of their power arises from the same backlash cultural template that undergirds the rest of contemporary conservatism—indeed, that shooting war and culture war are of a piece in the conservative mind. What makes national security such a winner for Republicans is that it dramatizes the same negative qualities of liberalism that we see in the so-called "values" issues, only much more forcefully. War casts in sharp relief the inauthenticity of the liberals, the insincerity of their patriotism, and their intellectual distance (always trying to "understand" the terrorists' motives) from the raw emotions felt by ordinary Americans—each quality an expression of the deracinated upperclassness that is thought to be the defining characteristic of liberalism.

The reason conservatives are always thought to be tough and liberals to be effete milquetoasts (two favorite epithets from the early days of the backlash) even when they aren't is the same reason Americans believe the French to be a nation of sissies and the same reason the Dead End Kids found it both easy and satisfying to beat up the posh boy from the luxury apartment building: the cultural symbolism of class. If you relish chardonnay/lattes/snowboarding, you will not fight. If you talk like a Texan, you are a two-fisted he-man who knows life's hardships and are ready to scrap at a moment's notice. This is the reason conservative authors and radio demagogues find it so easy to connect liberals and terrorists. It is the same reason, by extension, that old-time political nicknames like "the Fighting Liberal" make no sense to us anymore and that current foreign policy failures like North Korean nuclear proliferation do not bring lasting discredit on President Bush: in the face of such crises one is either a wimp or a hard guy, and we've already got a hard guy in there.

As the campaign dragged on, nearly every news story seemed to confirm the backlash fantasy. For example, when CBS News examined Dubya's years in the National Guard and based its conclusions on documents whose provenance could not be verified, the age-old charge of liberal bias suddenly became the topic of the day. While the distortions of the Swifties had brought no discredit on Republican campaign efforts, the CBS program was immediately understood not as an honest mistake but as a politically motivated hatchet job, the final proof that the nation's news organizations were out to get conservatives.

Then came what must rank as one of the most ill-conceived liberal electoral efforts of all time: in October the British *Guardian* newspaper launched a campaign to persuade one contested, blue-collar county in Ohio to vote against President Bush. The idea was to have *Guardian* readers in Britain write personal letters to voters in Ohio, whose names

and addresses the newspaper had secured from registration rolls. Unsur-
prisingly, the Ohioans strongly resented being lectured to on the foolish-
ness of their national leader by some random bunch of erudite Europeans.
Indeed, the episode was so outrageous that there was almost no need for
columnists and talk-radio hosts to sputter about the "pansy-ass, tea-sipping"
liberal elitists who thought they knew best—the arrogance of the wretched
thing spoke for itself.[8] The county had gone for Gore in 2000, but this
time, like the state, like the nation, it chose Bush. And why not? Biased
newscasters, conceited foreigners: to hell with them all.

But the most powerful evocation of the backlash spirit always comes from
personal testimony, a tale of how one man came to realize that liberals
weren't the friends of common folks but just the opposite. In the past it was
figures like George Wallace and Norman Podhoretz and Ronald Reagan
who declared that they hadn't left the Democratic Party, the party had left
them; in 2004 that traditional role fell to Zell Miller, Democratic senator
from Georgia, whose thunderous indictment of his liberal colleagues from
the podium of the Republican convention caused such excitement in conservative circles. Here was Miller to assure Republicans that everything
they'd ever suspected was true: that the real problem with American politics was that the Democrats had swerved too far to the left; that those same
Democrats were led by self-hating people who think "America is the
problem, not the solution"; that their presidential candidate was so
beguiled by Frenchness—a classic stand-in for devitalized upper-classness
—that he "would let Paris decide when America needs defending."[9]

Oddly enough, this same Zell Miller had once been known as a fairly formidable class warrior on the left, blasting Bush's father in a famous 1992
speech as a clueless "aristocrat" who knew nothing of hard work and then
dropping this memorable zinger on Dan Quayle: "Not all of us can be born
rich, handsome, and lucky, and that's why we have a Democratic Party."

But in the election of 2004 all the class anger was on the other side. Now
it was the Democrat whose aristocratic lifestyle was always coming into
question, who couldn't seem to take a step without detonating some explosive reminder of his exalted position. And it was Republican operatives
who were gleefully dropping the word "elitist" on the liberal at every turn
for his affected, upper-class ways. For his supposed love of brie cheese. For

his wealthy wife's supposed unfamiliarity with chili. For his mansion. His yacht. His windsurfing. His vacations with celebs on Nantucket Island. The secretary of commerce said he thought Kerry "looks French." The House majority leader made a habit of starting off speeches with the line, "Good afternoon, or, as John Kerry might say: 'Bonjour!' " The NRA came up with an image that brilliantly encapsulated the whole thing: an elaborately clipped French poodle in a pink bow and a Kerry-for-president sweater over the slogan "That dog don't hunt."[10]

And now it was the drawling son of 1992's aristocrat who was drawing the adoring throngs in the shuttered mill towns and coal-mining regions. It was the committed enemy of organized labor whose prayerful public performances persuaded so many that he "shares our values." It was the man who had slashed taxes on inherited fortunes and dividends who was said to be, in the election's most telling refrain, "one of us."

George W. Bush was authentic; John Forbes Kerry, like all liberals, was an affected toff, a Boston Brahmin who knew nothing of the struggles of average folks. Again and again, in the course of the electoral battle, I heard striking tales of this tragically inverted form of class consciousness: of a cleaning lady who voted for Bush because she could never support a rich man for president. Of the numerous people who lost their cable TV because of nonpayment but who nevertheless sported Bush stickers on their cars.

The most poignant, though, was one I saw with my own eyes: the state of West Virginia, one of the poorest in the nation, in the process of transforming itself into a conservative redoubt. This is a place where the largest private-sector employer is Wal-Mart and where decades of bloody fights between workers and mine owners gave rise to a particularly stubborn form of class consciousness. It does not stand to gain much from Bush's tax cuts and his crackdown on labor unions. But if class is a matter of cultural authenticity rather than material interests, John Kerry stood about as much of a chance there as the NRA's poodle did of retrieving a downed duck. As I toured the state's valleys and isolated mining towns, I spotted Bush posters adorning even the humblest of dwellings and mobile homes. Voters I spoke to told me they planned on voting Republican because of their beliefs regarding abortion or gun control.[11]

Every hamlet seemed to have a son or daughter on duty in Iraq, and wartime loyalty to the commander in chief was in the air. Running through each of these issues was the sense that Bush was somehow more authentic than his challenger. In the city of Charleston, West Virginia, I was told by a conservative activist that

> when you see those photos of [Bush] on his ranch down in Texas, with jeans and a cowboy hat, that's genuine. I was in Beckley when he was there a couple weeks ago, and that crowd, four thousand people, they loved the man. They loved the man. Personally. . . . You can't manufacture that; you can't fake it. They love him. They connect with him, they think he understands them, and I think he does, too.

West Virginia had been carried by Bill Clinton, Michael Dukakis, and almost every other Democratic candidate going back to Franklin Roosevelt, but this time it went Republican by a convincing thirteen percentage points.

2.

The illusion that George W. Bush "understands" the struggles of working-class people was only made possible by the unintentional assistance of the Democratic campaign. Once again, the "party of the people" chose to sacrifice the liberal economic policies that used to connect them to such voters on the altar of centrism. Advised by a legion of tired consultants, many of whom work as corporate lobbyists in off years, Kerry chose not to make much noise about corruption on Wall Street, or to expose the business practices of Wal-Mart, or to spend a lot of time talking about raising the minimum wage.[12]

The strategy had a definite upside: Kerry's fund-raising almost matched that of the Republican candidate, while the newspapers brimmed with exciting tales of New Economy millionaires volunteering to work their entrepreneurial magic for the Democrats, and the society sheets offered juicy details on fund-raising stunts pulled by wealthy women of fashion.[13] Yet there can be no question about this scheme's ultimate effects. As the savvy political journalist Rick Perlstein put it in a postelection report,

> For a party whose major competitive advantage over the opposition is its credibility in protecting ordinary people from economic insecurity, anything that compromises that credibility is disastrous.[14]

Swearing off economic liberalism also prevented Democrats from capitalizing on the great, glaring contradiction of their rivals' campaign, namely, the GOP's tendency to demote "values" issues once elections are over. Republicans may have seemed like God's authentic warriors when seen from the streets of Beckley, West Virginia, but as I wandered among the celebrations at the Republican convention in September it was obvious that they were still primarily soldiers for the business community, courting their most important constituency in the manner to which it was accustomed. Indeed, examples of the distinctly nonpopulist essence of Republicanism were hard to miss: the well-dressed GOP revelers pouring out into Fifth Avenue traffic as they left a party that had been held—so tastefully!—at the Cartier jewelry shop; or (my personal favorite) the Republicans celebrating tax cuts and laughing at Purple Heart winners[15] at a party in the New York Yacht Club, the kind of place that makes it easy for a fellow of means to pine for the nineteenth century.

At one party, held in a former bank building, I saw the relationship between the two GOP factions acted out in a manner so bluntly allegorical it could have been a Herblock cartoon. The party's nominal purpose was an episode of the talk-radio program hosted by Michael Reagan (the more conservative of the late president's sons), but the majority of the action seemed to be the generous dispensing of top-shelf liquor to satisfied corporate lawyers and Wall Street types. While these chosen ones sank comfortably into high-end inebriation, a string of famous right-wing talkers could be seen mounting the balcony where Reagan sat and taking their turns before his microphone, each one no doubt switching on the anger and giving virtuoso performances of their trademark anti-elitist routines for the listening hinterland. And high up on the stone wall of the building were inscribed these words, a sort of caption for the evening's doings: "Having little, you can not risk loss. Having much, you should the more carefully protect it."

Culture war most assuredly helped protect those who had much in 2004. George W. Bush carried the white working-class vote by 23 percentage points, according to pollster Ruy Teixeira. Then, on the morning after the election, the country's liberals were astonished to hear that, according to exit polls, at least, "moral values" outranked all other issues in determining voters' choices.[16] Later on that same day, the reelected President Bush set out his legislative objectives for his second term. Making America a more moral country was not one of them. Instead, his goals were mainly economic, and they had precious little to do with helping out the working-class people who had stood by them: he would privatize Social Security once and for all and "reform" the federal tax code. "Another Winner Is Big Business," declared a headline in *The Wall Street Journal* on November 4, as businessmen everywhere celebrated the election results as a thumbs-up on outsourcing and continued deregulation.

In the months since then the magnitude of the corporate victory has only become more apparent, with Republicans in Congress working to tighten up bankruptcy law at the request of the credit card companies, open up the Arctic National Wildlife Refuge to the oil companies, and crack down on class-action lawsuits for the greater glory of Wal-Mart. The clout of the U.S. Chamber of Commerce, the D.C. glamour lobbyist of the moment, is acclaimed by all as it raises millions to keep the pro-business bills coming. "Fortune 500 companies that invested millions of dollars in electing Republicans are emerging as the earliest beneficiaries of a government controlled by President Bush and the largest GOP House and Senate majority in a half century," wrote Jim VandeHei in *The Washington Post.*

And the values issues? They seemed to dissipate like so much smoke once the election was over and won. Republican Senator Arlen Specter, the chair-apparent of the powerful Senate Judiciary Committee, waited only a single day after his buddy Bush had been safely reelected before informing the nation that, no, his committee would not be approving judges who planned on overturning Roe v. Wade. The great crusade against gay marriage, which had worked such wonders for Republicans in so many states, was essentially abandoned by the President in January. After all, more important matters were beckoning: the war with the trial lawyers, for example, or the need to persuade people that our basically sound old-age insurance program was actually in crisis.[17]

In March the President and Republican congressional leaders chose to make much of the tragic Terri Schiavo affair, but the obvious futility of their legal demands and the patent self-interest of their godly grandstanding require little embellishment here.[18] Let us simply note how perfectly this incident, when paired with simultaneous GOP legislative action on big-business items, illustrates the timeless principles of the backlash. For its corporate backers, the

GOP delivers the goods; for its rank-and-file "values" voters it chooses a sturdy wall against which they are invited to bang their heads.

Meanwhile the stunned Democrats held introspective panel discussions in Washington, wrote weepy editorials protesting that they, too, had values, and headed home for Christmas to lick their wounds. But the Republicans took no time off in the season of goodwill. Far from declaring a Christmas truce, they pressed their advantage in the Christmas Panic of 2004. 'Twas suddenly the season to be indignant, and from conservative commentators across the land there arose a collective clatter about how the liberal elite had ruined everyone's favorite holiday with their infernal determination to suppress the innocent folkways of the good Christian people of Middle America. The provocation was the decision by a handful of towns and school districts (as usual, every node of the right-wing publicity apparatus relied on the same three or four examples) to keep Nativity scenes off the lawns of city halls and overtly religious songs out of public school pageants.

The response was a huge collective exercise in persecution mania, with radio hosts joining newspaper columnists and evangelical leaders in depicting themselves as unassuming common people crushed under the boot heel of arrogant liberalism, of "cultural fascists," of "leftist jihadis hunting down Jesus," of "liberal, anti-Christmas Nazis," of those who believe "God is the enemy." "Blatant religious bigotry," steamed one columnist. Denial of "the rights of people to practice religion freely," moaned another. "True freedom of worship for Christians is under increasing attack," shrieked a third. "Leftist organizations are aggressively seeking to redefine America in their own God-less image," wrote Jerry Falwell. "They hate the idea of Christmas with a deep abiding hate," declared Pat Buchanan.[19]

Sean Hannity teamed up with Michael Medved to issue a CD in which the two could be heard deploring, an advertisement claimed, "the recent onslaught of cultural attacks against the Christian aspects of Christmas."[20] Paul Weyrich imagined himself a victim of thugs who want to "get back at God" and advised readers to bravely confront the liberal bullies by saying, "We're here. We are not going away. Neither is Christmas. Deal with it." As usual Ann Coulter struck the perfect note of persecuted-majority sarcasm, confessing to her readers that she "belong[s] to a small religious cult that celebrates the birth of Jesus." Bill O'Reilly warned of a "well-organized movement" following a "strategy of minimizing the birth of Jesus" because, duh, religion "stands in the way of gay marriage, partial birth abortion, legalized narcotics, euthanasia and many other secular causes." (A less well-known conservative, one Noel Sheppard, added to this vision of conspiracy his startling discovery that the liberals commenced their "coordinated attack on Christmas almost immediately after Senator Kerry conceded," thus revealing it as part of their sinister plan to prevail in 2006 and 2008.)

All across America a good old-fashioned red-state Christmas—just like the ones we used to know, only much touchier—brought another year of liberal woe to a close. Righteous parents fantasized that they were striking back at the liberal Gestapo every time they uttered the subversive phrase "Merry Christmas." Visions of noble persecution danced in everyone's heads, as dazed Democrats wandered upstairs for yet another long winter's nap.

Notes

[1] As for O'Neill's "limited resources," it is now known that O'Neill was in fact recruited by the Nixon administration to battle the articulate antiwar leader Kerry. Even at that early date, when the backlash seemed to have all the hot-button spontaneity of a real working-class revolt, it was substantially scripted and funded by the most powerful people in the land.

[2] Quoted in a *Boston Globe* retrospective of Kerry's career, "First Campaign Ends in Defeat," by Brian C. Mooney, June 18, 2003.

[3] It is important to remember that Bauer is the son of a janitor and that the organization he heads today bears the distinctly proletarian name Campaign for Working Families. See "Democrats in Red States: Just Regular Guys," *The New York Times*, August 22, 2004.

[4] Brownback addressed the convention during prime time on August 31; the gathering of Christian conservatives was called the Faith, Family and Freedom Rally, and for a supposedly media-free event, it generated a great deal of media coverage. See David Kirkpatrick, "A Senator's Call to 'Win This Culture War,'" *The New York Times*, September 1, 2004, and Julia Duin, "GOP Keeps Faith, But Not in Prime Time," *Washington Times*, September 1, 2004. At that same gathering, Republicans premièred a movie called *George W. Bush: Faith in the White House*, later distributed to churches around the nation, which, in the words of *New York Times* columnist Frank Rich, characterizes the President as

"God's essential and irreplaceable warrior on Earth." See Frank Rich, "Now on DVD: The Passion of the Bush," *The New York Times*, October 3, 2004.

[5] On its Web site, AVIDD describes its mission by declaring that "American Veterans have defended America against its foreign enemies. We now have a number of domestic enemies loose in our beloved country." The organization also helpfully offers a list to clarify matters for the puzzled, naming as "Domestic Enemies" the judicial system, the Federal Reserve, the IRS, the NEA, the ACLU, the "Biased Liberal, Socialist News Media," and the "Conspiracy of an Immoral Film Industry." See www.avidd.org/template .php?page=enemies.

[6] The supposed affluence of the Sixties antiwar movement is nearly always mentioned in conservative complaints about that era. For example, the anti-Kerry booklet published by the American Conservative Union points out that, "like many children of affluent parents, John Kerry joined the so-called New Left in its relentless attack on America." See *Who Is John Kerry?*, p. 51.

[7] Class resentment simmered just below the surface of the SwiftVets' charges. The TV commercials aired by the group took pains to underscore the averageness of the men's occupations, and a *Washington Post* story on the group, after pointing out that the Swifties' real beef with Kerry was his involvement in the antiwar movement, notes that "while Kerry went on to make a prominent political career, they got jobs as teachers, accountants, surveyors and oil field workers. When he ran for president, partly on the strength of his war record, their resentment exploded." See Michael Dobbs, "Swift Boat Accounts Incomplete," August 22, 2004, p. 1.

[8] When I first heard about the British letter-writing campaign, I couldn't believe anyone was ignorant enough about American political sensibilities to do such a thing, or at least to do such a thing straight, on behalf of the candidate they really wanted to win. But they did. See Peronet Despeignes, "Brits' Campaign Backfires in Ohio," *USA Today*, November 4, 2004, and Andy Bowers, "Dear Limey Assholes..." *Slate*, November 4, 2004. The "pansy-ass, tea-sipping" epithet was one of the many responses sent by Ohio residents to the *Guardian*, according to *USA Today*.

[9] Just as interesting, to me anyway, was the fact that Zell Miller had taken until 2004 to figure all this out. The man had been a Democratic politician since the Fifties; each of his complaints had been part of the backlash repertoire for decades; and he had now come through the Sixties of Barry Goldwater and George Wallace, the Seventies of Archie Bunker and Dirty Harry, the Eighties

of Ronald Reagan, and the Nineties of Newt Gingrich before deciding it was time to make his move to the right.

[10] In fact, poodles are hunting dogs, bred hundreds of years ago to retrieve ducks from water. Their distinctive clipped coats were designed to aid them in this purpose, keeping the dog's body and joints warm as it splashes about but otherwise leaving it free from encumbrance. See Jill Hunter Pellettieri, "Why Are Poodle Haircuts So Weird?," *Slate*, February 10, 2004.

[11] In this sense they were heeding the advice of Charlton Heston, who toured the state during the 2000 campaign, exhorting voters to break with their traditional support for Democrats on the hallucinatory grounds that Democrats would violate their right to bear arms, and that this delusional fear far outranked "marginal" economic issues. As Heston put it in one speech, "You must forget what some shop steward or news anchor said . . . forget all the marginal issues and vote freedom."

  I toured West Virginia in the company of Serge Halimi, an editor at *Le Monde Diplomatique*. Read more about what we saw at mondediplo.com/2004/10 /02usa.

[12] On Kerry's campaign advisers, see Anna Sullivan, "Fire the Consultants," *Washington Monthly*, January/February 2005. On the consultants' corporate connections, see journalist Doug Ireland's blog for September 8, 2004, direland.typepad.com/direland/2004 /09/jesse_jackson_l.html. On the failure of Kerry to criticize Republicans for the many financial scandals of recent years, see the Op-Ed by Frank Partnoy, "Why Nobody Mentioned Markets," *Financial Times*, October 20, 2004. See also the essay by Eliot Spitzer in *The New Republic*, November 22, 2004, in which the same argument is made in greater detail, along with the point that John Kerry was, ironically, the perfect man to offer such criticism, since he had been one of the only national Democrats to support Spitzer's effort to clean up the mutual-fund industry.

[13] On New Economy millionaires, see Matt Bai, "Wiring the Vast Left-Wing Conspiracy," *The New York Times Magazine*, July 25, 2004. On wealthy women of fashion, see Diana Kapp, "Insider," *San Francisco*, June 2004, which details the efforts of two Bay Area "shoe horses" to persuade their fellow "stylistas" to donate their shoe budget to the Kerry campaign instead.

[14] See "The Wal-Mart Factor," *Boston Globe*, November 7, 2004, in which Perlstein chides the Democrats for missing the biggest issue-opportunity of the year: the public's widespread unhappiness with the Wal-Mart retail model.

[15] While at this party I was handed a Band-Aid decorated with a purple heart, stapled to a note mocking John Kerry's war wounds. The obvious message was that if a liberal could get a Purple Heart, then Purple Hearts were a joke. Many of the other revelers were wearing the Band-Aids as they partied the night away.

[16] "Moral values" mattered most to 22 percent of the electorate (80 percent of whom voted for President Bush) while "Economy/Jobs" mattered most to 20 percent and "Terrorism" and "Iraq" accounted for 19 percent and 15 percent respectively. This poll has since been much criticized for its vagueness, and rightfully so. For example, while all the other options were quite specific, the choice of "moral values" was not defined in any way. What was incorporated under "moral values"? Isn't concern about the economy or the Iraq war also a matter of morality? My own suspicion is that the question was designed to identify conservative culture-war voters specifically, since "values" has been a standard slogan of the Bush campaign. However we look at it, though, no amount of criticism can wash that 22 percent figure away. Furthermore, the astonishment with which it was met in liberal circles cannot be understated.

[17] On the abandonment of the Federal Marriage Amendment by the President, see Bush's instantly infamous interview with *The Washington Post*, January 15, 2005. See also Robert Borosage's essay "Shafting Kansas," which appeared on TomPaine.com on December 13, 2004.

[18] It is worth pointing out that the Schiavo matter, like every other culture-war skirmish over "values," was in fact suffused with the language of social class. For example, Daniel Henninger, a columnist for *The Wall Street Journal*, described the Schiavo case as a battle between the people and the elites in that it "ensures that these future questions of who lives and who dies won't be decided by the professional class alone in conferences and courtrooms."

[19] "Cultural fascists": from a press release issued by William Donohue of the Catholic League for Religious and Civil Rights, December 1, 2004, and widely circulated on the Internet (www.catholicleague.org/04press_releases/quarter4/041201_cword.htm). "Leftist jihadis" and "God is the enemy": from an essay by Mac Johnson on the Web site of *Human Events* (Human Events Online), December 1, 2004. "Liberal, anti-Christmas Nazis": from an essay by Chris Field also on Human Events Online, dated December 20, 2004. "Blatant religious bigotry": from a radio editorial written by Connie Mackey, produced by the Family

Research Council, December 6, 2004. "Rights of people to practice religion": from "ACLU Christmas Haters" by Kaye Grogan, December 10, 2004, and available on the Web site of RenewAmerica, an organization dedicated to the politics of Alan Keyes (www.renewamerica.us/columns/grogan/041210). "True freedom of worship": from "Mistletoe, Snow and Subpoenas?" by Eve Arlia, December 10, 2004, and available on the Web site of the Concerned Women for America (www.cwfa.org/articles/7013/LEGAL/freedom). Falwell: "The Impending Death of Christmas?" *Insight on the News*, December 13, 2004. Buchanan: "Do They Know It's Christmas?," *The American Conservative*, January 17, 2005 (the essay also appeared in numerous online outlets in December 2004).

[20] The Hannity/Medved CD, *Keeping Christ in Christmas*, was advertised in this way on one of the Focus on the Family Web sites. Weyrich: "Make a Difference with 'Merry Christmas,'" an essay dated December 20, 2004 that appeared on the Web site of GOPUSA in addition to *Insight on the News* and the Web site of Weyrich's own Free Congress Foundation. Coulter: "Merry Christmas, Red States!" Human Events Online, December 23, 2004. O'Reilly: "Christmas Haters Have an Agenda," *New York Daily News*, December 13, 2004. "Coordinated attack on Christmas": from "How (and Why) the Left Stole Christmas," written by Noel Sheppard, December 15, 2004, which can be found, curiously enough, at a Web site called IntellectualConservative.com. Sheppard's effort includes a humorous Christmas carol that goes, "It's appallingly looking NOT like Christmas/Ev'rywhere you go:/Leftists are at it once again, using their anchormen/ On a campaign to spread disdain you know."

The Unbranding
Jeffrey Goldberg

The New Yorker | March 21, 2005

Among other things, the 2004 presidential election reaffirmed the Republican Party's continuing preeminence in matters of national security. It didn't matter that John Kerry was a decorated Vietnam veteran, while George Bush had pulled strings as a young man to avoid combat duty. In the voters' minds, Bush was a tough-talking leader, flight suit and all, while Kerry and the Democrats simply weren't up to speed when it came to defending the country from attack.

In this New Yorker *piece, Jeffrey Goldberg takes a look a the Dems' early post-election attempts to refashion themselves as a party that is seen to be consistently strong on national defense. Not coincidentally, Goldberg's article showcases Senator Joseph Biden, one of the leading Democratic authorities on foreign policy (a strong advocate for intervening in Bosnia, Biden has been a vocal critic of the way the Iraq war is being prosecuted). At the time this article came out, Biden was considered a likely candidate for the Democratic presidential nomination in 2008. In mid-June of 2005 he made it quasi-official, announcing on* Face the Nation, *"If, in fact, I think I have a clear shot of winning the nomination by this November or December, then I'm going to seek the nomination." . . .*

Joseph Biden, the senior senator from Delaware, is the Democratic Party's main spokesman on international affairs; he is also a man who, on occasion, seems not to know, when sentences leave his mouth, where they are going or what they are meant to convey. Sometimes, when he thinks that he may shock or amuse his listener, he begins by stating, "I'm going to get in trouble if I say this," or, "This is a really outrageous thing to say, but . . ." And so when I asked Biden, as the ranking Democrat on the Senate Foreign Relations Committee, and one of John Kerry's chief advisers on foreign policy during last year's Presidential campaign, what advice he gave Kerry on how to convince voters that he was tough, Biden laughed and said, "I wish I could tell you. I wish I could tell you." Then he told me.

At sixty-two, Biden has a cheerful vanity and an exuberant restlessness that make him seem far younger. Since the election, he has become a leader of a modest-sized faction—"the national-security Democrats," in the words of Richard Holbrooke, an ambassador to the United Nations under President Clinton—that includes the most hawkish members in the Democratic Party. Among them are Senator Hillary Rodham Clinton, the former Vice-Presidential candidate John Edwards, Senator Evan Bayh, of Indiana, and Governor Bill Richardson, of New Mexico, along with a number of Clinton Administration foreign-policy officials, now in exile at think tanks scattered about Washington.

Biden can be eloquent in defense of his party, and in his criticism of President Bush, but his friends worry that his verbal indiscipline will sabotage any chance he might have to win the Democratic Presidential nomination in 2008. (Biden is an interested, but undeclared, candidate.) On the question of Kerry's mettle in the last campaign, for instance, Biden told me a story that was both entertaining and illuminating but did not capture the matter with complete accuracy.

On October 29th, Biden said, he was campaigning for Kerry in Pennsylvania, the state in which he was born, when he heard, on the radio, that Osama bin Laden had issued a videotape in which he belittled Bush and promised to continue to "bleed" America. Biden nearly panicked when he heard about the tape, he said, because he worried that Kerry's reaction might seem tepid or petty. His advice to Kerry throughout the campaign—which, he complained, went unheeded much of the time—was to harden his message, to focus, as Bush was doing, on terrorism alone: to sound, in short, more like the President and less like a Democratic senator from Massachusetts.

"I'm listening to the radio," Biden said. " 'Today' "—here he adopted a radio announcer's voice—" 'the President of the U.S. said *dah-dah, dah-dah, dah-dah,* and he said he's sure Senator Kerry agrees with him. Senator Kerry, unable to resist a dig'—that's what the announcer said, that was the phrase—'said today had we acted'—I'm paraphrasing—'had we acted properly in Tora Bora, we wouldn't have this problem.' "

Biden continued, "I'm on the phone, I e-mail, I say, 'John, please, say three things: "How dare bin Laden speak of our President this way." No. 2, "I know how to deal with preventing another 9/11." No. 3, "Kill him." ' Now, that's harsh. Kerry needed to be harsh. And it was—Jesus Christ." Here Biden threw up his hands. "He didn't make any of it. Let's get it straight. None of it. None of those three points were made."

This was not quite the case. In Kerry's first comment, made during an interview with a Milwaukee television station, he criticized Bush for missing an opportunity to kill bin Laden at Tora Bora, as he often had during the campaign. But, not long after that, Kerry spoke to the press, saying, "As Americans, we are absolutely united in our determination to hunt down and destroy Osama bin Laden and the terrorists. They're barbarians, and I will stop at absolutely nothing to hunt down, capture, or kill the terrorists wherever they are, whatever it takes, period."

Biden, apparently, did not actually reach Kerry until that night, so Kerry made this statement without Biden's help. In any case, Biden failed to recount the dénouement; leaving it out better served the point of his story, which concerned the troubles that faced the Kerry campaign and, by extension, the Democratic Party—a party that Biden hopes to see revived. It was then, Biden went on, that he realized Kerry would lose the election.

"That night, I got off that trip, from Scranton, I got off the plane, Wilmington airport, only private aircraft, get off, pick up a phone, call a local place called the Charcoal Pit before it closes. They have great steak sandwiches and a milkshake. Triple-thick milkshake. And I hadn't eaten. I'm going to pass it on the way home. They're literally sweeping the floors. A woman, overweight, forty years old, a little unkempt, had a tooth missing in the side, not in the front"—he showed his flashing white teeth, to demonstrate—"walks up to me to give me my steak sandwich. 'Senator Biden, I'm so glad you're here. I've got a problem.' And I take out a piece of paper, maybe Social Security for her mother, and she said, 'I heard you're for Kerry.' And she said, 'You're so strong and he's so weak.'"

Biden looked at me, to make sure I understood what he seemed to think was a point of considerable nuance. "I'm gonna tell you why I'm going to vote for someone," he said, addressing the woman of the story. "Look, you're working here tonight. If the Republicans have their way, you won't get paid overtime. When you stay here tonight, you're already closed. Besides that, what they want to do with your health care." Then he quoted what the woman had replied: "But you're so strong, and he's so weak. And President Bush—he seems strong."

In the peculiar vocabulary of Washington, Democrats who wish to be thought of as preoccupied with defense issues—and no one seeking elected office wants to be thought of as anything but firm on matters of national security—are frequently described by their staffs as "muscular," or "robust," or "hard-nosed," or "forward-leaning." Republicans do not often use words like these when describing their leaders, because the muscularity of the President and his partisans is assumed, just as Democrats don't find it necessary to refer to themselves as "compassionate."

The opposite of "muscular" is, of course, "weak," and it was, for a moment, surprising to hear Biden suggest—even in his marginally sly, I'm-just-repeating-what-someone-told-me sort of way—that Kerry was weak. After all, he calls Kerry a friend. (The reverse is also true: Kerry told me last week, after I briefly sketched for him Biden's critique, that he "loves" Biden and "welcomes his advice.")

But Biden and Kerry are also rivals—for primacy among the forty-four members of the Democratic caucus in the Senate and, presumably, for the Party's Presidential nomination in 2008 as well. "Weak" is a powerful epithet among the Democrats, who are still staggering as a result of last year's election, which, polls suggest, seems to have turned less on such issues as gay marriage and abortion than on the perception that Kerry and the Democrats were not quite up to the task of defending the nation. And most Democrats I've spoken to in the past month have said that this issue will be a determining factor in the next election, too. To paint a rival as weak on defense is to ruin his chance for national office. As Senator Bayh put it, "If the American people don't trust us with their lives, they're unlikely to trust us with much else."

Not all Democratic leaders agree that a credibility problem on national security exists. Kerry, for one, believes it doesn't. "The country had concluded that I was prepared to be Commander-in-Chief," he told me last week. The fifty-nine million votes he received, he said, should be proof enough that he was perceived as strong on the issue. "If we'd had a switch of sixty thousand votes"—in Ohio—"you'd have had a better outcome."

We met in his Capitol Hill office. In the reception area stood a model, under glass, of the Swift boat that he commanded in Vietnam. Kerry appeared drawn and pale, but he was animated in defense of his campaign. "The bottom line is that, if you look at the data, the appearance of the Osama bin Laden tape had a profound impact. The fact is, we flatlined on that day. I presented stronger arguments, but there was a visceral unwillingness to change Commander-in-Chief five days after the bin Laden tape."

Kerry considers himself to be a national-security-oriented Democrat—Holbrooke, too, puts him in that camp—and appeared to take no particular offense at Biden's criticisms. "I'm not going to dissect the campaign," he said. But he seemed displeased when I asked whether the Democrats had a credibility problem on defense issues, and he finally said, "Look, the answer is, we have to do an unbranding." By this he meant that the Democrats had to do a better job of selling to the American people what he believes is already true—that the Democrats are every bit as serious on the issue as Republicans. "We have to brand more effectively. It's marketing."

Most national-security Democrats believe that the Party's problems on the issue go deeper than marketing. They agree that the Party should be more open to the idea of military action, and even preëmption; and although they did not agree about the timing of the Iraq war and the manner in which Bush launched it, they believe that the stated rationale—Saddam's brutality and his flouting of United Nations resolutions—was ideologically and morally sound. They say that the absence of weapons of mass destruction was more a failure of intelligence than a matter of outright deception by the Administration; and although they do not share the neoconservatives' enthusiastic belief in the transformative power of military force, they accept the possibility that the invasion of Iraq might lead to the establishment of democratic institutions there.

In addition, national-security Democrats try to distance themselves from the Party's post-Vietnam ambivalence about the projection of American power. In other words, they are men and women who want to reach back to an age of Democratic resoluteness, embodied by Franklin D. Roosevelt, Harry Truman, and John F. Kennedy. Their mission may have been complicated earlier this year by Howard Dean's victory in the race for the chairmanship of the Democratic National Committee, although Dean, the most stridently antiwar of the major candidates in 2004, has promised to suppress the urge to comment on foreign policy.

Biden could find little to say about Dean, other than this: "No goddam chairman's ever made a difference in the history of the Democratic Party." His colleague Joseph Lieberman, who is perhaps the most conservative member of the Democratic caucus, said, "Dean was wrong on the war and what he was talking about was bad for the country. We'll see what he does as chairman. If he devotes his energies to building a party at the base, as he talked about doing, good for him. If he continues to be a prominent spokesman on defense policy, I would regret it."

Lieberman is a study in the dangers of steroidal muscularity, becoming an outlier in his own party. (He has edged to the right as his running mate in the 2000 election, Al Gore, has moved leftward.) His fate was sealed with a kiss, planted on his cheek by Bush, just after the President delivered his State of the Union address. "That may have been the last straw for some of the people in Connecticut, the blogger types," Lieberman told me. But he is unapologetic about his defense of Bush's Iraq policy, saying, "Bottom line, I think Bush has it right." When I asked if he was becoming a neoconservative, Lieberman smiled and said, "No, but some of my best friends are neocons."

For a Democrat who wants to cultivate an image of toughness on national security, the challenge is to adopt positions that, in some cases, are closer to those of Paul Wolfowitz than to those of Edward Kennedy while remaining loyal to the Party. This has become more difficult with the news from the Middle East over the past two months, which raises the possibility that the Bush Administration's core argument—that the antidote to Islamic-fundamentalist terrorism is democracy—might turn out to be something more than utopian theory.

It is far too early to claim that the Middle East is moving irreversibly toward tranquillity and freedom. Fifteen hundred American soldiers have been killed, and thousands more have been wounded; the insurgency within Iraq—the assassinations, the car bombings, the hostage-taking—has continued unabated. But, at the same time, something appears to have been shaken loose. The Iraqi election in late January; the election in the Palestinian territories and the rekindling of the Israeli-Palestinian peace process; the protests of the Lebanese against their Syrian occupiers; and the move by the Egyptian President, Hosni Mubarak, toward more direct elections have given the Bush Administration—and the neoconservatives who contribute much of its expansive ideology—its first good news in quite a while. Some of these events cannot plausibly be attributed to Bush. "This is a very lucky President," Biden said. "Why did Arafat die on his watch? I mean, give me a break."

Biden and other Democrats agreed, though, that their party should not appear stingy when the news favors Bush. "The Democrats need to stand with the President when he's right," Bill Richardson told me. "His emphasis on being more pro-democracy in the Middle East seems to have galvanized some movement. The Democrats need to establish their credentials on national security, and we get hurt by reflexive negativism."

Hillary Clinton says that she has been "forthright in agreeing with the Administration where I thought we could agree," but she believes that the Administration has taken advantage of Democratic support—particularly in the days after the terror attacks of September 11, 2001. "Joe and I and others offered our support to the President and stood unified with him in response to these attacks," Clinton said last week, referring to Biden. "The

Administration saw our actions as a sign of weakness," she said, adding that it "had a campaign strategy to exploit the legitimate fears of the American people." Clinton also said that the Democrats must criticize the Bush Administration for its foreign-policy failings—of which, she said, there are many—but that they are hindered by their role as the opposition party. "It's hard to describe a Democratic Party foreign-policy position, because we're not in charge of making policy," Clinton said. "We are, by the nature of the system, forced to critique and analyze and offer suggestions." This, she said, is where Biden comes in: he has managed to sound steady on terrorism, while still being able to criticize Bush policy. "He has a good sense of smell and touch about these issues, and so I often find myself wondering what Joe is thinking and saying."

Biden says he is reminded of the Party's difficult relationship with Ronald Reagan. "Everybody knew 'Reagan is dangerous,' remember? He talked about freedom, so what do we do? We say it's a bad speech, dangerous speech." Biden was referring to a 1982 speech delivered by Reagan to the British Parliament, in which he spoke of the power of democracy. Today, the Democrats are "making the same mistakes again," Biden said.

Antiwar Democrats dislike the suggestion that Bush's policies will lead to a democratic Middle East. Barbara Boxer, of California, who has been one of the most energetic critics of the Bush White House (she questioned Secretary of State-designate Condoleezza Rice aggressively during her confirmation hearing, suggesting that Rice had been dishonest in her arguments for taking the nation to war in Iraq), told me that she took "great offense" at Bush's inaugural speech. "He said that our freedom and our democracy depend on the freedom of other countries," she said. "I think that America is so strong, it has such a strong Constitution and a great history of freedom, that while we must, of course, be deeply concerned about what happens in other countries, what happens to this country is up to us. His words ring hollow because of the mess in Iraq, and all over the world. Every day, another terrible thing is happening."

I asked Boxer if events in Lebanon and Egypt had changed her views. "History will judge," she said, but added that in Lebanon "the streets are flooded with protesters today"—a reference to the Hezbollah-sponsored pro-Syria demonstration—"and you wonder if maybe a little quiet diplomacy there might have produced better results." She rejects the notion that her party is not in tune with voters on national-security issues. "We almost won the election," she said, and attributed Kerry's loss to superior Republican organizing and to Republican tactics, most notably the attacks last summer on Kerry's war record.

Ted Kennedy has called on President Bush to set an exit date for Iraq. He argued, in a speech delivered the week before the Iraqi election, that the insurgency is made stronger by the presence of American troops on Iraqi soil, and he compared the Iraq war to the war in Vietnam. "Our military and the insurgents are fighting for the same thing—the hearts and minds of the people—and that is a battle we are not winning," Kennedy declared.

When I spoke to Kennedy last month, he said that the election did not persuade him that the war was justified. He believes that it was fought under false pretenses, and is unconvinced that democracy can be brought by force to a place like Iraq. "How should democracy be exported?" he asked. "The First Amendment and food. We know how to grow it, and how to deliver it. The First Amendment is a pretty good starting point." Kennedy said that the United States does have national-security interests that must be insured by force, if necessary. "We need to keep Hormuz and the Molucca straits and the Suez Canal and the Panama Canal open." He does not, however, regret his 1991 vote opposing the first Gulf War. "I had not ruled out force, but I thought it was premature," he said. "I thought we ought to have tried economic sanctions. They worked in South Africa. It's breathtaking how fast they worked." (Kennedy, it should be noted, was not alone in opposing the 1991 Gulf War. At the time, he was joined by all but ten of the Democrats in the Senate, including Biden, Kerry, and the defense stalwarts Sam Nunn, of Georgia, and David Boren, of Oklahoma. Gore and Lieberman were two who voted in favor of the resolution.)

Kennedy and Boxer—and Dean—are to the left of the Democratic center on foreign policy, but their views are shared by many of the Party's active constituents. According to a recent Pew poll, seventy-four per cent of Democrats believe that it was wrong to go to war; twelve per cent of Republicans opposed the invasion. (The country as a whole, including independent voters, is evenly split on the issue.) Eli Pariser, the executive director of MoveOn.org, the antiwar group that helped propel Dean's campaign for

President, told me not long ago, "I don't see how Bush can create a state of fear in our country, and go off in a reckless rush to war in Iraq, and then take credit somehow for exporting democracy, which is a bizarre term, anyway, because democracy is about self-governance." In an e-mail to MoveOn members after the election, Pariser wrote, "It's our party. We bought it, we own it and we're going to take it back."

By at least one significant measure, though, it is not Pariser's party. Few of the most frequently mentioned contenders for the Party's Presidential nomination in 2008—including Clinton, Bayh, Edwards, and Biden—belong to the Democratic Party's left. Instead, the most likely would-be nominees are at pains to appear hawkish on defense. Hillary Clinton has been particularly skillful—not only on defense issues but also on such sensitive subjects as abortion rights. While she has been giving speeches in praise of the United Nations and multilateralism, she has been careful to assert the right of the United States to act without the support of allies when necessary.

Biden's views on the war have changed somewhat over the last several years—an evolution that reveals some of the dilemmas faced by the Democrats in responding to Bush's single-minded message. In November of 2002, in an interview with *USA Today*, Biden recalled a conversation with an unnamed chairman of a military service, who told him that a war with Iraq would be "the dumbest thing in the world." In the months leading up to the war, he often questioned the Bush Administration's timing, its planning, and the grandiose scope of its mission. But as the invasion neared—around the time when former Secretary of State Colin Powell told the United Nations Security Council that he had proof that Saddam Hussein was concealing an active weapons-of-mass-destruction program—Biden said, "The choice between war and peace is Saddam's. The choice between relevance and irrelevance is the U.N. Security Council's."

Biden, like nearly all Democrats, argues that the Administration's prosecution of the war has been inept. "The decision to go to war was the right one," Biden said recently, "but every decision they've made since Saddam fell was a mistake." In particular, Biden blames Secretary of Defense Donald Rumsfeld for the troubles of postwar Iraq—for the Abu Ghraib torture scandal, for the failure to anticipate an organized insurgency, and for the difficulties encountered in the training of Iraqi soldiers. He told Condoleezza Rice, at her confirmation hearing, "For God's sake, don't listen to Rumsfeld. He doesn't know what in the hell he's talking about on this."

Biden was once better known for his chairmanship of the Senate Judiciary Committee than for foreign-policy expertise; he oversaw the confirmation hearings of Robert Bork and Clarence Thomas, among others, and had established a reputation as a liberal in the mainstream of his party, and also as something of a grandstander.

His run for the 1988 Democratic Presidential nomination came to a sudden end when he was accused of borrowing, without attribution, from a television commercial by the former British Labour Party leader Neil Kinnock. This embarrassment did no permanent harm to his standing in the Senate, and he has remained highly visible there. Biden sponsored the Clinton Administration's 1994 crime bill, which funded a hundred thousand new police officers for local communities and helped neutralize the "law and order" issue that had hurt the Democrats in previous years.

By the mid-nineties, Biden had become more absorbed by foreign affairs, and he was deeply affected by the cruelty he saw on visits to Bosnia during the war there. He became a missionary in the cause of armed humanitarian intervention in Bosnia and, later, in Kosovo. "I came back to the Republicans and laid out the death camps in Kosovo, the rape camps in Bosnia—I laid it out in stark relief," he told me. "These guys"—the Republicans—"said, 'It's not our business.' What is so transformational in the last four years is that these assholes who wouldn't give President Clinton the authority to use force" have now become, he said, moral interventionists. "Give me a fucking break." (In fact, there were Republican senators who supported sending United States soldiers to Kosovo in 1999, including John McCain and John Warner, the chairman of the Armed Services Committee.)

Biden says that a "small faction" of the Party is mistrustful of even the occasional use of force. "There are some really bright guys and women in my party who underestimate the transformative capability of military power, when coupled with a rational policy that is both preventative and nation-building in nature," he said. He told me about a recent visit to Los Angeles, where he met with a group of wealthy liberals and laid out the following scenario: "Assume you're the President, and I'm your Secretary of Defense or State or C.I.A. director, and I come to you and tell you we know where bin Laden is, he and four hundred of his people, and they're in this portion of Pakistan the Pakistanis won't go into, and they told us not to go in. This is going to cost us five hundred to five thousand lives, of our soldiers, but we can get him. What do you do?" Biden said they had no answer. "The truth is, they put their heads down," he said.

Richard Holbrooke suggests that the Republicans have boxed in the Democrats, by stealing their ideas. "The Republicans, who always favored bigger defense budgets—we were the soft-power people, the freedom-and-democracy people—now seek to own both the defense side and the values side of the debate," Holbrooke said. He believes that if the Iraq war actually does bring about the hoped-for results it might help the Democrats. "We'd be better off as a country and better off as a party if Iraq is a success and we get it behind us. The Democrats can then talk about their traditional strengths, domestically and internationally."

Senator Clinton said that complaints about a lack of Democratic steadfastness are "always surprising to me, because so many of the disastrous mistakes in foreign policy over the past forty or fifty years have been made by Republicans." She went on, "I don't know all the reasons voters and observers might hold that view. I think a lot of it is unfounded, so part of our challenge is to reassert our voices with clarity in the debate on foreign policy and national security."

These days, Biden is touring the country, doing something that he hasn't done since his aborted Presidential campaign, seventeen years ago: meeting wealthy donors to measure their enthusiasm for him, and accepting offers to speak to Democratic groups far from Wilmington. He is now a senior man in the Party—he has served in the Senate for thirty-two years—and, among his supporters, there is the not unreasonable assumption that the statute of limitations on the Kinnock scandal has been reached.

He told me that he won't make a decision on a Presidential run for at least two years. "My honest-to-God answer is, I'm not going to go on a fool's errand," he said. "If I think I'm the horse that can pull the sleigh, I'll do it. But if there's someone else out there . . ." He trailed off. But he didn't leave the impression that he sees an overly crowded field.

He has come to realize, he said, that many Democrats still haven't grasped the political importance of September 11th, and again he recalled how he had urged Kerry to keep his campaign message focussed on terrorism. Kerry, Biden said, would tell voters that he would "fight terror as hard as Bush," but then he would add, "and I'll help you economically." "What is Bush saying?" Biden said. "Terror, terror, terror, terror, terror. I would say to John, 'Let me put it to you this way. The Lord Almighty, or Allah, whoever, if he came to every kitchen table in America and said, "Look, I have a Faustian bargain for you, you choose. I will guarantee to you that I will end all terror threats against the United States within the year, but in return for that there will be no help for education, no help for Social Security, no help for health care." What do you do?'

"My answer," Biden said, "is that seventy-five per cent of the American people would buy that bargain."

A Fighting Faith: An Argument for a New Liberalism

Peter Beinart

The New Republic | December 13, 2004

In this essay, New Republic *editor Peter Beinart puts the discussion of the Democrats' national-security woes in a broader historical context. He argues that the U.S. liberal base has largely forsaken the "hard" liberalism of Harry Truman and John Kennedy—which emphasized a strong military defense and a tough, anti-totalitarian foreign policy—for the "soft," reflexively anti-military liberalism embodied by Michael Moore and MoveOn.org. If liberals hope to remain an effective force in U.S. politics, says Beinart, they need to heed the wakeup call of 9/11 and the threat of Al Qaeda, and transform themselves into something more than "a collection of domestic interests and concerns."* . . .

In January 4, 1947, 130 men and women met at Washington's Willard Hotel to save American liberalism. A few months earlier, in articles in *The*

New Republic and elsewhere, the columnists Joseph and Stewart Alsop had warned that "the liberal movement is now engaged in sowing the seeds of its own destruction." Liberals, they argued, "consistently avoided the great political reality of the present: the Soviet challenge to the West." Unless that changed, "In the spasm of terror which will seize this country . . . it is the right—the very extreme right—which is most likely to gain victory."

During World War II, only one major liberal organization, the Union for Democratic Action (UDA), had banned communists from its ranks. At the Willard, members of the UDA met to expand and rename their organization. The attendees, who included Reinhold Niebuhr, Arthur Schlesinger Jr., John Kenneth Galbraith, Walter Reuther, and Eleanor Roosevelt, issued a press release that enumerated the new organization's principles. Announcing the formation of Americans for Democratic Action (ADA), the statement declared, "[B]ecause the interests of the United States are the interests of free men everywhere," America should support "democratic and freedom-loving peoples the world over." That meant unceasing opposition to communism, an ideology "hostile to the principles of freedom and democracy on which the Republic has grown great."

At the time, the ADA's was still a minority view among American liberals. Two of the most influential journals of liberal opinion, *The New Republic* and *The Nation*, both rejected militant anti-communism. Former Vice President Henry Wallace, a hero to many liberals, saw communists as allies in the fight for domestic and international progress. As Steven M. Gillon notes in *Politics and Vision*, his excellent history of the ADA, it was virtually the only liberal organization to back President Harry S Truman's March 1947 decision to aid Greece and Turkey in their battle against Soviet subversion.

But, over the next two years, in bitter political combat across the institutions of American liberalism, anti-communism gained strength. With the ADA's help, Truman crushed Wallace's third-party challenge en route to reelection. The formerly leftist Congress of Industrial Organizations (CIO) expelled its communist affiliates and *The New Republic* broke with Wallace, its former editor. The American Civil Liberties Union (ACLU) denounced communism, as did the NAACP. By 1949, three years after Winston Churchill warned that an "iron curtain" had descended across Europe, Schlesinger could write in *The Vital Center:* "Mid-twentieth century liberalism, I believe, has thus been fundamentally reshaped . . . by the exposure of the Soviet Union, and by the deepening of our knowledge of man. The consequence of this historical re-education has been an unconditional rejection of totalitarianism."

Today, three years after September 11 brought the United States face-to-face with a new totalitarian threat, liberalism has still not "been fundamentally reshaped" by the experience. On the right, a "historical re-education" has indeed occurred—replacing the isolationism of the Gingrich Congress with George W. Bush and Dick Cheney's near-theological faith in the transformative capacity of U.S. military might. But American liberalism, as defined by its activist organizations, remains largely what it was in the 1990s—a collection of domestic interests and concerns. On health care, gay rights, and the environment, there is a positive vision, articulated with passion. But there is little liberal passion to win the struggle against Al Qaeda—even though totalitarian Islam has killed thousands of Americans and aims to kill millions; and even though, if it gained power, its efforts to force every aspect of life into conformity with a barbaric interpretation of Islam would reign terror upon women, religious minorities, and anyone in the Muslim world with a thirst for modernity or freedom.

When liberals talk about America's new era, the discussion is largely negative—against the Iraq war, against restrictions on civil liberties, against America's worsening reputation in the world. In sharp contrast to the first years of the cold war, post-September 11 liberalism has produced leaders and institutions—most notably Michael Moore and MoveOn—that do not put the struggle against America's new totalitarian foe at the center of their hopes for a better world. As a result, the Democratic Party boasts a fairly hawkish foreign policy establishment and a cadre of politicians and strategists eager to look tough. But, below this small elite sits a Wallacite grassroots that views America's new struggle as a distraction, if not a mirage. Two elections, and two defeats, into the September 11 era, American liberalism still has not had its meeting at the Willard Hotel. And the hour is getting late.

The Kerry Compromise

The press loves a surprise. And so, in the days immediately after November 2, journalists trumpeted the revelation that "moral values" had cost John Kerry the election. Upon deeper investigation, however, the reasons for Kerry's loss don't look that surprising at all. In fact, they are largely the same reasons congressional Democrats lost in 2002.

Pundits have seized on exit polls showing that the electorate's single greatest concern was moral values, cited by 22 percent of voters. But, as my colleague Andrew Sullivan has pointed out ("Uncivil Union," *The New Republic*, November 22, 2004), a similar share of the electorate cited moral values in the '90s. The real change this year was on foreign policy. In 2000, only 12 percent of voters cited "world affairs" as their paramount issue; this year, 34 percent mentioned either Iraq or terrorism. (Combined, the two foreign policy categories dwarf moral values.) Voters who cited terrorism backed Bush even more strongly than those who cited moral values. And it was largely this new cohort—the same one that handed the GOP its Senate majority in 2002—that accounts for Bush's improvement over 2000. As Paul Freedman recently calculated in *Slate*, if you control for Bush's share of the vote four years ago, "a 10-point increase in the percentage of voters [in a given state] citing terrorism as the most important problem translates into a 3-point Bush gain. A 10-point increase in morality voters, on the other hand, has no effect."

On national security, Kerry's nomination was a compromise between a party elite desperate to neutralize the terrorism issue and a liberal base unwilling to redefine itself for the post-September 11 world. In the early days of his candidacy, Kerry seemed destined to run as a hawk. In June 2002, he attacked Bush from the right for not committing American ground troops in the mountains of Tora Bora. Like the other leading candidates in the race, he voted to authorize the use of force in Iraq. This not only pleased Kerry's consultants, who hoped to inoculate him against charges that he was soft on terrorism, but it satisfied his foreign policy advisers as well.

The Democratic foreign policy establishment that counseled the leading presidential candidates during the primaries—and coalesced behind Kerry after he won the nomination—was the product of a decade-long evolution. Bill Clinton had come into office with little passion for foreign policy, except as it affected the U.S. economy. But, over time, his administration grew more concerned with international affairs and more hawkish. In August 1995, Clinton finally sent NATO warplanes into action in Bosnia. And, four years later, the United States, again working through NATO, launched a humanitarian war in Kosovo, preventing another ethnic cleansing and setting the stage for a democratic revolution in Belgrade. It was an air war, to be sure, and it put few American lives at risk. But it was a war nonetheless, initiated without U.N. backing by a Democratic president in response to internal events in a sovereign country.

For top Kerry foreign policy advisers, such as Richard Holbrooke and Joseph Biden, Bosnia and Kosovo seemed like models for a new post-Vietnam liberalism that embraced U.S. power. And September 11 validated the transformation. Democratic foreign policy wonks not only supported the war in Afghanistan, they generally felt it didn't go far enough—urging a larger NATO force capable of securing the entire country. And, while disturbed by the Bush administration's handling of Iraq, they agreed that Saddam Hussein was a threat and, more generally, supported aggressive efforts to democratize the Muslim world. As *National Journal*'s Paul Starobin noted in a September 2004 profile, "Kerry and his foreign-policy advisers are not doves. They are liberal war hawks who would be unafraid to use American power to promote their values." At the Democratic convention, Biden said that the "overwhelming obligation of the next president is clear"—to exercise "the full measure of our power" to defeat Islamist totalitarianism.

Had history taken a different course, this new brand of liberalism might have expanded beyond a narrow foreign policy elite. The war in Afghanistan, while unlike Kosovo a war of self-defense, once again brought the Western democracies together against a deeply illiberal foe. Had that war, rather than the war in Iraq, become the defining event of the post-September 11 era, the "re-education" about U.S. power, and about the new totalitarian threat from the Muslim world that had transformed Kerry's advisers, might have trickled down to the party's liberal base, transforming it as well.

Instead, Bush's war on terrorism became a partisan affair—defined in the liberal mind not by images of American soldiers walking Afghan girls to school, but by John Ashcroft's mass detentions and Cheney's false claims about Iraqi WMD. The left's post-September 11 enthusiasm for an aggressive campaign against Al Qaeda—epitomized by students at liberal campuses signing up for jobs with the CIA—was overwhelmed by horror at the bungled Iraq war. So, when the Democratic presidential candidates began courting their party's activists in Iowa and New Hampshire in 2003, they found a liberal grassroots that viewed the war on terrorism in negative terms and judged the candidates less on their enthusiasm for defeating Al Qaeda than on their enthusiasm for defeating Bush. The three candidates who made winning the war on terrorism the centerpiece of their campaigns —Joseph Lieberman, Bob Graham, and Wesley Clark—each failed to capture the imagination of liberal activists eager for a positive agenda only in the domestic sphere. Three of the early front-runners—Kerry, John Edwards, and Dick Gephardt—each sank as Howard Dean pilloried them for supporting Ashcroft's Patriot Act and the Iraq war.

Three months before the Iowa caucuses, facing mass liberal defections to Dean, Kerry voted against Bush's $87 billion supplemental request for Iraq. With that vote, the Kerry compromise was born. To Kerry's foreign policy advisers, some of whom supported the supplemental funding, he remained a vehicle for an aggressive war on terrorism. And that may well have been Kerry's own intention. But, to the liberal voters who would choose the party's nominee, he became a more electable Dean. Kerry's opposition to the $87 billion didn't only change his image on the war in Iraq; it changed his image on the war on terrorism itself. His justification for opposing the $87 billion was essentially isolationist: "We shouldn't be opening firehouses in Baghdad and closing them down in our own communities." And, by exploiting public antipathy toward foreign aid and nation-building, the natural building blocks of any liberal anti-totalitarian effort in the Muslim world, Kerry signaled that liberalism's moral energies should be unleashed primarily at home.

Kerry's vote against the $87 billion helped him lure back the liberal activists he needed to win Iowa, and Iowa catapulted him toward the nomination. But the vote came back to haunt him in two ways. Most obviously, it helped the Bush campaign paint him as unprincipled. But, more subtly, it made it harder for Kerry to ask Americans to sacrifice in a global campaign for freedom. Biden could suggest "a new program of national service" and other measures to "spread the cost and hardship of the war on terror beyond our soldiers and their families." But, whenever Kerry flirted with asking Americans to do more to meet America's new threat, he found himself limited by his prior emphasis on doing less. At times, he said his primary focus in Iraq would be bringing American troops home. He called for expanding the military but pledged that none of the new troops would go to Iraq, the new center of the terror war, where he had said American forces were undermanned. Kerry's criticisms of Bush's Iraq policy were trenchant, but the only alternative principle he clearly articulated was multilateralism, which often sounded like a veiled way of asking Americans to do less. And, because he never urged a national mobilization for safety and freedom, his discussion of terrorism lacked Bush's grandeur. That wasn't an accident. Had Kerry aggressively championed a national mobilization to win the war on terrorism, he wouldn't have been the Democratic nominee.

The Softs

Kerry was a flawed candidate, but he was not the fundamental problem. The fundamental problem was the party's liberal base, which would have refused to nominate anyone who proposed redefining the Democratic Party in the way the ADA did in 1947. The challenge for Democrats today is not to find a different kind of presidential candidate. It is to transform the party at its grassroots so that a different kind of presidential candidate can emerge. That means abandoning the unity-at-all-costs ethos that governed American liberalism in 2004. And it requires a sustained battle to wrest the Democratic Party from the heirs of Henry Wallace. In the party today, two such heirs loom largest: Michael Moore and MoveOn.

In 1950, the journal *The New Leader* divided American liberals into "hards" and "softs." The hards, epitomized by the ADA, believed anti-communism was the fundamental litmus test for a decent left. Non-communism was not enough; opposition to the totalitarian threat was the prerequisite for membership in American liberalism because communism was the defining moral challenge of the age.

The softs, by contrast, were not necessarily communists themselves. But they refused to make anti-communism their guiding principle. For them, the threat to liberal values came entirely from the right—from militarists, from red-baiters, and from the forces of economic reaction. To attack the communists, reliable allies in the fight for civil rights and economic justice, was a distraction from the struggle for progress.

Moore is the most prominent soft in the United States today. Most Democrats agree with him about the Iraq war, about Ashcroft, and about Bush. What they do not recognize, or do not acknowledge, is that Moore does not oppose Bush's policies because he thinks they fail to effectively address the terrorist threat; he does not believe there is a terrorist threat. For Moore, terrorism is an opiate whipped up by corporate bosses. In *Dude, Where's My Country?*, he says it plainly: "There is no terrorist threat." And he wonders, "Why has our government gone to such absurd lengths to convince us our lives are in danger?"

Moore views totalitarian Islam the way Wallace viewed communism:

As a phantom, a ruse employed by the only enemies that matter, those on the right. Saudi extremists may have brought down the Twin Towers, but the real menace is the Carlyle Group. Today, most liberals naïvely consider Moore a useful ally, a bomb-thrower against a right-wing that deserves to be torched. What they do not understand is that his real casualties are on the decent left. When Moore opposes the war against the Taliban, he casts doubt upon the sincerity of liberals who say they opposed the Iraq war because they wanted to win in Afghanistan first. When Moore says terrorism should be no greater a national concern than car accidents or pneumonia, he makes it harder for liberals to claim that their belief in civil liberties does not imply a diminished vigilance against Al Qaeda.

Moore is a non-totalitarian, but, like Wallace, he is not an anti-totalitarian. And, when Democratic National Committee Chairman Terry McAuliffe and Tom Daschle flocked to the Washington premiere of *Fahrenheit 9/11*, and when Moore sat in Jimmy Carter's box at the Democratic convention, many Americans wondered whether the Democratic Party was anti-totalitarian either.

If Moore is America's leading individual soft, liberalism's premier soft organization is MoveOn. MoveOn was formed to oppose Clinton's impeachment, but, after September 11, it turned to opposing the war in Afghanistan. A MoveOn-sponsored petition warned, "If we retaliate by bombing Kabul and kill people oppressed by the Taliban, we become like the terrorists we oppose."

By January 2002, MoveOn was collaborating with 9-11peace.org, a website founded by Eli Pariser, who would later become MoveOn's most visible spokesman. One early 9-11peace.org bulletin urged supporters to "[c]all world leaders and ask them to call off the bombing," and to "[f]ly the UN Flag as a symbol of global unity and support for international law." Others questioned the wisdom of increased funding for the CIA and the deployment of American troops to assist in anti-terrorist efforts in the Philippines. In October 2002, after 9-11peace.org was incorporated into MoveOn, an organization bulletin suggested that the United States should have "utilize[d] international law and judicial procedures, including due process" against bin Laden and that "it's possible that a tribunal could even have garnered cooperation from the Taliban."

In the past several years, MoveOn has emerged, in the words of *Salon*'s Michelle Goldberg, as "the most important political advocacy group in Democratic circles." It boasts more than 1.5 million members and raised a remarkable $40 million for the 2004 election. Many MoveOn supporters probably disagree with the organization's opposition to the Afghan war, if they are even aware of it, and simply see the group as an effective means to combat Bush. But one of the lessons of the early cold war is scrupulousness about whom liberals let speak in their name. And, while MoveOn's frequent bulletins are far more thoughtful than Moore's rants, they convey the same basic hostility to U.S. power.

In the early days after September 11, MoveOn suggested that foreign aid might prove a better way to defeat terrorism than military action. But, in recent years, it seems to have largely lost interest in any agenda for fighting terrorism at all. Instead, MoveOn's discussion of the subject seems dominated by two, entirely negative, ideas. First, the war on terrorism crushes civil liberties. On July 18, 2002, in a bulletin titled "Can Democracy Survive an Endless 'War'?," MoveOn charged that the Patriot Act had "nullified large portions of the Bill of Rights." Having grossly inflated the Act's effect, the bulletin then contrasted it with the—implicitly far smaller—danger from Al Qaeda, asking: "Is the threat to the United States' existence great enough to justify the evisceration of our most treasured principles?"

Secondly, the war on terrorism diverts attention from liberalism's positive agenda, which is overwhelmingly domestic. The MoveOn bulletin consists largely of links to articles in other publications, and, while the organization says it "does not necessarily endorse the views espoused on the pages that we link to," the articles generally fit the party line. On October 2, 2002, MoveOn linked to what it called an "excellent article," whose author complained that "it seems all anyone in Washington can think or talk about is terrorism, rebuilding Afghanistan and un-building Iraq." Another article in the same bulletin notes that "a large proportion of [federal] money is earmarked for security concerns related to the 'war on terrorism,' leaving less money available for basic public services."

Like the softs of the early cold war, MoveOn sees threats to liberalism only on the right. And thus, it makes common cause with the most deeply illiberal elements on the international left. In its campaign against the Iraq war, MoveOn urged its supporters to participate in protests co-sponsored by International ANSWER, a front for the World Workers Party, which has defended Saddam, Slobodan Milosevic, and Kim Jong Il. When George Packer, in *The New York Times Magazine,* asked Pariser about sharing the stage with apologists for dictators, he replied, "I'm personally against defending Slobodan Milosevic and calling North Korea a socialist heaven, but it's just not relevant right now."

Pariser's words could serve as the slogan for today's softs, who do not see the fight against dictatorship and jihad as relevant to their brand of liberalism. When *The New York Times* asked delegates to this summer's Democratic and Republican conventions which issues were most important, only 2 percent of Democrats mentioned terrorism, compared with 15 percent of Republicans. One percent of Democrats mentioned defense, compared with 15 percent of Republicans. And 1 percent of Democrats mentioned homeland security, compared with 8 percent of Republicans. The irony is that Kerry—influenced by his relatively hawkish advisers—actually supported boosting homeland security funding and increasing the size of the military. But he got little public credit for those proposals, perhaps because most Americans still see the GOP as the party more concerned with security, at home and abroad. And, judging from the delegates at the two conventions, that perception is exactly right.

The Vital Center

Arthur Schlesinger Jr. would not have shared MoveOn's fear of an "endless war" on terrorism. In *The Vital Center,* he wrote, "Free society and totalitarianism today struggle for the minds and hearts of men. . . . If we believe in free society hard enough to keep on fighting for it, we are pledged to a permanent crisis which will test the moral, political and very possibly the military strength of each side. A 'permanent' crisis? Well, a generation or two anyway, permanent in one's own lifetime."

Schlesinger, in other words, saw the struggle against the totalitarianism of his time not as a distraction from liberalism's real concerns, or as alien to liberalism's core values, but as the arena in which those values found their deepest expression. That meant several things. First, if liberalism was to credibly oppose totalitarianism, it could not be reflexively hostile to military force. Schlesinger denounced what he called "doughfaces," liberals with "a weakness for impotence . . . a fear, that is, of making concrete decisions and being held to account for concrete consequences." Nothing better captures Moore, who denounced the Taliban for its hideous violations of human rights but opposed military action against it—preferring pie-in-the-sky suggestions about nonviolent regime change.

For Schlesinger (who, ironically, has moved toward a softer liberalism later in life), in fact, it was conservatives, with their obsessive hostility to higher taxes, who could not be trusted to fund America's cold war struggle. "An important segment of business opinion," he wrote, "still hesitates to undertake a foreign policy of the magnitude necessary to prop up a free world against totalitarianism lest it add a few dollars to the tax rate." After Dwight Eisenhower became president, the ADA took up this line, arguing in October 1953 that the "overriding issue before the American people today is whether the national defense is to be determined by the demands of the world situation or sacrificed to the worship of tax reductions and a balanced budget." Such critiques laid the groundwork for John F. Kennedy's 1960 campaign—a campaign, as Richard Walton notes in *Cold War and Counterrevolution*, "dominated by a hard-line, get-tough attack on communism." Once in office, Kennedy dramatically increased military spending.

Such a critique might seem unavailable to liberals today, given that Bush, having abandoned the Republican Party's traditional concern with balanced budgets, seems content to cut taxes and strengthen the U.S. military at the same time. But subtly, the Republican Party's dual imperatives have already begun to collide—with a stronger defense consistently losing out. Bush has not increased the size of the U.S. military since September 11 —despite repeated calls from hawks in his own party—in part because, given his massive tax cuts, he simply cannot afford to. An anti-totalitarian liberalism would attack those tax cuts not merely as unfair and fiscally reckless, but, above all, as long-term threats to America's ability to wage war against fanatical Islam. Today, however, there is no liberal constituency for such an argument in a Democratic Party in which only 2 percent of delegates called "terrorism" their paramount issue and another 1 percent mentioned "defense."

But Schlesinger and the ADA didn't only attack the right as weak on national defense; they charged that conservatives were not committed to defeating communism in the battle for hearts and minds. It was the ADA's ally, Truman, who had developed the Marshall Plan to safeguard European democracies through massive U.S. foreign aid. And, when Truman proposed extending the principle to the Third World, calling in his 1949 inaugural address for "a bold new program for making the benefits of our scientific advances and industrial progress available for the improvement and growth of underdeveloped areas," it was congressional Republicans who resisted the effort.

Support for a U.S.-led campaign to defeat Third World communism through economic development and social justice remained central to anti-totalitarian liberalism throughout the 1950s. Addressing an ADA meeting in 1952, Democratic Senator Brien McMahon of Connecticut called for an "army" of young Americans to travel to the Third World as "missionaries of democracy." In 1955, the ADA called for doubling U.S. aid to the Third World, to blunt "the main thrust of communist expansion" and to "help those countries provide the reality of freedom and make an actual start toward economic betterment." When Kennedy took office, he proposed the Alliance for Progress, a $20 billion Marshall Plan for Latin America. And, answering McMahon's call, he launched the Peace Corps, an opportunity for young Americans to participate "in the great common task of bringing to man that decent way of life which is the foundation of freedom and a condition of peace."

The critique the ADA leveled in the '50s could be leveled by liberals again today. For all the Bush administration's talk about promoting freedom in the Muslim world, its efforts have been crippled by the Republican Party's deep-seated opposition to foreign aid and nation-building, illustrated most disastrously in Iraq. The resources that the United States has committed to democratization and development in the Middle East are trivial, prompting Naiem Sherbiny of Egypt's reformist Ibn Khaldun Center to tell *The Washington Post* late last year that the Bush administration was "pussyfooting at the margin with small stuff."

Many Democratic foreign policy thinkers favor a far more ambitious U.S. effort. Biden, for instance, has called for the United States to "dramatically expand our investment in global education." But, while an updated Marshall Plan and an expanded Peace Corps for the Muslim world are more naturally liberal than conservative ideas, they have not resonated among post-September 11 liberal activists. A new Peace Corps requires faith in America's ability to improve the world, something that Moore— who has said the United States "is known for bringing sadness and misery to places around the globe"—clearly lacks. And a new Marshall Plan clearly contradicts the zero-sum view of foreign aid that undergirded Kerry's vote against the $87 billion. In their alienation over Iraq, many liberal activists seem to see the very idea of democracy-promotion as alien. When the *Times* asked Democratic delegates whether the "United States should try to change a dictatorship to a democracy where it can, or should the United States stay out of other countries' affairs," more than three times as many Democrats answered "stay out," even though the question said nothing about military force.

What the ADA understood, and today's softs do not, is that, while in a narrow sense the struggle against totalitarianism may divert resources from domestic causes, it also provides a powerful rationale for a more just society at home. During the early cold war, liberals repeatedly argued that the denial of African American civil rights undermined America's anti-communist efforts in the Third World. This linkage between freedom at home and freedom abroad was particularly important in the debate over civil liberties. One of the hallmarks of ADA liberals was their refusal to imply—as groups like MoveOn sometimes do today—that civil liberties violations represent a greater threat to liberal values than America's totalitarian foes. And, whenever possible, they argued that violations of individual freedom were wrong, at least in part, because they hindered the anti-communist effort. Sadly, few liberal indictments of, for instance, the Ashcroft detentions are couched in similar terms today.

Toward an Anti-Totalitarian Liberalism

For liberals to make such arguments effectively, they must first take back their movement from the softs. We will know such an effort has begun when dissension breaks out within America's key liberal institutions. In the late '40s, the conflict played out in Minnesota's left-leaning Democratic Farmer-Labor Party, which Hubert Humphrey and Eugene McCarthy wrested away from Wallace supporters. It created friction within the NAACP. And it divided the ACLU, which split apart in 1951, with anti-communists controlling the organization and non-communists leaving to form the Emergency Civil Liberties Committee.

But, most important, the conflict played out in the labor movement. In 1946, the CIO, which had long included communist-dominated affiliates, began to move against them. Over fierce communist opposition, the CIO endorsed the Marshall Plan, Truman's reelection bid, and the formation of

NATO. And, in 1949, the organization's executive board expelled eleven unions. As Mary Sperling McAuliffe notes in her book *Crisis on the Left: Cold War Politics and American Liberals, 1947–1954*, while some of the expelled affiliates were openly communist, others were expelled merely for refusing to declare themselves anti-communist, a sharp contrast from the Popular Front mentality that governed MoveOn's opposition to the Iraq war.

Softs attacked the CIO's action as McCarthyite, but it eliminated any doubt about the American labor movement's commitment to the anti-communist cause. And that commitment became a key part of cold war foreign policy. Already in 1944, the CIO's more conservative rival, the American Federation of Labor (AFL) had created the Free Trade Union Committee (FTUC), which worked to build an anti-totalitarian labor movement around the world. Between 1947 and 1948, the FTUC helped create an alternative to the communist-dominated General Confederation of Labor in France. It helped socialist trade unionists distribute anti-communist literature in Germany's Soviet-controlled zone. And it helped anti-communists take control of the Confederation of Labor in Greece. By the early '60s, the newly merged AFL-CIO was assisting anti-communists in the Third World as well, with the American Institute for Free Labor Development training 30,000 Latin American trade unionists in courses "with a particular emphasis on the theme of democracy versus totalitarianism." And the AFL-CIO was spending a remarkable 20 percent of its budget on foreign programs. In 1969, Ronald Radosh could remark in his book, *American Labor and United States Foreign Policy*, on the "total absorption of American labor leaders in the ideology of Cold War liberalism."

That absorption mattered. It created a constituency, deep in the grass-roots of the Democratic Party, for the marriage between social justice at home and aggressive anti-communism abroad. Today, however, the U.S. labor movement is largely disconnected from the war against totalitarian Islam, even though independent, liberal-minded unions are an important part of the battle against dictatorship and fanaticism in the Muslim world.

The fight against the Soviet Union was an easier fit, of course, since the unions had seen communism up close. And today's AFL-CIO is not about to purge member unions that ignore national security. But, if elements within American labor threw themselves into the movement for reform in the Muslim world, they would create a base of support for Democrats who put winning the war on terrorism at the center of their campaigns. The same is true for feminist groups, for whom the rights of Muslim women are a natural concern. If these organizations judged candidates on their commitment to promoting liberalism in the Muslim world, and not merely on their commitment to international family planning, they too would subtly shift the Democratic Party's national security image. Challenging the "doughface" feminists who opposed the Afghan war and those labor unionists with a knee-jerk suspicion of U.S. power might produce bitter internal conflict. And doing so is harder today because liberals don't have a sympathetic White House to enact liberal anti-totalitarianism policies. But, unless liberals stop glossing over fundamental differences in the name of unity, they never will.

Obviously, Al Qaeda and the Soviet Union are not the same. The USSR was a totalitarian superpower; Al Qaeda merely espouses a totalitarian ideology, which has had mercifully little access to the instruments of state power. Communism was more culturally familiar, which provided greater opportunities for domestic subversion but also meant that the United States could more easily mount an ideological response. The peoples of the contemporary Muslim world are far more cynical than the peoples of cold war Eastern Europe about U.S. intentions, though they still yearn for the freedoms the United States embodies.

But, despite these differences, Islamist totalitarianism—like Soviet totalitarianism before it—threatens the United States and the aspirations of millions across the world. And, as long as that threat remains, defeating it must be liberalism's north star. Methods for defeating totalitarian Islam are a legitimate topic of internal liberal debate. But the centrality of the effort is not. The recognition that liberals face an external enemy more grave, and more illiberal, than George W. Bush should be the litmus test of a decent left.

Today, the war on terrorism is partially obscured by the war in Iraq, which has made liberals cynical about the purposes of U.S. power. But, even if Iraq is Vietnam, it no more obviates the war on terrorism than Vietnam obviated the battle against communism. Global jihad will be with us long after American troops stop dying in Falluja and Mosul. And thus, liberalism will rise or fall on whether it can become, again, what Schlesinger called "a fighting faith."

Of all the things contemporary liberals can learn from their forebears half a century ago, perhaps the most important is that national security can be a calling. If the struggles for gay marriage and universal health care lay rightful claim to liberal idealism, so does the struggle to protect the United States by spreading freedom in the Muslim world. It, too, can provide the moral purpose for which a new generation of liberals yearn. As it did for the men and women who convened at the Willard Hotel.

The Once and Future President Clinton
Jennifer Senior

New York magazine | February 21, 2005

When names of potential Democratic candidates for president are bandied about, Hillary Clinton has always made the short list—but it has often been hard to tell if this reflected her own political appeal, or simply a Democratic nostalgia for husband Bill. After four years in the Senate, however, Hillary has taken on considerable stature in her own right. She's proved to be an able and well-liked senator, her approval ratings in her home state are high, and she's been raising money for her 2006 reelection campaign like nobody's business (almost $9 million through the first quarter of 2005).

Even more tellingly, as Jennifer Senior notes here, since Bush's reelection the junior senator from New York has been moving steadily toward the political center. In this article, Senior—whose profile of Hillary as a freshman senator was a selection in The Best American Political Writing 2002—*takes an up-close look at the ex–First Lady's presidential ambitions and comes away impressed. . . .*

A speech given by Hillary Rodham Clinton just four days after George W. Bush's second inauguration is never just a speech. On January 24, in an address notable for its elegant Clintonian geometry, Hillary told a room full of family-planning advocates that although she remained wholly committed to the freedom to choose, she also thought it was important for the pro-choice and anti-abortion movements to find common ground. The following day, her address got front-page coverage in the *New York Times*, and

Harold Ickes, with characteristic eloquence, showed up in a Washington, D.C., restaurant to crow about it.

"I'm sorry, but when push comes to fucking shove—not to turn a pun—my belief is that life begins at conception," he says, as he rips the tab of his tea bag into tiny little shreds. "And I think Hillary understands how hot-button this issue is for Democrats."

For a man who was fired by the Clinton administration and then rewarded with 32 subpoenas for his service, Ickes remains surprisingly close to the former First Family. As treasurer of her reelection committee, he speaks regularly with Hillary, and during the 2004 presidential campaign, when he ran two 527 organizations devoted to defeating George W. Bush, he spoke to Bill roughly every other day. "The issue of choice is deeply, deeply felt," he continues. "We progressives just can't dismiss people who feel to the contrary. This is a helpful dialogue Hillary's opened up."

He asks the waitress for more hot water. He rips the tab of his tea bag into even smaller chads. Then he adds a richer layer to this story. Hillary, as it turns out, isn't the only Clinton who believes the Democratic Party should soften its rhetoric on abortion. "During the presidential campaign," he says, "Bill Clinton's main plaint was that we Democrats, primarily Kerry, were ignoring the issues of abortion, guns, and gay marriage to our peril. He used to say, 'Abortions went down during my presidency. They went up after Bush II. We need to talk about that'—basically what Hillary said in her speech today."

So was the former president framing Hillary's message? I ask.

"I don't know," he says. "They're very, very close, not just personally but politically. He's not her only touchstone. But he's very much a touchstone."

He signals the waitress for the check.

"Her speech yesterday was a big speech," he concludes. "It's a positioning speech." For president?

"You can certainly argue that," he says. "I wouldn't necessarily disagree with you."

Most Democrats agree that Bill Clinton was the best thing to happen to their party in a generation. His wife may now be the best thing to happen to the next. How on earth did this happen? How did the reluctant cookie-baker, the socializer of health care, and the theorizer of a right-wing conspiracy become the presumptive nominee for the party in 2008?

"Well, unless someone can push you off the stage, you're on the stage," says John Breaux, the former Louisiana senator and confidant of Bill Clinton's. "No one has pushed her off. Is anyone even capable? That's the question."

What *isn't* the question is whether Hillary will run. In Washington, this fact is utterly taken for granted. Rather, the question is, who'll have the nerve to wrestle the nomination away from her? At the dedication of the Clinton library last November, which the press corps framed as a debutante ball for Hillary, Wesley Clark openly contemplated another run; this January, as I roamed the halls of the Senate, I heard plenty of other names being tossed about, some from the prospective candidates themselves. "Look, *I* may run against her for the nomination," said Joseph Biden, the Senate Democrat who's become a *Daily Show* favorite for his sense of humor and candor (and who already made a stab at the 1988 primaries, before he was caught plagiarizing from a speech by British Labour Party leader Neil Kinnock).

Really? I asked. *Seriously?*

"Yeah," he said. "I don't know if I'll do it, but I'm looking at it seriously. And she is, you know, the elephant in the living room. She's the big deal."

It's hard to imagine how spectacularly weird a Hillary candidacy would be. It raises the prospect of Bill Clinton, at one point the most humiliated man in America, being back in the White House—but this time, it'd be Hillary in the Oval Office late at night, ordering pizza. It raises the prospect of alternating political dynasties, one composed of husband and wife, the other of father and son.

Unlike Bush, though, who never seemed to wrestle with his political eligibility—that's the marvelous thing about family wealth, how it lends the illusion you've earned your privileges—Hillary would be dogged by the same questions that dogged a whole generation of feminists about power and how it's acquired. Sure, her candidacy would be the ultimate suffragette triumph, but it'd also send a complicated message: *So this is how we get to the White House? On a flagstone path laid by our husbands?* And what would Bill be, if she won? Co-president? Karl Rove? Just as her husband promised to end welfare as we knew it, Hillary, by definition, would have to end the office of the First Lady as we know it. Unless Bill were content to spend the next four years selecting china patterns.

In the meantime, there are the other contenders. Everyone assumes

John Kerry is making another stab. (And a brief exchange with him seemed to bear this out: When I asked him how Hillary had become such an attractive option for 2008, he gave me a look that'd tarnish silver, then told me he had a health-care bill to go work on—as if legislating had suddenly become a priority for him for the first time in twenty years.) Ditto for John Edwards. There are the dark-horse governors, like New Mexico's Bill Richardson, Iowa's Tom Vilsack, and Virginia's Mark Warner. And then there's Senator Evan Bayh, whom some regard as Bill Clinton's true heir— telegenic, moderate, a former governor. And he comes from the bright-red state of Indiana, currently eleven electoral votes rich.

"Yeah, but I don't know how you beat her for the Democratic nomination," says Bob Kerrey, the former Democratic senator from Nebraska, now the head of the New School. "She's a rock star." She's also way ahead in the most recent nationwide poll of Democrats, conducted by CNN, Gallup, and *USA Today:* 40 percent cite her as their first choice in 2008.

The whole subject makes Democratic Washington a bit jumpy. How can the party gamble on yet another liberal brainiac who lacks a tactile sense of politics and flair for speaking in the public square? Especially someone as polarizing as she is? Then again, she is *Hillary*. Think about how much money she could raise. How energized the base would be. And she'd have the world's best campaign strategist by her side, free of charge.

At the core of this debate, of course, is explaining the success of Bill Clinton. Was it his supernatural political gifts? Or was it his centrist politics? Though most Washington Democrats are having this argument now, no one seems to get anywhere with it. It's not like you can string the two apart.

Absent an answer, some very influential Democrats have found their default solution: Pick the other Clinton. And tell everyone she's just like Bill.

"I think the philosophies of Bill and Hillary are close," says Al From, head of the moderate Democratic Leadership Council, who talks fairly often with Hillary.

"She's not your classic New York Upper West Side liberal by any means," says Ickes.

"I don't sit home and worry about how Hillary will reinvent herself," says Donna Brazile, who managed Al Gore's 2000 campaign. "She understands she can't be pigeonholed. She won't be defined."

If you spend any time around Hillary's fans, supporters, or brain trust, this is more or less the refrain you come away with. And these people aren't necessarily being disingenuous. Since serving in public office, Hillary has scrupulously positioned herself as a centrist: She sits on the Armed Services Committee; she has spoken out in favor of the death penalty; she voted for the war in Iraq, then voted unambiguously for the $87 billion extra to sustain the troops (and without Kerry's grammatical sleight of hand—she voted for it before voting for it again). She has always spoken credibly about the role of religion and faith in her life. There are no love beads in sight: She wears the pantsuits, she's got the coif. And she's the human equivalent of a Thermos bottle—you have absolutely no clue what the temperature is of the contents roiling within.

But are we all supposed to believe this is the whole story? According to the *National Journal*, Hillary's voting record has gotten increasingly liberal as her senatorial career has worn on: Though she started in the center of the Democratic pack, she was the twelfth most liberal voter by 2002, and by 2003, she wound up in a three-way tie for eighth. When Al Gore threw a clumsy sop to Miami Cubans (using, of all ghastly things, a child as currency), Hillary couldn't bring herself to support legislation keeping Elián González in the country. There were the famous moments when the Wellesley feminist—"I'm no Tammy Wynette"—reared her head. And there's always the health-care debacle. Most Republican senators called it "Hillarycare" before she became one of their colleagues.

So let's say you were a Wellesley feminist. And let's say you had spent your life committed to public service. What greater achievement could there possibly be than to become the first female president of the United States? Probably none. And you'd probably sacrifice quite a few of your ideals to achieve this goal. "Back when Hillary was trying to be Hillary Rodham," recalls Joycelyn Elders, the former Clinton-administration surgeon general, "Arkansas almost destroyed her for speaking out. So if that meant shutting her mouth the next time, she was going to do that. It's hard to get elected and be completely up front about what you really think. We create a hypocrisy in our politicians."

Of course, many fine politicians contradict or reposition themselves. Bill Clinton did it all the time, and throughout Hillary's career, one can see traces of Clintonian triangulation, her abortion speech being only the latest example. But what separates good politicians from bad ones isn't their consistency. It's whether the electorate notices their pivoting. Can Hillary give the electorate what John Kerry couldn't—a coherent narrative about herself?

"I don't have the slightest clue who Hillary really is," says Charlie Rangel, the Harlem congressman who first encouraged Hillary to run for the Senate in 1999. "I don't think you ever find out who the real person is. All I see is a gal who knew she was as good as anyone else, and she saw this guy she could make something of, so she forfeited Illinois and went to Arkansas. That's a hell of a move to make for a redneck, which is all he was."

He thinks. "I've found that the human mind is so fragile, you can believe what you're doing is right if other people want you to do it," he adds. "If I was going to confession, and I had to talk about what adjustments I've made in public life, I don't know what I'd say. I don't remember contradicting myself, though I assume hundreds of reporters would say otherwise. Life's a changing thing."

A full four years after his presidency, it's still astounding how much hysteria a Bill Clinton appearance can generate. At Hamilton College in November, just a week after the election, I went to hear him speak, and the scene looked like a Stones concert: hordes lined up outside the door, smoking cigarettes to keep warm; buses from points far-flung; cops and checkpoints galore. The gym was packed to capacity (4,600), and the crowd, composed largely of undergraduates with unsettled skin and ski sweaters, was getting more unruly with every passing minute. The room burst into applause for the random fellow who flipped on the light over the lectern onstage, then groaned when the former president failed to materialize after a few moments. Women began shrieking. Men began stamping their feet. There were several unsuccessful attempts at a wave.

When Clinton finally arrived—late, of course—the crowd went nuts. There were howling, metronomic affirmations of his attractiveness ("Yeah, Bubba! Yeah, Bubba!"). But after the thunderous standing ovation, after the yelps and whoops died down, what his audience was left listening to was a rather conciliatory speech. He threw some red meat to the crowd— "every day, the United States of America borrows money from the central banks of China and Japan to cover my tax cut"—but he also gave Bush his due, noting his policies toward Israel have been "pretty good." He even said the results of the last election were encouraging because so many people showed up to vote.

It wasn't the speech many in the crowd had been expecting. Kerry had just lost the election, and Oneida County, Hamilton's home turf, had gone to George W. Bush. Caroline Lewis, a young creative-writing professor, summed it up best. "I kind of wish I'd heard some anger," she said. "Just a little. An edge. I almost forgot who I was watching. It was like Carter was up there. An elder statesman."

Hillary really is the preeminent Clinton now. Bill's still in the game, of course, but the dynamic has obviously shifted. She's the one in the spotlight, looking as good as she ever has, shiny in her prime; he, on the other hand, looks as if he's suddenly, violently capitulated to age, as if all the libidinal chaos—so central to his ambition, identity, and ultimate public unraveling—has drained right out of him. He still keeps a preposterous schedule (last week, an emerging-issues conference in North Carolina; two weeks before, Davos), but he tires in the afternoon, and he doesn't quite fill out his suits. Open-heart surgery is kind to no one, not even former presidents.

By most accounts, Bill and Hillary speak on the phone every day. They see each other mainly on weekends, though only when their schedules align. They recently attended a Broadway performance of Michael Frayn's *Democracy*, where they received a long standing ovation; they attended the Trump wedding reception; he followed her down to Florida three weekends ago while she spoke at a seminar and did a fund-raising loop. People can speculate all they want about their marriage, but it seems safe to say that something other than Chelsea keeps it together. Maybe it's a shared affection and obsession with politics and policy-making; maybe it's the fact that their lives are so utterly bizarre that they're the only ones who can truly relate to each other. But to suggest that their marriage is solely one of political convenience seems to miss something essential about their bond.

Most people assume that Bill Clinton, because he's Bill Clinton, still has his grubby mitts in every political pie. And that's partially true; his political instincts will never desert him. During this last election, Ickes recalls getting frustrated phone calls from Clinton, who'd tell him about ads he'd heard on black radio in Ohio. "They're talking about gay marriage," he'd fret. "We have to respond." (And sure enough, Bush got 16 percent of the black vote in Ohio—an unusually high number for a Republican.) During the DNC race, people went nuts attempting to discern traces of behind-the-scenes machinations: *James Carville had lunch with Wesley Clark and asked if he'd be interested in running the DNC—was that the work of the Clintons?*

But the truth is, there's only so much politicking Clinton can do, because to do so would erode the majesty of his position. Most of his public talks focus on sweeping themes: How the barons of this century will be the builders of a new energy economy, the way the barons of the last made their fortunes in petroleum. How important it is that everyone have access to clean water. How inescapable we all are from one another in an age of global interdependence. He's also busy running his foundation—fighting AIDS, encouraging urban renewal. And he's just accepted a job as the special U.N. envoy to regions devastated by the tsunami.

"Nobody will ever admit this," says Ickes, "but people resent being called and told what to do and say. Like, let's say someone's in the middle of the fray: Harry Reid or Nancy Pelosi or any of the congressional leaders. And Bill Clinton calls. Their immediate reaction is: *Great, he'll have a lot to say.* But there's also a subliminal reaction: *He's not in the mix here. I'm in the mix. I know the pressures and the nuances.* There's a time-distance problem."

Of all people, Ickes should know about this. Just days after our conversation, he endorsed Howard Dean for chairman of the Democratic National Committee, something he never would have done without the tacit approval of the Clintons. (And there are ancillary benefits: Dean's aggressive antiwar posturing will only make Hillary's hawkish voting record look moderate by comparison.)

"Bill Clinton has no bigger fish to fry than the overall welfare of this country," says Ickes. "But he's no longer president. So while I think he talks to a lot of Democratic leaders on a regular basis, ultimately, they have to be the vehicles, not him. Mrs. Clinton is a different kettle of fish. She's the one to watch in terms of articulation."

Pete King—raconteur, sometime fiction writer, and one of two House Republicans with the nerve to vote against the impeachment of Bill Clinton—has a great story about the former First Couple. Last April, he got beeped by President Clinton's office: Bill urgently needed to talk. It turned out the former president was starting the impeachment chapter of *My Life,* and he needed King to help reconstruct some of the details. Which was fine, of course, but King couldn't help but be puzzled: "I'm reading in the papers that the galleys of his book are already in," he says. "And here he is, talking to me—I can hear him going through papers, rustling through things, telling me, 'Hold on, hold on,' because he's gotta go upstairs, he wants to find some note. I imagined him like some crazy professor, racing around his Chappaqua house."

The conversation went perfectly well. Then, six weeks before the book came out, King got another phone call from the Clinton household—this time at six in the morning. "I'm sound asleep," says King. "My wife answers. And she hears a voice: 'This is the Capitol Hill operator. Are you ready to talk to Senator Clinton?' I take the phone, and Hillary says, 'I'm so sorry to wake you up, Pete, but Bill really had to speak to you.'" The next thing the congressman knew, the president was again on the line. "And he says, 'Hey, Pete! How ya doing?'" says King. "No mention that it's six in the morning. *Nothing.* And he's like, 'Hey, let me read you what I wrote about you, because if it'll cause you problems, I'll take it out.' But of course it wasn't going to cause me problems. It was basically about how I couldn't be bought. And he's like, 'Isn't it good? Isn't it good?' He was like a kid showing off a new Cadillac. Then, like a day or two later, Hillary called me at 8:30 in the morning. But that was prearranged. Official. Normal. Whatever."

These, perhaps, are the Clintons' characterological differences in a nutshell: Bill, the bounding cocker spaniel, panting for praise and attention no matter what the hour; Hillary, the groomed Cheshire cat, shrewdly observing boundaries. Dogs often become presidents—Kennedy, Johnson, and Clinton come to mind as recent examples—in part because their desperation to please, their sensitivity to human moods, makes them ravenously hungry for public approval. (And, as we unfortunately know, also a bit prone to acting like dogs.) But can a cat become a president?

"One thing I'll say about being successful in politics: People have to like you before they consider voting for you."

This is Breaux speaking again. Sly and good-natured, he retired from the Senate this January. He's now sitting in his office at Patton Boggs, an upscale law and lobbying firm in Washington. "If they like you," he continues, "they'll excuse you for positions that they don't agree with. Bill Clinton's a classic example of that."

And Hillary?

"Well, Hillary. I mean, she can charm a person very well. So she'll have to use those skills to talk to housewives and farmers and small-businessmen and -women around the country and say, *I'm the one who can represent your values and interests."*

The problem, he hastens to add, isn't that Hillary isn't likable. Quite the contrary. During the Democrats' Tuesday caucus lunches, he says Hillary used to stun colleagues by popping up for coffee and asking if anyone else wanted a cup—not exactly the reflex they were expecting from a woman who'd just had a giant White House staff at her disposal. But it's not like the rest of the world knows this.

"The problem is, when you're running for the first time for an office, you can help create your image," he says. "You can *tell* people who you are. But people already think they know who she is. So for a vast segment of the population, she'd have to change their opinion of her. And that's really . . . " he trails off. "She can keep the base, but that's all she has. And that's a real challenge. That's tough."

"Hillary's a bit of an anomaly," agrees Jay Timmons, former head of the National Republican Senatorial Committee. "She's an attractive candidate for both Democrats *and* Republicans. She's raised more money as the subject of both committees than anyone else."

In smaller settings, Hillary has proved she's capable of charming the most uncharmable sorts. But 99 percent of presidential politics is mediated through the television set, and Hillary's TV addresses are pure chloroform—they're positively narcotizing. And senators make lousy candidates. Their speech is larded with facts, figures, mysterious verbs that'd be better off as nouns; because they cast hundreds of votes, they're an opposition researcher's dream—nearly all of their votes can be reinterpreted in some unbecoming fashion.

Nor does the argument that Hillary has seduced the red parts of New York seem particularly convincing. Chuck Schumer has seduced red New York, too, and no one's suggesting for even five seconds that he run for president, or that his appeal will translate in Muncie, Indiana. Nor is it clear whether the American electorate will feel comfortable choosing a woman to run a country during a time of war, assuming the world feels as perilous in 2008 as it does now.

What if Hillary found her own wedge issue, her own Sister Souljah? I ask Breaux. Would it work?

"It has to happen."

But would it work? What does your gut tell you?

"It can work," he says. "But it's a helluva challenge."

Wouldn't it be ironic if the other politician with the name of Clinton couldn't triangulate?

"That's the challenge she has," he repeats for the third time, clearly straining under his own ambivalence—Breaux's very close to both Clintons, but he's also a moderate, and he's a blunt-spoken guy. It's what made him so popular both in his state and among his colleagues. He gives me a pained, sheepish look. "I'm being nice. But it's true." He struggles for the right way to frame it. "Hillary's the most exciting thing we have," he says. "The question is whether that excitement can transform people who have a built-in opposition to her. The question is whether it's enough."

Here's the grand irony about Hillary: She's already turned around her own worst enemies. She gets along famously with her GOP colleagues, is astoundingly well liked; it's almost a joke how popular she's become in the Senate. "This is the way I'd describe it," says Lindsey Graham, a puppy-eyed, mildly goofy Republican senator from South Carolina. "Hillary comes into an ego-driven body with a slew of bodyguards, which makes you different. If she changes her hairstyle, it makes news—in a body where everybody would like to make news. Yet there's a level of trust with her that's very real. When she does something with you, she makes sure that you're getting as much credit—or more—than she is. Which is politically smart, sure. But I also think it comes easy to her."

Graham is perhaps Hillary's most unlikely fan. In 1998, he was one of the twelve congressmen who managed her husband's impeachment.

"On the Armed Services Committee, Hillary has been anything but an ideologue," he continues. "*Anything* but that. When I've got a new piece of legislation, and I'm looking for an ally on the other side, she's one of the first people I call."

Of course, it's not unusual for senators to build all sorts of bizarre alliances. The rules of the place foster interdependence and compromise; it's an ecosystem where the donkey really does lie down with the elephant. Yet even by Senate standards, Hillary has demonstrated a stunning flair for bipartisanship. In just four years, she's managed to co-sponsor a bill with nearly every legislator who, at one time or another, professed to hate her guts. With Tom DeLay—that gerrymanderer of Texas, the House's very own Ichabod Crane—she collaborated on an initiative concerning foster children. With

Don Nickles, the former Oklahoma senator who breezily speculated in 1996 that Hillary would be indicted, she worked on a bill to extend jobless benefits. With Mississippi senator Trent Lott, who wondered aloud whether lightning might strike her before she arrived at the Senate, she worked on legislation to help low-income pregnant women. A Reuters story from April 2003 noted she'd already sponsored bills with more than 36 Republican senators.

"And she's a lot of fun," adds Graham. "That's the thing that shocked me. We've traveled a lot. I mean, we went, let's see . . . we went to Norway and Iceland and to the Arctic Circle. Estonia—"

Wait. She's *fun?*

"A lot of fun! She's got a great sense of humor." Can he give an example?

He gives me a cross look. "Hey, you're either funny or you're not, okay? And she's funny."

I ask what he thinks of Hillary as a presidential contender in '08.

"Some people would work morning, noon, and night to beat her," he says. "And some people would sell their firstborn for her to win. But I think there's also a sizable part in the middle that'd sit and listen to what she has to say. People are fair. I think she could win every state John Kerry won. And she'd probably be a better candidate in the swing states."

He smiles. "There are Republicans who are saying, 'Bring her on,'" he says. "But my counsel to them is, *Watch what you wish for.* Because I've worked with her. She's intelligent, she's classy, and she's comfortable with who she is and what she believes. The Hillary Clinton who's the subject of Republican campaign mail-outs and the Hillary Clinton who's the senator from New York are vastly different people."

Here's how the argument in favor of a Hillary candidacy goes: She has already been through two winning presidential campaigns. She has unrestricted access to the best Democratic strategist on planet Earth. As soon as she declared her candidacy, an infrastructure would immediately shuffle into place around her. And she can raise more money than God. "Can you *imagine* what Bill Clinton would have done in the Internet age?" asks Joe Trippi, architect of Dean's grassroots presidential-primary campaign. "Would it have been a quarter of a billion, a half a billion dollars? It'd have put Howard Dean and me to shame. So if you ask who out there would benefit most from this great sea change of grassroots mobilization, it's Hillary."

And sure, Hillary's polarizing, but according to a nationwide Quinnipiac University poll conducted on December 16, George Bush's negatives are even worse than hers—by six points. According to Opinion Research Associates, a Little Rock polling firm, her approval ratings in the recently red state of Arkansas remained well above 50 percent throughout some of her toughest years in the White House. (In 1998, they were at 65 percent.) In Florida, whose electoral significance need not be explained here, a Quinnipiac poll from December 7 revealed that 45 percent of all respondents wanted to see her run for president—a number that's ten points ahead of John Kerry, nine points ahead of John Edwards, one point ahead of John McCain (!), 25 points ahead of Arnold Schwarzenegger (assuming the Constitution were changed on his behalf), and only three points behind Rudolph Giuliani (who couldn't win the Republican nomination anyway, though he'll probably be so rich by 2008 that he could finance his own race as an independent).

And in New York, Hillary is certainly no longer Nurse Ratched. She has managed to transform her approval ratings from 36 percent (April 2000) to 65 percent (last week). Among married women, her most surprising problem-constituency in 2000, her numbers are now at 64 percent. The latest Quinnipiac polls even show she'd beat Rudy if he ran against her for Senate in 2006. Rope lines don't bother her now; she's more relaxed around the press. Pete King remembers going to a new-firehouse dedication with her not long after September 11. "I'm sure most of those guys voted for Bush," he says. "But by the time the event was over, there were more flashbulbs going off . . . One on one, she's very engaging."

It's also important to remember: In 1980, Democrats were praying Reagan would run in the Republican primary, believing he was too conservative. They were wrong. In 2000, they were thrilled that a man as seemingly vacuous and inexperienced as George W. Bush was on the ticket. That didn't work out so well either.

"A lot of my colleagues dream of running against her," says Ed Gillespie, the former chairman of the Republican National Committee. "I'm not one of them. I still think we beat her, but she's very smart, and she'd be a viable woman candidate for president, and that's a different dynamic—a lot of women and small-business owners who'd be inclined toward the Republican nominee could take a second look and say, 'Maybe we should have a woman president.' "

Campaigning against a woman can also be an interesting exercise in minefield-walking. Just ask Rick Lazio. Or George Allen, the Virginia governor turned senator who has twice run against female candidates (and just stepped down as head of the National Republican Senatorial Committee). "The truth is, it is different running against a woman," he says. "The phraseology is not the same, the language is not the same. You need to be a gentleman, but you can't just let them flat run over you either. I've seen folks run against women as if there's no difference. And it comes off bad."

I'll admit it. When I began writing this story, I dismissed Hillary-in-'08 supporters as utterly deranged. I chalked up their enthusiasm as sheer liberal folly—the folly of a party that never learns, the folly of a party that manages to self-immolate quadrennially. But I've since come to understand their enthusiasm. You can see how Hillary could thread the needle of the Electoral College, pulling along just enough people to carry Arkansas, Florida, New Mexico. She's astoundingly disciplined. She knows how to deflect the bad and the ugly. And she's one of those people who (like her colleague Chuck Schumer) are so hell-bent on getting what they want that it's hard to imagine them failing.

Here's how one could imagine it playing out: Hillary runs a Senate campaign in 2006 that focuses on how she helped rebuild New York after September 11. The topic, while of local importance, also allows her room to discuss her national-security bona fides, to mention her support for the Iraq war. She stakes out a few positions in opposition to Bush, like Social Security, that New Yorkers would relate to, yet she also stresses her various collaborations with colleagues from across the aisle, subtly suggesting that she's the true uniter, not a divider. The race gets covered as if it were a national race—this is Hillary, after all.

And at some point, the conventional wisdom tips. To a great many people, Hillary remains Eva Perón, Madame Chiang Kai-shek, whoever. But to *just* enough people, she's the Eleanor Roosevelt who finally found herself in the right generation—a woman who decided to commit herself to public service and found a life-partner who wanted to do the same. When he'd exhausted all his possibilities, she carried on in the same tradition, and she became the first First Lady ever to hold elected office.

It's a long shot, for sure. Even as I write, I'm not sure I buy it. But one thing I do know: No two people are more adept at writing their own story than the Clintons.

"Bill Clinton didn't just roll out of the crib with this talent," says Bob Kerrey. "He worked very, very hard at it. He knew the details of every congressional district in America, and he took great care with each one of his speeches—I debated this guy on several occasions, so I can tell you. We'd all be sitting there before the debates, joking around. Not him. He had his head down, his lips moving, rehearsing his answers. Then the camera went on. And he appeared relaxed, sure. *But he was prepared.*

"So it's not all magic," says Kerrey. "And Hillary's working on it. She's practicing and paying attention. And if you think oratory's important and body language is important, she's living with the best."

At the dedication of the William J. Clinton Presidential Center, the big joke was how much the library looked like a trailer park, rather than a bridge to the 21st century. But up close, it really doesn't look like either. Cantilevered over a river, its moorings far off to one end, the building looks more like a gangplank than anything else. The metaphor seems painfully apt. Clinton, the only two-term Democratic president since FDR, can't seem to shore up his legacy. Everyone who follows in his footsteps keeps taking a header off a narrow walkway.

The day was depressingly rich in symbolism and all-too-obvious metaphors. It was pouring—pouring in a wrathful, almost biblical way—and the rain drowned out everyone's words, once again making it impossible for Democrats to get their message out, and prompting one of my colleagues to note that this day, of all days, should have been the one for Democrats to find themselves a big tent. That evening, the original Clinton team threw a party in the original War Room—a space, it turns out, that's now vacant.

There was something bittersweet about that party. Kerry had just been defeated and the Senate Republican majority had just shot up, yet there were the architects, foot soldiers, and stalwarts of the Last Big Win—Stephanopoulos, Begala, Grunwald—nibbling on spinach dip, trying to figure out what next. A lot of them were passing around photos of their kids, though photos of their younger, '92 selves lined the wall, as well as pictures of the candidate they served, many of which only a die-hard fan of

Bubba could love: Bill playing the saxophone. Bill fans holding up an Elvis poster. Bill flopped out on the sofa, belly hanging out, his head in his wife's lap, remnants of a ravaged pastry by his side. Hillary looks a lot more presidential in that photo—though maybe they're just playing their parts, in the end. And they certainly look like partners. Is this the new Camelot? A Wellesley feminist in a headband, a Big Mac addict from a trailer park?

Bridges to the presidency have been paved with stranger stuff.

Part Four:
The State of the Union

Bipolar Disorder

Jonathan Rauch

The Atlantic Monthly | January–February 2005

Red states vs. blue states, Republicans vs. Democrats, conservatives vs. liberals—the common wisdom seems to be that the United States of America has never been as polarized politically as it is right now. However, when Jonathan Rauch examined what the scholars had to say on the subject for this Atlantic Monthly *article, he uncovered an America that's a lot less divided than you might think. In fact, Rauch suggests that the real divide may be between ordinary citizens and the nation's more partisan types. "At a time when the culture is notably calm," he writes, "politics is notably shrill." . . .*

Have fear, Americans. Ours is a country divided. On one side are those who divide Americans into two sides; on the other are all the rest. Yes, America today is divided over the question of whether America is divided.

All right, I'm joking. But the joke has a kernel of truth. In 1991 James Davison Hunter, a professor of sociology and religious studies at the University of Virginia, made his mark with an influential book called *Culture Wars: The Struggle to Define America*. The notion of a country deeply and fundamentally divided over core moral and political values soon made its way into politics; in 1992 Patrick Buchanan told the Republicans at their national convention that they were fighting "a cultural war, as critical to the kind of nation we will one day be as was the Cold War itself." By 1996, in his singeing dissent in the gay-rights case Romer v. Evans, Supreme Court Justice Antonin Scalia could accuse the Court of "tak[ing] sides in the culture wars," and everyone knew exactly what he meant.

In 2000 those ubiquitous election-night maps came along, with their red expanses of Bush states in the heartland and their blue blocks of Gore territory along the coasts and the Great Lakes. From then on everyone talked about red America and blue America as if they were separate countries. The 2004 post-election maps, which looked almost identical to the 2000 ones, further entrenched the conventional wisdom, to the point where most newspaper readers can recite the tropes: red America is godly, moralistic, patriotic, predominantly white, masculine, less educated, and heavily rural and suburban; blue America is secular, relativistic, internationalist, multicultural, feminine, college educated, and heavily urban and cosmopolitan. Reds vote for guns and capital punishment and war in Iraq, blues for abortion rights and the environment. In red America, Saturday is for NASCAR and Sunday is for church. In blue America, Saturday is for the farmers' market (provided there are no actual farmers) and Sunday is for *The New York Times*.

An odd thing, however, happened to many of the scholars who set out to map this culture war: they couldn't find it. If the country is split into culturally and politically distinct camps, they ought to be fairly easy to locate. Yet scholars investigating the phenomenon have often come back empty-handed. Other scholars have tried to explain why. And so, in the fullness of time, the country has arrived at today's great divide over whether there is a great divide.

One amusing example: In April of last year *The Washington Post* ran a front-page Sunday article headlined POLITICAL SPLIT IS PERVASIVE. It quoted various experts as saying, for example, "We have two parallel universes" and "People in these two countries don't even see each other." In June, *The New York Times* shot back with an article headlined A NATION DIVIDED? WHO SAYS? It quoted another set of experts who maintained that Americans' disagreements are actually smaller than in the past and shrinking.

Courageously, your correspondent set out into the zone of conflict. The culture-war hypothesis has generated some fairly rigorous scholarship in recent years, and I examined it. I wound up believing that a dichotomy holds the solution to the puzzle: American politics is polarized but the American public is not. In fact, what may be the most striking feature of the contemporary American landscape—a surprise, given today's bitterly adversarial politics—is not the culture war but the culture peace.

What, exactly, do people mean when they talk about a divided or polarized America? Often they mean simply that the country is evenly divided: split fifty-fifty, politically speaking. And so it indubitably and strikingly is. In 1979 Democratic senators, House members, governors, and state legislators commandingly outnumbered Republicans; since early in this decade the numbers have been close to equal, with Republicans slightly ahead. Opinion polls show that Republicans and Democrats are effectively tied for the public's loyalty. For the time being, America doesn't have a dominant party.

That may sound odd, given the Republicans' dominance in winner-take-all Washington. But in fact the 2004 elections confirmed that the parties are remarkably close to parity. The presidential election was tight, especially considering that an incumbent president was in the race. Republicans picked up four Senate seats, but the House of Representatives barely budged. The partisan allocation of state legislative seats (now close to parity) and of governorships (mildly favoring Republicans) also barely budged. As if to make parity official, in the main exit poll voters described themselves as Democrats and Republicans in precisely equal proportions.

To political analysts, who live in a world of zero-sum contests between two political parties, it seems natural to conclude that partisan division entails cultural division. Sometimes they elide the very distinction. In his book *The Two Americas* (2004), Stanley B. Greenberg, a prominent Democratic pollster, opens with the sentence *"America is divided"* (his italics) and goes on to say, "The loyalties of American voters are now almost perfectly divided between the Democrats and Republicans, a historical political deadlock that inflames the passions of politicians and citizens alike." In a two-party universe that is indeed how things look. But we do not live in a two-party universe. The fastest-growing group in American politics is independents, many of them centrists who identify with neither party and can tip the balance in close elections. According to the Pew Research Center for the People and the Press, since the Iraq War 30 percent of Americans have identified themselves as Republicans, 31 percent as Democrats, and 39 percent as independents (or "other"). Registered voters split into even thirds.

On election day, of course, independents who want to vote almost always have to choose between a Republican and a Democrat. Like the subatomic particles that live in a state of blurred quantum indeterminacy except during those fleeting moments when they are observed, on election day purple independents suddenly appear red or blue. Many of them, however, are undecided until the last moment and aren't particularly happy with either choice. Their ambivalence disappears from the vote tallies because the very act of voting excludes the nonpartisan middle.

By no means, then, does partisan parity necessarily imply a deeply divided citizenry. People who talk about culture wars usually have in mind not merely a close division (fifty-fifty) but a wide or deep division—two populations with distinct and incompatible world views. It was this sort of divide that Hunter said he had found in 1991. One culture was "orthodox," the other "progressive." The disagreement transcended particular issues to encompass different conceptions of moral authority—one side anchored to tradition or the Bible, the other more relativistic. Not only does this transcendental disagreement reverberate throughout both politics and everyday life, Hunter said, but *each side of the cultural divide can only talk past the other*" (his italics). In his book *The Values Divide* (2002) the political scientist John Kenneth White, of Catholic University, makes a similar case. "One faction emphasizes duty and morality; another stresses individual rights and self-fulfillment," he writes. The result is a "values divide"—indeed, a "chasm."

Both authors make their observations about culture and values—many of which are quite useful—by aggregating the attitudes of large populations into archetypes and characteristic world views. The question remains, however, whether actual people are either as extreme or as distinct in their views as the analysts' cultural profiles suggest. Might the archetypes really be stereotypes?

In 1998 Alan Wolfe, a sociologist at Boston College, said yes. For his book *One Nation, After All,* Wolfe studied eight suburban communities. He found a battle over values, but it was fought not so much between groups as within individuals: "The two sides presumed to be fighting the culture war do not so much represent a divide between one group of Americans and another as a divide between sets of values important to everyone." Intellectuals and partisans may line up at the extremes, but ordinary people mix and match values from competing menus. Wolfe found his subjects to be "above all moderate," "reluctant to pass judgment," and "tolerant to a fault." Because opinion polls are designed to elicit and categorize disagreements, he concluded, they tend to obscure and even distort this reality.

I recently came across an interesting example of how this can happen: In an August 2004 article Jeffrey M. Jones and Joseph Carroll, two analysts with the Gallup Organization, took note of what they called an election-year puzzle. Frequent churchgoers and men were much more likely to support George W. Bush than John Kerry. Non-churchgoers and women leaned the other way. That all jibed with the familiar archetypes of religious-male reds and secular-female blues. But here was the puzzle:

"Men—particularly white men—are much less likely to attend church than are women of any race or ethnicity." How, then, could churchgoers prefer Bush if women preferred Kerry?

The answer turns out to be that most individuals don't fit the archetypes. Men who go to church every week overwhelmingly favored Bush (by almost two to one), and women who stay home on Sundays favored Kerry by a similar margin. But these two archetypal categories leave out most of the population. Women who go to church weekly, men who stay home Sundays, and people of both sexes who go to church semi-regularly are all much more closely divided. The majority of actual Americans are in this conflicted middle.

To know how polarized the country is, then, we need to know what is happening with actual people, not with cultural or demographic categories. One thing we need to know, for example, is whether more people take extreme positions, such that two randomly chosen individuals would find less common ground today than in the past. In the fifty-fifty nation does the distribution of opinion look like a football, with Americans divided but clustered around the middle? Or has it come to look like a dumbbell, with more people at the extremes and fewer in the center?

In an impressive 1996 paper published in *The American Journal of Sociology*—"Have Americans' Social Attitudes Become More Polarized?"— the sociologists Paul DiMaggio, John Evans, and Bethany Bryson, of Princeton University, set out to answer that question using twenty years' worth of data from two periodic surveys of public opinion. They found no change in the "bimodality" of public opinion over the two decades. The football was not becoming a dumbbell.

DiMaggio and his colleagues then looked at particular issues and groups. On most issues (race and gender issues, crime and justice, attitudes toward liberals and conservatives, and sexual morality) Americans had become more united in their views, not more divided. (The exceptions were abortion and, to a lesser extent, poverty.) Perhaps more surprising, the authors found "dramatic *depolarization* in intergroup differences." That is, when they sorted people into groups based on age, education, sex, race, religion, and region, they found that the groups had become more likely to agree.

The authors did, however, find one group that had polarized quite dramatically: people who identified themselves as political partisans. There had been a "striking divergence of attitudes between Democrats and Republicans." In 2003 John Evans updated the study using data through 2000. He found, for the most part, no more polarization than before—except among partisans, who were more divided than ever.

Could it be that the structure of public opinion shows stability or convergence even as individuals hold their opinions in more vehement, less compromising ways? If so, that might be another kind of polarization. Getting inside individuals' heads is difficult, but scholars can look at so-called "feeling thermometers"—survey questions that ask respondents to rate other people and groups on a scale from "very cold" to "very warm." In his recent book *Culture War? The Myth of a Polarized America* the political scientist Morris P. Fiorina, of Stanford University (writing with Samuel J. Abrams and Jeremy C. Pope), finds little change in emotional polarization since 1980—except, again, among strong partisans.

A further possibility remains. Political *segregation* may be on the rise. Like-minded people may be clustering together socially or geographically, so that fewer people are exposed to other points of view. States, neighborhoods, and even bridge clubs may be turning all red or all blue. Is America becoming two countries living side by side but not together?

Fiorina and his associates approached that question by comparing blue-state and red-state opinion just before the 2000 election. What they found can only be described as a shocking level of agreement. Without doubt, red states were more conservative than blue ones; but only rarely did they actually disagree, even on such culturally loaded issues as gun control, the death penalty, and abortion. Rather, they generally agreed but by different margins. To take one example of many, 77 percent of red-state respondents favored capital punishment, but so did 70 percent of blue-state respondents. Similarly, 64 percent of those in blue states favored stricter gun control, but so did 52 percent of those in red states. Red-state residents were more likely to be born-again or evangelical Christians (45 percent, versus 28 percent in blue states), but strong majorities in both sets of states agreed that religion was very important in their lives. On only a few issues, such as whether to allow homosexuals to adopt children or join the military, did blue-state majorities part company with red-state majorities. Majorities in both red and blue states concurred—albeit by different margins—that Bill Clinton was doing a good job as president, that nonetheless they did not wish he could run again, that women's roles should be equal to men's, that the environment should take precedence over jobs, that English should be made the official language, that blacks should not receive preferences in hiring, and so on. This hardly suggests a culture war.

Red-state residents and blue-state residents agreed on one other point: most of them regarded themselves as centrists. Blue residents tipped toward describing themselves as liberal, and red residents tipped toward seeing themselves as conservative; but, Fiorina writes, "the distributions of self-placements in the red and blue states are very similar—both are centered over the 'moderate' or 'middle-of-the-road' position, whether we consider all residents or just voters." By the same token, people in both sets of states agreed, by very similar margins, that the Democratic Party was to their left and the Republican Party to their right. "In both red and blue states," Fiorina concludes, "a solid majority of voters see themselves as positioned between two relatively extreme parties."

Of course, one reason states look so centrist might be that most states aggregate so many people. A state could appear moderate, for example, even if it were made up of cities that were predominantly liberal and rural areas that were predominantly conservative. Indeed, media reports have suggested that a growing share of the population lives in so-called landslide counties, which vote for one party or the other by lopsided margins. Philip A. Klinkner, a professor of government at Hamilton College, examined this claim recently and found nothing in it. In 2000 the share of voters in landslide counties (36 percent) fell smack in the middle of the historical range for presidential elections going back to 1840. In 2000, Klinkner writes, "the average Democrat and the average Republican lived in a county that was close to evenly divided."

Of course, 36 percent of Americans living in landslide counties is a lot of people. But then, America has always been a partisan place. What John Adams's supporters said in 1796 about Thomas Jefferson, Bill Clinton pungently (and correctly) observed recently, would "blister the hairs off a dog's back." America is also no stranger to cultural fission. Think of Jeffersonians versus Hamiltonians, Jacksonians against the Establishment, the Civil War (now *there* was a culture war), labor versus capital a century ago, the civil-rights and Vietnam upheavals. No cultural conflict in America today approaches any of those. By historical standards America is racked with harmony.

My favorite indication of the culture peace came in a survey last July of unmarried Americans, conducted by the Gallup Organization for an online dating service called Match.com. Asked if they would be "open to marrying someone who held significantly different political views" from their own, 57 percent of singles said yes. Majorities of independents, Democrats, and (more narrowly) Republicans were willing to wed across political lines. Just how deep can our political disagreements be, I wonder, if most of us are willing to wake up next to them every morning?

A picture begins to emerge. A divide has opened, but not in the way most people assume. The divide is not within American culture but between politics and culture. At a time when the culture is notably calm, politics is notably shrill. Now, it bears emphasizing that culture peace, or war, is always a relative concept. America, with its cacophonous political schools and ethnic groups and religions and subcultures, will never be a culturally quiescent place, and thank goodness for that. Given the paucity of nation-splitting disagreements, however, what really needs explaining is the disproportionate polarization of American politics.

Reasons for it are not hard to find. They are almost bewilderingly numerous. When I burrow through the pile, I end up concluding that two are fundamental: America's politicians have changed, and so have America's political parties.

"Who sent us the political leaders we have?" Alan Ehrenhalt asked in 1991. Ehrenhalt is a respected Washington political journalist, the sort of person who becomes known as a "veteran observer," and the riddle is from his book *The United States of Ambition: Politicians, Power, and the Pursuit of Office.* "There is a simple answer," he continued. "They sent themselves." This, he argued persuasively, was something new and important.

Ehrenhalt, who was born in 1947, grew up in the dusk of a fading world that I, at age forty-four, am just a little too young to remember. In those days politicians and their supporters were like most other people, only more so. Ambition and talent always mattered, but many politicians were fairly ordinary people (think of Harry Truman) who were recruited into politics by local parties or political bosses and then worked their way up through the system, often trading on their ties to the party and on their ability to deliver patronage. Party machines and local grandees acted as gatekeepers. Bosses and elders might approach a popular local car dealer and ask him to run for a House seat, and they were frequently in a position to hand him the nomination, if not the job. Loyalty, not ideology, was the coin of the realm, and candidates were meant to be smart and ambitious but not, usually, *too* smart and ambitious.

In a society as rambunctious and egalitarian as America's, this system was probably bound to break down, and in the 1960s and 1970s it finally did. The smoke-filled rooms, despite their considerable (and often under-appreciated) strengths, were too cozy and homogenous and, yes, unfair to accommodate the democratic spirit of those times. Reformers, demanding a more open style of politics, did away with the gatekeepers of old. The rise of primary elections was meant to democratize the process of nominating candidates, and so it did; but hard-core ideologues—with their superior hustle and higher turnouts—proved able to dominate the primaries as they never could the party caucuses and conventions. As the power of the machines declined, ideology replaced patronage as the prime motivator of the parties' rank and file. Volunteers who showed up at party meetings or campaign offices ran into fewer people who wanted jobs and more who shared their opinions on Vietnam or busing.

With parties and patrons no longer able to select candidates, candidates began selecting themselves. The party nominee, Ehrenhalt wrote, gave way to the "self-nominee." Holding office was now a full-time job, and running for office was if anything even more grueling than holding it. "Politics is a profession now," Ehrenhalt wrote. "Many people who would be happy to serve in office are unwilling to think of themselves as professionals, or to make the personal sacrifices that a full-time political career requires. And so political office—political power—passes to those who want the jobs badly enough to dedicate themselves to winning and holding them." Those people, of course, are often left-wing and right-wing ideologues and self-appointed reformers. In the 1920s the town druggist might be away serving in Congress while the local malcontent lolled around the drugstore grumbling about his pet peeve. Today there's a good chance that the druggist is minding the store and the malcontent is in Washington.

• • •

The parties, too, have changed. Whereas they used to be loose coalitions of interests and regions, they are now ideological clubs. Northeastern Republicans were once much more liberal than Southern Democrats. Today more or less all conservatives are Republicans and more or less all liberals are Democrats. To some extent the sorting of parties into blue and red happened naturally as voters migrated along the terrain of their convictions, but the partisans of the political class have been only too happy to prod the voters along. Whereas the old party machines specialized in mobilizing masses of partisans to vote for the ticket, the newer breed specializes in "activating" (as the political scientist Steven E. Schier has aptly put it) interest groups by using targeted appeals, often inflammatory in nature. (This past year the Republican National Committee sent mailings in Arkansas and West Virginia suggesting that the Democrats would try to ban the Bible.) Both parties, with the help of sophisticated computer software and block-by-block demographic data, have learned to target thinner and thinner slices of the population with direct mail and telephone appeals.

Perhaps more significant, both parties also got busy using their computer programs and demographic maps to draw wildly complicated new district boundaries that furnished their incumbents with safe congressional seats. Today House members choose their voters rather than the other way around, with the result that only a few dozen districts are competitive. In many districts House members are much less worried about the general election than they are about being challenged in the primary by a rival from their own party. Partisans in today's one-party districts feel at liberty to support right-wing or left-wing candidates, and the candidates feel free (or obliged) to cater to the right-wing or left-wing partisans.

It's not such a surprise, then, that the ideological divide between Democrats and Republicans in Congress is wider now than it has been in more than fifty years (though not wide by pre-World War I standards). The higher you go in the hierarchies of the parties, the further apart they lean. The top leaders on Capitol Hill are the bluest of blues and the reddest of reds—left and right not just of the country but even of their own parties. (This is especially true on the Republican side. *National Journal,* a nonpartisan public-policy magazine and a sister publication of *The Atlantic,* rated House Speaker Dennis Hastert the most conservative member of the House in 2003; Majority Leader Tom DeLay tied for second place.) As party lines have hardened and drawn apart, acrimony has grown between Democratic and Republican politicians, further separating the parties in what has become a vicious cycle. The political scientist Gary C. Jacobson, of the University of California at San Diego, finds that Democrats and Republicans not only enter Congress further apart ideologically, but also become more polarized the longer they stay in Congress's fiercely partisan environment.

Not all of this had to happen—and indeed, happenstance has made matters worse in recent years. It is interesting to wonder how much less polarized American politics might be today if John McCain had won the presidency in 2000. Instead we got Bush, with his unyielding temperament and his strategy of mobilizing conservatives. Even more divisive was the fact that one party—the Republicans—has controlled the presidency and both chambers of Congress since 2003. In a fifty-fifty country, shutting one party out of the government can only lead to partisan excess on one side and bitter resentment on the other.

Centrist voters, of course, are unhappy, but what can they do? As Fiorina pithily puts it, "Given a choice between two extremes, they can only elect an extremist." Presented with a credible candidate who seemed relatively moderate, a McCain or a Ross Perot, many independents jumped at him; but the whole problem is that fewer moderates reach the ballot. The result, Fiorina writes, is that "the extremes are overrepresented in the political arena and the center underrepresented." The party system, he says, creates or inflames conflicts that are dear to the hearts of relatively small numbers of activists. "The activists who gave rise to the notion of a culture war, in particular, and a deeply polarized politics, in general, for the most part are sincere. *They* are polarized." But ordinary people—did someone say "silent majority"?—are not.

Well. A grim diagnosis. That it is largely correct is simply beyond question. I say this as one of the frustrated independent voters who feel left behind by two self-absorbed and overzealous major parties. In particular, the practice of gerrymandering congressional districts to entrench partisans (and thus extremists) is a scandal, far more insulting to popular sovereignty than anything to do with campaign finance. But that is not the note I wish to end on. Something may be going right as well.

It seems odd that cultural peace should break out at the same time that political contentiousness grows. But perhaps it is not so odd. America may be culturally peaceful *because* it is so politically polarized. The most irritating aspect of contemporary American politics—its tendency to harp on and heighten partisan and ideological differences—may be, as computer geeks like to say, not a bug but a feature.

America's polarized parties, whatever their flaws, are very good at developing and presenting crisp choices. How do you feel about abortion? A constitutional ban on same-sex marriage? Privatizing Social Security accounts? School vouchers? Pre-emptive war? Well, you know which party to vote for. Thanks to the sharply divided political parties, American voters—including the ones in the center—get clear alternatives on most issues that matter. By presenting those alternatives, elections provide a sense of direction.

Moreover, although party polarization may disgruntle the center (can't we be for stem-cell research *and* school vouchers?), it helps domesticate fanatics on the left and the right. Though you would be partly correct to say that the mainstream parties have been taken over by polarized activists, you could also say, just as accurately and a good deal more cheerfully, that polarized activists have been taken over by the mainstream parties. The Republican Party has acquired its distinctively tart right-wing flavor largely because it has absorbed—in fact, to a significant extent has organizationally merged with—the religious right. As Hanna Rosin reports elsewhere in this package [see p. 276], religious conservatives are becoming more uniformly Republican even as their faiths and backgrounds grow more diverse. On balance it is probably healthier if religious conservatives are inside the political system than if they operate as insurgents and provocateurs on the outside. Better they should write anti-abortion planks into the Republican platform than bomb abortion clinics. The same is true of the left. The clashes over civil rights and Vietnam turned into street warfare partly because activists were locked out by their own party establishments and had to fight, literally, to be heard. When Michael Moore receives a hero's welcome at the Democratic National Convention, we moderates grumble; but if the parties engage fierce activists while marginalizing tame centrists, that is probably better for the social peace than the other way around.

In the end what may matter most is not that the parties be moderate but that they be competitive—which America's parties are, in spades. Politically speaking, our fifty-fifty America is a divisive, rancorous place. The rest of the world should be so lucky.

A Lobbyist's Progress: Jack Abramoff and the End of the Republican Revolution

Andrew Ferguson

The Weekly Standard | December 20, 2004

They tend to keep a low media profile (if you read the article that follows, you'll understand why), but Washington, D.C.'s large network of lobbyists are the grease that lubricates the gears of our nation's capital. Essentially, their job is to help their clients, usually special interests of some sort, to get favorable treatment by the government—and the good ones get paid handsomely to do it.

This Weekly Standard *report is a rueful meditation on how Washington's Republicans have become just as compromised by the spoils of power as the Democrats ever were. It's also a primer on the mechanics of lobbying, and a cautionary tale of what happens when a lobbyist spins out of control. In this case, the protagonist, Jack Abramoff, is of special interest because of his close links to House Majority Leader Tom DeLay (who has taken expense-paid junkets arranged by Abramoff—a link that has prompted the Democrats to accuse DeLay of unethical behavior), and his friendship with Grover Norquist—now a leading force in the conservative movement—that dates back to their days as College Republicans. It was these sorts of connections that helped Abramoff rise to the top of his profession—until he got a little too greedy over some Indian casinos, and got himself hauled in front of the Senate Committee of Indian Affairs along with his colleague, Michael Scanlon (DeLay's former press secretary).*

Still, as Ferguson notes, "in the capital's lobbying culture, what's really fascinating isn't what's exceptional but what's typical. For apart from its price tag, which even lobbyists agree was excessive, the lobbying effort launched by Abramoff and Scanlon . . . was perfectly ordinary. Indeed, it's an almost textbook case of the sly manipulation of federal power on behalf of those who are willing to pay up— with the middlemen as the ultimate beneficiaries." . . .

In honor of the tenth anniversary of the fabled Republican Revolution—for precisely a decade has flown by since Republicans took control of the House of Representatives, following forty years of Democratic darkness— let us pause from our noise-making and silly-hat-wearing to ponder the story of Jack Abramoff and Michael Scanlon. They have lately been much in the news.

Abramoff was until recently a registered lobbyist, and Scanlon offers himself as a public affairs specialist, but more precisely they are what Republicans in Washington used to call "Beltway Bandits," profiteers who manipulate the power of big government on behalf of well-heeled people who pay them tons of money to do so. Sometime around 1995, Republicans in Washington stopped using the term "Beltway Bandits."

But they still exist, and how, and if you're a bandito of the Beltway variety, being "in the news" is a delicate matter. You want to be in the news, but not too much in the news. When the low-circulation, high-impact Washington magazine *National Journal* labels you, as it did Abramoff a couple years ago, "an object of awe on K Street," then that's exactly the kind of news you want to be in. (K Street, in downtown Washington, is where all the lobbyists have offices, just as securities traders used to be confined to Wall Street and drunks to Skid Row.) And when the low-circulation, high-impact Capitol Hill newspaper *Roll Call* underscores your close connections to powerful House Republicans, as it did for Scanlon a while back, that's excellent news to be in, too. But when, on the other hand, the high-circulation, high-impact *Washington Post* runs stories underneath headlines that say: "Lobbyist Quits as Firm Probes Work with Tribe," followed by "Ex-Lobbyist is Focus of Widening Investigations," well, then, you know you are too much in the wrong kind of news.

For Abramoff and Scanlon, the wrong kind of news has only intensified in the last couple months. In September and then in November, the Senate Committee on Indian Affairs held hearings on the pair's relations with a half-dozen Indian tribes who had hired them. Indian tribes have become big clients on K Street, believe it or not. In 1988, Congress authorized, and then established regulations over, casino gambling on Indian reservations. The result, from a lobbyist's perspective, couldn't have been happier. Gambling had two main effects. It made some tribes very rich—Indian casinos bring in as much as $30 million a month—and it permanently entangled those gambling tribes with a Washington bureaucracy that seemed, to an outsider anyway, at once all-powerful and impossible to understand. In hopes of not getting squashed by the sozzled federal giant it's gotten in bed with, a gambling tribe eager to defend its interests may spend $20,000 a month or more to retain the services of a Washington lobbying firm.

At least, that's the way it looked until the Abramoff story broke in the *Post*, and the world discovered that the $20,000 figure was for chumps. Several things are striking about the Abramoff story, as it has unfolded in the *Post* and in the documents released through the Senate investigation. One is the sheer lusciousness of the numbers involved. First-tier lobbying firms in Washington might bill a total of $20 million in fees a year. The Senate committee has reported that Abramoff and his partner Scanlon split as much as $82 million in fees from six tribes over three years. That figure doesn't include the additional millions that Abramoff told tribes to donate to charitable and political organizations. Moreover, these fees were collected during a period when Congress was considering scarcely any Indian-related legislation at all.

And then there is the identity of the people involved. For 25 years Abramoff has been a key figure in the conservative movement that led to the 1994 Republican Revolution, which once promised "to drain the swamp" in Washington, D.C. Abramoff is a mentor and close friend to the prominent activist Grover Norquist, and to Ralph Reed, founder of the Christian Coalition, highly successful political operative, and self-advertised adviser to the Bush White House. Both Reed and Norquist, in fact, lead organizations that were recipients of the tribes' generosity, through Abramoff's intercession.

All of these factors combine to make Abramoff's story worth pondering. They also go a long way towards explaining why Republicans in Washington stopped using the term "Beltway Bandits" sometime around 1995.

Jack Abramoff is 45. He grew up in Beverly Hills, son of a Diners Club executive, and went to college at Brandeis. A shared passion for conservative activism—not the most common passion on campuses in Massachusetts—let him to a friendship with Norquist, a Harvard graduate student. Together they organized students for the 1980 Reagan campaign in their state, which Reagan, miraculously, carried. After graduation they launched a campaign to take over a sleepy, Washington-based subsidiary of the Republican National Committee called College Republicans. Abramoff spent $10,000 of personal money winning the chairmanship. With Norquist as executive director, he transformed CR into a "right-wing version of a communist cell—complete with purges of in-house dissenters and covert missions to destroy the enemy left," as Nina Easton puts it in her useful history, *Gang of Five*.

Easton's sensibility may seem a bit delicate, but she well captures the revolutionary mood among the young idealists who came to Washington after Reagan's inauguration in 1981, among whom Abramoff and Norquist were the loudest and most energetic. They were soon joined by Reed, freshly graduated from the University of Georgia and looking even younger then than he does now, if you can imagine. Borrowing tactics from their leftist counterparts, College Republicans were particularly good at dramatizing the causes of limited government and anti-communism. When the Soviet Union invaded Poland, they swarmed the Polish Embassy in Washington and burned the Soviet flag for news cameras. They staged counter-demonstrations to those put on by the useful idiots of the nuclear-freeze movement. At late-night gatherings they sang age-old anarchist anthems that Norquist had taught them. You could tell a College Republican by the buttons he wore: "There's no government like no government," for example.

After College Republicans, Abramoff brought the same theatricality to his other activist jobs. "His greatest strength was his audacity," says the writer and political consultant Jeff Bell, who worked with Abramoff and Norquist at a Reaganite group called Citizens for America in the mid-1980s. "He and Grover were just wildmen. They always were willing to throw the long ball. Jack's speciality was the spectacular—huge, larger-than-life, almost Hollywood-like events." As the group's chairman, Abramoff staged his greatest spectacular in 1985, a "summit meeting" of freedom-fighters from around the world, held in a remote corner of the African bush. Among the summiteers was Adolfo Calero, a leader of the Nicaraguan contras, and playing host was a favorite of the 1980s conservative movement, the Angolan rebel Jonas Savimbi, who fought bravely against the Cuban occupiers of his country but turned out, alas, to be a Maoist cannibal. In her book Easton reports that both Abramoff and Norquist, who had been hired as Abramoff's assistant, were later dismissed from CFA for "lavish spending."

As the Reagan years wound down, the conservative movement's anti-communism, and the Reagan Doctrine it had encouraged, were being vindicated by the collapse of the Soviet Empire. Abramoff left Washington to become, improbably, a movie producer. In 1989, he produced *Red Scorpion*, an action thriller about anti-communist guerillas fighting and sweating in the African jungle. ("He's a human killing machine," said the advertisements. "Taught to stalk. Trained to kill. Programmed to destroy.

He's played by their rules . . . Until now.") The movie starred Dolph Lund-gren, who before drifting into total obscurity was a poor man's Jean Claude Van Damme, who was a poor man's Arnold Schwarzenegger. It was later reported that *Red Scorpion* was financed in part by the white South African government, which had also subsidized Savimbi, as well as an interna-tional student conference Abramoff had put on in the mid-1980s. *Red Scor-pion* was followed by *Red Scorpion 2.* According to jellyneckr, a reviewer on the Internet Movie Database website, *Red Scorpion 2* is even better than *Red Scorpion.*

The Republican victory in 1994 brought Abramoff back to Washington. "A year ago," *National Journal* wrote in 1995, "Abramoff was an obscure motion picture producer . . . and a political activist with a reputation only in the conservative camp. But in a Washington turned upside down by the 1994 elections, Abramoff has emerged as one of the biggest winners." The way a winner knows he's won is by cashing in his chips, and the press enthusiastically listed Abramoff's chips—the newly powerful Republican officeholders with whom he had longstanding ties, including Newt Gin-grich and Tom DeLay. "He has access to DeLay," DeLay's press secretary helpfully told *National Journal.* That's the good way of being in the news again—the kind of quote, as Abramoff was soon to discover, that's worth tens of thousands of dollars in fees.

Abramoff joined the law-lobbying firm of Preston Gates Ellis & Rou-velas Meeds (the name partner Gates is the father of Bill Gates) and later moved to the firm Greenberg Traurig. In both offices he was assisted by Scanlon, who had worked for DeLay as press secretary. Scanlon eventually left Greenberg to strike out on his own, relying on Abramoff for business referrals. And from the start there was a lot of business to go around. One of Abramoff's greatest early successes as a lobbyist was won on behalf of the casino-owning Choctaw tribe. Indian casino profits had been exempted from taxation, and when some in Congress suggested taxing them, just as the government taxes casino profits from Las Vegas and elsewhere, Abramoff managed to convince the Republican leadership that such a tax would be an outrageous violation of Republican principle. The issue nicely demonstrated the elasticity of conservative ideology when properly deployed. Any tax of any kind on Indians, Abramoff argued, would contra-dict the anti-tax position that had become a marker of House Republicans. The Indian reservations, bolstered by gambling, could serve instead as "free market laboratories"—a "low-tax, unregulated, sovereign economic model for communities around the nation." Moreover, Abramoff told his fellow Republicans, casino profits would wean Indians from their unhealthy dependence on Washington.

Abramoff's ingenuity quickly earned him a reputation as the premier lobbyist for Indians in Washington—though he only worked for casino-owning tribes, who were, after all, the only "free market laboratories" that could afford Washington lobbyists. He regularly arranged fact-finding trips for congressmen and their staffs to the casinos, especially those with golf courses.

Abramoff told the *Post* earlier this year that those Indian tribes "are engaged in the same ideological and philosophical efforts that conservatives are—basically saying, 'Look, we want to be left alone.' " Abramoff was echoing his old friend Norquist, who has dubbed the conservative movement, in its present manifestation, "the leave us alone coalition." Norquist has worked on behalf of casino tribes, too, and they have donated generously to his group Americans for Tax Reform, sometimes at Abramoff's insistence. And we should add that the tribes don't want to be left alone, you know, *all* the time. Abramoff has also bragged of the millions of dollars he has snagged for his Indian clients, in the form of more conventional pork-barrel appropriations for roads, schools, water projects, sewers, and the rest.

In Beltway lobbying, as elsewhere, diversification is the key to success. It is essential for a lobbyist like Abramoff—who boasts of his passion for ideology—to stretch his conservative arguments over as wide a variety of clients as possible. Channel One, the for-profit TV channel that pumps commercial-laden programming into public school classrooms, hired both Reed and Abramoff in the late 1990s to defend it against conservative criticism. Abramoff dismissed the channel's right-wing opponents for pursuing an "anti-free-market, anticommercial agenda." The textile industry in the Marianas islands, a U.S. protectorate, hired Abramoff when congressional Democrats tried to impose U.S. labor regulations on its sweatshops, where low-wage workers imported from China and the Philippines produced garments marked "Made in the USA." Abramoff arranged trips to the islands, where there was also a nice golf course. Among other congressional Republicans and Democrats, DeLay toured the sweatshops and pronounced the islands "a perfect Petri dish of capitalism." Before 9/11, Abramoff lobbied for the dictatorships in Pakistan and Malaysia. After

9/11, according to *National Journal,* he signed up as lobbyist for the General Council for Islamic Banks and Financial Institutions, a consortium of banks that operate according to *sharia,* or Islamic law.

None of this lucrative representation—I hurry to note—would raise an eyebrow among the capital's well-heeled political class. Democratic lobbyists have fattened off Washington for years. Abramoff was merely the first Republican to discover that pretending to advance the interests of conservative small-government could, for a lobbyist, be as insanely lucrative as pretending to advance the interests of liberal big-government; in reality, of course, lobbyists advance their own interests above all. It helped, too, when conservatives revised their philosophical commitments to embrace the nonsensical neologism "big government conservatism." Given this ideological elasticity, it was only a matter of time before Republicans achieved "parity" on K Street as they have in the country at large. No K Street firm can long endure without being half-Republican—thanks in large part to the exertions of Jack Abramoff.

Not surprisingly, then, it took an outsider to notice something fishy about the dealings between Indians and Abramoff.

In September 2003, a reporter for the daily *Town Talk* in Alexandria, Louisiana, wrote a story about a local Indian tribe, the Louisiana Coushattas, who run a casino in nearby Kinder. An internal audit, the reporter learned, had revealed that the tribe had been spending an inordinate sum on Washington lobbyists. In one year's time, they had paid $13.7 million to Michael Scanlon's firm Capitol Campaign Strategies, another half million to a "think tank" called the American International Center, $2.4 million to Abramoff's firm Greenberg Traurig, and another $485,000 to Abramoff himself. Though the tribe's casino generates about $300 million a year, the tribal government was running a $40 million deficit, and no tribe member, according to the newspaper, could quite explain what the lobbyists had done for the money. With a follow-up a month later, the *Town Talk* story found its way into the e-mail queues of Washington lobbyists early this year, and eventually inspired the stories in the *Washington Post,* which inspired the Senate hearings.

Abramoff and Scanlon appeared at the hearings separately, and both refused to answer questions, invoking the Fifth Amendment. True to

Senate traditions, however, their presence at the hearings was not really meant to elicit information; the two witnesses were there mostly so senators could browbeat them before the television cameras. "I don't know how you go to sleep at night," said Sen. Kent Conrad, in a typical rebuke.

In truth, Conrad's point was well taken. The story lines put together by the committee's investigators, and especially the e-mails and the memos they released as evidence, show a riot of presumption and greed on the part of Abramoff, Scanlon, and Reed. The activities covered by the committee involved six tribes. With variations from tribe to tribe, Abramoff and Scanlon's basic method in dealing with clients was this: Abramoff would urge a tribe to hire Scanlon for assistance in a "grass-roots" activity— helping to organize a tribal election, for example, or ginning up a letter-writing campaign to state legislators or congressional lawmakers. Scanlon would usually subcontract out the work, and collect the fees. These in turn would be shared with Abramoff—unbeknownst to the tribes or to Abramoff's own firm. Over three years, the tribes paid at least $66 million to Scanlon's firm, Capitol Campaign Strategies. At least $21 million of that was then routed to Abramoff.

"Jack Abramoff owed the tribes he represented a duty to disclose his financial stake in the multimillion dollar contract he was steering Michael Scanlon's way," said Sen. John McCain in an opening statement. McCain's dudgeon assumes that there is a code of honor among lobbyists that Abramoff had somehow breached. If such a code exists, it's not often consulted. There was, however, a legal logic behind the secrecy. By law anyone who spends at least 20 percent of his billable hours meeting with government officials on behalf of a client is a lobbyist. (Hence the wry Washington axiom: A lobbyist spends 20 percent of his time lobbying the government, 80 percent lobbying his client.) Lobbyists must publicly disclose their clients and fees. Abramoff is a lobbyist.

But Scanlon is not. He is a "political consultant," a "public affairs strategist," a "media relations specialist"—in Washington these phony-baloney job titles are interchangeable. As such he doesn't have to disclose his fees and clients. By directing Abramoff's clients to hire Scanlon, who then charged them enormous fees, the two men could make as much money as possible without having to disclose anything.

One 2003 e-mail from Abramoff to his accountant and released by the committee gave a small example of how the swag was divided:

"I think I understand what he [Scanlon] did. We received $5 million into CCS . . . he divided the $5 million into three piles: $1 M for actual expenses, and $2 M for each of us."

It helped, too, that there were several conduits the money could pass through. The most colorful, and mysterious, of these was Scanlon's think tank, the American International Center, into which the tribes paid millions of dollars. The prestige of real think tanks in Washington, quasi-academic research groups like the American Enterprise Institute and the Brookings Institution, has greatly increased the popularity of the term. Almost anything can be called a think tank nowadays. Scanlon started his in 2001. It's set up in a large house he bought (for $4.2 million, according to the *Post*) two blocks from the ocean, at the resort community of Rehoboth Beach, Delaware. A reporter for the *National Journal* visited its website shortly before it was taken down. The AIC, said the website, had the "global minded purpose of enhancing the methods of empowerment for territories, commonwealths, and sovereign nations in possession of and within the United States." Further, it sought "to expand the parameters of international discourse in an effort to leverage the combined power of world intellect." Living in the beach house were the two resident scholars: David Grosh had been named Rehoboth's "lifeguard of the year" in 1995, and Brian Mann, the *Post* reported, is a former yoga instructor.

Another recipient of the tribes' generosity was the Capital Athletic Foundation, a charitable organization founded by Abramoff and used to support a private boys school he opened in Maryland, the Eshkol Academy. Both Eshkol and the foundation are now defunct. When one of Abramoff's tribes, the Tigua of El Paso, Texas, had trouble paying its retainer, the lobbyist came up with an innovative solution—a "brand new deal," as he put it to the tribe's representative, Marc Schwartz. Abramoff suggested an "elderly legacy program": The tribe would take out term life insurance on its oldest members, naming the school as beneficiary. As the oldsters dropped off and the money rolled in, the school would pay Abramoff's retainer out of the proceeds. "Once the group of tribal elders has completed [a medical] exam and are accepted by the insurance company," Abramoff explained in a memo, "the financing phase will commence immediately." According to Schwartz, the elders of the tribe declined the arrangement. Too morbid, they said.

• • •

Because Abramoff and Scanlon have not yet had a chance to present their rebuttal to the committee's evidence, it's still unclear what services they performed in exchange for the millions they received. But the committee was able to illuminate one original mystery—why the Louisiana Coushatta tribe hired the pair to begin with.

As we've seen, Abramoff prized casino tribes as "low-tax sovereign economic models." But even "laboratories of free enterprise" don't like competition. Often tribes hired Abramoff to make sure that other tribes did not develop their own sovereign economic models which might drain away business. When three rival tribes in neighboring Texas opened casinos, drawing customers away from their casino in Kinder, the Louisiana Coushattas hired Abramoff and Scanlon. Their idea was to prod Texas Republicans to shut down the new casinos, either through the Texas legislature or the courts. Scanlon promised to launch a "grass-roots campaign" to pressure the Texans.

And he enlisted Abramoff's old colleague Ralph Reed to help. Since their salad days together in College Republicans, Reed had learned to prosper in politics, as Abramoff had. His firm, Century Strategies, specializes in "Strategic Business Development Assistance, Organizational Development, Direct Mail and Voter Contact Services, Fundraising Management, Research and Analysis, Creative Media Planning, Public and Media Relations, and List Management and Procurement." Whatever these terms may mean, they're expensive.

Though not yet as rich as his mentor, Reed is far more famous, and far more careful with his reputation. As a pillar among conservative evangelicals and an ardent foe of gambling, Reed refuses to take casino tribes as clients. The tribe therefore hired Scanlon, who hired Reed. Century Strategies was paid at least $4.2 million to organize a grass-roots campaign— working phone banks, writing letters—to shut down the Texas tribes' casinos and, as Reed put it in one e-mail, "get our pastors riled up." Half of the $4.2 million sum received by Reed's firm came from the American International Center, the think tank on the beach. Sure enough, in February 2002, the Texas casinos were shuttered by a Texas court, acting pursuant to an order sought by the Texas attorney general John Cornyn (now a U.S. senator).

The Texas tribes were devasted, of course, but Abramoff was energized. Shortly after the court order, through an intermediary, he approached one of the tribes, the Tigua of El Paso, offering to use his lobbying magic in Washington to get their casino reopened. The Tigua had no way of knowing that Abramoff and Scanlon had been involved in the campaign to shut down their casino.

On February 6, 2002, Abramoff e-mailed Scanlon under the header *I'm on the phone with Tigua:* "Fire up the jet, baby, we're going to El Paso!"

Scanlon responded: "I want all their MONEY!!!"

A few days later, Abramoff, in a more sober mood, addressed a proposal to a Tigua representative via e-mail. "Our motivations for this representation are manifold," Abramoff wrote. He wanted to protect "tribal sovereignty," he said. "While we are Republicans and normally want all Republicans to prevail in electoral challenges, this ill-advised decision on the part of the Republican leadership in Texas must not stand. And we intend to right this using, in part, Republican leaders from Washington."

Abramoff himself offered to help the Tigua for free—on two conditions. One, that "if we succeed, we can expect to have a long-term relationship with the tribe by representing their interests on the federal level"; and two, that the Tigua hire Michael Scanlon for "grass-roots lobbying." "He's the best there is in the business." Cost: $4.2 million.

The e-mails released by the committee, with their schoolyard vulgarities and adolescent chest-thumping, titillated Washington for days after excerpts were published in the *Post* this fall. (Abramoff to Reed: "I'd love us to get our mitts on that moolah!!") And the brazenness of the Abramoff-Scanlon maneuver with the Tigua—pushing the state government to shut down the tribe's casino, then offering to lobby the federal government to reopen it—was a jolt even to the most hardened Washington observers. (The e-mails and other documents can be seen in their entirety on the committee's website: www.indian.senate.gov)

Yet as often happens in the capital's lobbying culture, what's really fascinating isn't what's exceptional but what's typical. For apart from its price tag, which even lobbyists agree was excessive, the lobbying effort launched by Abramoff and Scanlon for the Tigua was perfectly ordinary. Indeed, it's an almost textbook case of the sly manipulation of federal power on behalf of those who are willing to pay up—with the middlemen as the ultimate beneficiaries.

On February 18, 2002, Scanlon and Abramoff flew by chartered jet to present the Tigua their proposal for "Operation Open Doors." In its breathless tone, its bogus self-confidence, its pompous phrasing, the document is a towering monolith of Beltway Baloney.

> The singular objective of our strategy is to open the doors of the Speaking Rock Casino within the next 4 months. . . . This political operation will result in a Majority of both federal chambers either becoming close friends of the tribe or fearing the tribe in a very short period of time. Simply put you need 218 friends in the U.S. House and 51 Senators on your side very quickly, and we will do that through both love and fear.

The idea was to persuade some accomodating lawmaker to attach a few sentences to an otherwise unrelated piece of legislation. The language would alter the tribe's federal charter, override the ruling of the Texas court, and make the tribe once again eligible to operate a casino.

And yet! "Make no mistake: the true value of this strategy is not the legislation. Quiet [sic] frankly the legislative solution itself is not what one would call rocket science." Generating "political support," however, is rocket science—and easily as expensive as anything NASA ever dreamed up. It involved constant polls, activated phone banks, and two (2) "fully customized databases"—one "Grassroots Database" and one "Qualitative Research Database"—"containing every piece of information fathomable." According to the committee, Abramoff and Scanlon also provided the tribe with a list of political "targets"—Republican congressmen, senators, political action committees, and organizations, such as Norquist's Americans for Tax Reform and Abramoff's Capital Athletic Foundation, to which they insisted the tribe give money. "If you execute this strategy in its entirety, your doors will be open and gaming [Indian for *gambling*] will return in the immediate future."

A few days after Abramoff and Scanlon's presentation to the Tigua, the El Paso newspaper ran a story about the closing of their casino: "450 Casino Employees Officially Terminated."

Via e-mail, Scanlon sent the story to Abramoff. "This is the front page of todays paper while they will be voting on our plan!"

Abramoff fired back: "Is life great or what!!!!"

But some things in life are too good to be true. Though the tribal council approved the plan and paid the money, in the end the Tigua "fix" didn't work out. The rocket science failed. For one thing, Scanlon's firm farmed out the database work to a subcontractor who charged less than $100,000, even though records obtained by the committee show that Scanlon charged the tribe $1.8 million for it. But even the sub-rocket science, the legislative solution, didn't work. It was not for lack of trying.

First Abramoff and Scanlon had to find a bill on which they could tack their "language." Abramoff e-mailed a subordinate: "I need to know asap which piece of legislation are likely to be passed through both House and Senate in the next three months. . . . How do we find silly little things which are moving which can have some technical corrections language attached?" In March 2002 they settled on an election reform bill, a silly little thing sponsored by Rep. Bob Ney, another onetime revolutionary from the House Republican Class of '94 and now firmly settled in the House leadership. Ney had also, just the month before, seen his chief of staff take a lucrative lobbying job with . . . Jack Abramoff. Abramoff e-mailed Scanlon the good news: "Just met with Ney!!! We're f'ing gold!!!!! He's going to do Tigua."

In a statement, Ney now says he was "duped by Jack Abramoff." But by all accounts, including one last week in *Roll Call*, it was a curious duping.

Ney says Abramoff had assured him that the Senate sponsor of the election reform bill, Sen. Christopher Dodd, would support the inclusion of the Tigua language. Indeed, Scanlon had already paid off three Democratic lobbyists, including a member of Dodd's campaign finance committee, to persuade Dodd to accept the insertion. In April, Abramoff took Tigua officials to meet Ney. The meeting lasted nearly two hours. Ney, one of the Tigua representatives testified, "was extremely animated about Mr. Abramoff and his ability as a representative lobbyist in the city [and] he had tremendous sympathy for the plight that the tribe had gone through." A few days later, the Tigua donated $30,000 to PACs controlled by Ney.

Then the Tigua got stingy. They declined to pay $50,000 to finance a skybox—all good lobbyists have skyboxes—for Abramoff at a Washington sports arena. In June, Abramoff e-mailed the Tigua again: "Our friend . . . asked if you could help (as in cover) a Scotland golf trip for him and some staff (his committee chief of staff) for August. The trip will be quite expensive (we did this for another member—you know who) 2 years ago. Let me know if you guys could do $50k . . . they would probably do the trip through the Capital Athletic Foundation as an educational mission." Already short of cash, the Tigua declined.

In July, Ney heard from Dodd that the senator would not support the inclusion of the Tigua language. "I had been misled by Jack Abramoff," Ney has said in his statement. "The matter was then closed from my perspective." A week later, however, he and the lobbyist had patched things up. Ney flew to Scotland on a charted jet with Abramoff, another lobbyist, an official of the General Services Administration, and their friend Ralph Reed. They played golf at St. Andrews. Abramoff had found someone else to pay for the trip. The Tigua never did get their "fix."

A funny thing happens whenever you talk to lobbyists, especially those with Indian casino clients, about the Senate investigation of Abramoff and Scanlon. None of them will talk for the record, of course, but they are surprisingly unanimous that all this unpleasantness will soon blow over.

"I think the story has about run its course," one told me the other day. "Really, after you get past Jack's excesses—which are Jack's—there's not much there."

"I'm hearing there won't be any more hearings," another told me. "It's done. They've nailed Jack. End of story."

This is just wishful thinking, though. The new chairman of the Indian Affairs committee, Sen. McCain, has made it clear he has much more material to ventilate in hearings that will continue next year. But the lobbyists' defensiveness is understandable. Stripped of its peculiar grossness, Abramoff's Indian story really is just another story of business as usual in the world of Washington lobbying, and the longer hearings like McCain's drag on, the more likely it is that even the Republican "grass-roots" will wise up. That closed, parasitic culture of convenience—with its revolving doors, front groups, pay-offs, expense-account comfort, and ideological cover stories—is as essential to the way Republican Washington works, ten years after the Revolution, as it ever was to Democratic Washington.

In an interview about Abramoff for National Public Radio a couple months ago, his old friend Norquist said, "To this day, I can't find anything he did or he's accused of doing that's illegal, immoral, or fattening." A few days later I came across another quote from Norquist, from a profile of Abramoff in the *National Journal* in 1995, soon after Abramoff had announced he would become a lobbyist, back when the Revolution was still young.

"What the Republicans need is 50 Jack Abramoffs," Norquist said. "Then this becomes a different town."

It was a bold statement, typical for the time, but even then it raised a question we now know the answer to: Would the Republicans change Washington, or would it be the other way around?

The Unregulated Offensive
Jeffrey Rosen

The New York Times Magazine | April 17, 2005

Following the surprise announcement this summer that Justice Sandra Day O'Connor will be stepping down—and with Chief Justice William Rehnquist widely expected to announce his own retirement sometime in 2005 as well—George W. Bush will have a chance to make at least one and possibly two appointments to the Supreme Court this year. O'Connor's replacement will mark the first change on the court since 1994—the second longest such stretch in U.S. history. While it's impossible to guess who the new justice might be, there's a good chance that his or her judicial philosophy will have been influenced by a growing trend in conservative jurisprudence: the Constitution in Exile movement, which aims to drastically scale back the federal government's role in running the country. In this article, Jeffrey Rosen, a law professor at George Washington University, reports on how the movement came into being, and how its adherents hope to reshape America. . . .

I. Justice Thomas's Other Controversy
If you think back to Clarence Thomas's Supreme Court confirmation hearings in 1991, what most likely comes to mind are the explosive allegations of sexual harassment made by the law professor Anita Hill. Years from now, however, when observers of the court look back on the hearings, they may well focus on a clash that preceded Hill's accusations—an acrimonious exchange that few remember today.

Early in the hearings, Joseph Biden, the Delaware Democrat who was chairman of the Senate Judiciary Committee, voiced a concern about Thomas's judicial philosophy. In particular, he singled out a speech that Thomas gave in 1987 in which he expressed an affinity for the ideas of legal scholars like Richard A. Epstein. A law professor at the University of Chicago, Epstein was notorious in legal circles for his thesis that many of the laws underpinning the modern welfare state are unconstitutional. Thomas tried to assure Biden that he was interested in ideas like Epstein's only as a matter of "political theory" and that he would not actually implement them as a Supreme Court justice. Biden, apparently unpersuaded, picked up a copy of Epstein's 1985 book, *Takings: Private Property and the Power of Eminent Domain,* and theatrically waved it in the air. Anyone who embraced the book's extreme thesis, he seemed to be suggesting, was unfit to sit on the court.

At the time, it was impossible to know whether Biden was right to worry. He was surely right, though, that Epstein was promoting a legal philosophy far more radical in its implications than anything entertained by Antonin Scalia, then, as now, the court's most irascible conservative. As Epstein sees it, all individuals have certain inherent rights and liberties, including "economic" liberties, like the right to property and, more crucially, the right to part with it only voluntarily. These rights are violated any time an individual is deprived of his property without compensation—when it is stolen, for example, but also when it is subjected to governmental regulation that reduces its value or when a government fails to provide greater security in exchange for the property it seizes. In Epstein's view, these libertarian freedoms are not only defensible as a matter of political philosophy but are also protected by the United States Constitution. Any government that violates them is, by his lights, repressive. One such government, in Epstein's worldview, is our government. When Epstein gazes across America, he sees a nation in the chains of minimum-wage laws and zoning regulations. His theory calls for the country to be deregulated in a manner not seen since before Franklin D. Roosevelt's New Deal.

After Thomas joined the Supreme Court, Biden's warnings seemed prescient. In 1995, echoes of Epstein's ideas could be clearly heard in one of Thomas's opinions. By a 5-4 majority in United States v. Lopez, the court struck down a federal law banning guns in school zones, arguing that the law fell outside Congress's constitutional power to regulate interstate commerce.

Lopez was a judicial landmark: it was the first time since the New Deal that the court had limited the power of the federal government on those grounds. Thomas, who sided with the majority, chose to write a separate opinion in which he suggested that even his conservative colleagues had not gone far enough. The real problem, he wrote, was not just with the law at hand but with the larger decision of the court during the New Deal to abandon the judicial doctrines of the 19th century that established severe limits on the government's power. He assailed his liberal colleagues for characterizing "the first 150 years of this Court's case law as a 'wrong turn.'" He continued, "If anything, the 'wrong turn' was the Court's dramatic departure in the 1930s from a century and a half of precedent."

Thomas did not cite Epstein directly in his opinion. But to anyone familiar with Epstein's writings, the similarities were striking. Indeed, Thomas's argument closely resembled one Epstein had made eight years earlier in "The Proper Scope of the Commerce Power" in the *Virginia Law Review*—so closely, in fact, that Sanford Levinson, a liberal law professor at the University of Texas, accused Thomas of outright intellectual theft. ("The ordinary standards governing attribution of sources—the violation of which constitutes plagiarism—seem not to apply in Justice Thomas's chambers," Levinson wrote in the *Texas Law Review*.) Biden's fear that Epstein's ideas might be written into law had apparently been realized. And the fear would continue to be realized in other courts throughout the '90s as a small but energetic set of lower-court judges, sympathetic to libertarian arguments, tried to strike down aspects of the Clean Water Act, the Endangered Species Act and other laws, challenging powers of the federal government that had come to be widely accepted during the second half of the 20th century.

Chief Justice William Rehnquist is expected to announce his resignation sometime this year, perhaps before the end of the court's current term in June. Rehnquist's retirement would create at least one confirmation hearing for a new justice, and two hearings if President George W. Bush chooses to nominate one of the current justices to be chief justice. At the same time, there is a political battle looming in the Senate over seven federal appellate-court candidates whose nominations were blocked by Senate Democrats during Bush's first term but who were renominated by the president after his reelection. Many liberals and centrists worry, and many conservatives hope, that the doctrine favored by these judicial candidates is originalism, the stated constitutional theory of Scalia. Originalists don't like interpreting the Constitution in light of present-day social developments and are generally skeptical of constitutional rights—like the right to have an abortion—that don't appear explicitly in the text of the Constitution. At least in theory, those in the originalist camp champion judicial restraint and states' rights.

But as Thomas's presence on the court suggests, it is perhaps just as likely that the next justice—or chief justice—will be sympathetic to the less well-known but increasingly active conservative judicial movement that Epstein represents. It is sometimes known as the Constitution in Exile movement, after a phrase introduced in 1995 by Douglas Ginsburg, a judge on the United States Court of Appeals for the D.C. Circuit. (Ginsburg is probably best known as the Supreme Court nominee, put forward by Ronald Reagan, who withdrew after confessing to having smoked marijuana.) By "Constitution in Exile," Ginsburg meant to identify legal doctrines that established firm limitations on state and federal power before the New Deal. Unlike many originalists, most adherents of the Constitution in Exile movement are not especially concerned about states' rights or judicial deference to legislatures; instead, they encourage judges to strike down laws on behalf of rights that don't appear explicitly in the Constitution. In addition to the scholars who articulate the movement's ideals and the judges who sympathize with them, the Constitution in Exile is defended by a litigation arm, consisting of dozens of self-styled "freedom-based" public-interest law firms that bring cases in state and federal courts, including the Supreme Court.

Critics of the movement note, with some anxiety, that it has no shortage of targets. Cass Sunstein, a law professor at the University of Chicago (and a longtime colleague of Epstein's), will soon publish a book on the Constitution in Exile movement called *Fundamentally Wrong*. As Sunstein, who describes himself as a moderate, recently explained to me, success, as the movement defines it, would mean that "many decisions of the Federal Communications Commission, the Environmental Protection Agency, the Occupational Safety and Health Administration and possibly the National Labor Relations Board would be unconstitutional. It would mean that the Social Security Act would not only be under political but also constitutional stress. Many of the Constitution in Exile people think there can't be

independent regulatory commissions, so the Security and Exchange Commission and maybe even the Federal Reserve would be in trouble. Some
applications of the Endangered Species Act and Clean Water Act would be
struck down as beyond Congress's commerce power." In what Sunstein
described as the "extreme nightmare scenario," the right of individuals to
freedom of contract would be so vigorously interpreted that minimum-
wage and maximum-hour laws would also be jeopardized.

Any movement with such ambitious goals must be patient and take the
long view about its prospects for success. Michael Greve, an active
defender of the Constitution in Exile at Washington's conservative American Enterprise Institute, argues that to achieve its goals, the movement
ultimately needs not just one or two but four more Supreme Court justices
sympathetic to its cause, as well as a larger transformation in the overall
political and legal culture. "I think what is really needed here is a fundamental intellectual assault on the entire New Deal edifice," he says. "We
want to withdraw judicial support for the entire modern welfare state. I'd
retire and play golf if I could get there."

II. Glory Days

All restoration fantasies have a golden age, a lost world that is based, at
least to a degree, in historical fact. For the Constitution in Exile movement,
that world is the era of Republican dominance in the United States from
1896 through the Roaring Twenties. Even as the Progressive movement
gathered steam, seeking to protect workers from what it saw as the ravages
of an unregulated market, American courts during that period steadfastly
preserved an ideal of free enterprise, routinely striking down laws that
were said to restrict economic competition.

The most famous constitutional battle of the time was the 1905
Supreme Court case Lochner v. New York, which challenged a law that was
passed by the New York State Legislature, establishing a maximum
number of working hours for bakers. The court struck down the law on the
grounds that it violated the bakers' freedom of contract, which was
arguably, but not explicitly, included in the 14th Amendment's protections
of "liberty" and "property." In a dissenting opinion, Justice Oliver Wendell
Holmes Jr. objected that "The Fourteenth Amendment does not enact Mr.
Herbert Spencer's Social Statics," referring to the celebrated Social Dar-
winist and advocate of laissez-faire economics.

Even after the election of Roosevelt in 1932, the Supreme Court continued to invoke laissez-faire economics to strike down federal laws, including signature New Deal legislation like the National Industrial Recovery Act. In February 1937, Roosevelt threatened to pack the court with justices who would presumably be more deferential to national regulation of the economy. Within a month, the court backed down, upholding a state law imposing a minimum wage for women and minors. (The majority opinion noted that "the unparalleled demands for relief which arose during the recent period of depression" had dislodged old laissez-faire nostrums about the equal bargaining power of workers and employers.) The following year, in the Carolene Products case, the court announced that it would uphold all economic regulations unless no reasonable person could believe them to be rational. Today, the conventional wisdom among liberal and conservative legal thinkers alike is that Lochner was decided incorrectly and that the court's embrace of judicial restraint on economic matters in 1937 was a triumph for democracy.

Members of the Constitution in Exile movement do not share this view. Not long ago, I visited Greve in his office on 17th Street in Washington. Greve, a witty and sardonic libertarian, is the American Enterprise Institute's John G. Searle Scholar (his benefactor was a pharmaceutical magnate), and over the course of a long conversation, he explained that 1937 was, in his opinion, an unmitigated disaster, resulting in the judicial abandonment of constitutional limits on government power that are inherent in the nature of a free society and the creation of a regulatory behemoth. As the administrative state ballooned during the '60s and '70s, judicial deference became even more pervasive: new independent regulatory agencies, from the Environmental Protection Agency to the Federal Communications Commission, began issuing a slew of regulations. To Greve's dismay, much of the regulatory state is politically quite popular; even a Republican Congress, he acknowledged, seems unlikely to roll back most post-New Deal programs and regulations. "Judicial activism will have to be deployed," he said. "It's plain that the idea of judicial deference was a dead end for conservatives from the get-go."

Now 48, Greve was born in Germany and came to embrace a libertarian outlook during his undergraduate years at the University of Hamburg, from which he graduated in 1981. That year, he visited the United States on a Fulbright and ended up at Cornell for a doctorate in government. ("I consider myself a refugee from the welfare state," he said with a chuckle.) His Ph.D. contrasted liberal environmental litigation in Germany and the United States. Greve was frustrated but also impressed by the way that well-financed liberal groups like Ralph Nader's Public Citizen worked in the courts to expand the reach of environmental laws, and he decided that the conservative movement needed to create organizations that would do exactly the opposite.

One of Greve's goals at the American Enterprise Institute is to convince more mainstream conservatives that traditional federalism—which is skeptical of federal, but not state, power—is only half right. In his view, states can threaten economic liberty just as significantly as the federal government. He is still exercised by the lawsuit brought in the '90s by 46 states against the tobacco companies, which resulted in a $246 billion settlement. "Taking the tobacco settlement down would have a huge public impact— that would push you in the right direction," he said, taking a long drag on a cigarette.

Although Greve's liberal critics have argued that resurrecting strict constitutional limits on federal and state powers would essentially mean a return to the unregulated climate of the Gilded Age, Greve emphasized that he doesn't have the Gilded Age in mind. The "modern, vibrant, mobile" and global economy of the 21st century, he argued, is competitive enough to regulate itself in most areas. Though he envisions a role for government in protecting against egregious forms of coercion, force and fraud, all other abuses would be regulated by private agreements among citizens. "I don't think much would be lost if we overturned federal wetlands regulations or if we repealed the Endangered Species Act, just by way of illustration," he said.

Greve expressed cautious optimism that his views will get a sympathetic hearing from some of the federal appellate judges renominated this year by the president. He said he is especially happy that Bush has tapped William Pryor, the former attorney general of Alabama. Greve noted that in one of the big Supreme Court cases involving the limits of federal power, which ultimately invalidated parts of the Violence Against Women Act, Pryor wrote a brief that Greve and other libertarians greatly admired. "Bill Pryor is the key to this puzzle; there's nobody like him," Greve said. "I think he's sensational. He gets almost all of it."

III. The Network

The idea of creating a network of activist conservative litigation groups was proposed in the early '70s by Lewis Powell, a corporate lawyer and future Supreme Court justice. In the years following the defeat of the Goldwater Republicans in 1964, conservatives were casting about for a new political strategy. At the same time, business interests were alarmed by the growth of the regulatory state and, in particular, the marked increase in environmental litigation. In 1971, Powell wrote a landmark memo for the United States Chamber of Commerce urging a counterattack. In addition to encouraging conservatives to develop a systematic and long-term effort to spread their ideas in the media, Powell recommended that conservatives should get over their aversion to judicial activism. "Especially with an activist-minded Supreme Court," he wrote, "the Judiciary may be the most important instrument for social, economic and political change."

At the time, Powell's idea was being echoed in California by a group of conservatives close to Ronald Reagan, who had recently been reelected governor. Reagan, who pledged to reform welfare in his 1970 campaign, set up a task force to do so, headed by his chief of staff, Edwin Meese III. The resulting reforms, which restricted welfare eligibility and cut the state's welfare rolls by more than 250,000 in three years, were attacked in the courts by liberal groups. Reagan's supporters were infuriated that there were no conservative groups that could respond in kind. "The liberals were using the courts," Meese recalled recently during a conversation in his office at the Heritage Foundation in Washington. "We wanted to make it a fair fight."

According to a history of conservative legal activism published by Heritage, *Bringing Justice to the People,* the first person to take up Powell's challenge, in the early 1970s, was John Simon Fluor, a wealthy Reagan supporter. Fluor was upset that environmental groups had managed to delay the construction of the Alaska pipeline and the initiation of offshore drilling in the Gulf of Mexico. After conversations with fellow Reagan supporters, including Meese, Fluor provided the seed money for the Pacific Legal Foundation, the first conservative property-rights litigation shop in the nation. It was staffed with members of the Reagan welfare-reform team and incorporated in 1973.

Other conservative business interests quickly replicated Fluor's model. In 1975, money from the major oil companies helped to create the National Legal Center for the Public Interest, an umbrella organization for several

regional litigation groups. Each group's focus was determined by its loca-
tion. The most influential spinoff group to emerge was the Mountain States
Legal Foundation, financed by the beer magnate Joseph Coors, which was
set up in 1977 to challenge federal land-use and natural-resources regulations, long a source of political resistance in the West. (The foundation's
distinguished alumni of the period include Gale Norton, now secretary of
the interior, and Jon Kyl, now a senator from Arizona.)

Though these conservative groups clearly served the interests of local
businesses, they also attracted a number of libertarians, many of whom
were not always consistent supporters of big business. One of the more
thoughtful of these is Chip Mellor, who joined the Mountain States Legal
Foundation in the late '70s and is now the head of the Institute for Justice,
a libertarian public-interest law firm in Washington. When I visited him
recently at his office near the White House (with an impressive corner view
of the Old Executive Office Building), he spoke engagingly of his youthful
idealism. "I came out of the protests of the 1960s," he recalled, "where I
was dissatisfied with the right and the left." He immersed himself in the
writings of Milton Friedman, the Nobel Prize-winning free-market economist, as well as those of the libertarian novelist Ayn Rand. "It was quite illuminating for me to read Friedman and Rand and to realize that you could
not divorce economic liberty and private property rights from the truly free
individual," Mellor said. "I came to see that societies where those rights
were taken away inevitably led to people impoverished in monetary wealth
and basic liberties."

When he was a law student at the University of Denver, Mellor saw a
recruiting flier for the Mountain States Legal Foundation and was
intrigued by its mention of property rights. Sporting long hair and a han-
dlebar mustache, he showed up without an appointment, but hit it off nevertheless with the foundation's president, James Watt. (Watt would later
achieve renown for his knockdown battles with environmentalists as
Reagan's secretary of the interior.) By 1982, Mellor had risen to become the
acting president of the foundation, and he soon hired a young law-school
graduate and fellow libertarian named Clint Bolick. The two became fast
friends and pledged to sustain their passion for libertarian principles above
partisan politics. (A fierce defender of Clarence Thomas during his nomination battle, Bolick left the Republican Party not long ago in protest over
its anti-immigrant policies and the Iraq war.)

Bolick, whose sunny idealism is hard to resist, still gets indignant when he recalls how Mellor came to part ways with Mountain States. It began when the foundation filed a free-speech lawsuit opposing an exclusive cable-TV franchise granted by the city of Denver to a local businessman who happened to be a friend of Joseph Coors. When Coors resigned from the board to protest the direction that Mountain States seemed to moving in, it set in motion a process that led, a year later, to Mellor being fired. "Chip and I discovered that there is a world of difference between an organization that is pro-business and an organization that is pro-free enterprise," Bolick told me recently. "We learned that some of the influential backers of the movement were more pro-business than pro-free enterprise." After the firing, Mellor said, he and Bolick sat in Mellor's backyard with tears in their eyes. "We pledged this is wrong, and someday we're going to do it right," he said.

They soon got their chance. After stints in Washington with the Reagan administration, in which Mellor was a deputy general counsel at the Department of Energy and Bolick was an assistant at the Equal Employment Opportunity Commission (then led by Clarence Thomas), the two men, in 1991, persuaded Charles Koch, an oil and gas magnate, to give them $350,000 a year in seed money from his private foundation to start the Institute for Justice. (To this day, the institute does not actively solicit corporate financing, and its $6.6 million annual budget is far lower than those of its liberal counterparts, like the A.C.L.U.) Before long, Mellor and Bolick had achieved victories in lower courts for clients without deep pockets. In a series of cases, they challenged state licensing laws that made it hard for small-business entrepreneurs to break into highly regulated professions. Their successful clients included limo drivers in Las Vegas, African-American hair braiders in San Diego and casket sellers in Tennessee. When Mellor gave me a tour of his office, he proudly pointed out an engraved tombstone of appreciation from the casket sellers, which sits in the institute's reception area.

IV. The (Other) Rights of Man

Defending the right of small businessmen to challenge local monopolies may have been necessary and noble, but for the movement it represented a small piece of the puzzle. If Mellor and Bolick and others like them were to transform the Supreme Court's approach to the entire post-New Deal regulatory state—to "resurrect the Constitution in Exile," as Bolick puts it—they would have to develop a sophisticated jurisprudential framework.

Early on, the movement found its intellectual guru in Richard Epstein. In the words of Michael Greve, Epstein is "the intellectual patron saint of everybody in this movement." Like Bolick, Epstein is too much of a libertarian purist to be a party loyalist. ("Our president is a most inconsistent classical liberal, to be charitable," he says. "He's terrible on trade and a huge spender and not completely candid about the parlous situation Social Security is in.") But his devotion to—and influence on—the Constitution in Exile is unsurpassed.

Takings: Private Property and the Power of Eminent Domain, still in print 20 years after its publication, purports to specify the conditions under which government can rightfully impose regulations and taxes that reduce the value of private property. Drawing on the political philosophy of John Locke, Epstein argues that before the existence of government, individuals in what political theorists call the "state of nature" have an inherent right of autonomy, which entitles them to acquire property by dint of their labor and to dispose of it only as they see fit through voluntary transfer of goods. Epstein also maintains that any form of government coercion—including taxation or other forced transfers of wealth—can be reconciled with the principles of personal freedom only if it makes individuals at least as well off as they were before the tax or regulation was imposed. Epstein's key insight, as the Constitution in Exile adherents see it, is that economic regulations are just as coercive as other involuntary wealth transfers. He insists that if the government wants to reduce the value of an individual's property—with zoning restrictions, for example—it has to compensate him for the lost value.

Moving from political theory to constitutional law, Epstein argues that the framers of the United States Constitution recognized these limitations on governmental power in the Takings Clause of the Constitution, which says that "private property" cannot be taken for public use "without just compensation." According to Epstein, the Takings Clause prevents the government from redistributing wealth in any form without appropriate compensation and that a proper understanding of the clause calls into question "many of the heralded reforms and institutions of the 20th century: zoning, rent control, workers' compensation laws, transfer payments," as well as "progressive taxation." Liberal governmental reforms could be sustained,

Epstein argues, only if the government were to compensate individuals for the lost value of their property or to make everyone better off in exchange for their taxes. "This simple theory of governance could be expanded to cover all taxes, all regulations, all shift in liability schemes," Epstein wrote in an intellectual autobiography. "It is also the recipe for striking down the New Deal."

Takings made Epstein a star on the Republican circuit, and he quickly became a favorite intellectual of Edwin Meese, then Reagan's attorney general. (Perhaps inspired by Epstein's arguments, Meese once announced at a Justice Department conference that a "revolution" in economic liberty was a possibility.) In 1986, Meese's office contacted Epstein and asked him to make a scholarly inquiry into Congress's power to regulate interstate commerce. The following year, Epstein published the results of his research in "The Proper Scope of the Commerce Power" (the article that Clarence Thomas would apparently later draw on in his Lopez opinion). Epstein argued that before the New Deal, Congress had the power to regulate only the *channels* of interstate commerce (railroads, for example) but not manufacturing, which doesn't qualify as commerce, or the trade of goods that don't cross state lines. The court, he maintained, was wrong, in its landmark 1942 ruling in Wickard v. Filburn, to allow the federal government to regulate the wheat production of a farmer who grew it for his own consumption. (The government had argued that private consumption was reducing demand for wheat that traveled across state lines.) Though he dutifully noted that his conclusion "seems radical," Epstein called on the court to reverse its error by returning to the more limited pre-New Deal understanding of Congress's power to regulate the economy.

From the outset, Epstein's ideas ran into resistance from traditional judicial conservatives. In October 1984, Epstein clashed publicly with Antonin Scalia, his former colleague at the University of Chicago, in a panel discussion convened at the libertarian Cato Institute. Scalia, speaking first before a standing-room-only crowd, defended the view that judges should restrain themselves from overturning legislation in the name of rights or liberties not clearly and expressly enumerated in the Constitution. "Every era raises its own peculiar threat to constitutional democracy," he said. "The reversal of a half-century of judicial restraint in the economic realm"—Epstein's stated project—"comes within that category." As a traditional federalist, Scalia had his own qualms about the unconstitutionality of unlimited federal power, but he was not in favor of striking down laws in the name of ambiguous and contestable economic rights. Scalia argued that conservatives who had criticized earlier courts, like the Warren court, for liberal judicial activism now faced a "moment of truth." They had to show the courage to reject conservative judicial activism as well.

When Epstein heard what Scalia had to say, he threw away his prepared remarks and delivered a spontaneous attack. Freely admitting that he was questioning the conservative "conventional wisdom," Epstein insisted that judges should be much more aggressive in protecting economic liberty. "There are many blatantly inappropriate statutes that cry out for a quick and easy kill," Epstein said, citing minimum-wage laws and other "legislative regulation of the economy." He excoriated the Supreme Court for refusing to strike these laws down. "One only has to read the opinions of the Supreme Court on economic liberties and property rights to realize that these opinions are intellectually incoherent," he concluded. "Some movement in the direction of judicial activism is clearly indicated."

V. Permanent Exile?

By 1995, the Constitution in Exile movement had reached what appeared to be a turning point. The Republicans had recently taken over both houses of Congress after pledging, in their Contract With America, to rein in the federal government. And the Supreme Court, by rediscovering limits on Congress's power in Lopez, seemed to be answering the call. For conservative advocacy groups and public-interest law firms, the possibilities for litigation looked encouraging.

In a reflection of the new mood, Douglas Ginsburg wrote an article in *Regulation,* a libertarian magazine published by the Cato Institute, calling for the resurrection of "the Constitution in Exile." He noted that for 60 years, proper constitutional limits on government power had been abandoned. "The memory of these ancient exiles, banished for standing in opposition to unlimited government," he wrote with a hint of wistful grandiosity, "is kept alive by a few scholars who labor on in the hope of a restoration, a second coming of the Constitution of liberty—even if perhaps not in their own lifetimes." While not all the leaders of the movement immediately embraced Ginsburg's catch phrase (Edwin Meese says that the phrase Constitution in Exile suggests incorrectly that they have retired from the field of battle), among some legal conservatives it became a rallying cry.

The restoration did not occur. The Rehnquist court in recent years has proved more sympathetic to enforcing limits on Congress's power than any court since 1937: between 1995 and 2003, the court struck down 33 federal laws on constitutional grounds—a higher annual rate than any other Supreme Court in history. But the so-called federalism revolution on the Rehnquist court did not deliver all of what the proponents of the Constitution in Exile had hoped. Every time a lower court appeared to be on the brink of successfully striking down a federal statute with substantial political support, like the Endangered Species Act, the Supreme Court wrote a hedging opinion reassuring the country that the justices intended to challenge Congressional power only at the margins.

"I think we failed," Michael Greve said flatly when I asked him about the past decade of Supreme Court litigation. "There are encouraging signs that with the right strategic moves you can make some headway, until the court looks the principle in the eye and says, 'Oh, my God,' and pulls back." He rattled off a series of property-rights cases in which the Supreme Court had declared (in his mocking paraphrase), "Oh, no, this would be too inconvenient, too constraining for government."

During the current term, the Supreme Court has heard three cases involving questions of economic liberty that, according to Greve, represent the most significant tests in a decade of the power of the Constitution in Exile movement. Kelo v. New London, which was argued before the court in February [2005], concerned Susette Kelo, a woman who sued the city of New London, Connecticut, after it used its power of eminent domain to seize 90 acres of property, including her house. The city planned to turn the parcel over to a private developer in order to increase the tax base and revitalize the city. Chip Mellor's organization, the Institute for Justice, represented Kelo, whom the institute's lawyers had sought out because she seemed like a sympathetic victim. Standing before the justices, Kelo's lawyer, Scott G. Bullock, asked the court to reject the claim that as long as the state could point to a plausible public purpose for the taking of private property (like increasing the tax base), it could appropriate people's homes. Justice Sandra Day O'Connor, however, seemed unimpressed by the suggestion that courts should second-guess the economic judgments of legislatures.

O'Connor and other justices seemed similarly skeptical during the second case, Lingle v. Chevron, U.S.A., which they heard later that same morning. Lingle involved a challenge to a rent-control regulation in

Hawaii. Richard Epstein filed a brief for the Cato Institute that argued that the court should abandon its longstanding presumption that economic regulations are rational and ask instead whether the law, in fact, makes economic sense or is simply a "naked wealth transfer."

Randy Barnett, a libertarian scholar at the Boston University School of Law and the Cato Institute, was the plaintiff's lawyer in Ashcroft v. Raich, another key Supreme Court showdown, which was argued before the court last fall. Raich is a challenge to the federal government's attempt to enforce drug laws that conflict with the effort by California (and 10 other states) to allow the use of medical marijuana. Barnett represented Angela Raich, a woman who suffered from cancer that often confined her to a wheelchair but who said she felt much better after being prescribed medical marijuana. The author of a provocative book, *Restoring the Lost Constitution*, Barnett argues that courts should evaluate economic regulations with a "presumption of liberty" rather than with a presumption of deference. His book identifies a series of regulations that he says the courts should consider constitutionally suspect, from environmental laws to laws forbidding the mere possession of ordinary firearms, therapeutic drugs or pornography. "The court has not really limited Congress's power very much," Barnett says. "But the fact that it was willing to limit it at all has been an important principle. If it now basically throws in the towel, it will be pretty demoralizing to this whole side."

In February, a day after the Kelo and Lingle cases were argued before the court, I phoned Epstein and asked him how he thought they had gone. "I think the exile's going to be a little longer after yesterday," he said with a sigh. "It's a very sad day to watch these guys work." Epstein expressed confidence that even if his side loses, the battle for the Constitution in Exile will continue at the state level—"the emotional grab of those eminent-domain cases is so strong," he said—but confessed that he had little hope, for now, in the Supreme Court. "They really have gone back to the extreme 1937 reaction that anything that concerns the economic well-being of this nation is simply a political matter," he said. "If the Constitution is an annoying obstacle, they'll just get it out of their way."

VI. Packing the Courts

If supporters of the Constitution in Exile lose all three cases now before the Supreme Court [Editor's note: they did], what happens next? The general consensus, according to Greve, is that the movement should focus its energies on the appointment of sympathetic judges. "I think the judicial appointments are what matters most of all," Greve says. "And Bush's renomination of the rejected judges is a way of saying, Let's cram the same judges back in their face. That's intended as a sign that they mean business."

Three candidates recently renominated by Bush for positions on the federal appellate courts are sympathetic to the ideas of the Constitution in Exile movement. In addition to William Pryor, the former attorney general of Alabama whom Greve praises, there is Janice Rogers Brown, a justice on the California Supreme Court and an outspoken economic libertarian. An African-American and a daughter of sharecroppers, Brown has been promoted by many libertarians as an ideal Supreme Court candidate. Known for her vigorous criticism of the post-New Deal regulatory state, Brown has called 1937, the year the Supreme Court began to uphold the New Deal, "the triumph of our socialist revolution," adding in another speech that "protection of property was a major casualty of the revolution of 1937." She has praised the court's invalidation of maximum-hour and minimum-wage laws in the Progressive era, and at her Senate confirmation hearing in 2003, she referred disparagingly to "the dichotomy that eventually develops where economic liberty—property—is put on a different level than political liberties."

From Greve's point of view, another sympathizer whom Bush has nominated for a federal appellate judgeship is William G. Myers III, who was the chief lawyer at the Department of the Interior and a lifelong advocate for mining and grazing interests. Democrats in the Senate have expressed special concern about Myers's narrow view of Congress's power to pass environmental regulations: he has criticized the "fallacious belief that the centralized government can promote environmentalism" and has denounced the Endangered Species Act and Clean Water Act as "regulatory excesses." He also helped to found Cattlemen Advocating Through Litigation, a conservative group that challenges environmental regulations in court. On March 17 [2005], he was the first candidate approved by the Judiciary Committee, on a party line vote.

For Democrats in the Senate, a main cause of concern is not only the principles that these judges embrace but also the potential conflicts of interests that their loyalties can create. For example, Douglas Ginsburg, the judge who introduced the phrase Constitution in Exile, serves on the board of a group called the Foundation for Research on Economics and the Environment, or FREE, which favors free-market solutions to environmental problems. As Douglas Kendall of the Community Rights Counsel, an environmental watchdog group, has reported, between 1992 and 2001 Ginsburg took more than a dozen all-expenses-paid trips, mainly to Montana, under FREE's auspices, where he often participated in its judicial-education seminars. In 1999, a constitutional challenge to emission regulations in the Clean Air Act was accepted for argument before Ginsburg. The lawyer who was challenging the regulations on behalf of several industry groups, Edward Warren, had also served on the board of FREE. Ginsburg joined an opinion accepting Warren's argument that the emission regulations were unconstitutional. A dissenting opinion charged the majority with ignoring "the last half century of Supreme Court jurisprudence," and the Supreme Court unanimously reversed the decision two years later in an acerbic opinion written by Scalia.

The battle over the ideologies and allegiances of appellate judges is, of course, something of a dress rehearsal for the Supreme Court nomination to come. Greve and his colleague Christopher DeMuth, the president of the American Enterprise Institute, say they are heartened by the judges reportedly on Bush's short list, many of whom they consider broadly sympathetic to their views. "I think the president and his top staff have shown really good taste in their court of appeals nominations," DeMuth told me during a visit to the institute, "and when the Supreme Court opening comes up, they will be very strongly inclined to nominate people from our side."

DeMuth was especially enthusiastic about the possible candidacy of Michael W. McConnell, a federal appellate judge in Denver and a former University of Chicago law professor who worked with DeMuth at the Office of Management and Budget in the Reagan administration. Greve explained that McConnell not only has "impeccable social conservative credentials" but also will "give you a vision of federalism that looks like the Constitution we once had, and he's intellectually powerful enough to pull it off on the court." Most of the other names on Bush's short list have similar qualities: J. Michael Luttig, a federal appellate judge in Virginia, is a vigorous proponent of the view that some federal environmental laws exceed Congress's powers to regulate interstate commerce; John Roberts, a federal judge in Washington, has also questioned whether some applications of the Endangered Species Act exceed Congress's regulatory powers.

The influence of the Constitution in Exile movement on judicial nominations is not always clear, since the concerns of the White House often overlap with concerns of conservatives broadly sympathetic to business interests or the concerns of more traditional federalists. "If you mentioned the phrase 'Constitution in Exile' in White House meetings I was in, no one would know what the hell you were talking about," a former White House official, who spoke on condition of anonymity because of the sensitivity of the topic, told me. "But a lot of people believe in the principles of the movement without knowing the phrase. And the nominees will reflect that." According to the former official, during Bush's first term, David S. Addington, the vice president's counsel, would often press the Justice Department to object that proposed laws and regulations exceeded the limits of Congress's power. "People like Addington hate the federal government, hate Congress," the former official said. "They're in a deregulatory mood," he added, and they believe that "the second term is the time to really do this stuff."

VII. America, Deregulated

If they win—if, years from now, the Constitution is brought back from its decades of arguable exile—and federal environmental laws are struck down, the movement's loyalists do not expect the levels of air and water pollution to rise catastrophically. They are confident that local regulations and private contracts between businesses and neighbors will determine the pollution levels that each region demands. Nor do they expect vulnerable workers to be exploited in sweatshops if labor unions are weakened: they anticipate that entrepreneurial workers in a mobile economy will bargain for the working conditions that their talents deserve. Historic districts, as they see it, will not be eviscerated if zoning laws are scaled back, but they do imagine there will be fewer brownstones and more McMansions. In exchange for these trade-offs, they insist, individual liberty—the indispensable guarantee of self-fulfillment and happiness—would flourish far more extensively than it does today.

Of course, there would be losers as well as winners in a deregulated market economy, and history provides plenty of reasons to be concerned about the possibility of abuse. Even the relatively modest deregulation of today's increasingly global and fluid U.S. economy may provide something of a cautionary tale. From Enron to illegal trading by mutual funds and bid-rigging in the insurance industry, corporate scandals are keeping consumer advocates like Eliot Spitzer quite busy. America, at the moment, is engaged in an important debate about the relative merits and dangers of the market economy, and the advocates of the Constitution in Exile are aware that they cannot achieve ultimate success without persuading a majority of the American people to embrace their vision.

But a political transformation in their favor remains, for the moment, remote, and they appear content, even eager, to turn to the courts to win the victories that are eluding them in the political arena. Advocates of the movement are entirely sincere in their belief that the regulatory state is unconstitutional as well as immoral and that a principled reading of the Constitution requires vigorous enforcement of fundamental limits on state power. Nevertheless, it is a troubling paradox that conservatives, who continue to denounce liberals for using courts to thwart the will of the people in cases involving abortion and gay marriage, now appear to be succumbing to precisely the same temptation. If the lessons of the past 60 years teach us anything, when judges try to short-circuit intensely contested democratic debates, from the New Deal cases to Roe v. Wade, they may provoke a fierce political backlash that sets back the movement they are trying to advance. In this sense, even if the Constitution in Exile movement manages to transform the courts before it has transformed the country, it may find that it has won less than it hoped.

Please Stand By While the Age of Miracles Is Briefly Suspended

James McManus

Esquire | August 2004

While the controversy over abortion continues to divide U.S. voters, technology has introduced a perplexing new moral issue into American politics: embryonic stem-cell research, which offers the hope of miracle medical cures, but only by sacrificing human embryos in the process. Following President Bush's decision in 2001 to limit federally-funded research to seventy-eight existing stem-cell lines, other *countries without such restrictions—most notably South Korea—have taken over as leaders in the field. Meanwhile, in October 2004, Californians approved a $3 billion bond issue to fund in-state stem-cell research, and other states have since moved to follow suit. This spring, the Republican-led Congress responded with their own legislation supporting stem-cell research. In May 2005, despite the president's warning that he would veto the bill, the House passed the Stem Cell Therapeutic and Research Act, establishing a national stem-cell bank to store embryos discarded by in vitro clinics. The Senate is expected to vote on similar legislation sometime this summer.*

In this piece (written before the House bill and the California initiative were passed), James McManus reviews the current status of the debate, and also provides a firsthand look at the president's bioethics committee—the same group that helped develop Bush's 2001 position on stem cells. McManus brings a keen personal interest to the subject: his twenty-nine-year-old daughter has diabetes, one of the diseases that scientists believe could be cured by stem-cell research—a fact underscored by the article's original Esquire *subtitle, "How the President Is Trying to Kill My Daughter." . . .*

A damp, nasty Thursday, January 15, 2004. The President's Council on Bioethics is meeting in the downstairs conference room of the Wyndham Hotel, four or five blocks from the White House. Minimal risk-to-benefit ratios for cutting-edge medical research are what the panel is trying to calibrate. Thumbs-up or thumbs-down, live or die. It's 8:45 in the morning, day one of week three of the most crucial election year since 1932, or perhaps 1860. Not to be melodramatic.

To get a better handle on the ethical objections to embryonic-stem-cell research, I've been listening with as much detachment as possible, given my twenty-nine-year-old daughter's ongoing slow death from juvenile (Type 1) diabetes, one of several diseases likely to be cured by this research. Bridget has already undergone a vitrectomy—open-eye surgery to remove vision-blocking blood clots and scar tissue from her vitreous humor—and several rounds of laser treatment to help keep her retinopathy in check. During these procedures, she needs to remain awake while a gonioscope is held against her eye and an ophthalmologic surgeon burns her pigment epithelium about eighteen hundred times with two hundred milliwatts of light. In each eye. Victims of juvenile diabetes can go blind because their elevated blood-sugar levels cause capillaries throughout their bodies, especially in their eyes and extremities, to leak and proliferate in unhealthy ways.

But like I said, I'm trying to listen to every voice here, even that of Alfonso Gómez-Lobo, the dapper metaphysician from Georgetown who proclaimed half an hour ago in his lilting Chilean accent that "all of us were once a blastocyst." His point was that no blastocyst, cloned or otherwise, should ever be destroyed for its cells, however great the possible benefits. I wanted to say that we all were once an ovum as well, yet we don't hold a funeral every time a woman who's made love has her period. That being evolved from amphibians doesn't keep us from deep-frying frog legs and washing them down with Corona. That defenders of animal rights fervently believe that eating meat, even fish, is a sacrilege, but we don't let them dictate to Smith & Wollensky or cut off government subsidies to the beef industry. . . .

To be fair, the Bush council straddles both sides of the fulcrum: ten members on Gómez-Lobo's side, seven on mine. Each is a brilliant and well-informed ethicist, doctor, or legal scholar; nearly all have an M.D. or Ph.D or sometimes, as in the case of chairman Leon Kass, both. Today they're presenting in public the ideas they've already fine-tuned and published.

Kass, Gómez-Lobo, columnist Charles Krauthammer, and the rest of the majority argue that embryonic-stem-cell research would put us on a slippery slope toward organ farms and cloned children. Their hostility focuses on a procedure called somatic cell nuclear transfer, in which the nucleus of an ovum is removed or deactivated and replaced with the nucleus from a human donor cell. After chemicals coax the doctored egg to reproduce itself, what forms after five days is a blastocyst, a cluster of one hundred to two hundred cells, including the stem cells prized by researchers. This early-stage embryo could be used for either reproductive cloning (to make a baby that's genetically identical to the donor), which almost no one favors, or therapeutic cloning (to isolate and harvest its stem cells) to advance the field of regenerative medicine.

Chapter 6 of *Human Cloning and Human Dignity*, published by the council in July 2002, is where its members most fully address the ethics of cloning. The majority recommends, "albeit with regret," that therapeutic cloning ought not be pursued. "The cell synthesized by somatic cell nuclear transfer, no less than the fertilized egg, is a human organism in its germinal stage." Somewhat defensively, the majority adds, "It is possible that some might suffer in the future because research proceeded more slowly. We cannot suppose that the moral life comes without cost."

No one wants cloned babies or fetuses cultured in hatcheries. But the council's minority is willing to let a small number of early-stage embryos— cloned embryos as well as those fertilized in vitro and now stored in the freezers of infertility clinics, bound for the Dumpster if not donated to science —be destroyed during medical research. Why? Because only embryonic—as opposed to adult—stem cells are "pluripotent," which means they're capable of morphing into any kind of cell in the human body. These "differentiated" cells could then be programmed to replace diseased neurons, heart-muscle tissue, or insulin-producing islet cells for diabetics. Genetically compatible with the patient, they would not be rejected by her immune system. Bona fide miracle cures are what we are talking about here. Even before they're perfected, they'll dispense potent medicine—hope. But only if the president's restrictions on this research are lifted.

In the summer of 1979, Bridget was four and a half, a pink-cheeked, blond kindergartner with a respectable forehand and a new baby brother. In the upper right side of her abdomen, though, her immune system suddenly attacked the islets of Langerhans in her pancreas, inexplicably mistaking them for foreign invaders. Within a couple of weeks, almost all of her islet cells had been obliterated. Her body no longer made enough insulin, the hormone that regulates the passage of nutrients into the cells, so she couldn't process food into energy. Long before we knew what was happening, Bridget's crystal-blue eyes began sinking into gray sockets, her ribs protruded through her flesh, and she started walking around in a daze. At a tryout to place her into the regular or advanced group of tennis students, she failed to even get a racket on balls she would have drilled a month earlier. In words that humiliate me even more now than they did in 1979, I criticized her from the sidelines for "doggin' it."

Her pediatrician referred us to an endocrinologist, who admitted her to Children's Memorial Hospital in Chicago. Bridget began receiving insulin intravenously. Within a week, she looked and felt back to normal. The only difference was that her islet cells couldn't be revived or replaced. As any macho dad would, I fainted and collapsed on the floor as the doctor was telling us that the disease is chronic and incurable. (Dozens of people visited

Bridget in the hospital, and the joke became to ask the nurses how Jim was doing.) I eventually managed to learn that the tip of one of Bridget's tiny fingers would now have to be stabbed with a stainless-steel lancet three or four times a day, allowing a droplet of her blood to be smeared across a chem strip that measured the glucose in her bloodstream; this determined the correct dosage of regular and timed-release insulin to be injected into her butt or thigh. She would no longer be able to eat the same treats her classmates' parents had packed in their Big Bird lunch boxes or served at their birthday parties. But at least Bridget was released fairly healthy from Children's. At least she had come home at all.

Full disclosure: Even if my daughter weren't ill, I would cheer on stem-cell research with gusto. Because that's the kind of Mick I am, brother. I was raised Roman Catholic but have lived the last forty years as a secular humanist. People like me get branded atheists, heretics, ethical relativists, French, and much worse; more affectionate terms include freethinker, agnostic, existentialist, beatnik. I have faith that our bodies—brain waves and action, commerce and science, art and language and children—are pretty much all there is to us. Or all there is to me, anyway. Once my EEG line goes flat, it's gonna be all she wrote. In the meantime, my one and only life will be awful in several respects, awesome in others. Later or sooner, a crosstown bus or a Hummer will squash me like Wile E. Coyote. Either that or an organ or two will break down and I'll suffer, piss and moan not a little, then purchase the farm. I've already made the down payment.

As far as the suffering goes—when it starts, how long it drags out—I used to be confident that Western medicine was riding full speed, or almost that fast, to the rescue. I pictured a rangy Asian cowgirl in a lab coat and Stetson, a bandolier of specimen vials jangling against her modest cleavage as she clutches in one hand the reins of a galloping stallion, in the other a filament delicate enough to boink a few islet cells into a failing pancreas. Not that I expect to live forever—just an extra decade or so, with a little more spring in my step. More important, I want people like Bridget to get a fair shot at their biblical threescore and ten. Our Bible-totin' president, however, has stripped my infinitely resourceful cowgirl of her most prom- ising protocols and forced her to ride sidesaddle on a stubborn Texas mule better equipped for wagon-train duty than galloping into the future.

Many of us who were willing to give Bush a chance, who voted for Al Gore but weren't terrified at the thought of a compassionate conservative in the Oval Office, now feel that the president isn't much less benighted than the Muslim fundamentalists he has engaged in an infinitely perilous clash of theocracies. Not that Bush is a dyed-in-the-wool Holy Roller himself. No, I believe he's a cold-blooded opportunist, able and willing to pander to our least-educated citizens—and that's much, much worse. After all, if, as Gallup recently reported, only 49 percent of Americans accept Darwin's theory of evolution, that number must hover near zero among certain blocs of red-state voters. What besides *shazam* can we say to these folks? But surely we can't let them hinder the momentum of biomedical research.

Not all conservative Christians attack science and reason while gorging on their fruits—laws, markets, medicine, weaponry, energy systems, computers—but the fanatical fringe surely does. Pretending to split the difference between these folks and the rest of us, the president's "compromise" effectively amounted to a ban on embryonic-stem-cell research. Announcing his decision from his ranch in Crawford, Texas, in August 2001, he claimed that "more than sixty genetically diverse stem-cell lines already exist" and that the NIH would be permitted to fund research on these existing lines only. Three years later, however, a mere nineteen of those lines have been made available to scientists, and most are genetically limited to people who tend to use in vitro clinics—the white, the infertile, the affluent. Not that there's anything wrong with these characteristics, but researchers will need hundreds—possibly thousands—of lines to provide genetic matches for the entire population. As the White House itself acknowledges in a fact sheet on the subject, "approximately 128 million Americans" stand to benefit from this research.

Fortunately, a movement to challenge or circumvent the Bush policy is now in full swing. On February 24 [2004], New Jersey governor James McGreevey submitted a budget that would make his state the first to fund embryonic-stem-cell research. In April, the privately funded Harvard Stem Cell Institute opened with a mandate to fill the void left by the ban against federal money. On April 28, 206 members of the House—including 36 Republicans, more than a few pro-lifers among them—sent the president a letter urging him to loosen restrictions on embryonic-stem-cell research. On June 4, the day before Ronald Reagan succumbed to Alzheimer's, a similarly bipartisan plea from fifty-eight senators landed in the president's in-box. And in November, Californians will vote on the Stem Cell Research and Cures Initiative, a hugely ambitious ballot measure that would allocate $3 billion in state money for research on stem cells, embryonic and otherwise. But so far, Bush hasn't blinked.

By supporting a bill proposed by Kansas senator Sam Brownback to send scientists engaged in embryonic-stem-cell research to prison and to outlaw treatments developed in other countries using such methods, the president has made this research downright unsavory, and he's done it on purpose. Even Dr. Kass regrets that young grad students won't go into stem-cell research as readily and that "maybe there's a certain chilling effect on the field as a whole."

Whatever is motivating President Bush, his policy has about it the stench of the witch doctor. It may be the most unenlightened position, with the most negative and far-reaching human consequences, ever taken by an American president.

In the 1980s, as Bridget's mother and I researched the possibilities for a cure, we were told to supervise Bridget's diet and insulin routine as closely as possible, and to teach her to maintain it herself. This would reduce the risk of complications ten or twenty years down the road. The better her control over her blood-sugar levels at each stage of her life, the healthier she'd be when a cure was discovered. It could even affect whether she'd be eligible for cutting-edge treatments.

During the eight or nine years after her diagnosis, our well-behaved little girl dutifully followed her regimens of shots, diet, and exercise. She almost never asked me, "How long do I have to take the shots, Dad? Do you know?" Having scrutinized every syllable of the Juvenile Diabetes Foundation literature and traveled to New York and St. Louis to interview researchers, I learned—or I chose to believe—that the disease would be conquered long before Bridget developed any serious complications. What I emphasized to her was that a cure would be found by the time she got her driver's license. "Just hold on until then," I would say with a hug, "and we'll have a ginormous double celebration."

At thirteen, Bridget was an A-minus student, a not-bad cello and piano and tennis player, and the starting shortstop for the Winnetka All-Stars, our town's traveling softball team. During the daylong tournaments on baked-clay diamonds in midwestern heat and humidity, she was usually the last player to run out of gas. We had to pack our Igloo with extra Gatorade and fruit and syringes, but by then we were used to that stuff. Bridget may have started sneaking the occasional candy bar or Pepsi with her teammates, but her overall health remained phenomenal. One mid-August Sunday, against the Deerfield Does, she snagged a line drive just behind second base, stepped on the bag to double off that runner, and ran down the runner advancing from first, completing an unassisted triple play.

Back at the Wyndham, the debate around the five-table pentagon has been framed, as it should be, in moral-philosophical terms. The tone remains cordial. Members forgo honorifics and refer to one another as Frank, Leon, Karen, "my friend." Yet the rock-bottom question persists: Should "man in his hubris" or some other entity write the ground rules for bio-medical research?

Chairman Kass has written, "In leading laboratories, academic and industrial, new creators are confidently amassing their powers and quietly honing their skills, while on the street their evangelists are zealously prophesying a posthuman future." A key notion for Kass is the Wisdom of Repugnance, also known as the Yuck Factor or, as I think of it, Ewisdom. "Repugnance is the emotional expression of a deep wisdom," he writes, referring to such things as rape, murder, incest . . . and somatic cell nuclear transfer. "Shallow are the souls that have forgotten how to shudder." But the shudder test is hardly foolproof and can lead to a slew of false positives. When Dr. Zabdiel Boylston used inoculation to thwart Boston's smallpox epidemic in 1721, one clergyman thundered, "For a man to infect a family in the morning with smallpox and pray to God in the evening against the disease is a blasphemy," language that caused bombs to be thrown into the homes of Dr. Boylston's cohorts. Whereas hamstringing researchers racing to cure diabetes makes me shudder with rage and disgust.

As a Jewish M.D. and humanities professor, Kass has no trouble pronouncing words like *nuclear* or *vekhen lo' ye'aseh* (Hebrew for "such as ought not to be done"). He hardly fits the stereotype of the born-again zealot embodied by John Ashcroft, Dick Armey, and the like. That said, his views may surprise you. Kass's seven-hundred-page tome, *The Beginning of Wisdom: Reading Genesis*, performs what he calls an "unmediated reading" of the first book of the Bible. Nature is morally neutral, but humans should not be. The "new way," according to Kass, is really the old way, and can be summarized in a single word: patriarchy. Man rules in this world, and woman obeys—to her benefit. From the president's point man on ethics, we read that "a prolonged period of barrenness" before childbirth is God's way of "taming the dangerous female pride in her generative powers," and that marriage as an "institution of stable domestic arrangements for rearing the young depends on some form of man's rule over woman." Again, this is no adjunct lecturer at Bob Jones University, an easier target of condescension for radical centrists like me. Nope, this is the Addie Clark Harding Professor of the University of Chicago's Committee on Social Thought, that bastion of pricey Nobelitude.

I sit down with Kass during a break at the Wyndham. Trim and energetic at sixty-five, scholarly without seeming fussy, he has a genial spirit to go with a thorough command of this complex scientific material. Much as I disagree with him, I have little reason to doubt his goodwill. I begin by congratulating him for leading such nuanced and respectfully argued discussions for and against therapeutic cloning. I also tell him up front that, mainly because of my daughter, I want the spigot open much wider than he and the president do.

He politely objects to my premise. "It's been misrepresented that the council came out in opposition to embryonic-stem-cell research by a vote of ten to seven," he says. "It did not. It came out in favor of a ban on all cloning, including the cloning of embryos." Speaking, as always, in muscular sentences and pausing for paragraph breaks, he goes on. "Congress has not declared stem-cell research illegal; it has said there should be no federal funding for research that involves the destruction of embryos." Pause. "The president found a way to fund embryonic-stem-cell research on the existing lines, which means he has liberalized the research opportunities."

Liberalized? Only if we're talking about the handful of lines he let slide in 2001 while banning federally funded work on the hundreds more lines researchers will need to succeed. But this is the schizoid position in which Kass and his boss have been in lockstep from the outset—or so I assume.

"Is it fair to say that the president appointed you chair of the council because he knew in advance you agreed with him about the proper limits of cell research?" I ask. "Or did he form his position after, or mainly because of, advice you have offered?"

"The truth is, I don't know," Kass responds. "I will say that I think it's improper to reveal conversations that we have had or to speculate on the mind of the president. I think I know what brought me to his attention. It was not my views on stem-cell research, about which I'd never written a word. I've been trying to stop human cloning for thirty-five years. The president wanted to hear a discussion of the ethical issues, to hear how one would lay out the various arguments. I think it's fair to say that I did not tell him what I thought he should do."

So it's not that the president wanted a council that would lend intellectual heft to whatever position wins red-state votes?

"Look," he says, holding my eye, "the president is pro-life. You've got to acknowledge it." He hooks a thumb back toward those of his colleagues still being interviewed. "But no previous bioethics council had anything like this diversity. It's not fair to say you've got a council that's opposed to embryonic-stem-cell research. You have some people on this council who'd be distressed to see lots of embryos destroyed before there was any proof of efficacy. I myself am very hopeful that over the next decade we will learn an enormous amount from the existing lines. The spigot is open."

"What about your opposition to in vitro fertilization?" I ask, referring to the fact that in 1971 he was speaking against it aggressively, predicting that it would lead to deformed infants. A million or so normal IVF births down the road, he's been branded everything from a "bio-Luddite" and "false prophet of doom" to "a sixteenth-century sensibility to guide us through twenty-first-century conundrums."

"I was an early critic of IVF because I didn't know it was going to be safe for children," he says. "I thought IVF might eventually lead to cloning, which it might. I had a change of heart in 1978, just when Louise Brown was born. On the question of IVF for infertility, at least if it's shown to be safe, I changed my mind."

It takes a good man to admit that. Even so, I believe Dr. Kass is dead wrong once again. Given his way thirty years ago, we never would have discovered the glories of IVF; countless families wouldn't even exist. If Kass, Brownback, and the president succeed in making therapeutic cloning a criminal act, American scientists not only won't discover the first round of cures for spinal-cord damage, diabetes, Alzheimer's, Parkinson's, and heart disease, we'll never know how many other cures we missed out on. The tragedy will become exponential.

In the meantime, a thunderclap. On February 13 [2004], scientists in Seoul, South Korea, announced they had succeeded in cloning human embryos and extracting stem cells from them. The team was led by Drs. Woo Suk Hwang and Shin Yong Moon, both of Seoul National University. Dr. Hwang emphasized that the research was subject to rigorous oversight by an ethics committee. It took place in test tubes and petri dishes; no embryo was, or could have been, implanted in a uterus. None of the sixteen volunteers who provided 242 unfertilized ova were paid. The project was funded by the government of South Korea, where reproductive cloning is illegal. The team's goal, Dr. Hwang stated forcefully, was not to clone human beings but to advance understanding of the causes and treatment of human disease.

Scientists and patients around the world hailed the results. A Chicago embryologist spoke for a lot of us by saying, "My reaction is, basically, wow." Dr. Kass's reaction came even before the Koreans' paper was published in *Science*. Speaking for the President's Council, he said, "The age of human cloning has apparently arrived: Today, cloned blastocysts for research; tomorrow, cloned blastocysts for baby-making. In my opinion, and that of the majority of the council, the only way to prevent this from happening here is for Congress to enact a comprehensive ban or moratorium on all human cloning." In much the same spirit, Carrie Gordon Earll of Focus on the Family branded the South Koreans' research "nothing short of cannibalism." But I'm here to tell you that *my* family—and, I assume, millions of others—was thrilled. Said Bridget, *"Finally!"*

The overarching fact that our president and the majority of his council seem unable to get their minds around is that human nature *evolves*. "Normal human" used to describe a four-foot-nine-inch club-wielding cretin draped in gore-spattered fur. It used to be "natural" for Tarzan, after impregnating Jane, to lope off in search of a new sperm receptacle, clubbing other men to death as he went, until—*blam!* And for his witch doctor to smear this wound with dung while grunting a few incantations. From the perspective of these early humans, we are what a Cro-Magnon Charles Krauthammer would fearfully denounce as "a class of superhumans," or the Addie Clark Harding caveman would hastily label "posthuman."

Glorious though it may be, evolution is also, as James Watson put it, "damn cruel," mainly because genetic mutations have introduced about fifteen hundred diseases into human DNA. What could we do about it? Not much until doctors like Rudolf Virchow (1821-1902) came along. Virchow was the German physician who finally convinced the medical establishment that the basic units of life were self-replicating cells. Building on François Raspail's axiom *Omnis cellula e cellula*—every cell, diseased or otherwise, originates from another cell—Virchow overturned the conventional wisdom that it was the entire body, or one of its "vapours," that became sick. Yet Virchow's most radiant brainchild may be that "medicine is a social science, and politics is nothing but medicine on a large scale." We still fall woefully short of this ideal, but as beneficent M.D.'s like Hwang, Moon, William Mayo, Jonas Salk, and Paul Farmer have shown, fighting back against disease is the most humane thing we can do. The most human.

Whatever epoch we live in, we all have to face getting caught at the worst possible point on the curve of medical progress: My cowgirl's campfire is visible on the horizon, yet I am accorded the honor of being the very last hombre to succumb to Syndrome X. "Remember when people had heart attacks?" some lucky duck in 2050 may guffaw, clutching her chest in mock agony. "I mean, can you *imagine?*" This fortunate woman would be exactly as human as any victim of plague or polio, and a lot more human, in my view, than the cretin with the club. However long it may seem to us now, her life span will still seem to *her* the way Nabokov and Beckett imagined it in the middle of the twentieth century: as a brief crack of light between two infinities of darkness.

Speaking of infinities of darkness, adolescence is the first prolonged test for people suffering with Type 1 diabetes. Physical routines readily followed by obedient ten-year-olds suddenly become a series of temptations to rebellion —against parents and authority in general, against the unrelenting regimens themselves. The flood of new hormones disrupting skin tone, academic performance, and household peace also wreak havoc on a diabetic's cardiovascular system. Psychological anxiety goes thermonuclear, which sets off more fuming rebellion. My doctors and parents say I can never smoke cigarettes? I'll retreble my efforts to buy them at 7-Eleven. And what harm can come from skipping my shot on homecoming night? When Bridget's doctor revealed that her sugar control wasn't nearly as tight as it should be, she started skipping blood tests as well. Her mantra became "Why should I struggle to take care of myself if I'm gonna die young anyway?"

In the meantime, I stepped up my visits to researchers, who by the early

1990s were working on ways to keep the islet cells of cows and pigs from being rejected by humans. I studied reports, wrote letters to congressmen, talked to more doctors. I imagined myself going blind; I found myself volunteering to "God" to deal with this fate instead of Bridget. My firstborn child, my talented and beautiful daughter, was being ravaged from the inside out by a rapist who was taking his time, and there was nothing I could do about it.

I began a novel about riding a bicycle from Chicago to Alaska. Narrated in the voice of a young woman with diabetes, it was my attempt to empathize as vividly as I could with the disease-ridden angst my daughter faced every day. *Going to the Sun* turned into a road trip connecting two love stories, and the character of Penny Culligan is an amalgam of myself, my sister Ellen, and Bridget. But Penny's diabetes is the plutonium rod— potent, relentless, explosive fueling each strand of the narrative. The ending is designed to evoke both the hope and desperation the young woman feels as she makes her way into adulthood.

The longer you have this disease, the more severe its complications become. It's a hassle from day one, to be sure, but after fifteen or twenty years your kidneys begin to break down and your retinopathy becomes more severe. Bridget's had diabetes for twenty-five years now. She's frightened, exhausted, and angry. She's also determined to overcome her long actuarial odds and live something resembling a normal life. But your self-esteem takes big hits when you have a chronic disease. Your skin becomes sallow and spongy from all the punctures; you also get to worry about whether you can get pregnant, carry a baby to term, then survive long enough to see your child enter kindergarten. "Why should I have to listen to the history of your cold," Bridget sometimes wants to know, "or how tough your meeting was? At least your freakin' pancreas works!"

If a cure isn't developed in the next few years or so, Bridget will become more and more susceptible to a heart attack or stroke, however diligently she takes care of herself. She may still go blind, and her kidneys might fail. As her circulatory system gets ravaged further, the dainty feet she used to lace into white size 5½ softball spikes may need to be amputated.

What scares me the most, of course, is the possibility that Bridget's disease will take its course just before the cure comes online. Which is why I so heartily agree with the council's minority. American society, it writes in *Human Cloning and Human Dignity*, has "an obligation to heal the sick and relieve their suffering." The minority accords "no special moral status to the early-stage cloned embryo," because it has no capacity for consciousness in any form. Even more to the point, "the potential to become something (or someone) is hardly the same as being something (or someone)."

As to whether somatic cell nuclear transfer would lead to cloned children or human-animal hybrids—the slippery-slope argument—Harvard's Michael Sandel proposes that the research should proceed "subject to regulations that embody the moral restraint appropriate to the mystery of the first stirrings of human life." Specifically: strict licensing criteria for labs, laws against commodifying ova or sperm, and measures to keep private firms from monopolizing access to cell lines. The minority concludes that it's "perfectly possible to treat a blastocyst as a clump of cells usable for lifesaving research, while prohibiting any such use of a later-stage embryo or fetus." We shouldn't outlaw all cloning, in other words, just because its therapeutic applications *could* be misused. Even Michael Jackson's face doesn't get plastic surgeons arrested.

Finally, because of advances in SCNT, *any* human cell could theoretically become a person if it were doctored aggressively enough in a lab. "If mere potentiality to develop into a human being is enough to make something morally human," the minority continues, "then every human cell has a special or inviolable moral status, a view that is patently absurd."

In addition to Sandel, the enlightened minority includes Janet Rowley, the Blum-Riese Distinguished Service Professor at the Pritzker School of Medicine at the University of Chicago. Dr. Rowley is blunt in her opposition: "Our ignorance is profound; the potential for important medical advances is very great. Congress should lift the ban and establish a broadly constituted regulatory board, *now*."

A few hours after my chat with the chairman, I sit down with Dr. Rowley. "Dr. Kass makes the case that the council hasn't done anything to inhibit embryonic-cell research," I begin. "He claims Bush has *opened* the spigot."

"Well, I would disagree," says Dr. Rowley, an elegant, hazel-eyed woman with undyed silver-brown hair. "For many people in the majority, a fertilized ovum is a human being, and therefore taking that single cell and doing anything with it is murder. Others of us believe that while a fertilized ovum has the potential to become a human being, if this potential human being could in fact lead us to something that could save the lives of many human beings, then we think it's a matter of competing goods. Helping many, many individuals is justification for taking a single cell or an early multiple-cell organism and using it to benefit more individuals."

Before I can hug her or put my fist in the air, she continues: "Now, to a purist, of course, that's immaterial. It's 'man in his hubris intervening,' not nature or God or whatever entity you want to invoke."

"Yet God is never mentioned explicitly. . . ."

"No," Rowley says. "They would generally cite moral and philosophical reasons. But in our early conversations, it was brought up that in Jewish and Islamic law, a developing embryo didn't become human for forty days—well within the limits of the time frame in which embryos would be used for therapeutic research."

Think back to that human-development continuum in your high school biology textbook. Sperm meets ovum on the left, full-term fetus to the right. No reasonable person would let researchers destroy anything recognizably human, just as no one objects to putting blood under an electron microscope. The points of contention fall somewhere between a blastocyst and the forty-day-old embryo of religious tradition. Exactly where we draw the line, and whether we make a distinction between what happens in a petri dish and what *could* happen in a uterus *but doesn't*, is determined by either spiritual/faith-based beliefs or rational/scientific principles.

In a democratic society, then, who gets to draw it? Why not George W. Bush, for example, with the backing of his eminent council? Well, one reason is that the person officially charged with helping Dr. Kass push the majority's agenda through Congress is executive director Dean Clancy, who spent eight years on the staff of Dick Armey. Not only is Clancy opposed to embryonic-stem-cell research, he virulently opposes public schools and federal taxes, which makes him what most folks would call a fanatic. Such appointments extend the Bush-Cheney pattern of loading any dice that get tossed down the policy table. In December 2002, for example, Bush appointed Dr. W. David Hager to an FDA committee on reproductive drugs. Hager is not only ferociously opposed to therapeutic cloning but has been accused of refusing to prescribe contraceptives to unmarried women; to women suffering from premenstrual syndrome, he counsels prayer and Bible reading. (You heard me.) In February, a group of sixty scientists—including twenty Nobel laureates—issued a statement that this administration repeatedly censors reports written by its own scientists, stacks its advisory councils, and disbands those offering unwanted advice. "Other administrations have, on occasion, engaged in such practices," the scientists wrote, "but not so systematically nor on so wide a front." Bush's response to such criticism? In late February, he and Dr. Kass replaced two members of the minority—Elizabeth Blackburn and William F. May—with three new members who all oppose therapeutic cloning. Dr. Kass's fair, diverse council is now tilted thirteen to five.

The majority of a different president's council—John Kerry's, for example, or the one Al Gore would have appointed—could make an equally strong case in favor of therapeutic cloning. At least as many alternate chairmen with bring-us-to-our-knees credentials—Janet Rowley, for example, or Douglas Melton, codirector of the Harvard Stem Cell Institute —stand ready to argue that position. Most of our scrutiny, then, should focus on the person who makes the appointments.

In January 2002, the president greeted members of his council in the Roosevelt Room of the White House, asking them to be mindful of "the notion that life is—you know, that there is a Creator." It's precisely this willful confusion of realms, this thumbing of his nose at the sworn constitutional duty to keep church and state separate, that keeps folks like me from stomaching the president but makes millions of others just crazy about the guy.

Isn't it inevitable, then, that sectarian dogma will tip the balance on every tough issue? Not really. Plenty of conservative Republicans, such as Trent Lott, Orrin Hatch, and Nancy Reagan, support embryonic-stem-cell research. Senator Hatch has said, "I just cannot equate a child living in a womb, with moving toes and fingers and a beating heart, with an embryo about to be taken from the freezer and which will be lawfully discarded if we don't use it."

Sooner or later, of course, a Bush will need cell-replacement therapy, and he or she may have to fly to California, New Jersey, or maybe even Seoul. Much worse, the necessary treatment may not be ready yet anywhere. But here's another thing I have faith in: Once the cures are available, those who opposed therapeutic cloning in 2004 will damn well find a way to get themselves and their families treated. It's not even hard to imagine them elbowing their way to the front of the line at the clinic. "Oh, yeah?" says my daughter. "Over my dead body."

American medicine has long been guided laymen and women of serious learning, not religiously correct politicians. We seem to understand that when science gets trumped by sectarianism, more bad things happen than good. The framers of our Constitution deliberately omitted *God* from its language, assigning supreme power to "We the People." They wanted to insulate us from holy wars, crusades, and oxymorons like "creation science."

Jimmy Carter, our first born-again president, faithfully kept religion and policy separate, and the intelligence of his heart gets more and more plain every year. In the early 1960s, moderate Democrat John Kennedy went out of his way to avoid giving even the slightest impression that his Catholicism might override his duties as chief executive. John Kerry, another Yankee Catholic, gives every indication he would do the same thing.

Back in July 2001, Kerry wrote a letter urging Bush to fully fund embryonic-stem-cell research. As Kerry said later, "Compassionate conservatism could have meant lifesaving treatments for those suffering from Parkinson's and Alzheimer's disease; instead it appears to be using words of compassion to mask efforts to keep a campaign promise to conservatives. . . . If, as he says, the president believes that stem-cell research may have lifesaving potential for millions, he should give scientists the tools to explore it rather than have the government impose burdensome restrictions." Kerry then cosponsored (with Republican Arlen Specter) a Senate bill to support embryonic-stem-cell research. The bill stalled in committee, but now, on the campaign trail, Kerry pounds away on this issue: "The medical discoveries that will come from stem-cell research are crucial next steps in humanity's uphill climb. . . . If we pursue the limitless potential of our science—and trust that we can use it wisely—we will save millions of lives and earn the gratitude of future generations."

In the meantime, here's how a wartime Republican balanced civic and spiritual responsibilities back in 1862, while thinking about the Emancipation Proclamation: "I am approached with the most opposite opinions and advice, and that by religious men who are equally certain that they represent the divine will. . . . I hope it will not be irreverent for me to say that if it is probable that God would reveal his will to others, on a point so connected with my duty, it might be supposed that he would reveal it directly to me. . . . These are not, however, the days of miracles, and I suppose it will be granted that I am not to expect a direct revelation. I must study the plain physical facts of the case, ascertain what is possible, and learn what appears to be wise and right." And he did.

National Conversation:
Politics, Morality, and Religion

Backward Christian Soldiers

Katha Pollitt

The Nation | April 18, 2005

As Hanna Rosin reports later in this section (see "Beyond Belief," p. 276), America's religions are all in the midst of an intra-denominational schism. On one side of the divide are those who hew to a sterner, fundamentalist view of religion and morality (i.e., social conservatives); on the other are those who tend to be more accepting of a variety of behaviors and moral codes (i.e., social liberals).

Whichever side of the divide you find yourself on, there's no question that the moral debate now going on between the two camps concerns some of the major ethical problems facing humanity. Abortion, embryonic-stem-cell research, end-of-life decisions, public prayer, and same-sex marriage are all issues that define our ethical and religious boundaries as a society.

One of the biggest fights has been over who gets to decide where these boundaries are drawn. In particular, conservatives have long railed against "out-of-control" judges who, they claim, are overturning the nation's traditional moral codes from the bench with rulings upholding the right to same-sex marriage, the ban on prayer in public schools, and other hot-button social issues. Liberals, meanwhile, worry that their own religious and personal freedoms are being threatened by conservative politicians who are backed by (and beholden to) the religious Right.

The bizarre and tragic story of Terri Schiavo brought many of these strands together in a mesmerizing tug-of-war over the life and a death of a single, badly brain-damaged woman (see "How Liberalism Failed Terri Schiavo," p. 268). Schiavo finally passed away two weeks after her feeding tube was removed, but only after Congress tried unsuccessfully to save her by passing a special law that allowed her parents to pursue their case in federal court. Here, Nation *columnist Katha Pollitt chews over the Schiavo episode—and asks how far Americans are willing to go in letting religious conservatives dictate the way they live (and end) their lives. . . .*

Maybe, just maybe, the religious right and its Republican friends have finally gone too far with the Terri Schiavo case. Americans may tell pollsters the earth was created in six days flat and dinosaurs shared the planet with Adam and Eve, but I don't believe they want Tom DeLay to be their personal physician. I don't think they want fanatics moaning and praying outside the hospital while they're making hard decisions. I don't think they want people getting arrested trying to "feed" their comatose relatives, or issuing death threats against judges and spouses in the name of "life." I don't think John Q. Public wants Jeb Bush to adopt his wife or Newt Gingrich to call her by her first name or Senator Frist to diagnose her by video, or Jesse Jackson to pop in at the last minute for a prayer and a photo-op.

The Terri Schiavo freak show is so deeply crazy, so unhinged, such a brew of religiosity and hypocrisy and tabloid sensationalism, just maybe it is clueing people in to where the right's moral triumphalism is leading us. Before Congress jumped into the act, Republicans may have seen a great opportunity to paint the Democrats as the "party of death." No thanks to the Dems, who mostly cowered, the stratagem backfired: The weekend after Schiavo's feeding tube was withdrawn, 75 percent of Americans told CBS pollsters they wanted government to stay out of end-of-life issues, and 82 percent thought Congress and the President should have kept away. Jesse Jackson seems not to have gotten the memo—he's calling for the Florida legislature to overturn thirty years of carefully crafted medical ethics and pass a previously rejected bill requiring patients in a persistent vegetative state to remain on life support forever, unless they've left a written directive to the contrary. If that's the "religious left," forget it.

It's about time Americans woke up. The Schiavo case only looks unprecedented: For decades, women seeking to terminate pregnancies have faced gantlets of screamers, invasions of privacy, violence in the name of "saving babies," charges of murder and of evil motives, politically motivated legal obstacles, spurious medical "expertise" (abortion causes breast cancer; Terri Schiavo just needs therapy). There is the same free-floating vitriol: Abortion is the "Silent Holocaust," while, according to Peggy Noonan, those who support Ms. Schiavo's right to die are on "a low road that twists past Columbine and leads toward Auschwitz" (that would be the same road that Tom DeLay and his family went down when they withheld life support from his critically injured father—the same road, in fact, that Robert Schindler, Terri's father, took when he turned off his mother's life support). Randall Terry, the Operation Rescue showman who wants to make America a "Christian nation" and to "execute" doctors who perform abortions, is the Schindlers' chief strategist; other Operation Rescuers in the hospice parking lot include the Rev. Pat Mahoney, who freely gives out Michael Schiavo's home address; Cheryl Sullenger, who served two years for conspiring to bomb an abortion clinic in 1987; and Scott Heldreth, a convicted sex offender who told an AP reporter that driving long hours to the hospice and getting arrested was all his 10-year-old son's idea.

In this transposition of the abortion drama, Terri Schiavo is the defenseless fetus; her husband, Michael, is the callous "convenience" aborter; and the Schindlers are the would-be adoptive couple doomed to childlessness by tyrannical judges. But there's a difference. Abortion happens to women —bad girls, sluts. Because of the shame and secrecy around abortion, you can believe, probably wrongly, that you don't know anyone who's had one and, thanks to your virtuous life, that you would never need one yourself. But anyone can fall into a permanent coma, and death comes to us all. Millions of people have had to make end-of-life decisions for loved ones or for themselves; they've had to think about what a life is—a pulse? a reflex? a thought?—and what a person is, and what that person would have wanted. And because of this collective experience, most Americans know that to "err on the side of life," as the enthusiastic death-penalty fan and Medicaid-cutter George W. Bush advises, is just a slogan. Your wife with Alzheimer's who's stopped eating and drinking is alive. Do you intubate or not? Your father in a stroke-induced coma is alive. Do you treat his pneumonia or see it as "the old man's friend"? When do you go for aggressive treatment, when do you let the person go, when do you decide the person has already gone and only their body is there in the bed? Over three decades, Americans won the right to make these painful, intimate decisions for themselves. That right—not disability rights or the possibility of medical miracles—is what is at stake in the Schiavo case. Most people, especially young people like Terri Schiavo, are never going to write living wills: Should no weight at all be given their spoken wishes or the conviction of their loved ones that, like Tom DeLay's father, they "would never have wanted to live like this"?

For many ordinary Americans, the stem cell debate was the first time the religious right strove to deprive them of something valuable. It's one thing to make women pay for sex with childbirth, or to deprive your children of modern scientific education, or to ostracize homosexuals, but it's going too far to value a frozen embryo more than Cousin Jim with Parkinson's. Now, with the Schiavo case, Americans have another opportunity to ask themselves if they really want to live in Randall Terry's world, where the next Michael and Terri Schiavo could be any one of us.

How Liberalism Failed Terri Schiavo

Eric Cohen

The Weekly Standard | April 4, 2005

In certain ways, the Terri Schiavo story is unique. Schiavo was not dying, but nei-ther was she "living" in the sense that most people would use the word. Instead, she lay in an unchanging limbo between life and death, kept alive by a feeding tube that her husband wanted removed—claiming it was what Terri would have had wanted—and that her parents were determined to keep in.

A tough ethical problem—and one that got plenty of attention, as Schiavo's husband and parents did battle through the Florida courts (which twice ruled that the feeding tube be removed) the Florida legislature (which passed a law reversing the first court ruling that was itself overturned), the Florida governor's office (Jeb Bush signed the Florida bill enthusiastically, then later tried to take personal cus-tody of Schiavo), the U.S. Congress (which scrambled to pass a law allowing Schiavo's parents to sue in federal court to have the tube reinserted), the White House (President Bush flew in from out of town solely to sign the new federal law), federal appeals court (which heard the Schiavos' suit, but refused to order the tube's reinsertion), and the U.S. Supreme Court (which, without comment, declined to hear the case).

In the end, a woman lay dying after spending fifteen years in an essentially non-functioning state (her autopsy later showed that Schiavo's brain had shrunk to half its normal size), and the rest of us were left to ponder the question explored by Eric Cohen in the following essay: When is (or isn't) a life worth preserving? . . .

The story of Terri Schiavo is both peculiar in its details and paradigmatic in its meaning. The legal twists, political turns, and central characters are so odd that one hesitates to draw any broader conclusions. But the Schiavo case is also a tragic example of the moral and legal confusions that govern how we care for those who cannot speak for themselves, especially those whose lives might seem less than fully human. And so we have a responsi-bility to confront what has happened and why—especially if we are to understand our moral obligation as caregivers for incapacitated persons, and our civic obligation to protect those who lack the capacity to express their will but are still human, still living, and still deserving of equal protection under the law.

In February 1990, a sudden loss of oxygen to the brain left Theresa Marie Schiavo in a coma and eventually in a profoundly incapacitated state. Terri's husband, Michael Schiavo, took care of her, working alongside Terri's parents. He took her to numerous doctors; he pursued experimental treatments; he sought at least some modest restoration of her self-awareness. In November 1992, he testified at a malpractice hearing that he would care for Terri for the rest of her life, that he "wouldn't trade her for the world," that he was going to nursing school to become a better caregiver. He explicitly reaffirmed his marriage vow, "through sickness, in health."

But the lonely husband eventually began seeing other women. His frustration with his wife's lack of improvement seemed to grow. When Terri suffered a urinary tract infection in the summer of 1993, he decided to cease all treatment, believing that her time to die had come, that this was what Terri would have wanted. But Terri's caregivers refused to let her die, and Michael Schiavo relented—for the time being. Not all Terri's doctors, however, saw their medical obligation in the same way; one physician declared that Terri had basically been dead for years, and told Michael that he should remove her feeding tube. Michael responded that he "couldn't do that to Terri," that he could never leave his wife to die of dehydration. But at some point, his heart changed. He decided that it was time for her final exit and his new beginning. He decided that his own wishes—for children, for a new family, for new love unclouded by old obligations—were also her wishes. He decided that she had a right to die and that he had a right to let her die.

Terri's parents, Robert and Mary Schindler, objected. They claimed that their son-in-law was no longer a fit guardian; that he was motivated by the money he would inherit at Terri's death; that Terri could improve with more love and better care. And so a long legal drama ensued, making its way through the Florida court system, centered on two sets of questions: First, what would Terri Schiavo have wanted? Would she want to die rather than live in a profoundly incapacitated condition? Was Michael Schiavo's decision to remove her feeding tube an act of fidelity to his wife's prior wishes or an act of betrayal of the woman entrusted to his care? Second, what was Terri Schiavo's precise medical condition? Did she have any hope of recovery or improvement? If her condition was unalterable—

the persistence of sleeping and waking, the inscrutable moans, the uncontrolled movement of her bladder, the apparent absence of any self-awareness —was her life still meaningful?

The first question—what would Terri Schiavo have wanted?—is the central question of modern liberalism when it comes to caring for those who cannot speak for themselves. It is the autonomy question, the self-determination question, the right to privacy question. At its best, the liberal autonomy regime protects the disabled from having other people's wishes wrongly imposed on them—whether in the form of over-treatment or under-treatment. And it affirms the "liberty interest" of those who no longer possess the capacity to act freely, by allowing the past self to speak for the present one. In legal terms, this is called the "substituted judgment" standard: We must do what the incompetent patient would have wanted; we must pretend that she could pass judgment on the worth of the person she is now, according to the interests and values of the person she once was.

The right to have medical treatment withheld on one's behalf was codified in a string of legal cases over the last few decades. Ideally, the individual's wishes would be laid out in an advance directive or living will, describing in detail what kind of care a person would want under various conditions. This is procedural liberalism's ideal of autonomy in action: The caregiver simply executes the dependent person's prior orders, like a lawyer representing his client. But even persons without living wills still have a legal right to have their wishes respected, so long as those wishes can be discovered. Each state establishes specific criteria and procedures for adjudicating the incompetent individual's wishes in cases where these wishes are not clear, especially when there is a dispute between family members (as in the Schiavo case) or between the family and the doctors.

Under the law of Florida, where the Schiavo case was adjudicated, the patient's prior wishes must be demonstrated with "clear and convincing evidence"—the highest standard of legal certainty in civil cases. In cases where this standard of proof is not met, the court must "err on the side of life," on the assumption that most people, even those who are profoundly disabled, would choose life rather than death. In other words, the state is not supposed to judge the comparative worth of different human beings, but to protect the right of individuals to decide for themselves when their lives would still have meaning. And in cases where the individual's wishes are uncertain, the state of Florida is charged to remain neutral by not imposing death. This is the aim of procedural liberalism—and this is where things went terribly wrong in the Schiavo case.

With scant evidence, a Florida district court concluded that Terri Schiavo would clearly choose death over life in a profoundly incapacitated state. There was no living will, no advance directive, no formal instructions left by Terri Schiavo about what to do for her under such circumstances. Instead, the court relied entirely on Michael Schiavo's recollection of a few casual conversations, on a train and watching television, in which Terri supposedly said that she wouldn't want to live "if I ever have to be a burden to anybody" or be kept alive "on anything artificial." This was evidence of her possible wishes, to be sure. But in light of Michael Schiavo's own earlier statements and behavior—including his pledge to care for Terri for the rest of her days, his unwillingness to remove her feeding tube when the idea was first suggested, his shifting sense of moral obligation as he realized that Terri's condition was probably permanent, and his romantic involvement with multiple other women—these recollections hardly constituted "clear and convincing evidence" of Terri's wishes. In this case, the court had a legal obligation to "err on the side of life." Instead, it chose to allow Michael Schiavo to choose death.

Part of the problem was simply judicial incompetence—especially the court's decision, in direct violation of Florida law, to act as Terri Schiavo's guardian at key moments of the case rather than appoint an independent guardian to represent her interests, separate from the interests of her husband and her parents. But the problem went deeper than incompetence: It also had to do with ideology—with a set of assumptions about what makes life worth living and thus worth protecting. *Procedural liberalism* (discerning and respecting the prior wishes of the incompetent person; preserving life when such wishes are not clear) gave way to *ideological liberalism* (treating incompetence itself as reasonable grounds for assuming that life is not worth living). When the district court's decision to allow Michael Schiavo to remove the feeding tube was challenged, a Florida appeals court framed the question before it as follows:

[W]hether Theresa Marie Schindler Schiavo, not after a few weeks in a coma, but after ten years in a persistent vegetative state that has robbed her of most of her cerebrum and all but the most instinctive neurological functions, with no hope of a medical cure but with sufficient money and strength of body to live indefinitely, would choose to continue the constant nursing care and the supporting tubes in hopes that a miracle would somehow recreate her missing brain tissue, or whether she would wish to permit a natural death process to take its course and for her family members and loved ones *to be free to continue their lives*. (emphasis added)

Now, one could surely read this as an effort to get inside Terri's once competent mind. But more likely, it expresses the court's own view of Terri's now incompetent and incapacitated existence as a meaningless burden, a barrier to her husband's freedom. The court's obligation to discern objectively what Terri's wishes were and whether they were clear—a question of fact—morphed into an inquiry as to whether she could ever get better, with the subjective assumption that life in her present condition was not meaningful life. The question became: Was she in a persistent vegetative state (PVS), and if so, can't we assume that Terri believed death to be preferable to life in such a state?

In response, both sides brought out their best medical experts: Michael Schiavo's doctors to quiet our consciences and assure us that Terri was already long gone, a mere ghost of her former self; the Schindlers' doctors to tell us that she was still responsive to her environment and still might get better, even after years of not improving. Clearly, for many years, Terri's treatment was subpar, and to this day many tests that could clarify her diagnosis have not been done. At the same time, a conservative estimate of her prospects for recovery suggests that her chances were slim, and that she would remain in her profoundly incapacitated state till the end of her days. The court finally ruled that she was indeed in a PVS, and that her feeding tube should be removed—which it was on October 15, 2003.

By then, of course, the Schiavo case had become a public drama, and the outcry at the prospect of leaving Terri to die was overwhelming. The Florida legislature sprang into action, and on October 21, 2003, it passed "Terri's Law," giving the governor authority to stay the court's judgment, order the feeding tube back in, and order a review of the case by an independent guardian charged to report on Terri's behalf. So began the next round of court fights and political battles. The ACLU joined Michael

Schiavo in challenging the constitutionality of Terri's Law. Terri's court-appointed guardian issued a largely unhelpful report. And eventually, the Florida court overturned Terri's Law, rejected the Schindlers' appeals, and ordered that the feeding tube once again be removed—which it was the other day, on March 18, 2005. And despite Congress's dramatic effort to restart the case in federal court and Governor Jeb Bush's continued encouragement to the Florida legislature to act again on her behalf, the most likely outcome at this writing is death by dehydration—the final triumph of Michael Schiavo's will, and supposedly what Terri Schiavo herself would have wanted.

For all the attention we have paid to the Schiavo case, we have asked many of the wrong questions, living as we do on the playing field of modern liberalism. We have asked whether she is really in a persistent vegetative state, instead of reflecting on what we owe people in a persistent vegetative state. We have asked what she would have wanted as a competent person imagining herself in such a condition, instead of asking what we owe the person who is now with us, a person who can no longer speak for herself, a person entrusted to the care of her family and the protection of her society.

Imagine, for example, that the Schindlers had agreed with Michael Schiavo that Terri's time had come, that she would never have wanted to live like this, that the feeding tube keeping her alive needed to come out. Chances are, there would have been no federal case, no national story, no political controversy. Terri Schiavo would have been buried long ago, mourned by the family that decided on her behalf that death was preferable to life in her incapacitated state. Under the law, such an outcome would have been unproblematic and uneventful, so long as no one had claimed that Terri Schiavo's previous wishes were being violated. But morally, the deepest problem would remain: What do we owe those who are not dead or dying but profoundly disabled and permanently dependent? And even if such individuals made their desires clearly known while they were still competent, is it always right to follow their instructions—to be the executors of their living wills—even if it means being their willing executioners?

For some, it is an article of faith that individuals should decide for themselves how to be cared for in such cases. And no doubt one response to the

Schiavo case will be a renewed call for living wills and advance directives—as if the tragedy here were that Michael Schiavo did not have written proof of Terri's desires. But the real lesson of the Schiavo case is not that we all need living wills; it is that our dignity does not reside in our will alone, and that it is foolish to believe that the competent person I am now can establish, in advance, how I should be cared for if I become incapacitated and incompetent. The real lesson is that we are not mere creatures of the will: We still possess dignity and rights even when our capacity to make free choices is gone; and we do not possess the right to demand that others treat us as less worthy of care than we really are.

A true adherence to procedural liberalism—respecting a person's clear wishes when they can be discovered, erring on the side of life when they cannot—would have led to a much better outcome in this case. It would have led the court to preserve Terri Schiavo's life and deny Michael Schiavo's request to let her die. But as we have learned, the descent from procedural liberalism's respect for a person's wishes to ideological liberalism's lack of respect for incapacitated persons is relatively swift. Treating autonomy as an absolute makes a person's dignity turn entirely on his or her capacity to act autonomously. It leads to the view that only those with the ability to express their will possess any dignity at all—everybody else is "life unworthy of life."

This is what ideological liberalism now seems to believe—whether in regard to early human embryos, or late-stage dementia patients, or fetuses with Down syndrome. And in the end, the Schiavo case is just one more act in modern liberalism's betrayal of the vulnerable people it once claimed to speak for. Instead of sympathizing with Terri Schiavo—a disabled woman, abandoned by her husband, seen by many as a burden on society—modern liberalism now sympathizes with Michael Schiavo, a healthy man seeking freedom from the burden of his disabled wife and self-fulfillment in the arms of another. And while one would think that divorce was the obvious solution, this was more than Michael Schiavo apparently could bear, since it would require a definitive act of betrayal instead of a supposed demonstration of loyalty to Terri's wishes.

Perhaps we can fashion better laws or better procedures to ensure that vulnerable persons get the care they deserve. But even truly loving caregivers will face hard decisions—decisions best left in their hands, not turned over to the state. And in reality, most decisions will be made at the bedside, where the reach of the law will always be limited, and usually should be. Moreover, the autonomy regime, at its best, prevents the worst abuses—like involuntary euthanasia, where doctors or public officials decide whose life is worth living. But the autonomy regime, even at its best, is deeply inadequate. It is based on a failure to recognize that the human condition involves both giving and needing care, and not always being morally free to decide our own fate.

In the end, the only alternative is a renewed understanding of both the family and human equality—two things ideological liberalism has now abandoned and modern conservatism now defends. Living in a family means accepting the burdens of caring for those bound to us in ties of fidelity—whether parent for child, child for parent, or spouse for spouse. The human answer to our dependency is not living wills but loving surrogates. And for those who believe in human equality, this means treating even the profoundly disabled—people like Terri Schiavo, who are not dead and are not dying—as deserving of at least basic care, so long as the care itself is not the cause of additional suffering. Of course, this does not mean that keeping our loved ones alive is our only goal. But neither can we treat a person's life as a disease in need of a cure, or aim at death as a means of ending suffering—even if a loved one asks us to do so.

Perhaps we should not be surprised at the immovable desire of Terri's parents to keep her alive and the willingness of Terri's husband to let her go. Parental love and spousal love take shape in fundamentally different ways. Parents first know their children as helpless beings, totally dependent on their care. Husbands first know their wives as attractive, autonomous beings who both give and receive love, and who enter into marriage as willing partners. But to marry means pledging one's fidelity despite the uncertainties of fortune. The beautiful wife may become disfigured, the wished-for mother may prove to be infertile, the young woman teeming with life may be plunged into a persistent vegetative state. Marriage often demands heroism, and we can hardly condemn those who fall short of it. But we can surely fault those, like Michael Schiavo, who claim to speak in the name of loved ones they have abandoned, and insist that letting them die is what they desire or deserve.

To question whether Michael Schiavo has his wife's best interests at heart is not to make this case ethically or humanely easy. The decision to continue feeding a person in a profoundly incapacitated state is always wrenching. We must at least wonder whether ensuring years or decades with a feeding tube, with no self-control, and with virtually no possibility of improvement is not love but torture, not respect for life but forced degradation. We, too, must tremble when we demand that people like Terri be fed. But in the end, the obligation to feed should win out, because the living humanity of the disabled person is undeniably real.

On March 18, 2005, the day her feeding tube was removed, Terri Schiavo was not dead or dying. She was a profoundly disabled person in need of constant care. And despite the hopes of her parents, it was unlikely that her medical condition would improve, even with the best possible care administered by those with her best interests at heart. But even in her incapacitated state, Terri Schiavo was still a human being, a member of the Schindler family and the human family. As such, she was still worthy of protection and care, even if some of those closest to her wished to deny it.

Beyond Belief
Hanna Rosin

The Atlantic Monthly | January–February 2005

In this Atlantic Monthly *piece, Hanna Rosin looks at a phenomenon that first emerged in the early 1970s but has been accelerating in recent years: the growing split between conservatives and liberals within America's various religions— including Christian evangelical churches. Lately, she detects another parallel trend: increasingly, conservative factions from different religions are allying themselves with each other, on the grounds that their religious differences matter less than their agreement on social issues like abortion and same-sex marriage. What's more, writes Rosin, "The divide between traditionalists and modernists is likely to widen in the coming years." . . .*

Richard Land is gloating, and who can blame him? When I called him a few weeks after the 2004 election, he said he'd been driving around his home town of Nashville with his cell phone ringing constantly, CNN on one line, *Time* magazine on the other—everyone wanting to ask the prominent Southern Baptist how his people had managed to win the election for George W. Bush. Yes, he told me, "we white evangelicals were the driving engine" of the president's victory. But then he veered into the kind of interview a quarterback gives in the locker room, in which he thanks the offensive line and the tight end and the coach and, well, really the whole team for bringing it home. "You'd be shocked," Land said, "at the number of Catholics who voted for this president. You'd be shocked at the number of Orthodox Jews, even observant Jews. This was a victory for all people of traditional moral values."

"Moral values." The phrase has turned into the hanging chad of the 2004 election, the cliché no one takes seriously. Do the debates over Iraq and the economy not involve moral values? Is everyone in the exit polls who didn't check that box a secular hedonist? As a way of explaining the outcome of the election, the "morality issue" has been amply debunked as all but meaningless.

But when Land uses the phrase to express his feeling of oneness with his Catholic (not to mention Jewish) brethren, it counts as a momentous development. Land does not, after all, come from some Quaker meetinghouse where all religious viewpoints are equally welcome. Rather, as the president of the Southern Baptists' Ethics and Religious Liberty Commission, he comes out of a tradition that has called the papacy the "mark of the beast." (It's no coincidence that in the Left Behind series so beloved by evangelicals, a former American cardinal serves as lackey to the Antichrist.) Yet Land is not shy about announcing now, "I've got more in common with Pope John Paul II than I do with Jimmy Carter or Bill Clinton." Of course, he still has theological differences with Catholics, but "these differences are *in addition to* the basics," he says. "Together we believe in the virgin-born son, who died on the cross and was resurrected on Easter Sunday—really resurrected, like *The Washington Post* could have reported it. We both say all human life is sacred, that marriage is between a man and a woman, that homosexual behavior is contrary to God's will." All this is just "more relevant," he says, "than whether I'm Catholic or Protestant."

Much of the post-election commentary about the "God gap" followed the old culture-war lines drawn by Pat Buchanan at the 1992 Republican National Convention, describing this presidential race as pitting the people of God against the godless. But although that has an epic sound to it, it's wrong—if only because there are far too few godless in the country to bring John Kerry to near parity. (Gallup polls show that only five percent of Americans don't believe in God or a higher power.) Rather, the election results confirmed an idea that sociologists have been dancing around for the past decade: that the more fundamental divide is *within* religious America, between different kinds of believers. Gradually the nation's spiritual map is being redrawn into two large blocs called traditionalist and modern—or orthodox and progressive, or rejectionist and accommodationist, or some other pair of labels that academics have yet to dream up.

For most of American history, of course, the important religious divides were between denominations—not just between Protestants and Catholics and Jews but between Lutherans and Episcopalians and Southern Baptists and the other endlessly fine-tuned sects. But since the 1970s fundamental disagreements have emerged within virtually all these denominations—over abortion, over gay rights, over modernity and religion's role in it. "There's a fault line running through American religions," Land says. "And that fault line is running not between denominations but through them."

Evidence for Land's claim pops up in newspapers every year starting around springtime, when many denominations hold their biennial or quadrennial meetings. In the past the subject of contention was typically abortion; of late it's more likely to have been homosexuality. The story line is remarkably consistent. A gay minister has been ordained, or a group of bishops have blessed a gay union. An internal trial is held, and sanctions are handed out. At the denomination meeting liberal protesters wearing rainbow stoles light candles; a conservative group called Solid Rock or First Principles threatens to break away and start a splinter faction unless the denomination holds fast to tradition. A vote is taken, and the denomination barely avoids schism. Last year the Episcopal Church got the most-dramatic headlines, after an openly gay bishop was ordained in New Hampshire and a coalition of congregations broke off from the American church. But similar rifts have appeared in the past few years within the United Methodists, the Presbyterians, the Lutherans—almost any denomination one can name. Nor is it just the mainline Protestant churches. At their June meeting the American Catholic bishops split over how strictly to hold politicians accountable for their positions on abortion. When Reform rabbis sanctioned gay unions, in 2000, Conservative and Orthodox rabbis issued statements objecting. And last year the Southern Baptists voted to pull out of the Baptist World Alliance, citing a move toward liberalism that includes tolerance of homosexuality and women clergy. The proximate cause was the acceptance into the alliance of a more liberal evangelical group, the Cooperative Baptists.

Every four years since 1992 a group of political scientists sponsored by the Pew Forum on Religion and Public Life has attempted to track these shifting loyalties; with each survey, says John C. Green, a professor of political science at the University of Akron and a member of the group, "the argument for the culture war in religion gets more convincing." The survey subdivides the three largest religious groups—evangelicals, mainstream Protestants, and Catholics—into "traditionalists," "centrists," and "modernists." Traditionalists are defined as having a "high view of the authority of the Bible" and worshiping regularly; they say they want to preserve "traditional beliefs and practices in a changing world." Centrists are defined as wanting to adapt beliefs to new times, while modernists have unabashedly heterodox beliefs, worship infrequently, and support upending traditional doctrines to reflect a modern view. The three categories are similar in size (centrists are a little larger and modernists a little smaller) and have remained about the same size over the dozen years of the survey.

On a wide range of issues, traditionalists agree with one another across denominations while strongly disagreeing with modernists in their own religion. For example, 32 percent of traditionalist evangelicals and 26 percent of traditionalist Catholics say abortion should always be illegal, compared with only seven percent of modernist evangelicals and three percent of modernist Catholics.

The current divide first became apparent in the 1970s, when evangelicals, who had largely retreated from public life following the Scopes trial of 1925, re-engaged after Roe v. Wade. "As the issues heated up, each side began organizing around them; then candidates picked up on them," Green says. Soon the religious landscape seemed like a copy of the political one.

Perhaps the survey's most surprising finding is the degree to which evangelicals are splintering along the same lines as all other denominations. About half the evangelicals surveyed in 2004 defined themselves as centrist or modernist. This reflects a new movement of what are sometimes called "freestyle evangelicals." They are often married women with children who attend one of those suburban megachurches where the doctrine is traditional but the style is modern. Their morals are conservative but their politics are more heterodox, featuring considerable support for education and the environment. In time they may erode the stereotype of evangelicals as overwhelmingly conservative.

The divide between traditionalists and modernists is likely to widen in the coming years. In a recent study of twenty- to thirty-four-year-olds Robert Wuthnow, the head of the Center for the Study of Religion at Princeton University, found that ideological splits were much more pronounced than they had been in a similar study he conducted in the mid-1970s. In particular he found that political and religious views were tracking more closely, with the most religious more avidly pro-life, and the spiritual but less traditionally religious more avidly pro-choice.

Even some who are skeptical of an American "culture war" concede that religious traditionalists are gelling into a united force. According to Alan Wolfe, the author of *One Nation, After All* (1998), "The theological differences between conservative Catholics and Protestants that created five hundred years of conflict and violence have been superseded by political agreement. They are simply not interested in citing theology so long as they agree on abortion. People like Wuthnow are saying this has been going on for fifteen, twenty years. But there's an intensity this time around, much more so than most of us were prepared for."

That intensity was not entirely spontaneous. From his first month in office President Bush focused on the emerging religious split and exploited it, systematically courting traditionalist religious leaders—not only the usual Republican checklist of evangelicals but also conservative Catholic bishops and Orthodox rabbis.

According to the *National Catholic Reporter*, last year Bush asked Vatican officials for help enlisting American bishops' support on conservative issues. He held regular conference calls with Catholic conservatives, and hired Catholics to turn out the vote in their communities. He created an atmosphere that enabled a small group of outspoken leaders—including Archbishop Charles Chaput of Denver, Archbishop John Myers of Newark, Archbishop Raymond Burke of St. Louis, Bishop Michael Sheridan of

Colorado Springs, and Bishop Paul Loverde of Arlington, Virginia—to make their case that public positions can't be separated from private faith.

Chaput in particular has emerged as a strong advocate of a politically engaged Catholicism. A sixty-year-old Native American, he has written stinging columns in the diocesan newsletter and an op-ed for *The New York Times* arguing that "if we believe in the sanctity of life . . . we need to prove that by our actions, including our political choices." A few weeks after the election he described his position to me at the U.S. Conference of Catholic Bishops, in Washington, D.C. As a bishop, he said, he couldn't be partisan. "We are not telling [parishioners] how to vote," he explained. "We are telling them how to take communion in good conscience." In practice that distinction can be a little hard to discern. Although in the run-up to the election Chaput never told his audiences to vote against John Kerry, he did argue that the killing of the unborn was a "non-negotiable" issue, and then reminded them that Kerry supports abortion rights and Bush doesn't.

"We've tried one approach for thirty years—to be against abortion but measured and contextualized," he explained to me. "But it hasn't rooted out abortion." Chaput says he doesn't spend much time thinking about what his position means for politics. "We're not with the Republican Party," he told *The New York Times*. "They're with us."

A still more surprising alliance seems to have arisen in the past few years between the Bush administration and the normally insular Orthodox Jewish community. Here, too, the administration's outreach has been aggressive. Bush has held Hanukkah parties at the White House with invitation lists heavy on actual rabbis—Orthodox rabbis in particular—rather than on leaders of Jewish interest groups. In 2002 the Seattle Hebrew Academy, destroyed in an earthquake, was denied federal relief funds because it was a religious institution. Soon after, Bush signed an order allowing such institutions to compete for federal funds. That year the Union of Orthodox Jewish Congregations, the largest umbrella group for Orthodox Jews, began signing on with the Southern Baptist Convention and the Christian Legal Society to support some of the administration's faith-based initiatives.

Bush closed the deal during the Republican convention last summer, with an event at the Waldorf-Astoria tailored especially to Orthodox Jews—the first such event ever held by a presidential campaign. Rabbis came in from all over the country. Senator Sam Brownback, of Kansas, and Tim

Goeglein, from the White House, spoke about their commitment to Israel and values. Tevi Troy, a campaign official and an Orthodox Jew, also spoke. "That event generated a lot of buzz in the Orthodox community," recalls Nathan Diament, a spokesman for the Union of Orthodox Jewish Congregations of America. "In the more insular segments of the community they don't watch TV, or get a newspaper outside the Orthodox papers. Suddenly there were headlines in the Jewish press saying the Bush campaign did this unprecedented thing, that for the first time they weren't lumping us in with the rest of the Jewish community."

The gambit worked. Thanks to Bush's attention (and, no doubt, his strong support of Israel), Hasidic enclaves—Kiryas Joel, north of Westchester; Lakewood, New Jersey; the Wickliffe suburb of Cleveland—voted as much as 95 percent for Bush, according to Diament, even though they had supported Al Gore by overwhelming percentages in 2000. (The enormous swings reflect voters' loyalty to the dictates of their rabbis.) Similarly, the Miami precinct with the largest Conservative synagogue voted 80 percent for Gore in 2000 and 57 percent for Bush this time around. A strong majority of Jews nationwide voted for Kerry, but Bush's focus on politically conservative rabbis helped increase his share of the Jewish vote from 19 percent in 2000 to 25 percent last year.

"We're starting to get an echo in our community of the divide Christians have, between traditionalists and progressives," Diament says. "We do, however, have a different theology than evangelical Christians, and that theology can lead to different positions on matters of public policy." For example, Orthodox Jews don't view "an embryo sitting in a petri dish" as having the same rights as a full human being, and the Jewish imperative to heal the sick puts them in favor of stem-cell research. But, Diament says, his community shares a general sense of the corruptive influence of the mainstream culture and appreciates "the role faith plays in Bush's life and the life of his community, and how he talks about it."

What does the country's religious divide mean for the future? Much depends on how modernists respond to the surge of activism on the traditionalist side. If religious America is truly undergoing a culture war, it is at the moment a lopsided one. "There's a sense of complete reversal from the late fifties and early sixties," says James Davison Hunter, the author of *Culture Wars: The*

Struggle to Define America (1991). "Conservatives within denominations are so well mobilized, while progressives within Protestantism and Catholicism find themselves flatfooted, without any coherent course of action or any way to make sense of what's going on." Typically, Hunter says, evangelicals are wary of mainstream society, and prone to doomsday predictions. But he found them brimming with a "stunning sense of optimism" when he recently visited an evangelical church in Houston. "Their understanding of their own hopes and dreams about the culture were entirely linked to getting out the vote for Bush. They seemed very pragmatic, very pleased."

For the moment, at least. It's an open question whether religious traditionalists will maintain the level of political engagement they showed in the 2004 election. The greatest obstacle here may be not a modernist backlash but the burden of high expectations. Already there are signs that evangelicals may be headed for a crushing disappointment. Following Bush's victory, James Dobson, of the evangelical group Focus on the Family, declared that if the Republicans don't deliver on issues such as abortion and gay marriage, "I believe they'll pay a price in the next election." Similarly, Bob Jones III, the president of Bob Jones University, read an open letter to Bush in chapel: "In your reelection, God has graciously granted America— though she doesn't deserve it—a reprieve from the agenda of paganism. You have been given a mandate . . . Don't equivocate. Put your agenda on the front burner and let it boil . . . Honor the Lord, and He will honor you."

It's not hard to imagine that perhaps six months, or a year, or three years down the road, religious traditionalists will face frustration and a sense of betrayal by the political system with which they are now engaging so enthusiastically. It wouldn't be the first time. After the election the conservative luminary Paul Weyrich issued a letter to evangelicals exulting, "God is indeed a Republican. He must be. His hand helped reelect a president, with a popular mandate." And yet only five years ago Weyrich, who in the 1970s helped found the Heritage Foundation and coined the phrase "Moral Majority," was disillusioned about conservative Christians' ability to influence the national agenda on abortion and other issues. "Politics has failed," he wrote then. His prescription at the time: "Drop out of this culture" and find places "where we can live godly, righteous and sober lives." In 2008 we'll see if Weyrich and other religious conservatives remain engaged or start dropping out again.

Part Five:
Iraq and the War on Terrorism

What Bush Got Right

Fareed Zakaria

Newsweek | March 14, 2005

As the first year of his second term wore on, President Bush found himself in a paradoxical position. The war against the insurgency in Iraq, which saw a spike in violence and U.S. casualties following the Iraqi elections in January, was becoming increasingly unpopular, and Republicans in Congress were talking openly about finding some way to pull American troops out sooner rather than later. And with his Social Security reform initiative in similar trouble (see "Personal Dispute," p. 117), Bush's own approval ratings, rarely high to begin with, had dipped perilously close to 40 percent, and the phrase "lame duck" was being tossed around with abandon.

Yet at the same time, there was a growing consensus that Bush's decision to push aggressively for democratic change in the Mideast as the best defense against Islamic terrorists was already bearing fruit. Recent popular uprisings in places like Ukraine, Kyrgyzstan, and Lebanon, if not inspired directly by the Iraq project, certainly benefited from the foreign policy Bush has constructed around it. In this Newsweek *column, Fareed Zakaria credits the president for the bold course he's charted—but cautions, "It is easier to imagine liberal democracy than to achieve it." . . .*

Events in the Middle East over the past few weeks have confirmed the theories of that great scholar of the region, Thomas (Tip) O'Neill. The late speaker of the House's most memorable aphorism was "All politics is local." It's true even of the politics of rage. As long-repressed societies in the Middle East open up, we are discovering that their core concerns are not global but local. Most ordinary Arabs, it turns out, are not consumed by grand theories about the clash between Islam and the West, or the imperialism of American culture, or even the Palestinian cause. When you let the Lebanese speak, they want to talk about Syria's occupation of their country. When Iraqis got a chance to congregate, they voted for a government, not an insurgency. When a majority of Palestinians were heard from, they endorsed not holy terror to throw Israel into the sea, but practical diplomacy to get a state.

Tomorrow, were the Egyptian Street to voice its views—I mean the real

Egyptian Street, not President Mubarak's state-controlled media—we would probably discover that its deepest discontent is directed not at the president of the United States, but at the president of Egypt. Perhaps Arabs and Muslims are not some strange species after all. It is their rulers who are strange.

The other noted political scientist who has been vindicated in recent weeks is George W. Bush. Across New York, Los Angeles and Chicago—and probably Europe and Asia as well—people are nervously asking themselves a question: "Could he possibly have been right?" The short answer is yes. Whether or not Bush deserves credit for everything that is happening in the Middle East, he has been fundamentally right about some big things.

Bush never accepted the view that Islamic terrorism had its roots in religion or culture or the Arab-Israeli conflict. Instead he veered toward the analysis that the region was breeding terror because it had developed deep dysfunctions caused by decades of repression and an almost total lack of political, economic and social modernization. The Arab world, in this analysis, was almost unique in that over the past three decades it had become increasingly unfree, even as the rest of the world was opening up. His solution, therefore, was to push for reform in these lands.

The theory did not originate with Bush's administration. Others had made this case: scholars like Bernard Lewis and Fouad Ajami, Thomas Friedman of *The New York Times*, the Arab intellectuals who wrote the United Nations' now famous "Arab Human Development Report" and even this writer. (Three weeks after 9/11 I wrote an essay titled "Why Do They Hate Us?" that made this case.) These ideas were gaining some ground in the Arab world, especially after 9/11. But Bush's adoption of them was absolutely crucial because he had the power to pressure the region's regimes. Efforts to change the dynamics of the Middle East had always collapsed in the past as its wily rulers would delay, obstruct and obfuscate. Bush has pushed them with persistence and, increasingly, he is trying to build a broader international effort. The results might surprise.

Repressive regimes are often extremely fragile. Syria is the perfect example. Bashar al-Assad's rule rests on the narrowest base of fear and coercion. His ruling clique, mostly coming from the country's small Alawite sect, is well aware that it lacks support in their society. That's why it is so easily rattled and why the events in Lebanon could snowball into something much, much bigger. The other Arab regimes are less fragile.

Mubarak, while unpopular, is not despised. The Saudi royal family is more stable than many think. It uses money, marriage and connections—and yet more money—to create an elaborate patronage network that sustains it. But everywhere, there is pressure to change.

The Middle East would do well with incremental but persistent reform, as is taking place in Jordan, Qatar and Dubai. But in too many places, small, gradual reforms have been a smoke screen for doing nothing. Economic reforms are the most crucial because they modernize the whole society. But they are also the most difficult because they threaten the power and wealth of the oligarchies that run these countries. So far there has been more talk than action on this front.

People have often wished that the president had traveled more over the years. But Bush's capacity to imagine a different Middle East may actually be related to his relative ignorance of the region. Had he traveled to the Middle East and seen its many dysfunctions, he might have been disheartened. Freed from looking at the day-to-day realities, Bush maintained a vision of what the region could look like.

But therein lies the danger. It is easier to imagine liberal democracy than to achieve it. Ronald Reagan imagined a Soviet Union that was politically and economically free. Twenty years later, except for the Baltic states, not one country of the former Soviet Union has achieved that. There have been more than 50 elections in Africa in the past 15 years—some as moving as those in Iraq, had we bothered to notice them—but only a few of those countries can be described as free. Haiti has had elections and American intervention, and still has foreign troops stationed there. Yet only a few of these elections have led to successful and free societies.

Every country, culture and people yearns for freedom. But building real, sustainable democracy with rights and protections is complex. In Lebanon, for example, the absence of Syria will not mean the presence of a stable democracy. It was the collapse of Lebanon's internal political order that triggered the Syrian intervention in 1976. That problem will have to be solved, even after Syrian forces go home. In Iraq, the end of the old order has produced growing tendencies toward separatism and intolerance. Building democracy takes patience, deep and specific knowledge and, most important, the ability to partner with the locals.

If Bush is to be credited for the benefits of his policies, he must also take responsibility for their costs. Over the past three years, his administration has racked up enormous costs, many of which could easily have been lowered or avoided altogether. The pointless snubbing of allies, the brusque manner in which it went to war in Iraq, the undermanned occupation and the stubborn insistence (until last summer) on pursuing policies that were fueling both an insurgency and anti-Americanism in Iraq—all have taken their toll in thousands of American and Iraqi lives and almost $300 billion.

Perhaps an even more lasting cost is the broad and deep shifts in public opinion against America around the world. Look at countries as disparate as Britain, Poland, Turkey and Japan, all allies of the United States. In every one of them, public views have changed significantly in the past few years, and being pro-American is now a political liability. Tony Blair, once the most popular British leader in decades, has fallen far in public esteem, largely because of his unflinching support for the Bush administration.

For most countries, the debate over Iraq was not really about Iraq. It was about how America would wield its enormous global power. And to many countries, it seemed that the Bush administration was doing it irresponsibly. On this front, the signs from Bush's second term are heartening. In the Middle East, however, everything will depend on success on the ground. If, five years from now, Iraq, Afghanistan and perhaps an independent Palestine and a democratic Lebanon are thriving countries with modern political and economic systems, America will be honored and respected—and the talk of anti-American terror will have dissipated considerably. If, on the other hand, these countries are chaotic and troubled—more like Central Asia than Central Europe—people there will blame America. Remember, all politics is local.

The Politics of Churlishness: Giving George W. Bush His Due on Democracy

Martin Peretz

The New Republic | April 11, 2005

One of the casualties of partisan politics, it seems, is the ability to root for your opponent in any way, shape, or form. This partisan antipathy is especially problematic during wartime, as illustrated by the politics over the conflict in Iraq. Liberal Democrats have found virtually nothing good to say about the White House's efforts to promote democracy there, or anywhere else, for that matter. In this essay, Martin Peretz, editor in chief of the New Republic, *scolds the American Left for their inability to acknowledge anything positive in Bush's pro-democracy agenda—an agenda he feels liberals should be applauding. "[T]he situation is certainly complex," he writes. "But complexity is not a warrant for despair. The significant fact is that Bush's obsession with the democratization of the region is working."* . . .

If George W. Bush were to discover a cure for cancer, his critics would denounce him for having done it unilaterally, without adequate consultation, with a crude disregard for the sensibilities of others. He pursued his goal obstinately, they would say, without filtering his thoughts through the medical research establishment. And he didn't share his research with competing labs and thus caused resentment among other scientists who didn't have the resources or the bold—perhaps even somewhat reckless— instincts to pursue the task as he did. And he completely ignored the World Health Organization, showing his contempt for international institutions. Anyway, a cure for cancer is all fine and nice, but what about AIDS?

No, the president has not discovered a cure for cancer. But there is a pathology, a historical pathology, that he has attacked with unprecedented vigor and with unprecedented success. I refer, of course, to the political culture of the Middle East, which the president may actually have changed. And he has accomplished this genuinely momentous transformation in ways that virtually the entire foreign affairs clerisy—the cold-blooded Brent Scowcroft realist Republicans and almost all the Democrats—never thought possible. Or, perhaps, in ways some of them thought positively undesirable. Bush, it now seems safe to say, is one of the great surprises in modern U.S. history. Nothing about his past suggested that he harbored these ideals nor the qualities of character required for their realization. Right up to the moment Bush became president, I was convinced that his mind, at least on matters Levantine, belonged to his father and to James Baker III, whose worldview seemed to be defined by the pecuniary prejudice of oil and Texas: Keep the ruling Arabs happy. But I was wrong, and, in light of what has already been achieved in the Middle East, I am glad to say so. Most American liberals, alas, enjoy no similar gladness. They are not exactly pleased by the positive results of Bush's campaign in the Middle East. They deny and resent and begrudge and snipe. They are trapped in the politics of churlishness.

The achievements of Bush's foreign policy abroad represent a revolution in the foreign policy culture at home. The traditional Republican mentality that was so perfectly and meanly represented by Bush père and Baker precluded the United States from pressing the Arabs about reform—about *anything*—for decades. Not Iraq about its tyranny and its record of genocide, not Syria about its military occupation of Lebanon and its own brutal Baathist dictatorship, not Egypt about loosening the crippling bonds of a statist economy and an authoritarian political system, not Saudi Arabia about its championing of the Wahhabi extremism that made its own country so desiccated and the world so dangerous, and certainly not the Palestinians about the fantasy that they had won all the wars that they had actually lost and were therefore entitled to the full rewards due them from their victories. This was the state of U.S.-Arab relations in 2001: The United States was actually more frightened of the Arabs than they were of us. The extraordinary report of the 9/11 Commission about the delinquent reactions to the decade-long lead-up to the catastrophe of September 11 only confirms this impression of official U.S. pusillanimity.

The Clinton administration seized on every possible excuse—from the first World Trade Center bombing in 1993, right through the atrocities in Kenya and Tanzania, to the attack on the USS *Cole*—not to respond meaningfully to Osama bin Laden. This aggressively dilatory approach was set early on, when Bill Clinton's first secretary of state, dead-man-walking Warren Christopher, proposed that a special bureau be set up to deal with drugs, crime, and terrorism in a single office, as if terrorism is a problem for policemen and not for strategists. The 9/11 Commission Report records that only congressional opposition aborted Christopher's concoction. Attorney General Janet Reno always worried about retaliation against any moves by the United States; Secretary of State Madeleine Albright, preoccupied with her "push for a peace agreement between the Palestinians and Israelis," was concerned that military strikes against the bin Laden operations in Afghanistan would strengthen the Taliban; National Security Adviser Sandy Berger fretted that a shoot-out might be seen as an assassination, and, always the trade lawyer, he consistently held out hope that some sort of carrot would turn the Taliban against bin Laden; General Anthony Zinni was more concerned about human rights abuses by the Taliban than by its hospitality to Al Qaeda and worried also that a mosque might be damaged in the course of bombing operations; Pentagon officials warned that a missile aimed at bin Laden might kill a visiting Emirati prince instead (but why was a UAE prince hanging out with bin Laden anyway?); and CIA Director George Tenet had so many objections to decisive action that it would be nearly impossible to enumerate them.

Clinton, it is true, resolved to eliminate bin Laden, but soon he eliminated his desire to eliminate him. The Clinton administration's true desire was to arrest bin Laden, to indict him, and to put him on trial—to "bring him to justice," as these men and women pompously exhorted each other. Except Berger also feared that bin Laden would be acquitted in a U.S. court of law. CIA personnel trying to cut a deal with the Northern Alliance to capture bin Laden warned that, if the Afghan "tribals"—that's the orientalism of liberals—did not bring him in alive but, heaven forbid, actually killed him, they would not be paid for their labors. The charismatic leader of the Afghan opposition and our best contact with it, Ahmed Shah Massoud, who was assassinated two days before September 11, thought he was dealing with madmen.

The new Bush presidency also found it hard to wrap its hands around the Al Qaeda phenomenon and preferred to focus instead on Star Wars redivivus—until, of course, a catastrophe in Lower Manhattan concentrated its mind. What the Bush administration gradually came to realize was that fighting the Muslim terrorist international could not be done in a vacuum. If the Islamic and Arab orbits were to continue to revolve around sanguinary tyrannies, there would be no popular basis in civil society to rob the cult of suicidal murder of its prestige. So, rather than being a distraction from the struggle against the armed rage suffusing these at once taut and eruptive polities, confronting their governments was actually intrinsic to that struggle. The Bush administration recognized that removing the effect means removing the cause. The 9/11 Commission seems to have grasped this, too, at least in its citations of Richard Clarke's assertion that bin Laden and Saddam Hussein, Al Qaeda and the Iraqi Baath could be natural allies.

History has never traveled in the Middle East as fast as it has during the last two years. In this place where time seems to have stopped, time has suddenly accelerated. It may be true (more likely, it is not) that a deep yearning for democracy has been latent throughout the region for a long time. There certainly was a basis in reality for skepticism about the Arabs' hospitability to the opening of their societies. Whatever the proper historical and cultural analysis of the past, however, the fact is that democracy did not begin even to breathe until the small coalition of Western nations led by the United States destroyed the most ruthless dictatorship in the area.

Democracy in Mesopotamia? A fantasy, surely. But not quite. Iraq was, despite its unbelievably bloody history, a rather sophisticated place. During the nineteenth century, many Baghdadis went abroad to study. Modern nationalism sank some roots. Baghdad itself had a plurality of Jews, learned and mercantile, until they fled to the new state of Israel. An ancient minority of Christians survived into the age of Sunni pogroms and survives—though in lesser numbers—still. The Kurds grew relatively tolerant in the areas they dominated. And the majority Shia, though viciously persecuted from the founding of the Iraqi state after World War I—with the not-so-passive consent of the British colonials—and condemned to near-genocide by Saddam's revolutionary republic, have generally maintained the restraint that piety sometimes allows. After a year and a half of nearly daily Sunni bloodletting among them, the Shia have not wreaked the vengeance they surely could and, equally as surely, some of them long to take.

The U.S. liberation-occupation has now tried to cobble together these diverging Iraqis into the beginnings of a democratic regime. Wonder of wonders, these estranged cousins have shown some talent in the art of compromise; and trying to make this polity work is hardly an effort undertaken without courage. The judge who was killed with his son outside his home on his way to work at the tribunal that will try Saddam knew that danger stalked him, and so did the rest of the victims of Sunni bloodlust. This bloodlust evokes an unmistakable but macabre schadenfreude among many critics of the war, who want nothing of history except to be proved right. It is as if suicide bombings and other sorts of helter-skelter murder were a just judgment on the wrongdoing—yes, there have been wrongdoings, some of them really disgusting—of the Bush administration. And, even if ridding western Asia of Saddam is reluctantly accepted as justified, what blogger couldn't have accomplished what came after more deftly?

In any case, this churlish orthodoxy tells us that the Sunnis need to be enticed into the political game lest it be deemed illegitimate. In this scenario, it is the murderers who withhold or bestow moral authority. John F. Burns, the defiantly honest *New York Times* journalist in Baghdad, who has consistently reported the ambiguous and truly tangled realities of the war, now sees the Baathist and Sunni warriors in retreat, if not actually beaten. What will probably happen in Iraq is a version of what endured for decades in Lebanon: a representative government rooted in sect—argumentative, perhaps even corrupt, but functioning. Lebanon was never perfect, but it worked reasonably well, until the aggressive Palestinian guests took to commanding Shia turf to establish a "state within a state." (This was a phenomenon that the nimble Thomas L. Friedman did not much report on in the first leg of his journey *From Beirut to Jerusalem*, confiding that fear for his life and livelihood kept him from deviating too far from the Palestinian story as they wanted it told. Eason Jordan *avant la lettre*.)

The fine fruits of the Bush administration's indifference to international opinion may be seen now in Lebanon, too. What is happening there is the most concrete intra-Arab consequence of the Iraq war. Nothing could be done in Lebanon without Syria's sanction, no government decision without the approval of Damascus, no business without a hefty Damascene percentage. Syrian troops and spies were everywhere. Lebanese of all sects and clans have been restive for years. But they lived in the fearful memory of their mad civil war, the civil war of the daily car bombs in the marketplace. Suddenly, the elections in Iraq, Bush's main achievement there, exhilarating and inspiring, sprung loose the psychological impediments that shackled the Lebanese to Syria. Even if the outcomes will not be exactly the same, this was Prague and Berlin at the end of the long subjugation to their neighbor to the east. More immediately, this was Kiev only a few months ago. The first mass protest against the Syrians and their satrap prime minister drew tens of thousands. Then there was the much larger crowd of pro-Syria Shia from the south, a disconcerting moment. But, after that, a multitude so huge that it defied counting, and so diverse. This was the true cedar revolution, a revolution of the young, for independence, for freedom from the failing but always brutal Damascus regime next door. Will Vladimir Putin be so stupid as to invest credit and arms in the stiff and callow son of Hafez Al Assad?

None of this happened by spontaneous generation. Yes, there were lucky breaks: Yasir Arafat died, Syria conspired somehow to have former Lebanese Prime Minister Rafik Hariri assassinated. And yes, the new directions are young, and the autocratic-theocratic political culture of the Middle East is old, and it is once again too early to proclaim that the mission has been accomplished. As the ancient Israelite king observed, let he who girds his harness not boast as he who takes it off. But the mission is nonetheless real, and far along, and it is showing thrilling accomplishments. It is simply stupid, empirically and philosophically, to assert that all or any of this would have happened without the deeply unpopular but historically grand initiative of Bush. The hundreds of thousands of young people in Martyrs' Square knew that they had Bush's backing. The president seems even to have enticed Jacques Chirac into a more active policy toward Lebanon: For him, too, Syria had to go. If this satisfies Chirac's yearning for *la gloire,* so be it. (But it will not be so easy to maintain such alliances: Already, Security Council members are said to be working up plans to put the future of Lebanon under the protective care of the United Nations Interim Force in Lebanon, when nothing in UNIFIL's past— nothing—should provide confidence that it is able, or even disposed, to act decisively against Arab brutality.)

What is occurring in Saudi Arabia and Egypt is also heartening, if more than a bit tentative. Under pressure from the Bush administration, the Saudis have allowed the first local elections in the country's history: an election to bodies that cannot make big decisions, and an election limited to male voters, naturally. But infidels (that is, Shia) may also vote. By Saudi standards, this is the revolution of 1848. In Egypt, responding to the insistence of the Bush people, President Hosni Mubarak has allowed that he will permit opponents to run in the presidential elections against him. Mubarak has no chance of losing . . . this time. Maybe, however, the son will not be the father's inevitable successor, and maybe the Arab custom of turning dictatorships into dynasties will also come to an end, at least in Cairo. And, in the brave figure of Ayman Nour, the world now has a hero of the anti-Mubarak forces to celebrate and to support. In both countries, to be sure, what we are seeing are the bare beginnings of a democratic process, the very bare beginnings. It will be years, maybe decades, before these become democratic polities. And there is always the chance—as was the case in Algeria, once the jewel in the shabby crown of the "non-aligned"—that the vox populi will vote wrong. In the Algerian instance, it had to vote wrong: The choice was between national fascists and pious fascists. Take your pick.

So the situation is certainly complex. But complexity is not a warrant for despair. The significant fact is that Bush's obsession with the democratization of the region is working. Have Democrats begun to wonder how it came to pass that this noble cause became the work of Republicans? They should wonder if they care to regain power. They should recall that Clinton (and the sanctimonious Jimmy Carter even more so) had absolutely no interest in trying to modify the harsh political character of the Arab world. What they aspired to do was to mollify the dictators—to prefer the furthering of the peace process to the furthering of the conditions that make peace possible. The Democrats were the ones who were always elevating Arafat. He was at the very center of *their* road map. After he stalked out of a meeting room in Paris during cease-fire talks in late 2000, Albright actually ran in breathless pursuit to lure him back. It was the Democrats who perpetuated Arafat's demonic sway over the Palestinians, and it was the Democrats who sustained him among the other Arabs. And so the cause of Arab democracy was left for the Republicans to pursue. After September 11, the cause became a matter also of U.S. national security.

The great diversion from the real politics of the Arab countries, and from the prospect of political reform, was the Palestinian grievance against Israel. In the early years of their conflict with the Zionists, the Palestinians thought that these countries would fight their battles for them, at the negotiating table and on the battlefield, which they did. But what happened in reality was that the various Arabs exploited the Palestinians as pawns in their own ambitions to pick off pieces of Palestine for themselves. That is why there was no Palestinian state in the West Bank or Gaza after the armistice of 1949, as one might have expected from the Partition Plan of 1947. The West Bank was annexed to Jordan. Gaza was not annexed but administratively attached to Egypt. Syria's armies won no decisive battles against the Jews; otherwise, they also would have taken a piece of Palestine. In any event, until the Six Days War, the Palestinian groan against the Jews was focused on the very existence of Israel within narrow and perilous borders, without strategic depth, without old Jerusalem, without the West Bank, without Gaza.

And Arab governments deflected the ample internal plaints of their own peoples with mobilized hysteria against the Jews. Every domestic grievance was dispersed with rousing rhetoric against Israel. The sun of Gamal Abdel Nasser rose and set with Cairo's failures in its wars with Israel. Hatred of the Zionists levitated the Baath dictatorships of both Iraq and Syria. In the end, after five wars and two intifadas, the Palestinians still seethed. But it had all come to nothing. And, finally, the angel of death unilaterally attacked Arafat. Bush had had the good sense to pay no attention to him, despite the urgent imprecations of the usual apologists: the European Union, the United Nations, France, Russia, and the editorial page of the *Times*. Had Bush made even a single accommodation to Arafat, Arafat's way in the world would have been enshrined in Palestinian lore for yet another generation as the only way.

But Bush didn't, and Ariel Sharon didn't, either. Now that there is some real hope among both Israelis and Palestinians about the future, let us examine the reasons for it. The first is that Bush made no gestures to the hyperbolic fantasies of Palestinian politics. He gave them one dose of reality after another. The second is that he gave Israel the confidence that he would not trade its security for anything—which means that Israel is now willing to cede much on its own. (Israeli dovishness for American hawkishness: This was always the only way.) The third is that Bush is holding Sharon to his commitments, and everyone who is at all rational on these issues now sees the Israeli prime minister as a man of his word and a man of history. After all, Sharon has broken with much of his own political party. Not for nothing is he now the designated assassination target of the Israeli hard right. Still, holding Sharon to his word also means holding Mahmoud Abbas to his. So far, the record is mixed. The serious shutting down of the terrorist militias has not yet begun, but the Palestinian Authority did run reasonably free local elections, and they were not accompanied by killing. It is true that Hamas won more of these races than makes either Sharon or Abbas comfortable, and its strength may even increase in the coming parliamentary voting. But this, too, is a part of the gamble of democracy; and, to the extent that the Palestinians are taking this gamble and following the newest fashion among the other Arabs, it is a tribute to the inked purple fingers of Iraq, which is to say, a tribute to Bush and his simplistic but effective trust in the polling place.

It has been heartening, in recent months, to watch some Democratic senators searching for ways out of the politics of churlishness. Some liberals appear to have understood that history is moving swiftly and in a good direction, and that history has no time for their old and mistaken suspicion of American power in the service of American values. One does not have to admire a lot about George W. Bush to admire what he has so far wrought. One need only be a thoughtful American with an interest in proliferating liberalism around the world. And, if liberals are unwilling to proliferate liberalism, then conservatives will. Rarely has there been a sweeter irony.

Iraq, the Press and the Election
Michael Massing

The New York Review of Books | Dec. 16, 2004

One of the ongoing debates around the Iraq conflict has been whether the U.S. press has been too negative in reporting what's really happening in Iraq, as conservatives assert, or, conversely, too willing to parrot the U.S. government's upbeat assessment of conditions there, as liberals claim.

In this essay on the U.S. media's coverage of the Iraq war in the period leading up to the 2004 election, Michael Massing argues the liberal case—and suggests that the tendency of the American media to tread lightly in their Iraq reporting was a significant factor in George Bush's victory. . . .

In the end, the war in Iraq did not have the decisive impact on the election that many had expected. In the weeks before the vote there were the massacre of forty-nine Iraqi police trainees; a deadly attack inside the previously impenetrable Green Zone in Baghdad; the refusal by an army unit to carry out a supply mission on the grounds that it was too dangerous; the explosion of several car bombs at a ceremony where soldiers were handing out candy, killing dozens of children; the abduction of contractors, journalists, and aid workers, including the director of the CARE office in Baghdad; the release of a report holding the highest reaches of the Pentagon and the military responsible for the abuses at Abu Ghraib; a report by President Bush's hand-picked investigator confirming that Iraq had long ago lost its ability to produce weapons of mass destruction; and the spread of the insurgency to every corner of the country, bringing reconstruction to a virtual halt. All of this, in the end, counted for less to voters (if the exit polls are to be believed) than such issues as whether homosexuals should be allowed to marry and whether discarded embryos should be used for stem cell research.

How did this happen? In many ways, George Bush's victory seems to have confirmed the fact that large numbers of voters in America today are very conservative, dominated by strong attachments to God, country, and the traditional family. At the same time, it's not clear to what extent the public was aware of just how bad things had gotten in Iraq. For while there was much informative reporting on the war, a number of factors combined to shield Americans from its most brutal realities. A look at these factors can help to understand some neglected aspects of George Bush's victory.

1.

Toward the end of September, Farnaz Fassihi, a correspondent for *The Wall Street Journal* in Baghdad, sent an e-mail to forty friends describing her working conditions in Iraq. Fassihi had been sending out such messages on a regular basis, but this one seethed with anger and frustration. "Being a foreign correspondent in Baghdad these days," she wrote,

> is like being under virtual house arrest. . . . I avoid going to people's homes and never walk in the streets. I can't go grocery shopping any more, can't eat in restaurants, can't strike a conversation with strangers, can't look for stories, can't drive in any thing but a full armored car, can't go to scenes of breaking news, can't be stuck in traffic, can't speak English outside, can't take a road trip, can't say I'm

an American, can't linger at checkpoints, can't be curious about what people are saying, doing, feeling. And can't and can't.

Citing the fall of Falluja, the revolt of Moqtada al-Sadr, and the spread of the insurgency to every part of the country, Fassihi declared that

despite President Bush's rosy assessments, Iraq remains a disaster. If under Saddam it was a "potential" threat, under the Americans it has been transformed to "imminent and active threat," a foreign policy failure bound to haunt the United States for decades to come. . . . The genie of terrorism, chaos and mayhem has been unleashed onto this country as a result of American mistakes and it can't be put back into a bottle.

Fassihi's e-mail soon ended up on the Internet, where it quickly spread, giving readers a vivid and unvarnished look at what it was like to live in the world's most dangerous capital. Somehow, Fassihi, in her informal message, had managed to capture the lurid nature of life in Iraq in a way that conventional reporting, with all its qualifiers and distancing, could not.

Other U.S. correspondents in Baghdad were startled at the attention her e-mail received. "All of us felt that we'd been writing that story," one journalist told me. "Everyone was marveling and asking what were we doing wrong if that information came as a surprise to the American public." Reporters rushed to file their own first-person accounts. Writing in the "Week in Review," for instance, *New York Times* reporter Dexter Filkins observed that

in the writing of this essay, a three-hour affair, two rockets and three mortar shells have landed close enough to shake the walls of our house. The door to my balcony opens onto an Iraqi social club, and the roar from the blasts set the Iraqis into a panic, their screams audible above the Arabic music wafting from the speakers.

Interestingly, no such account appeared in *The Wall Street Journal*. For Fassihi's criticism of Bush administration policy outraged some readers, who insisted that she could no longer write about Iraq with the necessary objectivity. In response, the *Journal* announced that Fassihi was going to take a previously scheduled vacation from Iraq and that this would keep her from writing anything more about it until after the U.S. election.

Both Fassihi and her editors insisted that this decision was not a criticism of her, but some detected a pulling back by the *Journal,* and an examination of its coverage tends to bear this out. In the weeks before Fassihi's departure, the paper ran a number of probing pieces on Iraq. On September 15, for instance, Fassihi and Greg Jaffe, in a front-page story, described how the steady rise in violence in Baghdad reflected growing cooperation among Iraq's once highly fragmented insurgent groups. After Fassihi's e-mail was circulated, however, such stories almost entirely disappeared from the *Journal's* front page, and they were hard to find inside as well. The resulting vacuum was filled by the *Journal's* stridently conservative opinion pages, which every day featured one or more editorials or columns insisting that the war was going well and that anyone who felt otherwise was a defeatist liberal uninterested in bringing democracy to the Middle East.

In one column, Daniel Henninger mentioned several Web sites that readers interested in learning what was truly going on in Iraq could consult. I looked up one of them, HealingIraq .com. It was written by an Iraqi dentist. His most recent posting began with an apology for the long hiatus since his last filing. "The daily situation in Baghdad is sadly too depressing to live through, let alone write about," he lamented. He told of one friend who had been shot in the stomach while working at an Internet café when an armed gang sprayed a nearby car belonging to a lawyer who was pursuing a case they wanted dropped. Another friend, a doctor, had been kidnapped along with a pharmacist by ten armed men storming a pharmacy that had supplied medications to the U.S. Army. Their decapitated bodies were later found outside Baghdad. Such grim reports were absent from the *Journal's* opinion pages, and, increasingly, its news pages. Thus one of the nation's top newspapers became effectively neutered as a source of reliable information about Iraq.

Meanwhile, pressure was building on other U.S. news organizations as a result of the visit to the United States of Iraqi Prime Minister Iyad Allawi in late September. In private, he was not optimistic. As Peter Boyer reported in the November 1 [2004] *New Yorker,* Allawi told President Bush of the conundrum facing him and the coalition—that the insurgency required

forceful action, but that any such action could further alienate the population, thus fueling the insurgency. In public, however, Allawi joined with
Bush in insisting that Iraq was making progress and in blaming the press
for making too much of the negative. Fourteen or fifteen of Iraq's eighteen
provinces, Allawi asserted, were "completely safe," and the others had
only "pockets of terrorism." And this threw editors and reporters on the
defensive.

"At the moment, there's real sensitivity about the perceived political
nature of every story coming out of Iraq," a Baghdad correspondent for a
large U.S. paper told me in mid-October. "Every story from Iraq is by definition an assessment as to whether things are going well or badly." In reality,
he said, the situation in Iraq was a "catastrophe," a view "almost unanimously" shared by his colleagues. But, he added, "editors are hypersensitive
about not wanting to appear to be coming down on one side or the other."

Allawi's visit to the United States was part of an intensive campaign by
the Bush administration to manage the flow of news out of Iraq. As a matter
of policy, any journalist wanting to visit the Green Zone, that vast swath of
Baghdad that is home to U.S. officialdom, had to be escorted at all times;
one could not simply wander around and chat with people in bars and cafés.
The vast world of civilian contractors—of Halliburton's Kellogg, Brown &
Root, of Bechtel, and of all the other private companies responsible for
rebuilding Iraq—was completely off-limits; employees of these companies
were informed that they would be fired if they were caught talking to the
press. During the days of the Coalition Provisional Authority, its adminis-
trator, L. Paul Bremer, and the top military commander, Ricardo Sanchez,
gave very few interviews to U.S. correspondents in Baghdad. They did, however, speak often via satellite with small newspapers and local TV stations,
which were seen as more open and sympathetic. "The administration has
been extremely successful in going around the filters, of getting their message directly to the American people without giving interviews to the
Baghdad press corps," one correspondent said.

The insurgents have done their part as well. In no prior conflict—not in
Vietnam, nor in Lebanon, nor in Bosnia—have journalists been singled out
for such sustained and violent attack. According to the Committee to Protect Journalists, thirty-six journalists have been killed in Iraq since the start
of the war—nineteen at the hands of the insurgents. Two French journalists seized in August remain missing. Until this fall, many journalists at

least felt safe while in their heavily guarded hotels. Then, in October, Paul Taggart, an American photographer, was seized by four gunmen after leaving the Hamra Hotel complex, one of the main residences for Western journalists. He was eventually released, but it was discovered that the captors had a floor plan of the hotel with the name of every journalist in every room. Facing such perils, many correspondents packed up and left.

2.

A number stayed, however, and, at considerable risk, set out to describe the Iraqi maelstrom. Leading the way were three top U.S. newspapers—*The New York Times*, *The Washington Post*, and the *Los Angeles Times*—backed by, among others, NPR, Knight Ridder, and the Associated Press. The newspapers, in particular, seemed driven by a sense that they had somehow let down their readers during the run-up to the war, that they had not sufficiently scrutinized the administration's case for war, and they now seemed determined to make up for it. *The New York Times*, for one, maintained a staff of forty to fifty people in Baghdad, including four or five reporters plus assorted drivers, housekeepers, security guards, and "fixers," those invaluable interpreter/journalists who help visiting reporters understand who's who, arrange interviews, and make sense of it all. With more and more of the country off-limits to Western reporters, these fixers were increasingly sent out into the field to find out what was going on, and some emerged as enterprising reporters in their own right.

In early October, *The New York Times*'s Edward Wong, accompanied by a fixer and a photographer, spent a day being guided through the streets of Baghdad's Sadr City by a mid-level aide to Moqtada al-Sadr. At the time, U.S. warplanes were pounding the district on a nightly basis, but Wong—whose itinerary included a kebab lunch at the aide's home, a street that had recently been bombed, and a hospital where the wounded were being treated—found that the strikes were not having their intended effect. "Loyalty to [Sadr] burns fierce here" in Sadr City, "a vast slum of 2.2 million people, despite frequent American raids and almost nightly airstrikes," he wrote on October 3. "The American military has stepped up its campaign to rout the Mahdi Army, Mr. Sadr's militia, on its home turf here, to drive him to the bargaining table. But it is often impossible here to distinguish between civilians and fighters."

After Prime Minister Allawi asserted that most of Iraq was safe, *The*

Washington Post's Rajiv Chandrasekaran—seeking a statistical measure—got hold of the daily security reports of Kroll, a private firm working for the U.S. government. These reports showed that Iraq was suffering an average of seventy attacks a day by insurgents, up from the forty to fifty that had occurred before the handover of political authority in late June. What is more, the reports showed, the attacks were occurring not only in the Sunni Triangle but in every province of Iraq. "In number and scope," Chandrasekaran wrote on the *Post*'s front page,

> the attacks compiled in the Kroll reports suggest a broad and intensifying campaign of insurgent violence that contrasts sharply with assessments by Bush administration officials and Iraq's interim prime minister that the instability is contained [in] small pockets of the country.

(Since he wrote, the number of attacks has increased to more than one hundred a day.)

In the face of Bush administration efforts to portray the Iraqi insurgency as made up exclusively of foreign fighters led by the Jordanian-born terrorist Abu Musab al-Zarqawi, several U.S. news organizations offered a more nuanced look. The AP's Jim Krane, for instance, reported in early October that the insurgents seemed to consist of four main groups, including not only "hardcore fighters" aligned with Zarqawi but also conservative Iraqis seeking to install an Islamic theocracy, Moqtada al-Sadr's Mahdi Army, and "Iraqi nationalists fighting to reclaim secular power lost when Saddam Hussein was deposed in April 2003." This last group, Krane wrote, was the largest. In other U.S. wars, he noted, "the enemy was clear." In Iraq, "the disorganized insurgency has no single commander, no political wing and no dominant group." As a result, "U.S. troops can't settle on a single approach" to the fighting.

In Washington, too, the press uncovered many significant stories about U.S. policy in Iraq. In one five-day period (October 22 to October 26), *The Washington Post*'s front page featured stories on

- a poll showing that U.S.-backed political figures were losing ground to religious leaders;
- how the war in Iraq had diverted energy and attention from the fight against al-Qaeda;

- how the CIA was secretly moving detainees out of Iraq—a "serious breach" of the Geneva Conventions; and

- administration plans to ask for an additional $70 billion to fund the wars in Iraq and Afghanistan.

The biggest bombshell, though, came on October 25 [2004], when the *Times*, in a two-column story on its front page, reported that nearly 380 tons of high-grade explosives had disappeared from a bunker south of Baghdad, and that this had likely occurred after the U.S. invasion. The story was quickly seized on by John Kerry, who for the remaining days of the campaign cited it as further evidence of the administration's mishandling of Iraq. On the day before the election, CNN analyst William Schneider said that the missing-explosives story seemed to be an "important" factor in a last-minute turning of the polls away from Bush.

3.

In the end, of course, the voters did not so turn. And leaving aside any possible problems with the polls themselves, it's clear that all those stories in the *Times* and the *Post*, and the discussion they generated, did not have the impact on the public that Schneider and many others had predicted. Understanding why requires a look at some of the constraints under which reporters at even the most aggressive papers worked. Just as reporters confronted physical no-go zones into which they could not venture, they also faced journalistic ones posing many perils.

Civilian casualties was one. Getting at this posed a number of obstacles for journalists, the most obvious being the lack of reliable figures. The U.S. military does not offer information about civilian casualties, and the estimates by private groups vary wildly. At the conservative end, Iraq Body Count, which offers on its Web site a running total based on news reports, places the number of civilian dead from military combat at between 14,300 and 16,500. At the upper end, a team of public health researchers from

Johns Hopkins University, using mortality estimates from both before and after the war, has estimated that 100,000 civilians have died either directly or indirectly as a result of the war. This finding, published by the British medical journal *The Lancet* in late October, was questioned by many other groups, including Human Rights Watch, which said that the real figure was probably much lower but still unacceptably high.

Amid such conflicting estimates, journalists—unable to visit most of the sites where civilian deaths occur— have been exceedingly cautious. A correspondent for a major U.S. paper described for me the dilemma he faced in a place like Falluja (this was before the current U.S. offensive). His paper, he said, has an Iraqi staffer in the city, and after each U.S. bombing he would go to the scene and report back that a certain number of civilians had died. "But," the correspondent said, "I want to see it myself." He elaborated:

> If you get a press release from the U.S. military saying it dropped four five-hundred-pound bombs on insurgents in Fallujah, and we know from our people that twelve people were killed, and they say it was Zarqawi's men, we'll print what they say—that it was Zarqawi. Al-Jazeera and al-Arabiya every night run interviews with hospital directors, who say a man, his wife, and their three children were killed. The U.S. military says that the director's been threatened. I don't know. It's very frustrating because we can't go in. You're left with "he said/she said."

Here, then, is another of those journalistic conventions—the need for "balance"—that deters papers from getting at one of the war's most disturbing dimensions.

Needless to say, the insurgents themselves have ruthlessly killed many civilians, in attacks that often target them. An admirable bid to weigh all this was made by Nancy Youssef of Knight Ridder. Youssef learned that the Iraqi Health Ministry had since early April been gathering statistics on civilian casualties from hospitals in fifteen of Iraq's eighteen provinces. Youssef obtained the numbers through September 19 [2004] and totaled them up. The number of dead came to 3,487, of which 328 were women and children. Another 13,720 Iraqis had been injured. Hospital officials believed that most of the dead were civilians, and Youssef, analyzing the circumstances of their death, was able to see a pattern, which she described in her lead: "Operations by U.S. and multinational forces and

Iraqi police are killing twice as many Iraqis —most of them civilians—as attacks by insurgents." Iraqi officials, she added,

> said the statistics proved that U.S. airstrikes intended for insurgents also were killing large numbers of innocent civilians. Some say these casualties are undermining popular acceptance of the American-backed interim government.

After Youssef's report appeared, other news organizations began clamoring for similar numbers. Within days, the interim government ordered the Health Ministry to stop issuing them. The silence again set in.

4.

The gingerly approach to civilian casualties in the U.S. press is part of a much larger hole in the coverage, one concerning the day-to-day nature of the U.S. occupation. Most of the soldiers in Iraq are young men who can't speak Arabic and who have rarely traveled outside the United States, and they have suddenly been set down in a hostile environment in which they face constant attack. They are equipped with powerful weapons and have authority over a dark-skinned people with alien customs. The result is constant friction, often leading to chronic abuses that, while not as glaring as those associated with Abu Ghraib, are no less corrosive in their effect on local sentiment.

One journalist who has seen this firsthand is Nir Rosen. A twenty-seven-year-old American freelance reporter, Rosen speaks Arabic (a rare skill among Western reporters in Iraq), has a dark complexion (allowing him to mix more easily with Iraqis), and prefers when in Iraq to hang out with locals rather than with other journalists. (In the late spring, he managed to get inside Falluja at a time when it was a death trap for Western reporters; he described his chilling findings in the July 5 issue of *The New Yorker*.) Seeing Iraq from the perspective of the Iraqis, Rosen got a glimpse of how persistently and routinely American actions alienated them. "People have to wait three hours in a traffic jam because a U.S. army convoy is going by," he notes. "Guns are pointed at you wherever you go. People are constantly shouting at you. Concrete walls are everywhere. Violence is everywhere."

In October 2003, Rosen spent two weeks embedded with a U.S. Army unit near the Syrian border. In sweeps through neighborhoods, he said, the Americans used Israeli-style tactics— making mass arrests in the hope that one or two of those scooped up will have something useful for them. "They'll hold them for ten hours in a truck without food or water," he told me. "And 90 percent of them are innocent." Writing of his experience in *Reason* magazine, Rosen described how a unit he accompanied on a raid broke down the door of a house of a man they suspected of dealing in arms. When the man, named Ayoub, did not immediately respond to their orders, they shot him with nonlethal bullets. "The floor of the house was covered with his blood," Rosen wrote. "He was dragged into a room and interrogated forcefully as his family was pushed back against their garden's fence."

Ayoub's frail mother, he continued, pleaded with the interrogating soldier to spare her son's life, protesting his innocence:

> He pushed her to the grass along with Ayoub's four girls and two boys, all small, and his wife. They squatted barefoot, screaming, their eyes wide open in terror, clutching one another as soldiers emerged with bags full of documents, photo albums and two compact discs with Saddam Hussein and his cronies on the cover. These CDs, called *The Crimes of Saddam,* are common on every Iraqi street and, as their title suggests, they were not made by Saddam supporters. But the soldiers couldn't read Arabic and saw only the picture of Saddam, which was proof enough of guilt. Ayoub was brought out and pushed on to the truck.

After holding Ayoub for several hours in a detention center, the soldiers determined that he was innocent, and they later let him go.

Rosen believes that such encounters are common. The American soldiers he saw "treat everybody as the enemy," he said, adding that they can be very abusive and violent. "If you're a boy and see soldiers beating the shit out of your father, how can you not hate the Americans?" He added: "Why doesn't anybody write about this in *The New York Times* or *The Washington Post?* The AP always has people embedded —why don't they write about it?"

One reason, he suggests, is that embedded journalists who write negatively about the U.S. military find themselves "blacklisted." It happened to Rosen: a series of stories he wrote for *Asia Times* about his experience while embedded elicited an angry letter from the commander and the public affairs officer of the unit he accompanied, and he has not been allowed to become embedded since. Other correspondents told me of similar experiences.

Another reason why news organizations don't write about such matters is suggested in the recently released DVD version of Michael Moore's movie *Fahrenheit 9/11*. It contains as an added feature an interview with Urban Hamid, a Swedish journalist who in late 2003 accompanied an American platoon on a raid in Samarra. Hamid's experience was similar to Nir Rosen's, with the difference that he caught his on tape. In it, we see soldiers using an armored personnel carrier to break down the gates of a house. We see the soldiers rush in with their rifles pointed ahead, and terrified women rushing out. An elderly man on crutches is rousted up and a plastic bag is placed over his head. The soldiers go through the family documents, trying to determine if this man is connected with the insurgency, but because they don't speak Arabic they can't really tell. Nonetheless, they take him to a detention center, where he joins dozens of others, their heads all sheathed in plastic. Celebrating the arrests, the soldiers take pictures of one another with their "trophies." One soldier admits that he's surprised they didn't find more weapons. "The sad thing for these guys is that we'll probably let them go because their names don't match up," he says.

In the interview, Hamid says he asked many Iraqis if they'd heard of things like this, and they all told him "of course." "It's preposterous," he says, "to think there is any way you win somebody's hearts and minds by imposing such a criminal and horrible policy." Hamid says that he tried to sell his tape to "mainstream media." First he approached the "Swedish media" but got no response. He then approached the "American media," with the same result. "It's obvious," he says, "that the mainstream media exercise some kind of self-censorship in which people know that this is a hot potato and don't touch it, because you're going to get burned."

5.

Is self-censorship among U.S. news organizations as widespread as Hamid says? The group he's referring to, of course, is television news, and it's here that most Americans get their news. For six weeks before the election I watched as much TV news as I could, constantly switching from one station to another.

Viewing the newscasts of the traditional networks—ABC, CBS, and NBC —I was surprised at how critical of Bush policy they could be. When Prime Minister Allawi claimed that fifteen of Iraq's eighteen provinces were fit for elections, Charles Gibson on ABC's *World News Tonight* asked Pentagon correspondent Martha Raddatz if this was true. "I can give you a two-word answer from a military commander I spoke to today," Raddatz replied. "He said, 'no way.' And one other commander said, 'Maybe nine, ten, of the eighteen, and that's being generous.'" On many nights, the networks aired "mayhem reels" out of Iraq, two minutes' worth of cars afire, blood stains on pavements, bodies being carried from rubble. In addition to relaying scoops from the daily press, the networks broke some stories of their own. On the Sunday before the election, for instance, *60 Minutes* ran a hard-hitting segment about a unit of the Oregon National Guard in Iraq that lacked such basic equipment as the armored plating needed to protect soldiers in Humvees from roadside bombs. Such reports appeared often enough to reinforce long-standing conservative complaints that the networks are inherently "liberal."

Yet even these "liberal" outlets had strict limits on what they would show. On September 12, for instance, a group of American soldiers patrolling Haifa Street, a dangerous avenue in central Baghdad, came under fire. Another group of soldiers in two Bradley fighting vehicles came to rescue them. They did, but one of the vehicles had to be abandoned, and a jubilant crowd quickly gathered around it. A banner from a group associated with Zarqawi was produced and placed on the vehicle. Arab TV crews arrived to record the event. At one point, two U.S. helicopters showed up and made several passes over the vehicle. With the crowd fully visible, one of the helicopters launched a barrage of rockets and machine-gun rounds. The vehicle was destroyed, and thirteen people were killed. Among them was Mazen al-Tumeizi, a Palestinian producer for the al-Arabiya network who was doing a TV report in front of the Bradley. Hit while on camera, his blood spattering the lens, Tumeizi doubled over and screamed that he was dying.

The video of Tumeizi's death was shown repeatedly on al-Arabiya and other Arabic-language networks. On American TV, it aired very briefly on NBC and CNN, then disappeared. On most other networks, it appeared not at all. Here was a dramatic piece of footage depicting in raw fashion the human toll of the fighting in Iraq, yet American TV producers apparently feared that if they gave it too much time, they would, in Urban Hamid's phrase, get burned. (I still have not heard of a single instance in which the killing of an American in Iraq has been shown on American TV.)

This fear seems especially apparent on cable news. Given the sheer number of hours CNN, MSNBC, and Fox have to fill, it's remarkable how little of substance and imagination one sees here. CNN still bills itself as "the most trusted name in news," but one wonders among whom. Its breakfast-time show, *American Morning*, offers a truly vapid mix of bromides and forced bonhomie. In mid-October, with a grinding war and bruising electoral campaign underway, the show spent a week in Chicago, providing one long, breathless promo for the city. Every hour or so, correspondent Brent Sadler would produce an update from Baghdad. For the most part, he offered rip-and-read versions of U.S. press releases, with constant references to "precision strikes" aimed at "terrorist targets" and "Zarqawi safehouses." Not once did I see Sadler make even a stab at an independent assessment.

For analysis, CNN leaned heavily on safe, establishment-friendly voices, including many of the same retired military officers who appeared in the run-up to the war. On October 15, for instance, former General George Joulwan discussed with Wolf Blitzer the need for Americans to do a better job of explaining to Muslims how much they'd done for them over the years. Blitzer agreed: "I don't think a lot of Muslims understand that over the past fifteen years, every time the U.S. has gone to war, whether in Kuwait, or Somalia, or Kosovo, or Bosnia, or Afghanistan or Iraq, it's to help Muslims." Joulwan: "We've saved tens of thousands of them. We need to understand that, and so do our Muslim friends."

Thankfully, not everything on CNN descended to this level. The network's reporting on the election in Afghanistan was crisp and informative, thanks largely to Christiane Amanpour's sharp reports. Aaron Brown's nightly show, while often slow-paced, offered a sober look at serious issues. And occasionally a truly stellar bit of reporting poked through, as when Jane Arraf, breaking loose from her embed with a U.S. unit laying siege to Samarra, found that many of the claims she'd been fed were untrue. "The U.S. said more than one hundred insurgents were killed, but residents saw it differently," Arraf reported. The signs of destruction all around her, she stated that "it was hard to find anyone who believes any of the people in hospitals are insurgents."

Rare on CNN, such reports are almost entirely absent from Fox News. The channel continues to insist that it is "fair and balanced," but hardly anyone takes this seriously anymore. Still, I was not prepared for just how blatant and pervasive its bias was. This was apparent throughout the presidential campaign, with George Bush forever portrayed as resolute, principled, and plainspoken, and John Kerry as equivocating, elitist, and French.

The slant was evident in the coverage of the war as well. Whenever news about Iraq came on, the urgent words "War on Terror" appeared on the screen, thus helping to frame the war exactly as the President did. "Did the President and his administration take their eye off the ball in the war on terror?" Brit Hume asked one night. For an answer, Hume spoke with Richard Miniter, the author of *Shadow War: The Untold Story of How Bush Is Winning the War on Terror.* No bias there. After the *Washington Times* reported the discovery in Iraq of a computer disk belonging to a Baath Party official that contained data showing the layout of six schools in the United States, Fox asked, "Can your school be a potential terrorist target?" This time, Fox turned to Jeffrey Beatty, a former Delta Force commander who, it so happens, runs an antiterrorist consulting firm. In fact, Beatty said, schools are potential terrorist targets, and they had better take precautionary measures *now.* On *The O'Reilly Factor,* the central question for weeks was "Should CBS fire Dan Rather?" Bill O'Reilly spent far more time dissecting Rather's mistakes at CBS than he did analyzing Bush's deeds in Iraq.

And that's how Fox wants it. The most striking feature of its coverage of the war in Iraq was, in fact, its *lack* of coverage. A good example occurred on the Saturday before the election. That morning, the U.S. military announced that eight Marines had been killed and nine others wounded in attacks in the Sunni Triangle. It was the highest U.S. death toll in nearly seven months. After reading the news on the Web, I tuned in to Fox's 11 A.M. news summary. It made no mention of the dead Marines. The next hour was taken up by a feverish program on hot stock picks. Then came the noon newscast. After spending ten minutes on the Osama bin Laden tape, the presidential campaign, and the tight race in Ohio, it finally got around to informing viewers of the Marines' deaths. It then spent all of twenty seconds on them. As it turned out, that Saturday was a particularly bloody day in Iraq, with a series of bombings, mortar attacks, and ambushes throughout the country. Viewers of Fox, however, saw little of it.

This formula has proved very popular. *The O'Reilly Factor* is currently the top-rated cable news show, and Fox's prime-time audience is on average twice as large as CNN's. That audience still trails far behind that of the traditional networks, but Fox has much more time to fill, and it does it with programming that is far more overtly ideological than anything else on TV. Its constant plugging of Bush, its persistent jabs at Kerry, its relentless insistence that Iraq is part of the war on terror and that both wars are going well—all have had their effect. According to election-day exit polls, 55 percent of voters regarded the Iraq war as part of the war on terrorism, as opposed to 42 percent who saw it as separate. And 81 percent of the former voted for George Bush.

In some ways, the coverage of the war featured a battle as fierce as the political one between Democrats and Republicans, with the "red" medium of Fox slugging it out with the "blue" outlets of the *Times* and the *Post*, CBS and ABC. CNN seemed somewhere in between, careening wildly between an adherence to traditional news values on the one hand and a surrender to the titillating, overheated, nationalistic fare of contemporary cable on the other. In the end, CNN—influenced by Fox's success—seemed firmly in the latter camp. It offered the superficiality of Fox without any of its conviction. This hollowing out of CNN was, in a sense, an enormous victory for the Bush campaign. Overall, in analyzing the reasons for Bush's triumph, the impact of Fox News should not be overlooked.

Now, with President Bush preparing for a second term, what can we expect from the press in Iraq? The initial signs, from Falluja, are not encouraging. Even allowing for the constraints imposed by embedding, much of the press seemed unduly accepting of U.S. claims, uncritically repeating commanders' assertions about the huge numbers of insurgents killed while underplaying the devastation in the city. And little attention was paid to the estimated 200,000 residents said to have fled Falluja in anticipation of the fighting. Amid U.S. claims that the city had been "liberated," these refugees seemed invisible. But, in light of the coverage in recent months, this should have come as no surprise.

Outsourcing Torture

Jane Mayer

The New Yorker | February 14 & 21, 2005

One of the most troubling aspects of America's war on terrorism has been the way the U.S. has treated detainees being held in Guantánamo, Afghanistan, Iraq, and untold other undisclosed locations. (The fact that the CIA has established a network of secret detention centers around the world has been reported on by many news outlets, including the New York Times *and* Washington Post.*) On the legal front, the Bush administration has challenged the norms of international law by claiming the right to hold people it deems "enemy combatants" indefinitely without trial or even access to a lawyer, and has also generated memos that appear to sanction torture. Their actual record on the ground is equally grim: a number of detainees have died while in U.S. custody, and government investigatory commissions have released horrific accounts and images of detainees being physically and mentally abused by American interrogators.*

Here, in a superb piece of reporting, Jane Mayer details another disturbing method used by both the Clinton and Bush administrations: the growing practice of handing prisoners over to foreign governments that are known to employ torture—a policy that goes by the chillingly bland name "extraordinary rendition." . . .

On January 27th, President Bush, in an interview with the *Times*, assured the world that "torture is never acceptable, nor do we hand over people to countries that do torture." Maher Arar, a Canadian engineer who was born in Syria, was surprised to learn of Bush's statement. Two and a half years ago, American officials, suspecting Arar of being a terrorist, apprehended him in New York and sent him back to Syria, where he endured months of brutal interrogation, including torture. When Arar described his experience in a phone interview recently, he invoked an Arabic expression. The pain was so unbearable, he said, that "you forget the milk that you have been fed from the breast of your mother."

Arar, a thirty-four-year-old graduate of McGill University whose family emigrated to Canada when he was a teen-ager, was arrested on September 26, 2002, at John F. Kennedy Airport. He was changing planes; he had been on vacation with his family in Tunisia, and was returning to Canada. Arar was detained because his name had been placed on the United States Watch List of terrorist suspects. He was held for the next thirteen days, as American officials questioned him about possible links to another suspected terrorist. Arar said that he barely knew the suspect, although he had worked with the man's brother. Arar, who was not formally charged, was placed in handcuffs and leg irons by plainclothes officials and transferred to an executive jet. The plane flew to Washington, continued to Portland, Maine, stopped in Rome, Italy, then landed in Amman, Jordan.

During the flight, Arar said, he heard the pilots and crew identify themselves in radio communications as members of "the Special Removal Unit." The Americans, he learned, planned to take him next to Syria. Having been told by his parents about the barbaric practices of the police in Syria, Arar begged crew members not to send him there, arguing that he would surely be tortured. His captors did not respond to his request; instead, they invited him to watch a spy thriller that was aired on board.

Ten hours after landing in Jordan, Arar said, he was driven to Syria, where interrogators, after a day of threats, "just began beating on me." They whipped his hands repeatedly with two-inch-thick electrical cables, and kept him in a windowless underground cell that he likened to a grave. "Not even animals could withstand it," he said. Although he initially tried to assert his innocence, he eventually confessed to anything his tormentors wanted him to say. "You just give up," he said. "You become like an animal."

A year later, in October, 2003, Arar was released without charges, after the Canadian government took up his cause. Imad Moustapha, the Syrian Ambassador in Washington, announced that his country had found no links between Arar and terrorism. Arar, it turned out, had been sent to Syria on orders from the U.S. government, under a secretive program known as "extraordinary rendition." This program had been devised as a means of extraditing terrorism suspects from one foreign state to another for interrogation and prosecution. Critics contend that the unstated purpose of such renditions is to subject the suspects to aggressive methods of persuasion that are illegal in America—including torture.

Arar is suing the U.S. government for his mistreatment. "They are outsourcing torture because they know it's illegal," he said. "Why, if they have suspicions, don't they question people within the boundary of the law?"

Rendition was originally carried out on a limited basis, but after

September 11th, when President Bush declared a global war on terrorism, the program expanded beyond recognition—becoming, according to a former C.I.A. official, "an abomination." What began as a program aimed at a small, discrete set of suspects—people against whom there were outstanding foreign arrest warrants—came to include a wide and ill-defined population that the Administration terms "illegal enemy combatants." Many of them have never been publicly charged with any crime. Scott Horton, an expert on international law who helped prepare a report on renditions issued by N.Y.U. Law School and the New York City Bar Association, estimates that a hundred and fifty people have been rendered since 2001. Representative Ed Markey, a Democrat from Massachusetts and a member of the Select Committee on Homeland Security, said that a more precise number was impossible to obtain. "I've asked people at the C.I.A. for numbers," he said. "They refuse to answer. All they will say is that they're in compliance with the law."

Although the full scope of the extraordinary-rendition program isn't known, several recent cases have come to light that may well violate U.S. law. In 1998, Congress passed legislation declaring that it is "the policy of the United States not to expel, extradite, or otherwise effect the involuntary return of any person to a country in which there are substantial grounds for believing the person would be in danger of being subjected to torture, regardless of whether the person is physically present in the United States."

The Bush Administration, however, has argued that the threat posed by stateless terrorists who draw no distinction between military and civilian targets is so dire that it requires tough new rules of engagement. This shift in perspective, labelled the New Paradigm in a memo written by Alberto Gonzales, then the White House counsel, "places a high premium on . . . the ability to quickly obtain information from captured terrorists and their sponsors in order to avoid further atrocities against American civilians," giving less weight to the rights of suspects. It also questions many international laws of war. Five days after Al Qaeda's attacks on the World Trade Center and the Pentagon, Vice-President Dick Cheney, reflecting the new outlook, argued, on *Meet the Press*, that the government needed to "work through, sort of, the dark side." Cheney went on, "A lot of what needs to be done here will have to be done quietly, without any discussion, using sources and methods that are available to our intelligence agencies, if we're going to be successful. That's the world these folks operate in. And so it's going to be vital for us to use any means at our disposal, basically, to achieve our objective."

The extraordinary-rendition program bears little relation to the system of due process afforded suspects in crimes in America. Terrorism suspects in Europe, Africa, Asia, and the Middle East have often been abducted by hooded or masked American agents, then forced onto a Gulfstream V jet, like the one described by Arar. This jet, which has been registered to a series of dummy American corporations, such as Bayard Foreign Marketing, of Portland, Oregon, has clearance to land at U.S. military bases. Upon arriving in foreign countries, rendered suspects often vanish. Detainees are not provided with lawyers, and many families are not informed of their whereabouts.

The most common destinations for rendered suspects are Egypt, Morocco, Syria, and Jordan, all of which have been cited for human-rights violations by the State Department, and are known to torture suspects. To justify sending detainees to these countries, the Administration appears to be relying on a very fine reading of an imprecise clause in the United Nations Convention Against Torture (which the U.S. ratified in 1994), requiring "substantial grounds for believing" that a detainee will be tortured abroad. Martin Lederman, a lawyer who left the Justice Department's Office of Legal Counsel in 2002, after eight years, says, "The Convention only applies when you know a suspect is more likely than not to be tortured, but what if you kind of know? That's not enough. So there are ways to get around it."

Administration officials declined to discuss the rendition program. But Rohan Gunaratna, a Sri Lankan expert on terrorist interrogations who has consulted with several intelligence agencies, argued that rough tactics "can save hundreds of lives." He said, "When you capture a terrorist, he may know when the next operation will be staged, so it may be necessary to put a detainee under physical or psychological pressure. I disagree with physical torture, but sometimes the threat of it must be used."

Rendition is just one element of the Administration's New Paradigm. The C.I.A. itself is holding dozens of "high value" terrorist suspects outside of the territorial jurisdiction of the U.S., in addition to the estimated five hundred and fifty detainees in Guantánamo Bay, Cuba. The Administration confirmed the identities of at least ten of these suspects to the 9/11 Commission —including Khalid Sheikh Mohammed, a top Al Qaeda operative, and

Ramzi bin al-Shibh, a chief planner of the September 11th attacks—but refused to allow commission members to interview the men, and would not say where they were being held. Reports have suggested that C.I.A. prisons are being operated in Thailand, Qatar, and Afghanistan, among other countries. At the request of the C.I.A., Secretary of Defense Donald Rumsfeld personally ordered that a prisoner in Iraq be hidden from Red Cross officials for several months, and Army General Paul Kern told Congress that the C.I.A. may have hidden up to a hundred detainees. The Geneva Conventions of 1949, which established norms on the treatment of soldiers and civilians captured in war, require the prompt registration of detainees, so that their treatment can be monitored, but the Administration argues that Al Qaeda members and supporters, who are not part of a state-sponsored military, are not covered by the Conventions.

The Bush Administration's departure from international norms has been justified in intellectual terms by elite lawyers like Gonzales, who is a graduate of Harvard Law School. Gonzales, the new Attorney General, argued during his confirmation proceedings that the U.N. Convention Against Torture's ban on "cruel, inhuman, and degrading treatment" of terrorist suspects does not apply to American interrogations of foreigners overseas. Perhaps surprisingly, the fiercest internal resistance to this thinking has come from people who have been directly involved in interrogation, including veteran F.B.I. and C.I.A. agents. Their concerns are as much practical as ideological. Years of experience in interrogation have led them to doubt the effectiveness of physical coercion as a means of extracting reliable information. They also warn that the Bush Administration, having taken so many prisoners outside the realm of the law, may not be able to bring them back in. By holding detainees indefinitely, without counsel, without charges of wrongdoing, and under circumstances that could, in legal parlance, "shock the conscience" of a court, the Administration has jeopardized its chances of convicting hundreds of suspected terrorists, or even of using them as witnesses in almost any court in the world.

"It's a big problem," Jamie Gorelick, a former deputy attorney general and a member of the 9/11 Commission, says. "In criminal justice, you either prosecute the suspects or let them go. But if you've treated them in ways that won't *allow* you to prosecute them you're in this no man's land. What do you do with these people?"

The criminal prosecution of terrorist suspects has not been a priority for the Bush Administration, which has focussed, rather, on preventing additional attacks. But some people who have been fighting terrorism for many years are concerned about unintended consequences of the Administration's radical legal measures. Among these critics is Michael Scheuer, a former C.I.A. counter-terrorism expert who helped establish the practice of rendition. Scheuer left the agency in 2004, and has written two acerbic critiques of the government's fight against Islamic terrorism under the pseudonym Anonymous, the most recent of which, *Imperial Hubris*, was a best-seller.

Not long ago, Scheuer, who lives in northern Virginia, spoke openly for the first time about how he and several other top C.I.A. officials set up the program, in the mid-nineties. "It was begun in desperation," he told me. At the time, he was the head of the C.I.A.'s Islamic-militant unit, whose job was to "detect, disrupt, and dismantle" terrorist operations. His unit spent much of 1996 studying how Al Qaeda operated; by the next year, Scheuer said, its mission was to try to capture bin Laden and his associates. He recalled, "We went to the White House"—which was then occupied by the Clinton Administration—"and they said, 'Do it.'" He added that Richard Clarke, who was in charge of counter-terrorism for the National Security Council, offered no advice. "He told me, 'Figure it out by yourselves,'" Scheuer said. (Clarke did not respond to a request for comment.)

Scheuer sought the counsel of Mary Jo White, the former U.S. Attorney for the Southern District of New York, who, along with a small group of F.B.I. agents, was pursuing the 1993 World Trade Center bombing case. In 1998, White's team obtained an indictment against bin Laden, authorizing U.S. agents to bring him and his associates to the United States to stand trial. From the start, though, the C.I.A. was wary of granting terrorism suspects the due process afforded by American law. The agency did not want to divulge secrets about its intelligence sources and methods, and American courts demand transparency. Even establishing the chain of custody of key evidence—such as a laptop computer—could easily pose a significant problem: foreign governments might refuse to testify in U.S. courts about how they had obtained the evidence, for fear of having their secret cooperation exposed. (Foreign governments often worried about retaliation from their own Muslim populations.) The C.I.A. also felt that other agencies sometimes stood in its way. In 1996, for example, the State Department stymied a joint effort by the C.I.A. and the F.B.I. to question one of bin Laden's cousins in America, because he had a diplomatic passport, which protects the holder from U.S. law enforcement. Describing the C.I.A.'s frustration, Scheuer said, "We were turning into voyeurs. We knew where these people were, but we couldn't capture them because we had nowhere to take them." The agency realized that "we had to come up with a third party."

The obvious choice, Scheuer said, was Egypt. The largest recipient of U.S. foreign aid after Israel, Egypt was a key strategic ally, and its secret police force, the Mukhabarat, had a reputation for brutality. Egypt had been frequently cited by the State Department for torture of prisoners. According to a 2002 report, detainees were "stripped and blindfolded; suspended from a ceiling or doorframe with feet just touching the floor; beaten with fists, whips, metal rods, or other objects; subjected to electrical shocks; and doused with cold water [and] sexually assaulted." Hosni Mubarak, Egypt's leader, who came to office in 1981, after President Anwar Sadat was assassinated by Islamist extremists, was determined to crack down on terrorism. His prime political enemies were radical Islamists, hundreds of whom had fled the country and joined Al Qaeda. Among these was Ayman al-Zawahiri, a physician from Cairo, who went to Afghanistan and eventually became bin Laden's deputy.

In 1995, Scheuer said, American agents proposed the rendition program to Egypt, making clear that it had the resources to track, capture, and transport terrorist suspects globally—including access to a small fleet of aircraft. Egypt embraced the idea. "What was clever was that some of the senior people in Al Qaeda were Egyptian," Scheuer said. "It served American purposes to get these people arrested, and Egyptian purposes to get these people back, where they could be interrogated." Technically, U.S. law requires the C.I.A. to seek "assurances" from foreign governments that rendered suspects won't be tortured. Scheuer told me that this was done, but he was "not sure" if any documents confirming the arrangement were signed.

A series of spectacular covert operations followed from this secret pact. On September 13, 1995, U.S. agents helped kidnap Talaat Fouad Qassem, one of Egypt's most wanted terrorists, in Croatia. Qassem had fled to Europe after being linked by Egypt to the assassination of Sadat; he had been sentenced to death in absentia. Croatian police seized Qassem in Zagreb and handed him over to U.S. agents, who interrogated him aboard a ship cruising the Adriatic Sea and then took him back to Egypt. Once there, Qassem disappeared. There is no record that he was put on trial. Hossam el-Hamalawy, an Egyptian journalist who covers human-rights issues, said, "We believe he was executed."

A more elaborate operation was staged in Tirana, Albania, in the summer of 1998. According to the *Wall Street Journal,* the C.I.A. provided the Albanian intelligence service with equipment to wiretap the phones of suspected Muslim militants. Tapes of the conversations were translated into English, and U.S. agents discovered that they contained lengthy discussions with Zawahiri, bin Laden's deputy. The U.S. pressured Egypt for assistance; in June, Egypt issued an arrest warrant for Shawki Salama Attiya, one of the militants. Over the next few months, according to the *Journal,* Albanian security forces, working with U.S. agents, killed one suspect and captured Attiya and four others. These men were bound, blindfolded, and taken to an abandoned airbase, then flown by jet to Cairo for interrogation. Attiya later alleged that he suffered electrical shocks to his genitals, was hung from his limbs, and was kept in a cell in filthy water up to his knees. Two other suspects, who had been sentenced to death in absentia, were hanged.

On August 5, 1998, an Arab-language newspaper in London published a letter from the International Islamic Front for Jihad, in which it threatened retaliation against the U.S. for the Albanian operation—in a "language they will understand." Two days later, the U.S. Embassies in Kenya and Tanzania were blown up, killing two hundred and twenty-four people.

The U.S. began rendering terror suspects to other countries, but the most common destination remained Egypt. The partnership between the American and the Egyptian intelligence services was extraordinarily close: the Americans could give the Egyptian interrogators questions they wanted put to the detainees in the morning, Scheuer said, and get answers by the evening. The Americans asked to question suspects directly themselves, but, Scheuer said, the Egyptians refused. "We were never in the same room at the same time."

Scheuer claimed that "there was a legal process" undergirding these early renditions. Every suspect who was apprehended, he said, had been convicted in absentia. Before a suspect was captured, a dossier was prepared containing the equivalent of a rap sheet. The C.I.A.'s legal counsel signed off on every proposed operation. Scheuer said that this system prevented innocent people from being subjected to rendition. "Langley would never let us proceed unless there was substance," he said. Moreover, Scheuer emphasized, renditions were pursued out of expedience—"not out of thinking it was the best policy."

Since September 11th, as the number of renditions has grown, and hundreds of terrorist suspects have been deposited indefinitely in places like Guantánamo Bay, the shortcomings of this approach have become manifest. "Are we going to hold these people forever?" Scheuer asked. "The policymakers hadn't thought what to do with them, and what would happen when it was found out that we were turning them over to governments that the human-rights world reviled." Once a detainee's rights have been violated, he says, "you absolutely can't" reinstate him into the court system. "You can't kill him, either," he added. "All we've done is create a nightmare."

On a bleak winter day in Trenton, New Jersey, Dan Coleman, an ex-F.B.I. agent who retired last July, because of asthma, scoffed at the idea that a C.I.A. agent was now having compunctions about renditions. The C.I.A., Coleman said, liked rendition from the start. "They loved that these guys would just disappear off the books, and never be heard of again," he said. "They were proud of it."

For ten years, Coleman worked closely with the C.I.A. on counter-terrorism cases, including the Embassy attacks in Kenya and Tanzania. His methodical style of detective work, in which interrogations were aimed at forging relationships with detainees, became unfashionable after September 11th, in part because the government was intent on extracting information as quickly as possible, in order to prevent future attacks. Yet the more patient approach used by Coleman and other agents had yielded major successes. In the Embassy-bombings case, they helped convict four Al Qaeda operatives on three hundred and two criminal counts; all four men pleaded guilty to serious terrorism charges. The confessions the F.B.I. agents elicited, and the trial itself, which ended in May, 2001, created an invaluable public record about Al Qaeda, including details about its funding mechanisms, its internal structure, and its intention to obtain weapons of mass destruction. (The political leadership in Washington, unfortunately, did not pay sufficient attention.)

Coleman is a political nonpartisan with a law-and-order mentality. His eldest son is a former Army Ranger who served in Afghanistan. Yet Coleman was troubled by the Bush Administration's New Paradigm. Torture, he said, "has become bureaucratized." Bad as the policy of rendition was before September 11th, Coleman said, "afterward, it really went out of control." He explained, "Now, instead of just sending people to third countries, we're holding them ourselves. We're taking people, and keeping them in our own custody in third countries. That's an enormous problem." Egypt, he pointed out, at least had an established legal system, however harsh. "There was a process there," Coleman said. "But what's our process? We have no method over there other than our laws—and we've decided to ignore them. What are we now, the Huns? If you don't talk to us, we'll kill you?"

From the beginning of the rendition program, Coleman said, there was no doubt that Egypt engaged in torture. He recalled the case of a suspect in the first World Trade Center bombing who fled to Egypt. The U.S. requested his return, and the Egyptians handed him over—wrapped head to toe in duct tape, like a mummy. (In another incident, an Egyptian with links to Al Qaeda who had cooperated with the U.S. government in a terrorism trial was picked up in Cairo and imprisoned by Egyptian authorities until U.S. diplomats secured his release. For days, he had been chained to a toilet, where guards had urinated on him.)

Under such circumstances, it might seem difficult for the U.S. government to legally justify dispatching suspects to Egypt. But Coleman said that since September 11th the C.I.A. "has seemed to think it's operating under different rules, that it has extralegal abilities outside the U.S." Agents, he said, have "told me that they have their own enormous office of general counsel that rarely tells them no. Whatever they do is all right. It all takes place overseas."

Coleman was angry that lawyers in Washington were redefining the parameters of counter-terrorism interrogations. "Have any of these guys ever tried to talk to someone who's been deprived of his clothes?" he asked. "He's going to be ashamed, and humiliated, and cold. He'll tell you anything you want to hear to get his clothes back. There's no value in it." Coleman said that he had learned to treat even the most despicable suspects as if there were "a personal relationship, even if you can't stand them." He said that many of the suspects he had interrogated expected to be tortured, and were stunned to learn that they had rights under the American system. Due process made detainees more compliant, not less, Coleman said. He had also found that a defendant's right to legal counsel was beneficial not only to suspects but also to law-enforcement officers. Defense lawyers frequently persuaded detainees to cooperate with prosecutors, in exchange for plea agreements. "The lawyers show these guys there's a way out," Coleman said. "It's human nature. People don't cooperate with you unless they have some reason to." He added, "Brutalization doesn't work. We know that. Besides, you lose your soul."

The Bush Administration's redefinition of the standards of interrogation took place almost entirely out of public view. One of the first officials to offer hints of the shift in approach was Cofer Black, who was then in charge of counter-terrorism at the C.I.A. On September 26, 2002, he addressed the House and Senate Intelligence Committees, and stated that the arrest and detention of terrorists was "a very highly classified area." He added, "All you need to know is that there was a 'before 9/11' and there was an 'after 9/11.' After 9/11, the gloves came off."

Laying the foundation for this shift was a now famous set of internal legal memos—some were leaked, others were made public by groups such as the N.Y.U. Center for Law and National Security. Most of these documents were generated by a small, hawkish group of politically appointed lawyers in the Justice Department's Office of Legal Counsel and in the office of Alberto Gonzales, the White House counsel. Chief among the authors was John C. Yoo, the deputy assistant attorney general at the time. (A Yale Law School graduate and a former clerk to Justice Clarence Thomas, Yoo now teaches law at Berkeley.) Taken together, the memos advised the President that he had almost unfettered latitude in his prosecution of the war on terror. For many years, Yoo was a member of the Federalist Society, a fellowship of conservative intellectuals who view international law with skepticism, and September 11th offered an opportunity for him and others in the Administration to put their political ideas into practice. A former lawyer in the State Department recalled the mood of the Administration: "The Twin Towers were still smoldering. The atmosphere was intense. The tone at the top was aggressive—and understandably so. The Commander-in-Chief had used the words 'dead or alive' and vowed to bring the terrorists to justice or bring justice to them. There was a fury."

Soon after September 11th, Yoo and other Administration lawyers began advising President Bush that he did not have to comply with the Geneva Conventions in handling detainees in the war on terror. The lawyers classified these detainees not as civilians or prisoners of war—two categories of individuals protected by the Conventions—but as "illegal enemy combatants." The rubric included not only Al Qaeda members and supporters but the entire Taliban, because, Yoo and other lawyers argued, the country was a "failed state." Eric Lewis, an expert in international law who represents several Guantánamo detainees, said, "The Administration's lawyers created a third category and cast them outside the law."

The State Department, determined to uphold the Geneva Conventions, fought against Bush's lawyers and lost. In a forty-page memo to Yoo, dated January 11, 2002 (which has not been publicly released), William Taft IV, the State Department legal adviser, argued that Yoo's analysis was "seriously flawed." Taft told Yoo that his contention that the President could disregard the Geneva Conventions was "untenable," "incorrect," and "confused." Taft disputed Yoo's argument that Afghanistan, as a "failed state," was not covered by the Conventions. "The official United States position before, during, and after the emergence of the Taliban was that Afghanistan constituted a state," he wrote. Taft also warned Yoo that if the U.S. took the war on terrorism outside the Geneva Conventions, not only could U.S. soldiers be denied the protections of the Conventions— and therefore be prosecuted for crimes, including murder—but President Bush could be accused of a "grave breach" by other countries, and be prosecuted for war crimes. Taft sent a copy of his memo to Gonzales, hoping that his dissent would reach the President. Within days, Yoo sent Taft a lengthy rebuttal.

Others in the Administration worried that the President's lawyers were wayward. "Lawyers have to be the voice of reason and sometimes have to put the brakes on, no matter how much the client wants to hear something else," the former State Department lawyer said. "Our job is to keep the train on the tracks. It's not to tell the President, 'Here are the ways to avoid the law.'" He went on, "There is no such thing as a non-covered person under the Geneva Conventions. It's nonsense. The protocols cover fighters in everything from world wars to local rebellions." The lawyer said that Taft urged Yoo and Gonzales to warn President Bush that he would "be seen as a war criminal by the rest of the world," but Taft was ignored. This may be because President Bush had already made up his mind. According to top State Department officials, Bush decided to suspend the Geneva Conventions on January 8, 2002—three days before Taft sent his memo to Yoo.

The legal pronouncements from Washington about the status of detainees were painstakingly constructed to include numerous loopholes. For example, in February, 2002, President Bush issued a written directive stating that, even though he had determined that the Geneva Conventions did not apply to the war on terror, all detainees should be treated "humanely." A close reading of the directive, however, revealed that it referred only to military interrogators—not to C.I.A. officials. This exemption allowed the C.I.A. to continue using interrogation methods, including rendition, that stopped just short of torture. Further, an August, 2002, memo written largely by Yoo but signed by Assistant Attorney General Jay S. Bybee argued that torture required the intent to inflict suffering "equivalent in intensity to the pain accompanying serious physical injury, such as organ failure, impairment of bodily function, or even death." According to the *Times*, a secret memo issued by Administration lawyers authorized the C.I.A. to use novel interrogation methods—including "water-boarding," in which a suspect is bound and immersed in water until he nearly drowns. Dr. Allen Keller, the director of the Bellevue/N.Y.U. Program for Survivors of Torture, told me that he had treated a number of people who had been subjected to such forms of near-asphyxiation, and he argued that it was indeed torture. Some victims were still traumatized years later, he said. One patient couldn't take showers, and panicked when it rained. "The fear of being killed is a terrifying experience," he said.

The Administration's justification of the rough treatment of detainees appears to have passed down the chain of command. In late 2003, at Abu Ghraib prison, in Iraq, photographs were taken that documented prisoners being subjected to grotesque abuse by U.S. soldiers. After the scandal became public, the Justice Department revised the narrow definition of torture outlined in the Bybee memo, using language that more strongly prohibited physical abuse during interrogations. But the Administration has fought hard against legislative efforts to rein in the C.I.A. In the past few months, Republican leaders, at the White House's urging, have blocked two attempts in the Senate to ban the C.I.A. from using cruel and inhuman interrogation methods. An attempt in the House to outlaw extraordinary rendition, led by Representative Markey, also failed.

In a recent phone interview, Yoo was soft-spoken and resolute. "Why is it so hard for people to understand that there is a category of behavior not covered by the legal system?" he said. "What were pirates? They weren't fighting on behalf of any nation. What were slave traders? Historically, there were people so bad that they were not given protection of the laws. There were no specific provisions for their trial, or imprisonment. If you were an illegal combatant, you didn't deserve the protection of the laws of war." Yoo cited precedents for his position. "The Lincoln assassins were treated this way, too," he said. "They were tried in a military court, and executed." The point, he said, was that the Geneva Conventions' "simple binary classification of civilian or soldier isn't accurate."

Yoo also argued that the Constitution granted the President plenary powers to override the U.N. Convention Against Torture when he is acting in the nation's defense—a position that has drawn dissent from many scholars. As Yoo saw it, Congress doesn't have the power to "tie the President's hands in regard to torture as an interrogation technique." He continued, "It's the core of the Commander-in-Chief function. They can't prevent the President from ordering torture." If the President were to abuse his powers as Commander-in-Chief, Yoo said, the constitutional remedy was impeachment. He went on to suggest that President Bush's victory in the 2004 election, along with the relatively mild challenge to Gonzales mounted by the Democrats in Congress, was "proof that the debate is over." He said, "The issue is dying out. The public has had its referendum."

A few months after September 11th, the U.S. gained custody of its first high-ranking Al Qaeda figure, Ibn al-Sheikh al-Libi. He had run bin Laden's terrorist training camp in Khalden, Afghanistan, and was detained in Pakistan. Zacarias Moussaoui, who was already in U.S. custody, and Richard Reid, the Shoe Bomber, had both spent time at the Khalden camp. At the F.B.I.'s field office in New York, Jack Cloonan, an officer who had worked for the agency since 1972, struggled to maintain control of the legal process in Afghanistan. C.I.A. and F.B.I. agents were vying to take possession of Libi. Cloonan, who worked with Dan Coleman on anti-terrorism cases for many years, said he felt that "neither the Moussaoui case nor the Reid case was a slam dunk." He became intent on securing Libi's testimony as a witness against them. He advised his F.B.I. colleagues in Afghanistan to question Libi respectfully, "and handle this like it was being done right here, in my office in New York." He recalled, "I remember talking on a secure line to them. I told them, 'Do yourself a favor, read the guy his rights. It may be old-fashioned, but this will come out if we don't. It may take ten years, but it will hurt you, and the bureau's reputation, if you don't. Have it stand as a shining example of what we feel is right.' "

Cloonan's F.B.I. colleagues advised Libi of his rights and took turns with C.I.A. agents in questioning him. After a few days, F.B.I. officials felt that they were developing a good rapport with him. The C.I.A. agents, however, felt that he was lying to them, and needed tougher interrogation.

To Cloonan's dismay, the C.I.A. reportedly rendered Libi to Egypt. He was seen boarding a plane in Afghanistan, restrained by handcuffs and ankle cuffs, his mouth covered by duct tape. Cloonan, who retired from the F.B.I. in 2002, said, "At least we got information in ways that wouldn't shock the conscience of the court. And no one will have to seek revenge for what I did." He added, "We need to show the world that we can lead, and not just by military might."

After Libi was taken to Egypt, the F.B.I. lost track of him. Yet he evidently played a crucial background role in Secretary of State Colin Powell's momentous address to the United Nations Security Council in February, 2003, which argued the case for a preemptive war against Iraq. In his speech, Powell did not refer to Libi by name, but he announced to the world that "a senior terrorist operative" who "was responsible for one of Al Qaeda's training camps in Afghanistan" had told U.S. authorities that Saddam Hussein had offered to train two Al Qaeda operatives in the use of "chemical or biological weapons."

Last summer, *Newsweek* reported that Libi, who was eventually transferred from Egypt to Guantánamo Bay, was the source of the incendiary charge cited by Powell, and that he had recanted. By then, the first anniversary of the U.S. invasion of Iraq had passed and the 9/11 Commission had declared that there was no known evidence of a working relationship between Saddam and Al Qaeda. Dan Coleman was disgusted when he heard about Libi's false confession. "It was ridiculous for interrogators to think Libi would have known anything about Iraq," he said. "I could have told them that. He ran a training camp. He wouldn't have had anything to do with Iraq. Administration officials were always pushing us to come up with links, but there weren't any. The reason they got bad information is that they beat it out of him. You never get good information from someone that way."

Most authorities on interrogation, in and out of government, agree that torture and lesser forms of physical coercion succeed in producing confessions. The problem is that these confessions aren't necessarily true. Three of the Guantánamo detainees released by the U.S. to Great Britain last year, for example, had confessed that they had appeared in a blurry video, obtained by American investigators, that documented a group of acolytes meeting with bin Laden in Afghanistan. As reported in the London *Observer*, British intelligence officials arrived at Guantánamo with evidence that the accused men had been living in England at the time the video was made. The detainees told British authorities that they had been coerced into making false confessions.

Craig Murray, the former British Ambassador to Uzbekistan, told me that "the U.S. accepts quite a lot of intelligence from the Uzbeks" that has been extracted from suspects who have been tortured. This information was, he said, "largely rubbish." He said he knew of "at least three" instances where the U.S. had rendered suspected militants from Afghanistan to Uzbekistan. Although Murray does not know the fate of the three men, he said, "They almost certainly would have been tortured." In Uzbekistan, he said, "partial boiling of a hand or an arm is quite common." He also knew of two cases in which prisoners had been boiled to death.

In 2002, Murray, concerned that America was complicit with such a regime, asked his deputy to discuss the problem with the C.I.A.'s station chief in Tashkent. He said that the station chief did not dispute that intelligence was being obtained under torture. But the C.I.A. did not consider this a problem. "There was no reason to think they were perturbed," Murray told me.

Scientific research on the efficacy of torture and rough interrogation is limited, because of the moral and legal impediments to experimentation. Tom Parker, a former officer for M.I.5, the British intelligence agency, who teaches at Yale, argued that, whether or not forceful interrogations yield accurate information from terrorist suspects, a larger problem is that many detainees "have nothing to tell." For many years, he said, British authorities subjected members of the Irish Republican Army to forceful interrogations, but, in the end, the government concluded that "detainees aren't valuable." A more effective strategy, Parker said, was "being creative" about human intelligence gathering, such as infiltration and eavesdropping. "The U.S. is doing what the British did in the nineteen-seventies, detaining people and violating their civil liberties," he said. "It did nothing but exacerbate the situation. Most of those interned went back to terrorism. You'll end up radicalizing the entire population."

• • •

Although the Administration has tried to keep the details of extraordinary renditions secret, several accounts have surfaced that reveal how the program operates. On December 18, 2001, at Stockholm's Bromma Airport, a half-dozen hooded security officials ushered two Egyptian asylum seekers, Muhammad Zery and Ahmed Agiza, into an empty office. They cut off the Egyptians' clothes with scissors, forcibly administered sedatives by suppository, swaddled them in diapers, and dressed them in orange jumpsuits. As was reported by *Kalla Fakta,* a Swedish television news program, the suspects were blindfolded, placed in handcuffs and leg irons; according to a declassified Swedish government report, the men were then flown to Cairo on a U.S.-registered Gulfstream V jet. Swedish officials have claimed that they received assurances from the Egyptians that Zery and Agiza would be treated humanely. But both suspects have said, through lawyers and family members, that they were tortured with electrical charges to their genitals. (Zery said that he was also forced to lie on an electrified bed frame.) After spending two years in an Egyptian prison, Zery was released. Agiza, a physician who had once been an ally of Zawahiri but later renounced him and terrorism, was convicted on terrorism charges by Egypt's Supreme Military Court. He was sentenced to twenty-five years in prison.

Another case suggests that the Bush Administration is authorizing the rendition of suspects for whom it has little evidence of guilt. Mamdouh Habib, an Egyptian-born citizen of Australia, was apprehended in Pakistan in October, 2001. According to his wife, Habib, a radical Muslim with four children, was visiting the country to tour religious schools and determine if his family should move to Pakistan. A spokesman at the Pentagon has claimed that Habib—who has expressed support for Islamist causes— spent most of his trip in Afghanistan, and was "either supporting hostile forces or on the battlefield fighting illegally against the U.S." Last month, after a three-year ordeal, Habib was released without charges.

Habib is one of a handful of people subjected to rendition who are being represented pro bono by human-rights lawyers. According to a recently unsealed document prepared by Joseph Margulies, a lawyer affiliated with the MacArthur Justice Center at the University of Chicago Law School, Habib said that he was first interrogated in Pakistan for three weeks, in part at a facility in Islamabad, where he said he was brutalized. Some of his interrogators, he claimed, spoke English with American accents.

(Having lived in Australia for years, Habib is comfortable in English.) He was then placed in the custody of Americans, two of whom wore black short-sleeved shirts and had distinctive tattoos: one depicted an American flag attached to a flagpole shaped like a finger, the other a large cross. The Americans took him to an airfield, cut his clothes off with scissors, dressed him in a jumpsuit, covered his eyes with opaque goggles, and placed him aboard a private plane. He was flown to Egypt.

According to Margulies, Habib was held and interrogated for six months. "Never, to my knowledge, did he make an appearance in any court," Margulies told me. Margulies was also unaware of any evidence suggesting that the U.S. sought a promise from Egypt that Habib would not be tortured. For his part, Habib claimed to have been subjected to horrific conditions. He said that he was beaten frequently with blunt instruments, including an object that he likened to an electric "cattle prod." And he was told that if he didn't confess to belonging to Al Qaeda he would be anally raped by specially trained dogs. (Hossam el-Hamalawy said that Egyptian security forces train German shepherds for police work, and that other prisoners have also been threatened with rape by trained dogs, although he knows of no one who has been assaulted in this way.) Habib said that he was shackled and forced to stand in three torture chambers: one room was filled with water up to his chin, requiring him to stand on tiptoe for hours; another chamber, filled with water up to his knees, had a ceiling so low that he was forced into a prolonged, painful stoop; in the third, he stood in water up to his ankles, and within sight of an electric switch and a generator, which his jailers said would be used to electrocute him if he didn't confess. Habib's lawyer said that he submitted to his interrogators' demands and made multiple confessions, all of them false. (Egyptian authorities have described such allegations of torture as "mythology.")

After his imprisonment in Egypt, Habib said that he was returned to U.S. custody and was flown to Bagram Air Force Base, in Afghanistan, and then on to Guantánamo Bay, where he was detained until last month. On January 11th, a few days after the *Washington Post* published an article on Habib's case, the Pentagon, offering virtually no explanation, agreed to release him into the custody of the Australian government. "Habib was released because he was hopelessly embarrassing," Eric Freedman, a professor at Hofstra Law School, who has been involved in the detainees' legal defense, says. "It's a large crack in the wall in a house of cards that is midway through tumbling down." In a prepared statement, a Pentagon spokesman, Lieutenant Commander Flex Plexico, said there was "no evidence" that Habib "was tortured or abused" while he was in U.S. custody. He also said that Habib had received "Al Qaeda training," which included instruction in making false abuse allegations. Habib's claims, he suggested, "fit the standard operating procedure."

The U.S. government has not responded directly to Habib's charge that he was rendered to Egypt. However, several other men who were recently released from Guantánamo reported that Habib told them about it. Jamal al-Harith, a British detainee who was sent home to Manchester, England, last March, told me in a phone interview that at one point he had been placed in a cage across from Habib. "He said that he had been in Egypt for about six months, and they had injected him with drugs, and hung him from the ceiling, and beaten him very, very badly," Harith recalled. "He seemed to be in pain. He was haggard-looking. I never saw him walk. He always had to be held up."

Another piece of evidence that may support Habib's story is a set of flight logs documenting the travels of a white Gulfstream V jet—the plane that seems to have been used for renditions by the U.S. government. These logs show that on April 9, 2002, the jet left Dulles Airport, in Washington, and landed in Cairo. According to Habib's attorney, this was around the same time that Habib said he was released by the Egyptians in Cairo, and returned to U.S. custody. The flight logs were obtained by Stephen Grey, a British journalist who has written a number of stories on renditions for British publications, including the London *Sunday Times*. Grey's logs are incomplete, but they chronicle some three hundred flights over three years by the fourteen-seat jet, which was marked on its tail with the code N379P. (It was recently changed, to N8068V.) All the flights originated from Dulles Airport, and many of them landed at restricted U.S. military bases.

Even if Habib is a terrorist aligned with Al Qaeda, as Pentagon officials have claimed, it seems unlikely that prosecutors would ever be able to build a strong case against him, given the treatment that he allegedly received in Egypt. John Radsan, a law professor at William Mitchell College of Law, in St. Paul, Minnesota, who worked in the general counsel's office of the C.I.A. until last year, said, "I don't think anyone's thought through what we do with these people."

Similar problems complicate the case of Khalid Sheikh Mohammed, who was captured in Pakistan in March, 2003. Mohammed has reportedly been "water-boarded" during interrogations. If so, Radsan said, "it would be almost impossible to take him into a criminal trial. Any evidence derived from his interrogation could be seen as fruit from the poisonous tree. I think the government is considering some sort of military tribunal somewhere down the line. But, even there, there are still constitutional requirements that you can't bring in involuntary confessions."

The trial of Zacarias Moussaoui, in Alexandria, Virginia—the only U.S. criminal trial of a suspect linked to the September 11th attacks—is stalled. It's been more than three years since Attorney General John Ashcroft called Moussaoui's indictment "a chronicle of evil." The case has been held up by Moussaoui's demand—and the Bush Administration's refusal—to let him call as witnesses Al Qaeda members held in government custody, including Ramzi bin al-Shibh and Khalid Sheikh Mohammed. (Bin al-Shibh is thought to have been tortured.) Government attorneys have argued that producing the witnesses would disrupt the interrogation process.

Similarly, German officials fear that they may be unable to convict any members of the Hamburg cell that is believed to have helped plan the September 11th attacks, on charges connected to the plot, in part because the U.S. government refuses to produce bin al-Shibh and Mohammed as witnesses. Last year, one of the Hamburg defendants, Mounir Motassadeq, became the first person to be convicted in the planning of the attacks, but his guilty verdict was overturned by an appeals court, which found the evidence against him too weak.

Motassadeq is on trial again, but, in accordance with German law, he is no longer being imprisoned. Although he is alleged to have overseen the payment of funds into the accounts of the September 11th hijackers—and to have been friendly with Mohamed Atta, who flew one of the planes that hit the Twin Towers—he walks freely to and from the courthouse each day. The U.S. has supplied the German court with edited summaries of testimony from Mohammed and bin al-Shibh. But Gerhard Strate, Motassadeq's defense lawyer, told me, "We are not satisfied with the summaries. If you want to find the truth, we need to know who has been interrogating them, and under what circumstances. We don't have any answers to this."

The refusal by the U.S. to produce the witnesses in person, Strate said, "puts the court in a ridiculous position." He added, "I don't know why they won't produce the witnesses. The first thing you think is that the U.S. government has something to hide."

In fact, the Justice Department recently admitted that it had something to hide in relation to Maher Arar, the Canadian engineer. The government invoked the rarely used "state secrets privilege" in a motion to dismiss a lawsuit brought by Arar's lawyers against the U.S. government. To go forward in an open court, the government said, would jeopardize the "intelligence, foreign policy and national security interests of the United States." Barbara Olshansky, the assistant legal director of the Center for Constitutional Rights, which is representing Arar, said that government lawyers "are saying this case can't be tried, and the classified information on which they're basing this argument can't even be shared with the opposing lawyers. It's the height of arrogance—they think they can do anything they want in the name of the global war on terrorism."

Nadja Dizdarevic is a thirty-year-old mother of four who lives in Sarajevo. On October 21, 2001, her husband, Hadj Boudella, a Muslim of Algerian descent, and five other Algerians living in Bosnia were arrested after U.S. authorities tipped off the Bosnian government to an alleged plot by the group to blow up the American and British Embassies in Sarajevo. One of the suspects reportedly placed some seventy phone calls to the Al Qaeda leader Abu Zubaydah in the days after September 11th. Boudella and his wife, however, maintain that neither he nor several of the other defendants knew the man who had allegedly contacted Zubaydah. And an investigation by the Bosnian government turned up no confirmation that the calls to Zubaydah were made at all, according to the men's American lawyers, Rob Kirsch and Stephen Oleskey.

At the request of the U.S., the Bosnian government held all six men for three months, but was unable to substantiate any criminal charges against them. On January 17, 2002, the Bosnian Supreme Court ruled that they should be released. Instead, as the men left prison, they were handcuffed, forced to put on surgical masks with nose clips, covered in hoods, and herded into waiting unmarked cars by masked figures, some of whom appeared to be members of the Bosnian special forces. Boudella's wife had come to the prison to meet her husband, and she recalled that she recognized him, despite the hood, because he was wearing a new suit that she had brought him the day before. "I will never forget that night," she said. "It was snowing. I was screaming for someone to help." A crowd gathered, and tried to block the convoy, but it sped off. The suspects were taken to a military airbase and kept in a freezing hangar for hours; one member of the group later claimed that he saw one of the abductors remove his Bosnian uniform, revealing that he was in fact American. The U.S. government has neither confirmed nor denied its role in the operation.

Six days after the abduction, Boudella's wife received word that her husband and the other men had been sent to Guantánamo. One man in the group has alleged that two of his fingers were broken by U.S. soldiers. Little is publicly known about the welfare of the others.

Boudella's wife said that she was astounded that her husband could be seized without charge or trial, at home during peacetime and after his own government had exonerated him. The term "enemy combatant" perplexed her. "He is an enemy of whom?" she asked. "In combat where?" She said that her view of America had changed. "I have not changed my opinion about its people, but unfortunately I have changed my opinion about its respect for human rights," she said. "It is no longer the leader in the world. It has become the leader in the violation of human rights."

In October, Boudella attempted to plead his innocence before the Pentagon's Combatant Status Review Tribunal. The C.S.R.T. is the Pentagon's answer to the Supreme Court's ruling last year, over the Bush Administration's objections, that detainees in Guantánamo had a right to challenge their imprisonment. Boudella was not allowed to bring a lawyer to the proceeding. And the tribunal said that it was "unable to locate" a copy of the Bosnian Supreme Court's verdict freeing him, which he had requested that it read. Transcripts show that Boudella stated, "I am against any terrorist acts," and asked, "How could I be part of an organization that I strongly believe has harmed my people?" The tribunal rejected his plea, as it has rejected three hundred and eighty-seven of the three hundred and ninety-three pleas it has heard. Upon learning this, Boudella's wife sent the following letter to her husband's American lawyers:

Dear Friends, I am so shocked by this information that it seems as if my blood froze in my veins, I can't breathe and I wish I was dead. I can't believe these things can happen, that they can come and take your husband away, overnight and without reason, destroy your family, ruin your dreams after three years of fight. . . . Please, tell me, what can I still do for him? . . . Is this decision final, what are the legal remedies? Help me to understand because, as far as I know the law, this is insane, contrary to all possible laws and human rights. Please help me, I don't want to lose him.

John Radsan, the former C.I.A. lawyer, offered a reply of sorts. "As a society, we haven't figured out what the rough rules are yet," he said. "There are hardly any rules for illegal enemy combatants. It's the law of the jungle. And right now we happen to be the strongest animal."

Part Six:
America in an Uncertain World

Mr. President, Here's How to Make Sense of Your Second Term, Secure Your Legacy, and, Oh Yeah, Create a Future Worth Living

Thomas P. M. Barnett

Esquire | February 2005

If you're the president of the United States, the strange thing about achieving reelection is that, suddenly, there are no more elections for you to look forward to. And since they no longer have to worry about pleasing potential voters, goes the thinking, America's chief executives, as they embark on their second terms, start giving increasing thought to their place in history—presumably elevating the wisdom of their policies to new heights, as they shed their partisan bonds and strive for the universal good.

In this entertaining and provocative essay, Thomas P. M. Barnett, a military strategist who is a professor at the U.S. Naval War College and the author of the best-selling book The Pentagon's New Map: War and Peace in the Twenty-first Century, *gives George Bush some free advice on how to manage the world's affairs over the next four years. His operative topic: how can the president make the best use—and get the biggest possible historical bang for the buck—out of the brief time he has left? . . .*

So you say you have no concern for your legacy. That some historian eighty years from now will figure out if you were a good president or not. Fair enough, but let's review so far.

Your big-bang strategy to reform the Middle East took down Saddam, which was good; you've completely screwed up the Iraq occupation, which is bad; and now you don't seem to know exactly where you're going, which is not so great.

This brings me to the bad news. The two players with the greatest potential for hog-tying your second term and derailing your big-bang strategy don't even live in the Middle East. Instead, they're located on little islands of unreality much like Washington, D. C.: Taiwan and North Korea. When either Taipei or Pyongyang decide to sneeze, it's gonna be your legacy that catches a cold, and here's why: Either country can effectively pull all your attention away from the Middle East while simultaneously torpedoing the most important strategic relationship America has right now.

Yeah, I'm talking about China, a country your old man knows a thing or two about (hint, hint), even if the neocons don't have a clue. Your posse rode into town four years ago convinced that China was the rising military threat to America, only to be proven wrong by bin Laden on 9/11. Enough said.

What I'm here to tell you is this: You can achieve the fabled Middle East peace, but only if you lay down an effective fire wall between that region and the two potential flash points that can still ignite East Asia and send this whole global economy up in flames in a heartbeat. China is the baby you can't throw out with the bathwater you've dubbed the "global war on terrorism." You lose China, you might just kill globalization, and if that happens, it won't be just a matter of what historians write eighty years from now; you'll spend the rest of your days wondering why the world thinks you personally destroyed the planet's best hope for ending war as we know it.

So here's the package you need to pursue: Co-opt Iran, lock in China, and take down North Korea. Let's get started, shall we?

Nixon Goes to Tehran

Work with me on this one. Iran getting the bomb could be the best thing that's ever happened to the Middle East peace process.

Whoa! Don't put down the magazine before I've had a chance to explain.

Iran is the one country standing between you and peace in the Middle East. You can't solve the Israeli-Palestinian conflict without its say-so, because the mullahs are the biggest potential spoilers in the region. They fund the terrorist groups that can effectively veto peace efforts in both Jerusalem and Baghdad. Iran is the one regional power that can still menace the Gulf militarily. Everyone else there operates in Tehran's shadow.

You and I both know Nixon would have inevitably headed to Tehran by now, absent 9/11 and your subsequent Axis of Evil speech. The Shiite revolution is a spent force in that country, whose sullen majority pretends to obey the mullahs while they pretend to rule over a very young population that's frighteningly ambitious for a better life. We're looking at a very late-Brezhnev-type situation here, with the Gorby already on the scene in the person of reformist president Mohammad Khatami. His version of perestroika took one step forward and then ten steps back once we lumped him in with Saddam and Kim, but even though his preferred course of treatment is on hiatus, the political diagnosis remains the same for Iran.

I know, I know. If the mullahs are so weak and scared, then why do they reach so obviously for the bomb?

Look at it from their perspective, Mr. President. Those scary neocons just toppled regimes to Iran's right (Afghanistan) and left (Iraq), and our military pulled off both takedowns with ease. Moreover, your administration has demonstrated beyond all doubt that you don't fear leaving behind a god-awful mess in your war machine's wake. Frankly, you're as scary as Nixon was in his spookiest White House moments on Vietnam. All I'm saying is now's the time to cash in on that reputation with Iran.

And don't tell me we can't do that rapprochement thing with a hostile regime that supports international terrorism. If we could do it with the Evil Empire back in 1973, we can do it with the Axis of Evil's number two today.

Our offer should be both simple and bold. I would send James Baker, our last good secretary of state, to Tehran as your special envoy with the following message: "We know you're getting the bomb, and we know there isn't much we can do about it right now unless we're willing to go up-tempo right up the gut. But frankly, there's other fish we want to fry, so here's the deal: You can have the bomb, and we'll take you off the Axis of Evil list, plus we'll re-establish diplomatic ties and open up trade. But in exchange, not only will you bail us out on Iraq first and foremost by ending your support of the insurgency, you'll also cut off your sponsorship of Hezbollah and other anti-Israeli terrorist groups, help us bully Syria out of Lebanon, *finally* recognize Israel, and join us in guaranteeing the deal on a permanent Palestinian state. You want to be recognized as *the* regional player of note. We're prepared to do that. But that's the price tag. Pay it now or get ready to rumble."

This is a win-win for everybody. The ruling mullahs desire survival most of all, and once Iran opens up economically, its people will stop blaming them for all that's wrong with the country because they'll be too busy taking advantage of all that opportunity. Israel wins because Tel Aviv finally gets someone on the Muslim side who is big enough and scary enough to sit down with the "Little Devil" as a real nuclear equal but still willing to guarantee Israel's existence. I know, it might seem insane to Israel (especially the Likud party), but mutually assured destruction really works and, frankly, Mr. President, now's the time to use some of that political capital you've built up with Ariel Sharon.

No doubt some neocons will try to sell you on a military option in Iran, but don't pull that thread under any circumstances, because if you do, you'll find yourself having to go medieval across an "arc of crisis" stretching from Riyadh to Islamabad, and nobody's got cojones that big. Trust me, Afghanistan and Iraq alone are enough to tap Central Command and Special Operations Command.

I'm also aware that there are plenty of regional experts who'll tell you we've got to do this or that with Egypt or Saudi Arabia, but, frankly, neither of those regimes has shown the ability to do squat when it comes to forging a lasting Middle East peace. Iran's the key. Squeeze it now while it's scared—and while Arafat's still dead. America has played bad cop long enough with Iran. For crying out loud, Iranians are the only people in the Middle East who actually like us!

What's more, Iran is the gateway for bringing both India and China into the mix. Both countries have recently cut huge oil and gas deals with Tehran. You know you want India and China to feel secure about their energy flow, and you know Iran's simply too big a player on both counts for either country to pass up. Plus, India considers itself both a major Gulf security player and Iran's natural mentor, while China's emerging alliance with Tehran (not to mention its ties with Pakistan) should be exploited for all it's worth. New Delhi and Beijing *want* to stabilize the Islamic arc of crisis as much as you do.

If détente with Iran secures Iraq to the south, then it's clear whom we need to romance in the north on the issue of the Kurds—Turkey. Yes, the role of the Kurds in Turkey is a long and complex tale, but who the hell else is going to step up to the plate on that one?

The price tag is not hard to dream up. You twist some arms in the European Union until they either fall off or Turkey's admission gets fast-tracked. If NATO won't come to our rescue in the Sunni triangle, it's the least Old Europe can do.

Speaking of the triangle, that stinker's going to remain ours for the long term, but with Israel and Palestine off the table and real cooperation from both Iran and Syria in clamping down on all those jihadists with a one-way ticket to paradise, we'll extinguish the dream of the Saddam Baathists who are still fighting hard by effectively killing Iraq as a unitary state. Eventually, Iraq's Sunni population will realize that it can either become the recognized master of the triangle and nothing else (the same narrowing solution we forced on the Serbs in the Balkans), or it can choose to live in the region's new West Bank, surviving on intifada for the rest of its days.

Lock in China at Today's Prices

To understand China today, you have to remember what it was like for the United States back in the early years of the twentieth century. Here we were, this burgeoning economic powerhouse with a rising yet still relatively small military package, and all the old-school powers worried about us as an up-and-coming threat. While the European form of globalization predominated at that time, our upstart version ("We don't need no stinkin' empire!") would come to dominate the landscape by the century's midpoint, primarily because Europe decided to self-destruct all its empires via two "world" wars that in retrospect look like the European Union's versions of the American Civil War.

China is the United States of the early twenty-first century: rising like crazy, but not really a threat to anyone except small island nations off its coast. (God, I miss T. R. and the Rough Riders.) Hu Jintao, China's current president and party boss of the country's fourth generation of leaders, has tried to calm global fears by proposing his theory of Peacefully Rising China, a tune that, frankly, none of the Pentagon's hardcore neocons can carry.

Why? The far Right is still gunning for China, and precious Taiwan is its San Juan Hill. Nixon burned Taiwan's ass back in the early seventies when he effectively switched official recognition from Taipei to the mainland, so the price it demanded was the continued "defense guarantee" that said we'd always arm Taiwan to the teeth and rush to its rescue whenever China unleashed its million-man swim of an invasion.

That promise is still on the books, like some blue law from a bygone era. Does anyone seriously think we'd sacrifice tens of thousands of American troops to stop China from reabsorbing Taiwan?

I know, I know. China's still "communist" (like I still have a full head of hair if the lighting's just so), whereas Taiwan is a lonely bastion of democracy in an otherwise . . . uh . . . increasingly democratic Asia. So even though the rest of Asia, including Japan, is being rapidly sucked into China's economic undertow (as "running dogs of capitalism" go, China's a greyhound), somehow the sacredness of Taiwan's self-perceived "independence" from China is worth torching the global economy over? Does that strike anybody as slightly nuts?

Here's the weirdest part: China's been clearly signaling for years that it's perfectly willing to accept the status quo, basically guaranteeing Taiwan's continued existence, so long as Taipei's government maintains the appearance of remaining open to the possibility of rejoining the mainland someday.

Now I know people say you don't read books, Mr. President, but being a Southerner, you know something about the Civil War. Imagine if Jefferson Davis and the leftovers of the Confederacy had slipped away to Cuba in 1865 to set up their alternative, nose-thumbing version of America on that island. Then fast-forward to, say, 1905 and imagine how much the U. S. would have tolerated some distant, imperial power like England telling us what we could or could not do vis-à-vis this loser sitting just off our shore. Imagine where old Teddy Roosevelt would have told the Brits they could shove their defense guarantee.

My point is this: In a generation's time, China will dominate the global economy just as much as the United States does today. (Don't worry, we'll be co-dominatrices.) The only way to stop that is to kill this era's version of globalization—something I worry about those neocons actually being stupid enough to do as part of their fanciful pursuit of global "hegemony." That nasty, far poorer future is not the one I want to leave behind for my kids, and I expect you feel the same about yours. China won't go down alone; it'll take most of the advanced global economy with it. So on this one, let's go with those vaunted American interests I keep hearing about and look out for number one.

This may seem a back-burner issue, but there's credible talk of Taipei doing something provocative like adding the word *Taiwan* in parentheses behind its official name, the Republic of China. That may not seem like much to us, but Beijing's reluctant hand may be forced by this act. Seems crazy, doesn't it?

Again, how much of the global economy—how many American lives—are you prepared to sacrifice on your watch just so Taiwan can rejoice in this moment of self-actualization?

I vote for zero. Zip. Nada.

Take America's defense guarantee to Taiwan off the table and do it now, before some irrational politician in Taipei decides he's ready to start a war between two nuclear powers. Trust me, you'd be doing Taiwan a favor, because it's my guess that our defense guarantee would evaporate the moment any Taiwan Straits crisis actually boiled over, leaving Taipei severely embarrassed and Beijing feeling excessively emboldened.

Let's lock in a strategic alliance with rising China at today's prices, because it's got nowhere to go but up over the coming years. Buying into this relationship now is like stealing Alaska from the czars for pennies on the dollar; it'll never be this cheap again.

More to the point, preemptively declaring a permanent truce in the Taiwan Straits is the quid we offer for Beijing's quo in the solution set that really matters in East Asia today: the reunification of Korea following Kim Jong Il's removal from power.

Kill Kim: Volumes 1, 2 & 3

Now we get to the good part. The Koreas issue is the tailbone of the cold war: completely useless, but it can still plunge you into a world of pain if middle-aged Asia slips and falls on it. North Korea is the evil twin, separated at birth, and yet, because it's still joined at the hip with its sibling, its better half grows ever more irrationally distraught as time passes, contemplating the inevitable invasive surgery that lies ahead.

So while it might seem at first glance like a job for *Team America: World Police,* you'll want something less *South Park* in its comic simplicity and a little more Tarantinoesque in its B-movie grandeur. That's right, we need a Deadly Viper Assassination Squad to make Kim an offer he can't refuse. Kim Jong Il's checked all the boxes: He'll sell or buy any weapons of mass destruction he can get his hands on, he's engaged in bizarre acts of terrorism against South Korea, and he maintains his amazingly cruel regime through the wholesale export of both narcotics and counterfeit American currency. Is he crazy? He once kidnapped two of South Korea's biggest movie stars and held them hostage in his own personal DreamWorks studio. But if that doesn't do it for you, then try this one on for size: The Kim-induced famine of the late 1990s killed as many as two million North Koreans. If that doesn't get you a war-crimes trial in this day and age, then what the hell will?

Here's the squad we need to assemble: China, Japan, South Korea, Australia, and New Zealand, plus Russia.

You just shook hands with China over Taiwan. Japan's there because both China and America are on the team and because it's got the most cash to finance the reconstruction. The Aussies and Kiwis are invited out of respect for their longtime security role in Asia, and the Russians are in because they might just run a pipeline to Japan through the Korean peninsula when it's all said and done. As for the wobbly South Koreans, just smack 'em upside the head and tell them it's strictly business—nothing personal.

Those are the Seven Samurai that walk into Kim Jong Il's palace and offer him three possible endings to this thriller: the Good, the Bad, and the Ugly.

Version #1 (Good) is the Baby Doc Duvalier package. Keep your money, keep your women, keep your entourage, keep it all . . . just somewhere else. China can offer Kim a fabulous forbidden city somewhere in Inner Mongolia. Hell, promise this Cecil B. Demented a five-picture deal and tell him Steven Spielberg wants to do lunch.

If he doesn't bite on that one, then show Kim Version #2 (Bad). He goes on trial in the Hague for years on end, paraded around like the freak job he is, and once he's thoroughly stripped of what passes for his "majesty," we'll let him rot in a jail cell for the rest of his days.

Version #3 (Ugly) is delivered sotto voce. Just have Paul Wolfowitz show Kim the "six-month reconstruction plan" the Pentagon neocons drew up for the postwar occupation. If he thinks you're bluffing, then instruct Wolfie to slip him some of those morgue shots of Uday and Qusay looking all stitched up like a pair of Frankensteins. Kim'll get the hint. Your administration has proven that you're willing to wage war with almost no concern for the resulting VIP body count, the subsequently incompetent occupation, or the inevitable political uproar back home. I say when you've got it, flaunt it.

If it comes to trigger-pulling, can we pull it off? You know we can, and even here we've got a choice between the stripped-down package (i.e., just kill Kim) and the tricked-up models (e.g., smash-and-grab WMD, decapitating command-and-control, pounding ground forces). North Korea's military will prove less brittle than Saddam's Republican Guard but hardly invulnerable. Plus, on this one the local players will provide plenty of boots on the ground (South Korea, China) and humanitarian aid (Japan) just to prevent refugees from flooding across their borders. Moreover, Kim's slim power base sits atop a Mafia-like criminal empire that features the usual "honor" among thieves, so bribing his fellow kleptocrats with golden parachutes is quite feasible. Finally, the postconflict investment flow will be heavy on this one, because there will be no insurgency, no jihad, no nothing, just a gulag's worth of political prisoners to set free.

But the truth is, it probably won't come to that simply because both you and the neocons have such a scary reputation that you can likely stare down

Lil' Kim, so long as you've got China glaring at him disapprovingly over your shoulder. You know China would just as soon jettison Kim because he's a genuine nut and he's terrible for property values. So what you really need to offer the Chinese on the far side is something truly useful, and that something is an Asian NATO. That's right: Kim's tombstone should mark the spot where a NATO-like security alliance for East Asia is born.

If you terminate Taiwan's defense guarantee in order to bring Beijing to Kim's table, then you offer to kill all your plans for missile defense to get the Chinese to pull the chair out from under him. Star Wars has been the single worst boondoggle in the history of the Pentagon—nearly $100 billion wasted and not even Tang to show for it. By securing America's military alliance with China, Japan, and Korea, you not only kill the concept of great-power war in Asia for good, you've just ended Osama bin Laden's bid to pit East against West.

That's it. And you've got about ten months to get it all rolling, with maybe another twenty months to wrap most of it up. By the summer of 2007, your presidency and all the power you wield right now will begin to be severely discounted by politicians both at home and abroad.

Mr. President, I know you're committed to following through on what you've set in motion in the Middle East, and I know you're hell-bent to prove all the eggheads wrong about the possibility of democracy taking root there—and I like your certitude on both points. You're the just-do-it president. You react from your gut more than either your heart or your brains, and you know what? You're as big a gift from history as 9/11's wakeup call turned out to be—and almost equally hard for many Americans to swallow.

You believe that America will defeat global terrorism only if it is willing to transform the Middle East in the process, and I agree. But just as we had to make peace with the Soviets before we could "tear down that wall," your administration will have to make peace with Iran's mullahs before we can begin dismantling the many walls that still isolate that insular region from the global economy and the mutually assured dependence that defines its long-term stability and peace. The road to lasting security in both Jerusalem and Baghdad starts in Tehran, and ultimately it must run through Beijing as well.

You lock down Asia by putting a leash on Taiwan, inviting China into the copilot seat and shoving Kim underground, and you'll not only free up America's military resources for more-urgent tasks in the Middle East, you'll create a sense of strategic despair in the minds of bin Laden and Zarqawi that they'll never be able to overcome. Their dream is to split up the advancing core of globalization and stop its creeping embrace of their idealized Islamic world, which they know will be forever altered by that integration process. Their best strategic hope in this conflict is that some hostile great power will rise in the East to challenge the American-led West. You lock in China today, Mr. President, and you will corner and kill transnational terrorism tomorrow.

And not that you care, Mr. President, but there's your legacy.

Grand Strategy in the Second Term
John Lewis Gaddis

Foreign Affairs | January–February 2005

In this essay, which appeared in Foreign Affairs *(the influential publication of the Council on Foreign Relations) John Lewis Gaddis, a professor of history at Yale University, takes a long-range view of the Bush administration's foreign policy. "George W. Bush," he writes, ". . . has presided over the most sweeping redesign of U.S. grand strategy since the presidency of Franklin D. Roosevelt."*

Like FDR, notes Gaddis, the Bush redesign was prompted by a surprise attack—in this case 9/11, which showed "that deterrence against states affords insufficient protection from attacks by gangs." But while he gives Bush high marks for setting the right course in response to the attacks—particularly his attempts to shatter the existing status quo, and open up the nations of the Mideast to democracy—Gaddis takes the administration to task for showing little concern or aptitude for persuading others to follow its lead, and suggests that pursuit of a more multilateral foreign policy should be a top priority for Bush in his second term. Equally disturbing to Gaddis was the assumption on the part of the Bush team that once the international status quo has been shaken up, "the pieces would realign themselves in patterns favorable to U.S. interests," without any in-depth oversight or planning on the part of the U.S. government. This assumption, he adds, "was the single greatest misjudgment of the Bush administration." . . .

Reconsiderations

Second terms in the White House open the way for second thoughts. They provide the least awkward moment at which to replace or reshuffle key advisers. They lessen, although nothing can remove, the influence of domestic political considerations, since reelected presidents have no next election to worry about. They enhance authority, as allies and adversaries learn—whether with hope or despair—with whom they will have to deal for the next four years. If there is ever a time for an administration to evaluate its own performance, this is it.

George W. Bush has much to evaluate: he has presided over the most sweeping redesign of U.S. grand strategy since the presidency of Franklin D. Roosevelt. The basis for Bush's grand strategy, like Roosevelt's, comes from the shock of surprise attack and will not change. None of F.D.R.'s successors, Democrat or Republican, could escape the lesson he drew from the events of December 7, 1941: that distance alone no longer protected Americans from assaults at the hands of hostile states. Neither Bush nor his successors, whatever their party, can ignore what the events of September 11, 2001, made clear: that deterrence against states affords insufficient protection from attacks by gangs, which can now inflict the kind of damage only states fighting wars used to be able to achieve. In that sense, the course for Bush's second term remains that of his first one: the restoration of security in a suddenly more dangerous world.

Setting a course, however, is only a starting point for strategies: experience always reshapes them as they evolve. Bush has been rethinking his strategy for some time now, despite his reluctance during the campaign to admit mistakes. With a renewed and strengthened electoral mandate, he will find it easier to make midcourse corrections. The best way to predict their extent is to compare what his administration intended with what it has so far accomplished. The differences suggest where changes will—or at least should—take place.

Pre-Emption and Prevention

The narrowest gap between Bush's intentions and his accomplishments has to do with preventing another major attack on the United States. Of course, one could occur at any moment, even between the completion of this article and its publication. But the fact that more than three years have passed without such an attack is significant. Few Americans would have thought it likely in the immediate aftermath of September 11. The prevailing view then was that a terrorist offensive was underway, and that the nation would be fortunate to get through the next three months without a similar or more serious blow being struck.

Connecting causes with consequences is always difficult—all the more so when we know so little of Osama bin Laden's intentions or those of his followers. Perhaps al Qaeda planned no further attacks. Perhaps it anticipated that the United States would retaliate by invading Afghanistan and deposing the Taliban. Perhaps it foresaw U.S. military redeployments from Saudi Arabia to Afghanistan, Uzbekistan, Kyrgyzstan, and Iraq. Perhaps it expected a worldwide counterterrorist campaign to roll up substantial portions of its network. Perhaps it predicted that the Bush administration would abandon its aversion to nation building and set out to democratize the Middle East. Perhaps bin Laden's strategy allowed for all of this, but that seems unlikely. If it did not, then the first and most fundamental feature of the Bush strategy—taking the offensive against the terrorists and thereby surprising them—has so far accomplished its purposes.

A less obvious point follows concerning pre-emption and prevention, a distinction that arose from hypothetical hot-war planning during the Cold War. "Pre-emption" meant taking military action against a state that was about to launch an attack; international law and practice had long allowed such actions to forestall clear and immediately present dangers. "Prevention" meant starting a war against a state that might, at some future point, pose such risks. In mounting its post-September 11 offensive, the Bush administration conflated these terms, using the word "pre-emption" to justify what turned out to be a "preventive" war against Saddam Hussein's Iraq.

It did so on the grounds that, in a post-September 11 world, both terrorists and tyrants threatened the security of the United States. Al Qaeda could not have acted without the support and sanctuary the Taliban provided. But the traditional warnings governments had used to justify pre-emption—the massing of armed forces in such a way as to confirm aggressive intent—would not have detected the September 11 attacks before they took place. Decisions made, or at least circumstances tolerated, by a shadowy regime in a remote country halfway around the world produced an act of war that killed more Americans than the one committed six decades earlier by Japan, a state known at the time to pose the clearest and most present of dangers.

Pre-emption in its older and narrower sense might have worked against the Japanese fleet as it approached Pearl Harbor—had it been detected in time. Pre-emptive arrests would have stopped Mohammed Atta and his 18 co-conspirators as they approached their respective airports—if it had been possible to read their minds. No nation's safety, however, can depend on such improbable intelligence breakthroughs: as the Pearl Harbor historian Roberta Wohlstetter pointed out years ago and as the 9/11 Commission Report has now confirmed, detecting telltale signals in a world full of noise requires not just skill, but also extraordinary luck.

That is why the Bush administration's strategists broadened "pre-emption" to include the Cold War meaning of "prevention." To wait for terrorist threats to become clear and present was to leave the nation vulnerable to surprise attacks. Instead, the United States would go after states that had harbored, or that might be harboring, terrorist gangs. It would at first seek to contain or deter such regimes—the familiar means by which the Cold War had been fought—but if those methods failed, it reserved the right to pre-empt perceived dangers by starting a preventive war.

The old distinction between pre-emption and prevention, therefore, was one of the many casualties of September 11. That event revealed a category of threats so difficult to detect and yet so devastating if carried out that the United States had little choice but to use pre-emptive means to prevent their emergence. John Kerry made it clear during the 2004 campaign that he would not have relinquished that option had he won the presidency. His successful opponent certainly will not do so, nor are his successors likely to. This feature of the Bush grand strategy is here to stay.

Speaking More Softly—and More Clearly

Pre-emption defined as prevention, however, runs the risk—amply demonstrated over the past two years—that the United States itself will appear to much of the world as a clear and present danger. Sovereignty has long been a sacrosanct principle in the international system. For the world's most powerful state suddenly to announce that its security requires violating the sovereignty of certain other states whenever it chooses cannot help but make all other states nervous. As the political scientist G. John Ikenberry has pointed out, Washington's policy of pre-emption has created the image of a global policeman who reports to no higher authority and no longer allows locks on citizens' doors. However shocking the September 11 attacks may have been, the international community has not found it easy to endorse the Bush administration's plan for regaining security.

Bush and his advisers anticipated this problem. After brushing aside offers of help in Afghanistan from NATO allies, the administration worked hard to win multilateral support for its first act of pre-emption for preventive purposes: the invasion of Iraq. It expected success. After all, who, apart from the United States, could organize the overthrow of Saddam Hussein, a dictator who had abused his people, started wars, flouted UN resolutions, supported terrorists, and, in the view of intelligence agencies everywhere, probably possessed weapons of mass destruction (WMD)? The use of U.S. power to depose such a monster, Bush's strategists assumed, would be welcomed, not feared.

They were wrong. The war in Iraq gained far less international support than the administration had anticipated. One can debate at length the reasons why: the outdated structure of the U.N. Security Council, which better reflected the power balance of 1945 than 2003; the appearance Bush gave of having decided to go to war with or without that body's consent; the difficulty of establishing a credible connection between Saddam Hussein and al Qaeda; the absence of incontrovertible evidence that the Iraqi dictator really did have WMD; the distrust that lingered from Bush's unnecessarily harsh rejections of the Kyoto Protocol, the International Criminal Court, and the Anti-Ballistic Missile Treaty. Whatever the explanation, his strategy of pre-emption by consent did not get consent, and this was a major failure.

President Bush's decision to invade Iraq anyway provoked complaints that great power was being wielded without great responsibility, followed by an unprecedented collapse of support for the United States abroad. From nearly universal sympathy in the weeks after September 11, Americans within a year and a half found their country widely regarded as an international pariah.

It is easy to say that this does not matter—that a nation as strong as the United States need not worry about what others think of it. But that simply is not true. To see why, compare the American and Soviet spheres of influence in Europe during the Cold War. The first operated with the consent of those within it. The second did not, and that made an enormous difference quite unrelated to the military strength each side could bring to bear in the region. The lesson here is clear: influence, to be sustained, requires not just power but also the absence of resistance, or, to use Clausewitz's term, "friction." Anyone who has ever operated a vehicle knows the need for lubrication, without which the vehicle will sooner or later grind to a halt. This is what was missing during the first Bush administration: a proper amount of attention to the equivalent of lubrication in strategy, which is persuasion.

The American claim of a broadly conceived right to pre-empt danger is not going to disappear, because no other nation or international organization will be prepared anytime soon to assume that responsibility. But the need to legitimize that strategy is not going to go away, either; otherwise, the friction it generates will ultimately defeat it, even if its enemies do not. What this means is that the second Bush administration will have to try again to gain multilateral support for the pre-emptive use of U.S. military power.

Doing so will not involve giving anyone else a veto over what the United States does to ensure its security and to advance its interests. It will, however, require persuading as large a group of states as possible that these actions will also enhance, or at least not degrade, their own interests. The United States did that regularly—and highly successfully—during World War II and the Cold War. It also obtained international consent for the use of predominantly American military force in the 1991 Persian Gulf War, in Bosnia in 1995, in Kosovo in 1999, and in Afghanistan in 2001. Iraq has been the exception, not the rule, and there are lessons to be learned from the anomaly.

One is the need for better manners. It is always a bad idea to confuse power with wisdom: muscles are not brains. It is never a good idea to insult potential allies, however outrageous their behavior may have been. Nor is it wise to regard consultation as the endorsement of a course already set. The Bush administration was hardly the first to commit these errors. It was the first, however, to commit so many so often in a situation in which help from friends could have been so useful.

Another lesson relates to language. The president and his advisers preferred flaunting U.S. power to explaining its purpose. To boast that one possesses and plans to maintain "strengths beyond challenge" may well be accurate, but it mixes arrogance with vagueness, an unsettling combination. Strengths for what purpose? Challenges from what source? Cold War presidents were careful to answer such questions. Bush, during his first term, too often left it to others to guess the answers. In his second, he will have to provide them.

A final and related lesson concerns vision. The terrorists of September 11 exposed vulnerabilities in the defenses of all states. Unless these are repaired, and unless those who would exploit them are killed, captured, or dissuaded, the survival of the state system itself could be at stake. Here lies common ground, for unless that multinational interest is secured, few other national interests—convergent or divergent—can be. Securing the state will not be possible without the option of pre-emptive military action to prevent terrorism from taking root. It is a failure of both language and vision that the United States has yet to make its case for pre-emption in these terms.

Iraq Is Not Vietnam

The Bush administration believed that it could invade Iraq without widespread consent because it expected a replay of the Afghanistan experience: military resistance would quickly evaporate, Iraqis would welcome the Americans and their allies, and the victorious coalition would quickly install an Iraqi regime capable of controlling and rebuilding the country. Success on the ground, together with confirmation that Saddam Hussein did indeed have WMD, would yield the consensus that diplomacy had failed to produce. The occupation of Iraq would become a broadly supported international effort, even if the invasion had not been.

The military campaign proceeded as anticipated, but nothing else did. Enough troops were deployed to defeat the Iraqi army, but not to restore order, suppress looting, and protect critical infrastructure. Iraqis did not step forward to form a new government, however grateful they may have been to have their old one removed. Pentagon planners misjudged how quickly many Iraqis would begin to see their liberators as oppressors. They even hastened that process through a laissez-faire attitude toward the rights of prisoners that produced sickening abuses. WMD were not found. And the expanded multilateral assistance Bush had hoped for in running the occupation never arrived. To note gaps between intentions and accomplishments in Iraq is to understate: they littered the landscape.

The Bush administration has been scrambling ever since to close those gaps. It has done so with an indecisiveness that is quite at odds with its normal method of operation: it has seemed, far too often, simply not to know what to do. As a consequence, it has come close, more than once, to losing the initiative in Iraq. Visions of a Vietnam-like quagmire have begun to loom.

Such visions are, however, premature. After a year and a half of fighting, U.S. casualties in Iraq have yet to exceed what the monthly total in the Vietnam War frequently was. Iraqi losses, although much greater, are nowhere near what the Vietnamese suffered. The insurgents receive far less external aid than the Soviet Union and China provided to the North Vietnamese and the Viet Cong. There is no Iraqi equivalent to Ho Chi Minh: Iraq's division among Sunnis, Shia, and Kurds has created a balance of antagonisms, not a unified resistance.

It is also the case that the U.S. military tends to learn from its mistakes. Historians now acknowledge that American counterinsurgency operations in Vietnam were succeeding during the final years of that conflict; the problem was that support for the war had long since crumbled at home. Military learning is also taking place in Iraq, but the domestic opposition is not even approaching Vietnam-era proportions: 2004 was nothing like 1968. There is still time, then, to defeat the insurgency—even though the insurgents are no doubt also learning from their own mistakes.

Victory, in the end, will go to the side that can rally the "silent majority" of Iraqis who have so far not taken sides. Here an advantage lies with the Americans and their allies, for they can offer elections. The insurgents cannot. Opportunities to vote in equally dangerous circumstances—in El Salvador, Cambodia, and most recently Afghanistan—have punctured the pretensions of terrorists by diminishing the fears on which they depend. There are, to be sure, no guarantees. Elections could produce governments that are weak, incompetent, unrepresentative, brutal, or even fanatically opposed to the occupiers themselves. The risks of holding them, however, are preferable to the alternatives of swamping Iraq with U.S. troops or abandoning it altogether.

And what if the United States, despite its best efforts, ultimately fails in Iraq? It is only prudent to have plans in place in case that happens. The best one will be to keep Iraq in perspective. It seems to be the issue on which everything depends right now, just as Vietnam was in 1968. Over the next several years, however, President Richard Nixon and National Security Adviser Henry Kissinger showed that it was possible to "lose" Vietnam while "gaining" China. What takes place during the second Bush term in

Afghanistan, Egypt, Iran, Libya, Morocco, Pakistan, Saudi Arabia, Syria, Turkey, and especially the Israeli-Palestinian relationship may well be as significant for the future of the Middle East as what occurs in Iraq. And what happens in China, India, Russia, Europe, and Africa may well be as important for the future of the international system as what transpires in the Middle East. All of which is only to say that Iraq must not become, as Vietnam once was, the single lens through which the United States views the region or the world.

Winning the War on Terrorism

Grand strategy is as much about psychology as it is facts on the ground. The Bush administration intended that a demonstrated capacity for retaliation, pre-emption, and/or prevention in Afghanistan and Iraq would convince al Qaeda that the United States could not be run out of the Middle East. "Shock and awe" would dry up recruiting for that organization. And it would deter other states in the region and elsewhere from supporting terrorism in the future. The record of accomplishments here is mixed.

Not even bin Laden can now expect a diminished U.S. presence in the Middle East: in political, economic, and certainly military terms, the United States is more firmly entrenched there than it was prior to September 11. It is less clear, though, that the Bush strategy has impeded al Qaeda's recruiting. The toppling of Saddam Hussein humiliated at least as many Arabs as it pleased. The occupation of Iraq revealed irresolution and inefficiency as often as the firmness it was meant to convey. The Israeli-Palestinian conflict remains a festering grievance: military victory in Iraq removed a threat to Israel, but it has yet to speed a settlement. On balance, U.S. power has become more respected in the Middle East. But respect for U.S. culture, institutions, and leadership has significantly declined.

Efforts to deter dangerous states have also produced mixed results. Whatever Colonel Muammar al-Qaddafi's reasons for abandoning Libya's quest for WMD, his decision was just what the Bush strategists hoped would happen on a wider scale. They can also claim, as a success, Pakistan's dismantling of Abdul Qadeer Khan's network for marketing nuclear weapons components. In Iran and North Korea, however, the picture is bleaker: the invasion of Iraq appears to have convinced leaders in those countries that they must have a nuclear capability of their own. Far from deterring them, the United States may have pushed them into finding ways to deter it.

Grand strategies always have multiple audiences: actions aimed at particular adversaries can (and usually do) make unintended impressions on others. A major priority for the second Bush administration, then, will be to determine the extent to which its aggressive use of U.S. military power in Afghanistan and Iraq has produced results it did not want elsewhere, and to adjust strategy accordingly.

It will be necessary, in doing this, to avoid extremes of pessimism and optimism. The Bush team made the worst of Saddam Hussein's alleged WMD, while making the best of the more credible capabilities Iran and North Korea have been developing. Whatever the reasons behind this disparity, it is not sustainable. For even if the United States should succeed in Iraq, its larger strategy will have failed if it produces a nuclear-capable Iran or North Korea, and those countries behave in an irresponsible way.

This is not to predict that they will. States that have acquired nuclear weapons have so far handled them carefully. To take comfort in this pattern, however, is like trying to find reassurance in an extended game of Russian roulette: sooner or later the odds will turn against you. The same is true of the risk that nuclear, chemical, and biological weapons could make the leap, like some lethal virus, from potentially deterrable states to undeterrable terrorists. It may take the use of such weapons to awaken the world to this danger. That too, however, is a Russian roulette solution, which makes it not worth waiting for.

There are opportunities, then, for a renewed U.S. commitment to the task of keeping WMD out of the hands of tyrants and terrorists—by multilateral means. The prospects for such an effort, like those for the Iraqi occupation, are better than they might at first seem. U.N. sanctions do appear to have prevented the rebuilding of Saddam Hussein's WMD after the Gulf War. That organization has shown itself effective as well in publicizing, if not resolving, the crisis over Iran's nuclear program. Cooperative initiatives elsewhere have also shown promise: examples include the Nunn-Lugar program to dismantle nuclear stockpiles, the Proliferation Security Initiative to intercept illegal weapons shipments, and the tacit agreement North Korea's neighbors have reached that none has an interest in seeing Pyongyang develop the capacity for mass destruction.

The Bush administration has been proceeding in this direction. Its multilateralism outside of Afghanistan and Iraq is insufficiently acknowledged—probably because it has been inadequately explained. What is needed now is a clear and comprehensive statement of which international organizations and initiatives the United States can cooperate with, which it cannot, and why. It is as bad to promise too much, as the Clinton administration did, as to propose too little, as happened during Bush's first term. But with tact, flexibility, and a willingness to listen—as well as the power to pre-empt if such strategies fail—Americans could by these means regain what they have recently lost: the ability to inspire others to want to follow them.

Sowing the Seeds of Change

President Bush has insisted that the world will not be safe from terrorists until the Middle East is safe for democracy. It should be clear by now that he is serious about this claim: it is neither rhetorical nor a cloak for hidden motives. Democratization, however, is a long-term objective, so it is too early to assess accomplishments. What one can evaluate is the extent to which the Bush strategists have succeeded in a more immediate task they set for themselves: to clear the way for democratization by shattering a status quo in the Middle East that they believed had victimized the people of the region and had become a threat to the rest of the world.

The regimes responsible for this situation had three characteristics. They were authoritarian: liberation from colonialism and its equivalents had left the region in a new kind of bondage to tyrannical or at least unrepresentative rule. Most of them benefited from the geological accident of where oil lay beneath the surface of the earth, so that the need to remain competitive within a global economy did not produce the political liberalization that it did almost everywhere else. And several of these regimes had cut deals with an Islamist religious establishment that had its own reasons for resisting change, thereby reinforcing a long-standing trend toward literal readings of the Koran that left little room for alternative interpretations. This unhealthy combination of authoritarianism, wealth, and religious literalism, the Bush administration maintained, fed frustrations for many and fueled rage in a few: that was enough to bring about September 11. Breaking this status quo would make the world safer in the short run and facilitate democratization in the long run.

The shock and awe that accompanied the invasions of Afghanistan and Iraq were meant to begin this process, but Bush and his advisers did not rely solely on military means to sustain its momentum. They expected that September 11 and other terrorist excesses would cause a majority of Muslims to recoil from the extremists among them. They anticipated that the United States would be able to plant the seeds of democracy in the countries where it had deposed dictators, and that these would spread. They also assumed that the Middle East could not indefinitely insulate itself from the democratization that had already taken hold in much of the rest of the world.

Divisions have indeed surfaced among Muslims over the morality and effectiveness of terrorism. Saudis have seen the terrorists they financed strike back at them. Well before Yasir Arafat's death, Palestinians were questioning what suicide bombing and a perpetual intifada had accomplished; now there is even more room for second thoughts. Iraqis have begun to speak out, if cautiously, against the hostage-taking and televised beheadings that have afflicted their country. And the Beslan massacre—the taking of a school in southern Russia, with the subsequent slaughter of more than 300 children and teachers—has raised doubts throughout the Middle East that terror directed against innocents can ever be justified when decoupled from any apparent political objective.

Whether democracy can be "planted" through military occupation in that part of the world is not yet clear, however, and may not be for some time. Three years after the invasion of Afghanistan, that country still is not secure. Taliban and al Qaeda elements remain, economic recovery is spotty, warlords rule, opium cultivation thrives, and Westerners cannot travel safely much beyond Kabul. And yet, on October 9, 2004, millions of Afghans lined up to vote in an election that had no precedent in their nation's long history. Had anyone predicted this three years ago, the response would have been incredulity—if not doubts about sanity.

What this suggests is that forces of disruption and construction coexist in Afghanistan: their shifting balance is beyond precise measurement. If that is true there, then it is all the more so in Iraq, where the contradictions are greater, the stakes are higher, and the standards for making optimistic or pessimistic judgments are even more opaque. The best one can say at the moment, of both countries, is that they defy generalization. That is less than the Bush administration hoped for. It is far more, however, than any previous American administration has achieved in the Middle East. For better or for worse, the status quo exists no longer.

And what of the region's insulation from the wave of democratization that has swept the globe? According to Freedom House statistics, no countries allowed universal suffrage in 1900. By 1950, 22 did, and by 2000, the number had reached 120, a figure that encompassed 62.5 percent of the world's population. Nor, as the examples of Bangladesh, India, Indonesia, and Turkey suggest, is there reason to think that representative government and Islam are incompatible. Democratization has indeed been delayed in the Arab world, as Arabs themselves have begun to acknowledge. To conclude that it can never take hold there, however, is to neglect the direction in which the historical winds have been blowing. And the best grand strategies, like the most efficient navigators, keep the winds behind them.

The second Bush administration will now have the opportunity to reinforce the movement—the shift in the status quo—that the first Bush administration started in the Middle East. A Kerry administration would probably have done the same. What September 11 showed was that the United States can no longer insulate itself from what happens in that part of the world: to do so would be to ignore clear and present danger. A conservative Republican administration responded by embracing a liberal Democratic ideal—making the world safe for democracy—as a national security imperative. If that does not provide the basis for a renewed grand strategic bipartisanship, similar to the one that followed Pearl Harbor so long ago, then one has to wonder what ever would.

What Would Bismarck Do?

Finally, one apparent assumption that runs through the Bush grand strategy deserves careful scrutiny. It has to do with what follows shock and awe. The president and his advisers seem to have concluded that the shock the United States suffered on September 11 required that shocks be administered in return, not just to the part of the world from which the attack came, but to the international system as a whole. Old ways of doing things no longer worked. The status quo everywhere needed shaking up. Once that had happened, the pieces would realign themselves in patterns favorable to U.S. interests.

It was free-market thinking applied to geopolitics: that just as the removal of economic constraints allows the pursuit of self-interest automatically to advance a collective interest, so the breaking up of an old international order would encourage a new one to emerge, more or less spontaneously, based on a universal desire for security, prosperity, and liberty. Shock therapy would produce a safer, saner world.

Some such therapy was probably necessary in the aftermath of September

11, but the assumption that things would fall neatly into place after the shock was administered was the single greatest misjudgment of the first Bush administration. It explains the failure to anticipate multilateral resistance to pre-emption. It accounts for the absence of planning for the occupation of Iraq. It has produced an overstretched military for which no "revolution in military affairs" can compensate. It has left official obligations dangerously unfunded. And it has allowed an inexcusable laxity about legal procedures—at Guantanamo, Abu Ghraib, and elsewhere—to squander the moral advantage the United States possessed after September 11 and should have retained.

The most skillful practitioner ever of shock and awe, Otto von Bismarck, shattered the post-1815 European settlement in order to unify Germany in 1871. Having done so, however, he did not assume that the pieces would simply fall into place as he wished them to: he made sure that they did through the careful, patient construction of a new European order that offered benefits to all who were included within it. Bismarck's system survived for almost half a century.

The most important question George W. Bush will face in his second term is whether he can follow Bismarck's example. If he can shift from shock and awe to the reassurance—and the attention to detail—that is necessary to sustain any new system, then the prospects for his post-September 11 grand strategy could compare favorably to Bismarck's accomplishments, as well as to those of U.S. presidents from Roosevelt through Clinton. For their post-Pearl Harbor grand strategy, over more than half a century, persuaded the world that it was better off with the United States as its dominant power than with anyone else. Bush must now do the same.

Bush's Lost Year

James Fallows

The Atlantic Monthly | October 2004

Among the national security community, the chief criticism of the Iraq war is that it has diverted U.S. attention and resources away from other, more pressing threats—including Al Qaeda and Osama bin Laden (who is reportedly alive and well somewhere in the border region between Afghanistan and Pakistan), as well as North Korea and Iran, both of whom appear to be actively pursuing nuclear weapons programs. In this Atlantic Monthly *article, James Fallows, a veteran reporter on defense-related topics, investigates whether the U.S. might be less safe today as a result of the decision to invade Iraq. . . .*

I remember distinctly the way 2002 began in Washington. New Year's Day was below freezing and blustery. The next day was worse. That day, January 2, I trudged several hundred yards across the vast parking lots of the Pentagon. I was being pulled apart by the wind and was ready to feel sorry for myself, until I was shamed by the sight of miserable, frozen Army sentries at the numerous outdoor security posts that had been manned nonstop since the September 11 attacks.

I was going for an interview with Paul Wolfowitz, the deputy secretary of defense. At the time, Wolfowitz's name and face were not yet familiar worldwide. He was known in Washington for offering big-picture explanations of the Administration's foreign-policy goals—a task for which the President was unsuited, the Vice President was unavailable and most other senior Administration officials were, for various reasons, inappropriate. The National Security Adviser, Condoleezza Rice, was still playing a background role; the Secretary of Defense, Donald Rumsfeld, was mainly dealing with immediate operational questions in his daily briefing about the war in Afghanistan; the Secretary of State, Colin Powell, was already known to be on the losing side of most internal policy struggles.

After the interview I wrote a short article about Wolfowitz and his views for the March 2002 issue of this magazine In some ways the outlook and choices he described then still fit the world situation two and a half years later. Even at the time, the possibility that the Administration's next move in the war on terror would be against Iraq, whether or not Iraq proved to be involved in the 9/11 hijackings, was under active discussion. When talking with me Wolfowitz touched briefly on the case for removing Saddam Hussein, in the context of the general need to reduce tyranny in the Arab-Islamic world.

But in most ways the assumptions and tone of the conversation now seem impossibly remote. At the beginning of 2002 the United States still operated in a climate of worldwide sympathy and solidarity. A broad range of allies supported its anti-Taliban efforts in Afghanistan, and virtually no international Muslim leaders had denounced them. President Bush was still being celebrated for his eloquent speech expressing American resolve, before a joint session of Congress on September 20. His deftness in managing domestic and international symbols was typified by his hosting an end-of-Ramadan ceremony at the White House in mid-December, even as battle raged in the Tora Bora region of Afghanistan, on the Pakistani border. At the start of 2002 fewer than 10,000 U.S. soldiers were deployed overseas as part of the war on terror, and a dozen Americans had died in combat. The United States had not captured Osama bin Laden, but it had routed the Taliban leadership that sheltered him, and seemed to have put al-Qaeda on the run.

Because of the quick and, for Americans, nearly bloodless victory over the Taliban, the Administration's national security team had come to epitomize competence. During our talk Wolfowitz referred to "one reason this group of people work very well together," by which he meant that Cheney, Rumsfeld, Powell, and many others, including himself, had collaborated for years, from the Reagan Administration through the 1991 Gulf War and afterward. From this experience they had developed a shared understanding of the nuances of "how to use force effectively," which they were now applying. In retrospect, the remarkable thing about Wolfowitz's comment was the assumption—which I then had no reason to challenge—that Bush's foreign-policy team was like a great business or sporting dynasty, which should be examined for secrets of success.

As I listen to the tape of that interview now, something else stands out: how expansive and unhurried even Wolfowitz sounded. "Even" Wolfowitz because since then he has become the symbol of an unrelenting drive toward war with Iraq. We now know that within the Administration he was urging the case for "regime change" there immediately after 9/11. But when speaking for the record, more than a year before that war began, he stressed how broad a range of challenges the United States would have to address, and over how many years, if it wanted to contain the sources of terrorism. It would need to find ways to "lance the boil" of growing anti-Americanism, as it had done during the Reagan years by supporting democratic reform in South Korea and the Philippines. It would have to lead the Western world in celebrating and welcoming Turkey as the most successfully modernized Muslim country. It would need to understand that in the long run the most important part of America's policy was its moral example—that America stands for things "the rest of the world wants for itself."

I also remember the way 2002 ended. By late December some 200,000 members of the U.S. armed forces were en route to staging areas surrounding Iraq. Hundreds of thousands of people had turned out on the streets of London, Rome, Madrid, and other cities to protest the impending war. That it was impending was obvious, despite ongoing negotiations at the United Nations. Within weeks of the 9/11 attacks President Bush and Secretary Rumsfeld had asked to see plans for a possible invasion of Iraq. Congress voted to authorize the war in October. Immediately after the vote, planning bureaus inside the Pentagon were told to be ready for combat at any point between then and the following April. (Operation Iraqi Freedom actually began on March 19.) Declaring that it was impossible to make predictions about a war that might not occur, the Administration refused to discuss plans for the war's aftermath—or its potential cost. In December the President fired Lawrence Lindsey, his chief economic adviser, after Lindsey offered a guess that the total cost might be $100 billion to $200 billion. As it happened, Lindsey's controversial estimate held up very well. By this summer, fifteen months after fighting began in Iraq, appropriations for war and occupation there totaled about $150 billion. With more than 100,000 U.S. soldiers still based in Iraq, the outlays will continue indefinitely at a rate of about $5 billion a month—much of it for fuel, ammunition, spare parts, and other operational needs. All this is at striking variance with the pre-war insistence by Donald Rumsfeld and Paul Wolfowitz that Iraq's oil money, plus contributions from allies, would minimize the financial burden on Americans.

Despite the rout of al-Qaeda in Afghanistan, terror attacks, especially against Americans and Europeans, were rising at the end of 2002 and would continue to rise through 2003. Some 400 people worldwide had died in terror attacks in 2000, and some 300 in 2001, apart from the 3,000-plus killed on September 11. In 2002 more than 700 were killed, including 200 when a bomb exploded outside a Bali nightclub in October.

Whereas at the beginning of the year Paul Wolfowitz had sounded expansive about the many avenues the United States had to pursue in order to meet the terror threat, by the end of the year the focus was solely on Iraq, and the Administration's tone was urgent. "Simply stated, there is no doubt that Saddam Hussein now has weapons of mass destruction," Vice President Cheney said in a major speech to the Veterans of Foreign Wars just before Labor Day. "There is no doubt he is amassing them to use against our friends, against our allies, and against us." Two weeks later, as Congress prepared for its vote to authorize the war, Condoleezza Rice said on CNN, "We do know that [Saddam Hussein] is actively pursuing a nuclear weapon . . . We don't want the smoking gun to be a mushroom cloud."

On the last day of the year President Bush told reporters at his ranch in Texas, "I hope this Iraq situation will be resolved peacefully. One of my New Year's resolutions is to work to deal with these situations in a way so that they're resolved peacefully." As he spoke, every operating branch of the government was preparing for war.

September 11, 2001, has so often been described as a "hinge event" that it is tempting to think no other events could rival its significance. Indeed, as a single shocking moment that changed Americans' previous assumptions, the only modern comparisons are Pearl Harbor and the assassination of John F. Kennedy. But as 9/11 enters history, it seems likely that the aftermath, especially the decisions made during 2002, will prove to be as significant as the attack itself. It is obviously too early to know the full historical effect of the Iraq campaign. The biggest question about post-Saddam Iraq—whether it is headed toward stability or toward new tyranny and chaos—may not be answered for years.

But the biggest question about the United States—whether its response to 9/11 has made it safer or more vulnerable—can begin to be answered. Over the past two years I have been talking with a group of people at the working level of America's anti-terrorism efforts. Most are in the military, the intelligence agencies, and the diplomatic service; some are in think tanks and nongovernmental agencies. I have come to trust them, because most of them have no partisan ax to grind with the Administration (in the nature of things, soldiers and spies are mainly Republicans), and because they have so far been proved right. In the year before combat started in Iraq, they warned that occupying the country would be far harder than conquering it. As the occupation began, they pointed out the existence of plans and warnings the Administration seemed determined to ignore.

As a political matter, whether the United States is now safer or more vulnerable is of course ferociously controversial. That the war was necessary—and beneficial—is the Bush Administration's central claim. That it was not is the central claim of its critics. But among national-security professionals there is surprisingly little controversy. Except for those in government and in the opinion industries whose job it is to defend the Administration's record, they tend to see America's response to 9/11 as a catastrophe. I have sat through arguments among soldiers and scholars about whether the invasion of Iraq should be considered the worst strategic error in American history—or only the worst since Vietnam. Some of these people argue that the United States had no choice but to fight, given a pre-war consensus among its intelligence agencies that Iraq actually had WMD supplies. Many say that things in Iraq will eventually look much better than they do now. But about the conduct and effect of the war in Iraq one view prevails: it has increased the threats America faces, and has reduced the military, financial, and diplomatic tools with which we can respond.

"Let me tell you my gut feeling," a senior figure at one of America's military-sponsored think tanks told me recently, after we had talked for twenty minutes about details of the campaigns in Afghanistan and Iraq. "If I can be blunt, the Administration is full of shit. In my view we are much, much worse off now than when we went into Iraq. That is not a partisan position. I voted for these guys. But I think they are incompetent, and I have had a very close perspective on what is happening. Certainly in the long run we have harmed ourselves. We are playing to the enemy's political advantage. Whatever tactical victories we may gain along the way, this will prove to be a strategic blunder."

This man will not let me use his name, because he is still involved in military policy. He cited the experiences of Joseph Wilson, Richard Clarke, and

Generals Eric Shinseki and Anthony Zinni to illustrate the personal risks of openly expressing his dissenting view. But I am quoting him anonymously — as I will quote some others—because his words are representative of what one hears at the working level.

To a surprising extent their indictment doesn't concentrate on the aspect of the problem most often discussed in public: exactly why the United States got the WMD threat so wrong. Nor does it involve a problem I have previously discussed in this magazine (see "Blind Into Baghdad," January/February [2004] *Atlantic*): the Administration's failure, whether deliberate or inadvertent, to make use of the careful and extensive planning for postwar Iraq that had been carried out by the State Department, the CIA, various branches of the military, and many other organizations. Rather, these professionals argue that by the end of 2002 the decisions the Administration had made—and avoided making—through the course of the year had left the nation less safe, with fewer positive options. Step by step through 2002 America's war on terror became little more than its preparation for war in Iraq.

Because of that shift, the United States succeeded in removing Saddam Hussein, but at this cost: The first front in the war on terror, Afghanistan, was left to fester, as attention and money were drained toward Iraq. This in turn left more havens in Afghanistan in which terrorist groups could reconstitute themselves; a resurgent opium-poppy economy to finance them; and more of the disorder and brutality the United States had hoped to eliminate. Whether or not the strong international alliance that began the assault on the Taliban might have brought real order to Afghanistan is impossible to say. It never had the chance, because America's premature withdrawal soon fractured the alliance and curtailed postwar reconstruction. Indeed, the campaign in Afghanistan was warped and limited from the start, by a pre-existing desire to save troops for Iraq.

A full inventory of the costs of war in Iraq goes on. President Bush began 2002 with a warning that North Korea and Iran, not just Iraq, threatened the world because of the nuclear weapons they were developing. With the United States preoccupied by Iraq, these other two countries surged ahead. They have been playing a game of chess, or nerves, against America—and if they have not exactly won, they have advanced by several moves. Because it lost time and squandered resources, the United States now has no good options for dealing with either country. It has fewer deployable soldiers and weapons; it has less international leverage through the "soft power" of its alliances and treaties; it even has worse intelligence, because so many resources are directed toward Iraq.

At the beginning of 2002 the United States imported over 50 percent of its oil. In two years we have increased that figure by nearly 10 percent. The need for imported oil is the fundamental reason the United States must be deferential in its relationship with Saudi Arabia. Revenue from that oil is the fundamental reason that extremist groups based in Saudi Arabia were so rich. After the first oil shocks, in the mid-1970s, the United States took steps that reduced its imports of Persian Gulf oil. The Bush Administration could have made similar steps a basic part of its anti-terrorism strategy, and could have counted on making progress: through most of 2002 the Administration could assume bipartisan support for nearly anything it proposed. But its only such suggestion was drilling in the Arctic National Wildlife Refuge.

Before America went to war in Iraq, its military power seemed limitless. There was less need to actually apply it when all adversaries knew that any time we did so we would win. Now the limits on our military's manpower and sustainability are all too obvious. For example, the Administration announced this summer that in order to maintain troop levels in Iraq, it would withdraw 12,500 soldiers from South Korea. The North Koreans, the Chinese, the Iranians, the Syrians, and others who have always needed to take into account the chance of U.S. military intervention now realize that America has no stomach for additional wars. Before Iraq the U.S. military was turning away qualified applicants. Now it applies "stop-loss" policies that forbid retirement or resignation by volunteers, and it has mobilized the National Guard and Reserves in a way not seen since World War II.

Because of outlays for Iraq, the United States cannot spend $150 billion for other defensive purposes. Some nine million shipping containers enter American ports each year; only two percent of them are physically inspected, because inspecting more would be too expensive. The Department of Homeland Security, created after 9/11, is a vast grab-bag of federal agencies, from the Coast Guard to the Border Patrol to the former Immigration and Naturalization Service; ongoing operations in Iraq cost significantly more each month than all Homeland Security expenses combined. The department has sought to help cities large and small to improve their "first responder" systems, especially with better communications for their fire and emergency medical services. This summer a survey by the U.S. Conference of Mayors found that fewer than a quarter of 231 major cities under review had received any of the aid they expected. An internal budget memo from the Administration was leaked this past spring. It said that outlays for virtually all domestic programs, including homeland security, would have to be cut in 2005—and the federal budget deficit would still be more than $450 billion.

Worst of all, the government-wide effort to wage war in Iraq crowded out efforts to design a broader strategy against Islamic extremists and terrorists; to this day the Administration has articulated no comprehensive long-term plan. It dismissed out of hand any connection between policies toward the Israeli-Palestinian conflict and increasing tension with many Islamic states. Regime change in Iraq, it said, would have a sweeping symbolic effect on worldwide sources of terror. That seems to have been true— but in the opposite way from what the President intended. It is hard to find a counter-terrorism specialist who thinks that the Iraq War has reduced rather than increased the threat to the United States.

And here is the startling part. There is no evidence that the President and those closest to him ever talked systematically about the "opportunity costs" and tradeoffs in their decision to invade Iraq. No one has pointed to a meeting, a memo, a full set of discussions, about what America would gain and lose.

The Prelude: Late 2001

Success in war requires an understanding of who the enemy is, what resources can be used against him, and how victory will be defined. In the immediate aftermath of 9/11 America's expert agencies concluded that Osama bin Laden and al-Qaeda were almost certainly responsible for the attacks—and that the Taliban regime in Afghanistan was providing them with sanctuary. Within the government there was almost no dispute, then or later, about the legitimacy and importance of destroying that stronghold. Indeed, the main criticism of the initial anti-Taliban campaign was that it took so long to start.

In his book *Against All Enemies* the former terrorism adviser Richard Clarke says it was "plainly obvious" after September 11 that "al Qaeda's sanctuary in Taliban-run Afghanistan had to be occupied by U.S. forces and the al Qaeda leaders killed." It was therefore unfortunate that the move against the Taliban was "slow and small." Soon after the attacks President

Bush created an interagency Campaign Coordination Committee to devise responses to al-Qaeda, and named Clarke its co-chairman. Clarke told me that this group urged a "rapid, no-holds-barred" retaliation in Afghanistan—including an immediate dispatch of troops to Afghanistan's borders to cut off al-Qaeda escape routes.

But the Administration was unwilling to use overwhelming power in Afghanistan. The only authorized account of how the "principals"—the big shots of the Administration—felt and thought at this time is in Bob Woodward's books *Bush at War* (2002) and *Plan of Attack* (2004), both based on interviews with the President and his senior advisers. To judge by *Bush at War*, Woodward's more laudatory account, a major reason for delay in attacking the Taliban had to do with "CSAR"—combat search and rescue teams. These were meant to be in place before the first aerial missions, so that they could go to the aid of any American pilot who might be downed. Preparations took weeks. They involved negotiations with the governments of Tajikistan and Uzbekistan for basing rights, the slow process of creating and equipping support airstrips in remote mountainous regions, and the redeployment of far-flung aircraft carriers to the Persian Gulf.

"The slowness was in part because the military weren't ready and they needed to move in the logistics support, the refueling aircraft, all of that," Richard Clarke told me. "But through this time the President kept saying to the Taliban, 'You still have an opportunity to come clean with us.' Which I thought—and the State Department thought—was silly. We'd already told them in advance that if this happened we were going to hold them personally responsible." Laurence Pope, a former ambassador to Chad, made a similar point when I spoke with him. Through the late 1990s Pope was the political adviser to General Zinni, who as the head of U.S. Central Command was responsible for Iraq and Afghanistan. Pope had run war games concerning assaults on both countries. "We had warned the Taliban repeatedly about Osama bin Laden," he told me, referring to the late Clinton years. "There was no question [after 9/11] that we had to take them on and deny that sanctuary to al-Qaeda. We should have focused like a laser on bin Laden and taking down al-Qaeda, breaking crockery in the neighborhood if necessary."

The crockery he was referring to included the government of Pakistan, which viewed the Pashtun tribal areas along the Afghan border as ungovernable. In the view of Pope and some others, the United States should have insisted on going into these areas right away, either with

Pakistani troops or on its own—equipped with money to buy support, weapons, or both. This might have caused some regional and international disruption—but less than later invading Iraq.

It was on October 6, three and a half weeks after the attacks, that President Bush issued his final warning that "time was running out" for the Taliban to turn over bin Laden. The first cruise-missile strikes occurred the next day. The first paramilitary teams from the CIA and Special Forces arrived shortly thereafter; the first regular U.S. combat troops were deployed in late November. Thus, while the United States prepared for its response, Osama bin Laden, his deputy Ayman al-Zawahiri, and the rest of their ruling Shura Council had almost two months to flee and hide.

Opinions vary about exactly how much difference it would have made if the United States had killed or captured al-Qaeda's leaders while the World Trade Center ruins were still smoldering. But no one disputes that the United States needed to move immediately against al-Qaeda, and in the most complete and decisive way possible. And there is little disagreement about what happened next. The military and diplomatic effort in Afghanistan was handicapped from the start because the Administration had other concerns, and it ended badly even though it started well.

Winter 2001-2002: War on the Cheap

By the beginning of 2002 U.S. and Northern Alliance forces had beaten the Taliban but lost bin Laden. At that point the United States faced a consequential choice: to bear down even harder in Afghanistan, or to shift the emphasis in the global war on terror (GWOT, as it is known in the trade) somewhere else.

A version of this choice between Afghanistan and "somewhere else" had in fact been made at the very start of the Administration's response to the 9/11 attacks. As Clarke, Woodward, and others have reported, during the top-level meetings at Camp David immediately after the attacks Paul Wolfowitz forcefully argued that Saddam Hussein was so threatening, and his overthrow was so "doable," that he had to be included in the initial military response. "The 'Afghanistan first' argument prevailed, basically for the reasons that Colin Powell advocated," Richard Clarke told me. "He said that the American people just aren't going to understand if you don't do something in Afghanistan right away—and that the lack of causal connection between Iraq and 9/11 would make it difficult to make the case for that war."

But Afghanistan first did not mean Afghanistan only. Clarke reminded me that he had prepared a memo on anti-terrorism strategy for the President's review before September 11. When it came back, on September 17, Clarke noticed only one significant change: the addition of a paragraph asking the Defense Department to prepare war plans for Iraq. Throughout the fall and winter, as U.S. troops were deployed in Afghanistan, Bush asked for and received increasingly detailed briefings from General Tommy Franks about the forces that might later be necessary in Iraq. According to many people who observed the process, the stated and unstated need to be ready for Saddam Hussein put a serious crimp in the U.S. effort against bin Laden and the Taliban.

The need to reserve troops for a likely second front in Iraq was one factor, though not the only one, in the design of the U.S. battle plan for Afghanistan. Many in the press (including me) marveled at America's rapid move against the Taliban for the ingenuity of its tactics. Instead of sending in many thousands of soldiers, the Administration left much of the actual fighting to the tribes of the Northern Alliance. Although the U.S. forces proved unable to go in fast, they certainly went in light—the Special Forces soldiers who chose targets for circling B-52s while picking their way through mountains on horseback being the most famous example. And they very quickly won. All this was exactly in keeping with the "transformation" doctrine that Donald Rumsfeld had been emphasizing in the Pentagon, and it reflected Rumsfeld's determination to show that a transformed military could substitute precision, technology, and imagination for sheer manpower.

But as would later become so obvious in Iraq, ousting a regime is one thing, and controlling or even pacifying a country is something else. For a significant group of military and diplomatic officials within the U.S. government, winning this "second war," for post-combat stability in Afghanistan, was a crucial step in the Administration's longterm efforts against al-Qaeda. Afghanistan had, after all, been the site of al-Qaeda's main training camps. The Taliban who harbored al-Qaeda had originally come to power as an alternative to warlordism and an economy based on extortion and drugs, so the United States could ill afford to let the country revert to the same rule and economy.

In removing the Taliban, the United States had acted as a genuine liberator. It came to the task with clean hands and broad international support.

It had learned from the Soviet Union the folly of trying to hold Afghanistan by force. But it did not have to control the entire country to show that U.S. intervention could have lasting positive effects. What it needed, according to the "second war" group, was a sustained military, financial, and diplomatic effort to keep Afghanistan from sinking back toward chaos and thus becoming a terrorist haven once again.

"Had we seen Afghanistan as anything other than a sideshow," says Larry Goodson, a scholar at the Army War College who spent much of 2002 in Afghanistan, "we could have stepped up both the economic and security presence much more quickly than we did. Had Iraq not been what we were ginning up for in 2002, when the security situation in Afghanistan was collapsing, we might have come much more quickly to the peacekeeping and 'nation-building' strategy we're beginning to employ now." Iraq, of course, *was* what we were ginning up for, and the effects on Afghanistan were more important, if subtler, than has generally been discussed.

I asked officials, soldiers, and spies whether they had witnessed tradeoffs—specific transfers of manpower—that materially affected U.S. success in Afghanistan, and the response of Thomas White was typical: not really. During the wars in Afghanistan and Iraq, White was Secretary of the Army. Like most other people I spoke with, he offered an example or two of Iraq-Afghanistan tradeoffs, mainly involving strain on Special Forces or limits on electronic intelligence from the National Security Agency. Another man told me that NSA satellites had to be "boreholed" in a different direction—that is, aimed directly at sites in Iraq, rather than at Afghanistan. But no one said that changes like these had really been decisive. What did matter, according to White and nearly everyone else I spoke with, was the knowledge that the "center of gravity" of the anti-terrorism campaign was about to shift to Iraq. That dictated not just the vaunted "lightness" of the invasion but also the decision to designate allies for crucial tasks: the Northern Alliance for initial combat, and the Pakistanis for closing the border so that al-Qaeda leaders would not escape. In the end neither ally performed its duty the way the Americans had hoped. The Northern Alliance was far more motivated to seize Kabul than to hunt for bin Laden. The Pakistanis barely pretended to patrol the border. In its recent "after-action reports" the U.S. military has been increasingly critical of its own management of this campaign, but delegating the real work to less motivated allies seems to have been the uncorrectable error.

The desire to limit U.S. commitment had at least as great an effect on what happened after the fall of the Taliban. James Dobbins, who was the Bush Administration's special envoy for Afghanistan and its first representative in liberated Kabul, told me that three decisions in the early months "really shaped" the outcome in Afghanistan. "One was that U.S. forces were not going to do peacekeeping of any sort, under any circumstances. They would remain available to hunt down Osama bin Laden and find renegade Taliban, but they were not going to have any role in providing security for the country at large. The second was that we would oppose anybody else's playing this role outside Kabul. And this was at a time when there was a good deal of interest from other countries in doing so." A significant reason for refusing help, according to Dobbins, was that accepting it would inevitably have tied up more American resources in Afghanistan, especially for airlifting donated supplies to foreign-led peacekeeping stations in the hinterland. The third decision was that U.S. forces would not engage in any counter-narcotics activities. One effect these policies had was to prolong the disorder in Afghanistan and increase the odds against a stable government. The absence of American or international peacekeepers guaranteed that the writ of the new Karzai government would extend, at best, to Kabul itself.

"I can't prove this, but I believe they didn't want to put in a lot of regular infantry because they wanted to hold it in reserve," Richard Clarke explains. "And the issue is the infantry. A rational military planner who was told to stabilize Afghanistan after the Taliban was gone, and who was not told that we might soon be doing Iraq, would probably have put in three times the number of infantry, plus all the logistics support 'tail.' He would have put in more civil-affairs units, too. Based on everything I heard at the time, I believe I can make a good guess that the plan for Afghanistan was affected by a predisposition to go into Iraq. The result of that is that they didn't have enough people to go in and stabilize the country, nor enough people to make sure these guys didn't get out."

The Administration later placed great emphasis on making Iraq a showcase of Islamic progress: a society that, once freed from tyranny, would demonstrate steady advancement toward civil order, economic improvement, and, ultimately, democracy. Although Afghanistan is a far wilder, poorer country, it might have provided a better showcase, and sooner. There was no controversy about America's involvement; the rest of the world was ready to provide aid; if it wasn't going to become rich, it could become demonstrably less poor. The amount of money and manpower sufficient to transform Afghanistan would have been a tiny fraction of what America decided to commit in Iraq. But the opportunity was missed, and Afghanistan began a descent to its pre-Taliban warlord state.

Spring 2002: Chaos and Closed Minds

Early 2002 was the Administration's first chance to look beyond its initial retaliation in Afghanistan. This could have been a time to think broadly about America's vulnerabilities and to ask what problems might have been overlooked in the immediate response to 9/11. At this point the United States still had comfortable reserves of all elements of international power, "hard" and "soft" alike.

As the fighting wound down in Tora Bora, the Administration could in principle have matched a list of serious problems with a list of possible solutions. In his State of the Union speech, in late January, President Bush had named Iran, Iraq, and North Korea as an "axis of evil." The Administration might have weighed the relative urgency of those three threats, including uncontested evidence that North Korea was furthest along in developing nuclear weapons. It might have launched an all-out effort to understand al-Qaeda's strengths and weaknesses—and to exploit the weak points. It might have asked whether relations with Pakistan, Egypt, and Saudi Arabia needed fundamental reconsideration. For decades we had struck an inglorious bargain with the regimes in those countries: we would overlook their internal repression and their role as havens for Islamic extremists; they would not oppose us on first-order foreign-policy issues—demonstrating, for instance, a relative moderation toward Israel. And the Saudis would be cooperative about providing oil. Maybe, after serious examination, this bargain would still seem to be the right one, despite the newly manifest dangers of Islamic extremism. But the time to ask the question was early in 2002.

The Administration might also have asked whether its approach to Israel and the Palestinians needed reconsideration. Before 9/11 it had declared a hands-off policy toward Israel and the PLO, but sooner or later all Bush's predecessors had come around to a "land for peace" bargain as the only plausible solution in the Middle East. The new Administration would never have more leverage or a more opportune moment for imposing such a deal than soon after it was attacked.

Conceivably the Administration could have asked other questions—

about energy policy, about manpower in the military, about the fiscal base for a sustained war. This was an opportunity created by crisis. At the top level of the Administration attention swung fast, and with little discussion, exclusively to Iraq. This sent a signal to the working levels, where daily routines increasingly gave way to preparations for war, steadily denuding the organizations that might have been thinking about other challenges.

The Administration apparently did not consider questions like "If we pursue the war on terror by invading Iraq, might we incite even more terror in the long run?" and "If we commit so many of our troops this way, what possibilities will we be giving up?" But Bush "did not think of this, intellectually, as a comparative decision," I was told by Senator Bob Graham, of Florida, who voted against the war resolution for fear it would hurt the fight against terrorism. "It was a single decision: he saw Saddam Hussein as an evil person who had to be removed." The firsthand accounts of the Administration's decision-making indicate that the President spent most of his time looking at evidence of Saddam Hussein's threat, and significant but smaller amounts of time trying to build his coalition and hearing about the invasion plans. A man who participated in high-level planning for both Afghanistan and Iraq—and who is unnamed here because he still works for the government—told me, "There was absolutely no debate in the normal sense. There are only six or eight of them who make the decisions, and they only talk to each other. And if you disagree with them in public, they'll come after you, the way they did with Shinseki."

The three known exceptions to this pattern actually underscore the limits on top-level talks. One was the discussions at Camp David just after 9/11: they led to "Afghanistan first," which delayed rather than forestalled the concentration on Iraq. The second was Colin Powell's "You break it, you've bought it" warning to the President in the summer of 2002: far from leading to serious questions about the war, it did not even persuade the Administration to use the postwar plans devised by the State Department, the Army, and the CIA. The third was a long memo from Rumsfeld to Bush a few months before the war began, when a campaign against Iraq was a foregone conclusion. As excerpted in *Plan of Attack*, it listed twenty-nine ways in which an invasion could backfire. "Iraq could successfully best the U.S. in public relations and persuade the world that it was a war against Muslims" was one. "There could be higher than expected collateral damage" was another. But even this memo was couched in terms of "making sure that we had done everything humanly possible to prepare [the President] for what could go wrong, to prepare so things would go right," Rumsfeld explained to Bob Woodward. And its only apparent effect was that Bush called in his military commanders to look at the war plans.

Discussions at the top were distorted in yet another way—by an unspoken effect of disagreements over the Middle East. Some connections between Iraq policy and the Israeli-Palestinian dispute are obvious. One pro-war argument was "The road to Jerusalem runs through Baghdad"—that is, once the United States had removed Saddam Hussein and the threat he posed to Israel, it could lean more effectively on Ariel Sharon and the Likud government to accept the right deal. According to this logic, America could also lean more effectively on the Palestinians and their supporters, because of the new strength it would have demonstrated by liberating Iraq. The contrary argument—"The road to Baghdad leads through Jerusalem"—appears to have been raised mainly by Tony Blair. Its point was that if the United States first took a tougher line with Sharon and recognized that the Palestinians, too, had grievances, it would have a much easier time getting allied support and Arab acquiescence for removing Saddam Hussein. There is no evidence that this was ever significantly discussed inside the Administration.

"The groups on either side of the Iraq debate basically didn't trust each other," a former senior official in the Administration told me—and the people "on either side" he was speaking of all worked for George Bush. (He, too, insisted on anonymity because he has ongoing dealings with the government.) "If it wasn't clear *why* you were saying these skeptical things about invading Iraq, there was naturally the suspicion that you were saying [them] because you opposed the Israeli position. So any argument became suspect." Suspicion ran just as strongly the other way—that officials were steadfast for war because they supported the Israeli position. In this (admittedly oversimplified) schema, the CIA, the State Department, and the uniformed military were the most skeptical of war—and, in the view of war supporters, were also the most critical of Israel. The White House (Bush, Cheney, Rice) and the Defense Department's civilian leadership were the most pro-war—and the most pro-Israel. Objectively, all these people agreed far more than they differed, but their mutual suspicions further muted dissenting views.

At the next level down, different problems had the same effect: difficulty in thinking broadly about threats and responses. An obscure-sounding bureaucratic change contributed. At the start of his second term Bill

Clinton had signed FDD 56, a presidential decision directive about handling international emergencies. The idea was that, like it or not, a chaotic world would continually involve the United States in "complex contingency operations." These were efforts, like the ones in the Balkans and East Africa, in which soldiers, diplomats, relief workers, reconstruction experts, economists, legal authorities, and many other officials from many different institutions would need to work together if any of them were to succeed. The directive set up a system for coordinating these campaigns, so that no one organization dominated the others or operated unilaterally.

When it took office, the Bush Administration revoked this plan and began working on a replacement. But nothing was on hand as of September 11. For months the response to the attacks was managed by a variety of ad hoc groups. The Campaign Coordination Committee, run by Richard Clarke and his colleague Franklin Miller, oversaw strategies against al-Qaeda. The new Domestic Preparedness Committee, run by John Ashcroft's deputy, Larry Thompson, oversaw internal-security measures. And the "principals"—Bush, Cheney, Rumsfeld, Powell, Rice, Director of Central Intelligence George Tenet, and a few others, including Wolfowitz, Powell's deputy Richard Armitage, and Cheney's aide Lewis "Scooter" Libby—met frequently to plan the showdown with Iraq. There was no established way to make sure that State knew what Defense was doing and vice versa, as became disastrously obvious after the fall of Baghdad. And there was no recognized venue for opportunity-cost discussions about the emerging Iraq policy, even if anyone had wanted them.

In the absence of other plans, initiative on every issue was increasingly taken in the Pentagon. And within the Pentagon the emphasis increasingly moved toward Iraq. In March of 2002, when U.S. troops were still engaged in Operation Anaconda on the Afghan-Pakistani border, and combat in Iraq was still a year away, inside the government Afghanistan had begun to seem like yesterday's problem. When asked about Iraq at a press conference on March 13, Bush said merely, "All options are on the table." By that time Tommy Franks had answered Bush's request for battle plans and lists of potential bombing targets in Iraq.

The more experienced in government the people I interviewed were, the more likely they were to stress the importance of the mental shift in the spring of 2002. When I asked Richard Clarke whether preparations for Iraq had really taken anything crucial from Afghanistan or other efforts, he said yes, unquestionably. "They took one thing that people on the outside find hard to believe or appreciate," he said. "Management time. We're a huge government, and we have hundreds of thousands of people involved in national security. Therefore you would think we could walk and chew gum at the same time. I've never found that to be true. You've got one National Security Adviser and one CIA director, and they each have one deputy. The same is true in Defense. Interestingly in terms of the military, both of these wars took place in the same 'CINCdom' "—by which Clarke meant that both were in the realm of Tommy Franks's Central Command, rather than in two different theaters. "It just is not credible that the principals and the deputies paid as much attention to Afghanistan or the war against al-Qaeda as they should have."

According to Michael Scheuer, a career CIA officer who spent the late 1990s as head of the agency's anti-bin Laden team, the shift of attention had another destructive effect on efforts to battle al-Qaeda: the diversion of members of that team and the Agency's limited supply of Arabic-speakers and Middle East specialists to support the mounting demand for intelligence on Iraq. (Because Scheuer is still on active duty at the CIA, the Agency allowed him to publish his recent book, *Imperial Hubris*, a harsh criticism of U.S. approaches to controlling terrorism, only as "Anonymous." After we spoke, his identity was disclosed by Jason Vest, in the *Boston Phoenix*; when I met him, he declined to give his name and was introduced simply as "Mike.") "With a finite number of people who have any kind of pertinent experience," Scheuer told me, "there is unquestionably a sucking away of resources from Afghanistan and al-Qaeda to Iraq, just because it was a much bigger effort."

Scheuer observed that George Tenet had claimed early in 2003 that there was enough expertise and manpower to handle both Iraq and al-Qaeda. "From inside the system that sounded like a very questionable judgment," Scheuer said. "You start with a large group of people who have worked bin Laden and al-Qaeda and Sunni terrorism for years—and worked it every day since 9/11. Then you move a lot of people out to work the Iraq issue, and instead you have a lot of people who come in for ninety days or one hundred and twenty days, then leave. It's like any other profession. Over time you make connections. A name comes up, and there's nothing on file in the last two years—but you remember that five years ago there was a guy with that name doing acts in the Philippines. If you don't have an institutional memory, you don't make the connection. When they talk about connecting the dots, the computers are important. But at the end of the day, the most important thing is that human being who's been working this issue for five or six years. You can have the best computers in the world, and you can have an ocean of information, but if you have a guy who's only been there for three weeks or three months, you're very weak."

Laurence Pope, the former ambassador, told me that Iraq monomania was particularly destructive in the spring of 2002 because of the opportunity that came and went in Afghanistan. "There was a moment of six months or so when we could have put much more pressure on the tribal areas [to get al-Qaeda], and on Pakistan, and done a better job of reconstruction in Afghanistan," he said. "In reality, the Beltway can only do one thing at a time, and because of the attention to Iraq, what should have happened in Afghanistan didn't."

So by the spring, after six months in which to consider its strategy, the Administration had radically narrowed its choices. Its expert staffers were deflected toward Iraq—and away from Afghanistan, Iran, North Korea, Israel-Palestine, the hunt for bin Laden, the assault on al-Qaeda, even China and Taiwan. Its diplomats were not squeezing Pakistan as hard as possible about chasing al-Qaeda, or Saudi Arabia about cracking down on extremists, because the United States needed their help—or at least acquiescence—in the coming war with Iraq. Its most senior officials were working out the operational details of a plan whose fundamental wisdom they had seldom, if ever, stopped to examine.

Summer and Fall: The One-Front War

President Bush's first major statement about his post-9/11 foreign policy had come in his State of the Union address. His second came on June 1, when he gave the graduation speech at West Point. It carefully laid out the case for a new doctrine of "pre-emptive" war. Bush didn't say "Iraq" or "Saddam Hussein," but his meaning was unmistakable. "Containment is not possible when unbalanced dictators with weapons of mass destruction can deliver those weapons on missiles or secretly provide them to terrorist allies," he said. "We cannot put our faith in the word of tyrants who solemnly sign non-proliferation treaties and then systemically break them. If we wait for threats to fully materialize, we will have waited too long." A few weeks later Condoleezza Rice presented a fuller version of the concept, and Dick Cheney hammered home his warnings that Saddam Hussein had, beyond all doubt, acquired weapons of mass destruction. In September, Donald Rumsfeld said at a news conference that the link between Saddam Hussein and al-Qaeda was "not debatable." By October, Bush had practically stopped referring to Osama bin Laden in his press statements; he said of Saddam Hussein, "This is the guy that tried to kill my dad."

The Democrats still controlled the Senate, but on October 11 Majority Leader Tom Daschle led John Kerry, John Edwards, and twenty-six other Democrats in voting to authorize the war. (Authorization passed the Senate 77-23; most Democrats in the House voted against it, but it still carried there, by 296 to 133.) Democratic officials were desperate to get the vote behind them, so that in the impending midterm elections they could not be blamed for hampering the war on terrorism—in which, the Administration said, war in Iraq played an integral part.

The Cyclops-like nature of the Administration's perception of risk became more evident. Uncertain evidence about Iraq was read in the most pessimistic fashion; much more reliable evidence about other threats was ignored. Of the three members of the "axis of evil," Iraq had made the sketchiest progress toward developing nuclear weapons. In October, just before the Iraq War vote, a delegation of Americans in Pyongyang found that North Korea's nuclear-weapons program was actually up and running. As the weeks wore on, North Korea became more and more brazen. In December it reactivated a nuclear processing plant it had closed eight years earlier as part of a deal with the United States. Soon thereafter it kicked out inspectors from the International Atomic Energy Agency and announced that it would withdraw from the Nuclear Non-Proliferation Treaty. North Korea was dropping even the pretense that it was not developing nuclear bombs.

Meanwhile, in August of 2002, an Iranian opposition group revealed the existence of two previously secret nuclear facilities, in Natanz and Arak. The first was devoted to uranium enrichment, the second to heavy-water production, which is a step toward producing plutonium. Months before the vote on war with Iraq, then, the United States had very strong indications that Iran was pursuing two paths toward atomic weaponry: uranium and plutonium. The indications from North Korea were at least as strong. If the very worst pre-war suspicions about Saddam Hussein's weapons of mass destruction had turned out to be true, the nuclear stakes would still have been lower than those in North Korea or Iran.

"How will history judge this period, in terms of the opportunity costs of invading Iraq?" said John Pike, the director of GlobalSecurity.org, when we spoke. "I think the opportunity cost is going to be North Korea and Iran. I mean, in 2002 it became obvious that Iran has a full-blown nuclear-weapons program under way, no ifs or buts. For the next eighteen months or so, before it's running, we have the opportunity to blow it up. But this Iraq adventure will give blowing up your enemies a bad name. The concern now has to be that the 'Iraq syndrome' will make us flinch from blowing up people who really need to be blown up."

Bombing North Korea's reactor has never been an option, since North Korea has so many retaliatory forces so close to Seoul. But whatever choices the United States had at the beginning of 2002, it has fewer and worse ones now. The North Koreans are that much further along in their program; the U.S. military is under that much more strain; international hostility to U.S. policies is that much greater. "At the rate North Korea is pumping out bomb material," Pike said, "the Japanese will realize that the missile defense we've sold them will not save them. And they will conclude that only weaponizing their plutonium will enable them to sleep easily at night. And *then* you'll have South Korea and Taiwan . . ." and on through other ripple-effect scenarios. Pike says that the United States has little leverage to prevent any of this, and therefore can't afford to waste any more time in acting against North Korea.

"Are we better off in basic security than before we invaded Iraq?" asks Jeffrey Record, a professor of strategy at the Air War College and the author of the recent *Dark Victory,* a book about the Iraq War. "The answer is no. An unnecessary war has consumed American Army and other ground resources, to the point where we have nothing left in the cupboard for another contingency—for instance, should the North Koreans decide that with the Americans completely absorbed in Iraq, now is the time to do something."

"We really have four armies," an Army officer involved in Pentagon planning for the Iraq War told me. "There's the one that's deployed in Afghanistan and Iraq. There's the one that's left back home in Fort Hood and other places. There's the 'modular Army,' of new brigade-sized units that are supposed to be rotated in and out of locations easily. There's the Guard and Reserve. And every one of them is being chewed up by the ops tempo." "Ops tempo" means the pace of operations, and when it is too high, equipment and supplies are being used faster than they can be replaced, troops are being deployed far longer than they expected, and training is being pared back further than it should. "We're really in dire straits with resourcing," he said. "There's not enough armor for Humvees. There's not enough fifty-caliber machine guns for the Hundred and First Airborne or the Tenth Mountain Division. A country that can't field heavy machine guns for its army—there's something wrong with the way we're doing business."

"The stress of war has hit all the services, but none harder than the Army," Sydney Freedberg wrote recently in *National Journal*. "The crucial shortfall is not in money or machines, but in manpower." More than a third of the Army's 500,000 active-duty soldiers are in Iraq or Kuwait. Freedberg referred to a study showing that fifteen of the Army's thirty-four active-duty combat units were currently deployed overseas, and wrote, "That means that nearly as many units are abroad as at home, when historical experience shows that a long-term commitment, as with the British in Northern Ireland, requires three or four units recuperating and training for each one deployed." In the long run the U.S. military needs either more people or fewer responsibilities. At the moment, because of Iraq, it has very little slack for dealing with other emergencies that might arise.

Winter: Misreading the Enemy

President Bush's first major speech after 9/11, on September 20, 2001, was one of the outstanding addresses given by a modern President. But it introduced a destructive concept that Bush used more and more insistently through 2002. "Why do they hate us?" he asked about the terrorists. He answered that they hate what is best in us: "They hate what we see right here in this chamber—a democratically elected government . . . They hate our freedoms—our freedom of religion, our freedom of speech, our freedom to vote and assemble and disagree with each other." As he boiled down this thought in subsequent comments it became "They hate us for who we are" and "They hate us because we are free."

There may be people who have studied, fought against, or tried to infiltrate al-Qaeda and who agree with Bush's statement. But I have never met any. The soldiers, spies, academics, and diplomats I have interviewed are unanimous in saying that "They hate us for who we are" is dangerous claptrap. Dangerous because it is so lazily self-justifying and self-deluding: the only thing we could possibly be doing wrong is being so excellent. Claptrap because it reflects so little knowledge of how Islamic extremism has evolved.

"There are very few people in the world who are going to kill themselves so we can't vote in the Iowa caucuses," Michael Scheuer said to me. "But there's a lot of them who are willing to die because we're helping the Israelis, or because we're helping Putin against the Chechens, or because we keep oil prices low so Muslims lose money." Jeffrey Record said, "Clearly they do not *like* American society. They think it's far too libertine, democratic, Christian. But that's not the reason they attack us. If it were, they would have attacked a lot of other Western countries too. I don't notice them putting bombs in Norway. It's a combination of who we are and also our behavior."

This summer's report of the 9/11 Commission, without associating this view with Bush, was emphatic in rejecting the "hate us for who we are" view. The commission said this about the motivation of Khalid Sheikh Muhammad, whom it identified as the "mastermind of the 9/11 attacks": "KSM's animus toward the United States stemmed not from his experiences there as a student, but rather from his violent disagreement with U.S. foreign policy favoring Israel." In discussing long-term strategies for dealing with extremist groups the commission said, "America's policy choices have consequences. Right or wrong, it is simply a fact that American policy regarding the Israeli-Palestinian conflict and American actions in Iraq are dominant staples of popular commentary across the Arab and Muslim world." The most striking aspect of the commission's analysis is that it offered any thoughts at all about the right longterm response to Islamic extremists. The 9/11 Commission was one of several groups seeking to fill the void left by the Administration's failure to put forward any comprehensive battle plan for a long-term campaign against terrorism. By its actions the Administration showed that the only terrorism problem it recognized was Saddam Hussein's regime, plus the al-Qaeda leaders shown on its "most wanted" lists.

The distinction between who we are and what we do matters, because it bears on the largest question about the Iraq War: Will it bring less or more Islamic terrorism? If violent extremism is purely vengeful and irrational, there is no hope except to crush it. Any brutality along the way is an unavoidable cost. But if it is based on logic of any sort, a clear understanding of its principles could help us to weaken its appeal—and to choose tactics that are not self-defeating.

A later article will describe insights about controlling terrorism. For now the point is the strong working-level consensus that terrorists are "logical," if hideously brutal, and that the steps in 2002 that led to war have broadened the extremists' base. In March of 2003, just after combat began in Iraq, President Hosni Mubarak, of Egypt, warned that if the United States invaded, "instead of having one bin Laden, we will have one hundred bin Ladens." Six months later, when the combat was over, Rumsfeld wrote in a confidential memo quoted in *Plan of Attack*, "We lack metrics to know if we are winning or losing the global war on terror. Are we capturing, killing or deterring and dissuading more terrorists every day than the madrassas [Islamic schools] and the radical clerics are recruiting, training and deploying against us? . . . The cost-benefit ratio is against us! Our cost is billions against the terrorists' costs of millions." Six months after that, as violence surged in occupied Iraq, the International Institute for Strategic Studies, in London, reported that al-Qaeda was galvanized by the wars in Afghanistan and Iraq. As of mid-2004 it had at least 18,000 operatives in sixty countries. "Al Qaeda has fully reconstituted [and] set its sights firmly on the USA and its closest Western allies in Europe," the report said. Meanwhile, a British parliamentary report warns that Afghanistan is likely to "implode" for lack of support.

"I have been saying for years, Osama bin Laden could never have done it without us," a civilian adviser to the Pentagon told me this summer. "We have continued to play to his political advantage and to confirm, in the eyes of his constituency, the very claims he made about us." Those claims are that the United States will travel far to suppress Muslims, that it will occupy their holy sites, that it will oppose the rise of Islamic governments, and that it will take their resources. "We got to Baghdad," Michael Scheuer said, "and the first thing Rumsfeld said is, 'We'll accept any government as long as it's not Islamic.' It draws their attention to bin Laden's argument that the United States is leading the West to annihilate Islam." The Administration had come a long way from the end-of-Ramadan ceremony at the White House.

What Happened in a Year
To govern is to choose, and the choices made in 2002 were fateful. The United States began that year shocked and wounded, but with tremendous strategic advantages. Its population was more closely united behind its leadership than it had been in fifty years. World opinion was strongly

sympathetic. Longtime allies were eager to help; longtime antagonists were silent. The federal budget was nearly in balance, making ambitious projects feasible. The U.S. military was superbly equipped, trained, and prepared. An immediate foe was evident—and vulnerable—in Afghanistan. For the longer-term effort against Islamic extremism the Administration could draw on a mature school of thought from academics, regional specialists, and its own intelligence agencies. All that was required was to think broadly about the threats to the country, and creatively about the responses.

The Bush Administration chose another path. Implicitly at the beginning of 2002, and as a matter of formal policy by the end, it placed all other considerations second to regime change in Iraq. It hampered the campaign in Afghanistan before fighting began and wound it down prematurely, along the way losing the chance to capture Osama bin Laden. It turned a blind eye to misdeeds in Saudi Arabia and Pakistan, and to WMD threats from North Korea and Iran far more serious than any posed by Saddam Hussein, all in the name of moving toward a showdown with Iraq. It overused and wore out its army in invading Iraq—without committing enough troops for a successful occupation. It saddled the United States with ongoing costs that dwarf its spending for domestic security. And by every available measure it only worsened the risk of future terrorism. In every sense 2002 was a lost year.

Contributors

Eric Alterman is the media columnist for the *Nation* and the author of the blog *Altercation*. A professor of English at Brooklyn College of the City University of New York, he has written numerous books including, most recently, *When Presidents Lie: A History of Deception and its Consequences.*

Matt Bai is a contributing writer at the *New York Times Magazine.*

Thomas P. M. Barnett is a professor and senior military analyst at the U.S. Naval War College, and is the author of *The Pentagon's New Map: War and Peace in the Twenty-first Century.*

Peter Beinart is the editor of the *New Republic.*

Jonathan Chait is a senior editor at the *New Republic.*

Eric Cohen is the editor of the *New Atlantis* and a resident scholar at the Ethics and Public Policy Center.

Nicholas Confessore is a reporter for the *New York Times,* and a former editor at the *Washington Monthly.*

James Fallows is a national correspondent for the *Atlantic Monthly,* where his writing has won a National Magazine Award.

Andrew Ferguson is a senior editor at the *Weekly Standard.*

Thomas Frank is a contributing editor for *Harper's* magazine, and the author of *What's the Matter with Kansas?: How Conservatives Won the Heart of America.*

Daniel Franklin is a consulting editor for the *Washington Monthly.*

John Lewis Gaddis is Robert A. Lovett Professor of History at Yale University. He is the author of several books, including the soon-to-be published *The Cold War: A New History.*

Nancy Gibbs is an editor at large for *Time.*

Jeffrey Goldberg writes the regular "Letter from Washington" feature for the *New Yorker.*

John Heilemann writes frequently for *New York,* and is a regular contributor to the magazine's "The National Interest" column.

Wil S. Hylton is a correspondent for *GQ.* His writing has also appeared in numerous other publications, including *Esquire* and *Harper's* magazine.

Tom Junod is a writer at large for *Esquire.* His work has also appeared in *Life, Sports Illustrated,* and *GQ,* where his writing has won two National Magazine Awards.

N. Gregory Mankiw is a professor of economics at Harvard University and the former chairman of President George W. Bush's Council of Economic Advisers.

Michael Massing, a contributing editor at the *Columbia Journalism Review,* writes frequently on the press and foreign affairs.

Jane Mayer is a staff writer for the *New Yorker* and the coauthor of two books, *Strange Justice: The Selling of Clarence Thomas* and *Landslide: The Unmaking of the President, 1984-1988.*

James McManus is a frequent contributor to *Esquire* and other publications. He is the author of several books including, most recently, *Positively Fifth Street: Murderers, Cheetahs, and Binion's World Series of Poker.*

Louis Menand is a staff writer for the *New Yorker* and a professor of English at Harvard University. He is the author of numerous books including, most recently, *American Studies.*

A. G. Newmyer III is managing director of U.S. Fiduciary Advisors.

Martin Peretz is editor in chief of the *New Republic*.

Katha Pollitt is a columnist for the *Nation* and the author of several books, including *Antarctic Traveller*, winner of the 1982 National Book Critics Circle Award for Poetry, and *Subject to Debate: Sense and Dissents on Women, Politics, and Culture*.

Jonathan Rauch is a correspondent for the *Atlantic Monthly* and the author of several books including, most recently, *Gay Marriage: Why It Is Good for Gays, Good for Straights, and Good for America*.

Jeffrey Rosen is a law professor at George Washington University and a frequent contributor to the *New York Times Magazine*. He is the author of several books including, most recently, *The Judical Branch and American Democracy*.

Hanna Rosin writes for the Style section of the *Washington Post*.

Jennifer Senior is a contributing editor for *New York* magazine.

Mimi Swartz is an executive editor at *Texas Monthly* magazine, where, in a previous stint, her writing won a National Magazine Award. She has also worked as a staff writer at *Talk* magazine and the *New Yorker*. Her articles have also appeared in the *New York Times*, *Slate*, *Vanity Fair*, and *Esquire*, among other publications.

Jeffrey Toobin is a staff writer for the *New Yorker* and a legal analyst for CNN, where he has won an Emmy award for his reporting. He is the author of several books, including *Too Close to Call: The 36-Day Battle to Decide the 2000 Election*.

Fareed Zakaria is the editor of *Newsweek International* and a columnist for *Newsweek*. He is also a regular member of the roundtable on *This Week with George Stephanopolous* on ABC, and the author of several books including, most recently, *The Future of Freedom: Illiberal Democracy at Home and Abroad*.

Permissions